The Longitudin:
Advanced L2 Ca_l

The present edited volume explores the connection between longitudinal study and advanced language capacities, two under-researched areas in investigations of language learning and teaching, and proposes an agenda for future research. Five chapters probe theoretical and methodological reflections about the longitudinal study of advanced L2 capacities, followed by eight chapters that report on empirical longitudinal investigations spanning descriptive, quasi-experimental, qualitative, and quantitative longitudinal methodologies. In addition, the co-editors offer a detailed introduction to the volume and a coda chapter in which they explore what it would take to design systematic research programs for the longitudinal investigation of advanced L2 capacities. Acknowledging that advancedness is increasingly important in our multicultural societies and globalized world, the diverse contributions revolve around two central questions: How does learning over time evolve toward advanced capacities in a second language? What tools and constructs can enable researchers to illuminate change toward advancedness longitudinally?

The volume will be of great interest to scholars and students in the field of applied linguistics and in the related fields of foreign language education, second language acquisition, and educational linguistics.

Lourdes Ortega is Associate Professor of Second Language Studies at the University of Hawai'i at Mānoa. Her research interests include second language acquisition, second language writing, and research methods. Recent publications are *Synthesizing Research on Language Learning and Teaching* (co-edited with John Norris, Benjamins) and *Understanding Second Language Acquisition* (Arnold).

Heidi Byrnes is George M. Roth Distinguished Professor of German at Georgetown University. Her research focus is the acquisition of L2 academic literacy by adult instructed learners. Recent publications include *Educating for Advanced Foreign Language Capacities: Constructs, Curriculum, Instruction, Assessment* (co-edited with Heather Weger-Guntharp and Katherine A. Sprang, Georgetown University Press); and *Advanced Language Learning: The Contribution of Halliday and Vygotsky* (Continuum).

Second language acquisition research: theoretical and methodological issues
Edited by Susan M. Gass and Alison Mackey

The Longitudinal Study of Advanced L2 Capacities

Edited by
Lourdes Ortega and Heidi Byrnes

Routledge
Taylor & Francis Group

NEW YORK AND LONDON

First published 2008
by Routledge
270 Madison Ave, New York, NY 10016

Simultaneously published in the UK
by Routledge
2 Park Square, Milton Park, Abingdon, Oxon OX14 4RN

Routledge is an imprint of the Taylor & Francis Group, an informa business

Transferred to Digital Printing 2010

© 2008 Taylor & Francis

Typeset in Baskerville by
RefineCatch Limited, Bungay, Suffolk

Library of Congress Cataloging in Publication Data
The longitudinal study of advanced L2 capacities / [edited] by Lourdes Ortega
and Heidi Byrnes.
    p. cm.
  Language and languages—Study and teaching.   2. Second language
acquisition.   I. Ortega, Lourdes.   II. Byrnes, Heidi.
P51.L598 2008
418.0071—dc22

                                                            2007034958

ISBN 10: 0-8058-6173-4 (hbk)
ISBN 10: 0-415-88219-2 (pbk)
ISBN 10: 1-4106-1532-4 (ebk)

ISBN 13: 978-0-8058-6173-0 (hbk)
ISBN 13: 978-0-415-88219-4 (pbk)
ISBN 13: 978-1-4106-1532-9 (ebk)

Contents

Illustrations

Tables

Figures

Excerpts

Exhibits

Contributors

Mariana Achugar, Carnegie Mellon University USA
machugar@andrew.cmu.edu

Claudia V. Angelelli, San Diego State University, USA
cangelel@mail.sdsu.edu

Géraldine Blattner, Florida Atlantic University, USA
gblattne@fau.edu

Jana Bressem, Freie Universität Berlin, Germany
jb_uni@hotmail.com

Heidi Byrnes, Georgetown University, USA
byrnesh@georgetown.edu

M. Cecilia Colombi, University of California Davis, USA
cmcolombi@ucdavis.edu

Norbert Dittmar, Freie Universität Berlin, Germany
diso@zedat.fu-berlin.de

Linda Harklau, University of Georgia, USA
lharklau@uga.edu

Marie Källkvist, Lund University, Sweden
marie.kallkvist@englund.lu.se

Celeste Kinginger, The Pennsylvania State University, USA
cxk37@psu.edu

John Klapper, The University of Birmingham, UK
j.m.klapper@bham.ac.uk

Olga Liamkina, Georgetown University, USA
oliamkina@yahoo.com

Florence Myles, Newcastle University, UK
Florence.Myles@ncl.ac.uk

Lourdes Ortega, University of Hawai'i at Mānoa
lortega@hawaii.edu

Jonathan Rees, The University of Birmingham, UK
J.I.Rees@bham.ac.uk

Castle Sinicrope, University of Hawaiʻi, USA
csinicrope@gmail.edu

Romuald Skiba, Max-Planck-Institute for Psycholinguistics, The Netherlands
R.Skiba@mpi.nl

Allison J. Spenader, Concordia College, USA
spenader@cord.edu

Katherine A. Sprang, Foreign Service Institute, USA
sprangk@rstarmail.com

Naoko Taguchi, Carnegie Mellon University, USA
taguchi@andrew.cmu.edu

Introduction

1 The longitudinal study of advanced L2 capacities: An introduction

Lourdes Ortega and Heidi Byrnes

Abstract

In this chapter we argue for the main connection between the two areas of longitudinal research and advancedness and we introduce the chapters in the present volume. Our goal is to draw readers' attention to the main contributions each chapter makes to longitudinal research into advanced L2 capacities.

Introduction

Both researchers and educators routinely call for longitudinal research on language learning and teaching. Many researchers believe that longitudinal findings can uniquely bolster our knowledge of language acquisition processes, and many practitioners find longitudinal insights particularly convincing as a basis on which to justify recommendations for educational practice. Obviously, developing advanced capacities in any language, but particularly in a second, foreign, or heritage language (hereafter, L2), is a process that inherently involves time, and a long time at that. The need for longitudinal research is particularly acute when the goals are to generate cutting-edge insights about the nature of advanced L2 capacities and to formulate sound educational practices that may enable more of our language students to attain them.

Yet, few systematic efforts have been made to support and foment longitudinal research on L2 learning and teaching. To be sure, scattered across books, dissertations, and journal articles is an untapped body of longitudinal applied linguistics research on L2 learning. Some of those studies were conducted in our disciplinary awakenings and have become classic citations in second language acquisition (SLA) research (e.g., Hakuta, 1976; Huebner, 1983; Schmidt, 1983; Schumann, 1978). Other recent longitudinal studies are testimony of the great expansion the field has undergone in the last decade (e.g., Han, 2005; Jia and Aaronson, 2003; Leki, 2003; Marx, 2002; Ushioda, 2001; Vavrus, 2002). Nevertheless, the lack of an explicit or sustained focus on longitudinal questions has meant that, after some 40 years of disciplinary history, we know little about the longitudinal pace and pattern of development in second language and literacy, much less when development is understood to span the lifetime of multilingual and multicultural people who set out to function in several languages, including an L2. The bulk of research practices and disciplinary discussions within the field of applied linguistics, too, favors a cross-sectional view of language learning and, as a consequence, discussions about longitudinal research are scarce. A telling indication is the treatment that longitudinal research receives in applied linguistics research methods textbooks. In Hatch and Lazaraton (1991), a 628-page compendium that is now out of print, readers will find four pages devoted to any such discussion. In a more recent volume that is 349 pages long, Mackey and Gass (2005) do not include the term in their glossary and devote slightly more than two pages (under the header "Participant mortality") to longitudinal considerations.

Given this dearth in substantive as well as methodological focus, our purpose with the present volume is to inspire others to explore the theoretical, methodological, and epistemological demands of various longitudinal empirical approaches and to evaluate how the available options can aid in the pursuit of future research programs that investigate the longitudinal course towards L2 advancedness. To our knowledge, this is the first time the connection between the two areas of "longitudinal study" and "advanced capacities" is made. In fact, the field has only recently begun to explore either theme, and both are currently underresearched. Thus, the collection itself is designed to prompt an exploration of the connection of the two themes that can set the agenda for future research in the area.

To this end, we have gathered in this volume five chapters that probe theoretical and methodological reflections about the longitudinal study of advanced L2 capacities, followed by eight chapters that report on empirical longitudinal investigations of L2 learning. In addition, as co-editors, in Chapter 15 we explore what it would take to design systematic research programs for the longitudinal investigation of advanced L2 capacities. In this opening chapter, we first make the case for linking longitudinalness with advancedness. In order to do so, we also examine the range of meanings that can be evoked under the labels of "longitudinal" and "advanced L2 capacities." We then introduce the contributions gathered in the volume.

The case for longitudinal research

The case for a longitudinal methodology is sufficiently well established, at least conceptually and in general terms. Simply put, L2 learning takes a long time, and it is only by investigating the phenomenon through time that we may attain better and fuller insights into L2 learning and the development of advanced capacities.

We have compelling descriptions in the SLA literature of how long it may take learners to traverse even beginning and intermediate levels of competence in an L2. Without instruction, a period of one to three years may enable us to capture only minimal progress towards intermediate levels at best. Ge, Huebner's (1983) Hmong learner of English in Hawai'i, did not use the article *the* at all for half a year, after which he began using *da* (his rendition of *the*) across undifferentiated noun contexts, a so-called flooding effect that lasted another half a year at least. JDB, Duff's (1993) Cambodian learner of English in Canada, took even longer (about two and a half years) to move from the use of *have* as an existential topic marker to the use of the form *'s* (pronounced as /z/) that perhaps foreshadowed the possible emergence of the English existential *there is*. Indeed, a mere 9 (or 24 percent) of the 38 Italian adult immigrants in Scotland studied by Pavesi (1986) appeared to use relativization in English at the level of object of preposition or beyond, even after six years on average of living in the L2 environment. The best and most successful uninstructed adult learners may still require a period of about two and a half years to reach their full potential for advancedness, judging from the case of Julie, Ioup *et al.*'s (1994) exceptional British learner of Arabic in Egypt. However, perhaps in optimal conditions of naturalistic but supported acquisition, half a year may be enough to observe considerable progress, as was witnessed for one of the two US learners of Swedish investigated by Spenader (Chapter 13, this volume).

In naturalistic contexts that offer no special first language support, even young L2 learners may exhibit only slow development, contrary to popular belief. For example, Thanh and Tai, the two Vietnamese brothers studied by Sato (1990), produced only a few instances of high-frequency irregular past tense verbs in natural conversation and never in ten months gave any indication of using the grammatical past tense marker -*ed*; similarly, Ana, a 12-year-old Spanish learner of English investigated by Mellow (2006), began producing relative clauses quite early (after two months of observations, or three months of stay in the US), but only of the simplest subject type. She produced only two direct object relative clauses, each at the end of months 3 and 4, in the span of seven months of reading and writing sessions.

With formal instruction, as well, the time demands of L2 development are substantial. Thus, in a foreign language classroom context investigated by Myles *et al.* (1998), it took about two years for 10 (or 63 percent) of 16 beginning learners of French to restructure chunks into productive French-like questions. In a second language classroom context investigated by Bardovi-Harlig (1994), it took about half of that time, but nevertheless still a full year, for 10 (or 63 percent) of 16 pre-advanced college students of English to begin using the past perfect. In the context of the college-level four-year German curriculum investigated in three chapters in the present volume, Byrnes and Sinicrope (Chapter 7, this volume) found that 14 (or 61 percent) of 23 L2 writers of German deployed evidence of the object of preposition relative clause at levels 2 or 3, whereas only one writer did so during the first semester and only two during the highest level investigated; and Sprang (Chapter 8, this volume) and Liamkina (Chapter 9, this volume) reported that learners in the same program at the upper levels of the curriculum (i.e., level 4) did not yet handle well certain derivational morphology and dative case marking, respectively.

It may be that areas of language where development has been documented to emerge rather late for L1 users, such as narrative competencies (Berman and Nir-Sagiv, 2004), figurative language (Levorato and Cacciari, 2002) or intonation (Wells *et al.*, 2004) develop even more slowly in the L2 across diverse contexts (e.g., pragmatic competence as described by Taguchi, Chapter 11, this volume; sociolinguistic competence as described by Kinginger and Blattner, Chapter 12, this volume; translation and interpretation capabilities as those described in Källkvist, Chapter 10, this volume; and Angelelli, Chapter 14, this volume).

Judging from the extended time L2 learners require to traverse even rather basic developmental stages, let alone more sophisticated areas, it seems natural for SLA researchers to want to examine longitudinal development along the full course of language learning, from beginning all the way to advanced learning. After many years of repeated calls for longitudinal studies—calls that are nearly ritualized in the discussion and implications sections of existing cross-sectional investigations—it would appear natural for SLA research to explicitly embrace a longitudinal orientation. And yet, the full longitudinal course against which advancedness needs to be understood is left rather unexplored in current SLA thinking. In fact, as Ortega and Iberri-Shea (2005) discuss, it is not easy to determine what exactly counts as longitudinal in L2 research.

Defining longitudinal, making the link with advancedness

Ortega and Iberri-Shea (2005) argue for a flexible definition of "longitudinalness" that focuses not on the sheer length of study (which often depends on the appropriacy of scaling time on biologically, chronologically, or institutionally meaningful units), but rather on the joint contribution of study length and three other criteria: the presence of multi-wave data collection, the conceptual focus on capturing change by design, and the focus on establishing antecedent–consequent relationships through prolonged tracking of the phenomenon in its context rather than through experimental controls or comparisons.

How long is long enough for a study to be considered longitudinal? Harklau (Chapter 2, this volume) mentions the conventional one-year benchmark established for the social sciences by Young, Savola, and Phelps (1991). In applied linguistics, researchers have identified their studies as "longitudinal" for lengths that would be considered rather short in other fields, as short as three or four months and as long as six years, in a very few cases (Ortega and Oberri-Shea, 2005). Longitudinal observation spans in this collection ranged from seven weeks (Taguchi, Chapter 11) to the curricular equivalent of four years (Byrnes and Sinicrope, Chapter 7). In most cases the motivation for choice of length was practical and ecological. For example, natural lengths of time in formal education contexts are the intensive seven-week summer course, the typical 15-week semester, or the traditional one-semester or one-year study abroad program.

However long the "longitudinal" outlook of particular studies and initiatives, we argue that we need insights into an extended course of second language development. This means capturing beginning competencies, as learners strive to attain basic meaning-making capacities and grasp for essential vocabulary and grammar knowledge, through tracing intermediate levels where some more sophisticated aspects of second language knowledge and use gradually emerge in varied areas, up to mapping the development of late-emerging capacities in areas we would consider characteristic of "advanced learners."

By gathering the chapters in this collection, we make no claims that longitudinal study will inherently uncover advancedness on the part of the learners. It is well known that some learners may attain "advancedness," whereas many do not, and some of the chapters in this volume clearly show this. Longitudinal study would merit our serious consideration just the same, for its projected ability to uncover interesting phenomena regarding the attainment of "intermediate" or "beginning" levels in the development towards mature meaning-making capacities. We do wish to claim, however, that SLA longitudinal research will be the richer, theoretically and empirically, if a trajectory toward advancedness is part of its conceptualization right from the beginning and, in reverse, that advancedness is a particularly interesting acquisitional level at which to observe the evolving claims and recommendations associated with the longitudinal study of language development.

Defining advancedness

If definitions of longitudinal study are less straightforward than they seem at first sight, crafting a definition of advancedness that can be taken as definitive or complete at this point in our field is an equally complex task. We examine here four alternative but also partially overlapping operationalizations of advancedness: institutional status, characterizations gleaned from standardized tests, late-acquired language features, and—the one we ultimately favor—sophisticated language use in context. In Chapter 15, we will return to these four definitions and problematize them. Here, we briefly introduce each in turn.

Within the community of foreign language researchers, "advanced" learners are often defined by reference to their institutional status, a practice that is also widespread in L2 research more generally (Thomas, 2006). For example, college-level students enrolled in third-year courses beyond the minimum foreign language requirement are inherently considered "advanced." In this volume, for instance, the German learners investigated by Sprang (Chapter 8) and Liamkina (Chapter 9) and the French learners investigated by Kinginger and Blattner (Chapter 12) were at the post-foreign language requirement stage and thus can be thought of as having chosen to pursue more advanced levels of L2 competence. Källkvist (Chapter 10) and Taguchi (Chapter 11) also note that university students in Sweden and Japan, respectively, are considered to be advanced because they have accrued the proficiency expected after compulsory English education during junior and senior high school.

Advancedness can also be measured by information gleaned from standardized tests, that is, tests that come with conventionalized and publicly available regulations for administration, scoring, and reporting. Many of the authors in this volume make use of this approach as one of several ways of gauging advancedness. Kinginger and Blattner (Chapter 12) use the *Test de Français International* developed in the late 1990s at the University of Ottawa and adopted since then by the Educational Testing Service. Spenader (Chapter 13) uses the Oral Proficiency Interview scoring protocol developed by the Foreign Service Institute (FSI) for Swedish, and its equivalent American Council on the Teaching of Foreign Languages levels (ACTFL, 1999). Sometimes this definition of advancedness is framed by reference to competent or effective functioning in specific workplace or academic contexts. For example, the levels 3+, 4, and 5 of the Interagency Language Roundtable (ILR) scale developed by the FSI are based on the assumption that, at these levels, second language users are capable of functioning effectively in Foreign Service jobs. Likewise, the cut-off point of 600 on the TOEFL, often established as a prerequisite for enrollment in higher education in the United States, is based on the premise that learners at this level or higher are well equipped to meet the demands of advanced academic study. Certification into jobs, such as the certification for interpretation in medical contexts associated with the *Language Proficiency* and *Interpreter Readiness* tests developed for Cantonese, Hmong, and Spanish by Angelelli (Chapter 14), is also a way in which advancedness is gauged through well-designed standardized tests.

A different definition of advancedness can be found in the SLA literature. There, advanced development may be claimed when learners exhibit certain late-acquired features of the language, such as object of preposition relative clauses, passive voice, past perfect, and so on. These language features are thought to be late-acquired, and one can expect them to develop slowly even when they are expressly targeted by instruction. Myles (Chapter 4) and Byrnes and Sinicrope (Chapter 7), and to some extent Skiba *et al.* (Chapter 5), Rees and Klapper (Chapter 6), Källkvist (Chapter 10), and Taguchi (Chapter 11), all orient towards this definition of advancedness. Alternatively, a dual orientation can be taken, in which outstanding acquisitional concerns are identified and inventoried, first, and theoretically motivated instructional interventions are specified and implemented later. This position characterizes the approach espoused by Sprang (Chapter 8) and Liamkina (Chapter 9).

Finally, advancedness is also framed as sophisticated language use in context, with the concomitant realization that the construct needs to accommodate both purely linguistic accomplishments but also more encompassing notions that transcend linguistic phenomena. Thus, "advancedness" is linked also to aspects of literacy, to diverse manifestations of cultural competence, choice among registers and multiple speech community repertoires, voice, and identity in cross-cultural communicative settings. Several chapters contribute empirical insights into this area—particularly Achugar and Colombi; Angelelli; Harklau; and Kinginger and Blattner. This definition of advancedness is increasingly important in multicultural societies and a globalized environment. These latter features of choice and identity suggest the need to explore the notion of advancedness through an understanding of competence that extends not only Chomskyan notions of both performance and competence (Brown, Malmkjær, and Williams, 1996) but also notions generally associated with "communicative competence" in the Canale and Swain tradition (e.g., Kramsch, 2006). As we will argue in Chapter 15, the language theories of Hallidayan linguistics are particularly useful when exploring this definition of advancedness (see Byrnes, 2006a, b).

Given this variety of definitions, in this volume we have chosen the term "advanced *capacities*" (rather than *proficiency* or *skills*, among other choices) because it encompasses all the possibilities outlined above, while making the construct wide enough to accommodate notions of sophisticated language use in context, including issues of literacy development and development of other nonlinguistic (e.g., sociopragmatic, identity) dimensions of development.

We hope this collection serves as encouragement and invitation for other L2 researchers to imagine central characteristics of advancedness and to link these to principled approaches through which L2 development might be studied longitudinally. In the remainder of the chapter, we introduce each contribution in the collection, highlighting some initial interconnections and differences. We begin with the five theoretical and methodological chapters. We then offer commentaries on the eight empirical chapters.

The theoretical and methodological chapters

In Chapter 2, Harklau argues for the use of qualitative longitudinal case study methodology as an ideal window into understanding advancedness. She advocates more specifically for longitudinal case studies that are interpretive-qualitative and ethnographic in orientation, an approach to which she has devoted her research efforts for nearly two decades. This epistemological commitment has several entailments. As in other interpretive-qualitative research, a constructivist orientation demands that "findings" be understood as constructed knowledge rather than found explanations and that the subjectivities of the researchers be recognized and accounted for in the design, analysis, interpretation, and reporting of the research. An interpretive-qualitative perspective also calls for naturalistic, inductive, and iterative research processes. In addition, as in other ethnographic research, the focus is on the relationships among actors, context, and culture. More specifically, taking an ethnographic perspective means theorizing how actors are "participants in and products of the cultural context" (p. 24) and how "learning is mediated by participants' understandings of and interactions with context over time" (p. 26). Harklau offers an honest acknowledgement of several big challenges that longitudinal qualitative case study research poses. The biggest challenge of all, perhaps, is the contested legitimacy of the approach in certain social science circles, including sectors of applied linguistics and a large part of second language acquisition as a field. In the end, Harklau is hopeful that this approach can yield unique and fine-grained theoretical knowledge about advanced multicompetence.

In Chapter 3, Achugar and Colombi move the lens onto a theory of language learning, Systemic Functional Linguistics (SFL), which views language as a socially grounded meaning-making system. SFL provides a coherent framework for the study of language development (we will expand on this point in Chapter 15), and one that these authors have applied with success to the longitudinal study of academic literacy development among Spanish heritage language learners. By virtue of its linguistic focus, the SFL framework offers some unique contributions that many L2 researchers may find useful. For one, it provides a theoretically compelling set of concrete linguistic tools to analyze and explicate L2 development. One such tool is the construct of grammatical metaphor, which is considered to be a hallmark of advancedness, illustrated in the following example from Achugar and Colombi's chapter (p. 40):

> Peor aún es la *emigración* masiva del campo a las ciudades, el *abandono* de las granjas . . . [emigrar/emigración, abandonar/abandono]
>
> Even worse is the massive *migration* from the country to the city, the *abandonment* of the farms . . . [to migrate/migration, to abandon/abandonment]

Second, SFL conceives of language learning and content learning as inseparable and mutually constitutive. Hence, it is particularly powerful as a framework for the longitudinal study of advanced schooled capacities, where content and language learning are also inseparable (e.g., Mohan and Beckett, 2001; Shohamy, 2006). Finally, Achugar and Colombi also illustrate a less discussed application of SFL, namely the study of language as an index and tool that construes social roles and reflects negotiation of types of social participation over time. By employing the SFL apparatus to explicate longitudinal heritage language development, Achugar and Colombi pose transformative understandings of what advancedness means, particularly in educational settings.

The next two chapters, by Myles (Chapter 4) and Skiba, Dittmar, and Bressem (Chapter 5), tighten the focus on linguistic analytical issues. Together, the two chapters present a compelling case for the creation and maintenance of publicly available electronic longitudinal corpora of learner language. In both cases the authors speak from their substantial experience with longitudinal investigations of linguistic development.

In Chapter 4, Myles makes a call for SLA researchers who work on longitudinal L2 analyses to take advantage of the computer-aided framework of CHILDES (MacWhinney, 2000), which has had an enormous impact on the field of first language acquisition but has been seldom explored in SLA. She provides a number of reasoned arguments for her call. Perhaps the most compelling is that high-quality longitudinal L2 data are so expensive and demanding to collect that it is imperative that they be shared freely by the research community so that they can be explored and exploited by other research programs beyond the ones for which the data are initially collected. She then describes FLLOC, an L2 French initiative spearheaded by Myles herself in the 1990s at the University of Southampton in the United Kingdom, and she exemplifies how CHILDES was used in this initiative to gather and make public longitudinal as well as cross-sectional L2 French corpora.

In Chapter 5, on the other hand, Skiba, Dittmar, and Bressem furnish readers interested in heeding Myles' call with concrete methodological and logistic guidance for designing and implementing linguistically oriented and computer-supported longitudinal studies of L2 development. They do so, as they note in the beginning of their chapter, on the basis of their experiences in the P-MoLL project, a three-year longitudinal study of L2 German led by Dittmar from 1987 until 1992 at the Free University of Berlin in Germany. The authors first discuss fundamental questions of longitudinal design: How can researchers determine overall study length, ideal density of data collection intervals, and balanced coverage of L2 performance through the principled selection of genres and tasks? How can they deal with attrition over a long-lasting study? What may representativeness and comparability mean in the context of longitudinal investigations, and how do they contribute to the validity of longitudinal designs? They then offer even more specific guidance regarding the logistics of collecting, transcribing, and preparing the data for analyses not only by the original researchers but also by potential future users of the electronic L2 corpora. Together, Chapters 4 and 5 compel SLA researchers who collect L2 corpora for their longitudinal investigations to make them public and available to the wider SLA research community.

Chapter 6, by Rees and Klapper, which is the last in this first part of the collection, turns the methodological lens onto a widely researched but not yet fully understood context for the development of L2 capacities—study abroad. As the authors note, study abroad is a singularly important context for advanced L2 learning, both from the viewpoint of national educational policies and because it is often found to be one of few strong predictors of ultimate levels of L2 attainment (e.g., Carroll, 1967; see also Sasaki, 2004). Rees and Klapper examine study abroad longitudinal research critically, implicitly drawing from their own engagement with a four-year longitudinal assessment of the linguistic gains that come about before and after studying abroad (Klapper and Rees, 2003). They first offer a map of the research domain, identifying key types of designs for the investigation of language learning during study abroad. They then examine several types of longitudinal design critically. In their conclusions they offer strong recommendations for future longitudinal researchers to strive for more rigor and creative thinking in four areas: genuine or at least fair and meaningful comparisons of study abroad; awareness and sophistication in the conceptualization and coverage of what counts as "proficiency" or linguistic gains; judicious use of mixed methods research and of qualitative longitudinal data; and better informed use of statistical procedures in quantitative longitudinal investigations. Readers will leave Rees and Klapper's critical overview chapter with a healthy awareness that more research on the linguistic gains during study abroad will be needed before the language education professions can proclaim with confidence what contributions study abroad makes in the pathway to develop advanced competencies.

The empirical chapters

Instructed advanced L2 development

Our empirical studies section opens with Byrnes and Sinicrope (Chapter 7), who describe the longitudinal development of an allegedly advanced area of L2 development: relativization. Their investigation spans the first four levels of a college German curriculum in the United States that overtly fosters the development of advanced L2 abilities through writing. Using a particularly explicit theoretical framework about language development, Keenan and Comrie's (1977) Noun Phrase Accessibility Hierarchy, the study tracks learners' progress along the implicationally scaled developmental stages for relativization. Taking a longitudinal perspective on the group data, Byrnes and Sinicrope find noteworthy departures from this progression, in terms of occurrence along the implicational hierarchy, of range and frequency of use, of embeddedness, and of relative clause length. More important, the findings question both the status of advancedness for relativization—for some learners, these forms occur remarkably early in their language learning—and the implicit assumption that more frequent and more diverse use would characterize learners that otherwise show certain characteristics of advancedness. Not only is this not the case for this group of L2 German learners; a focused analysis of two learners shows highly intricate and variant paths that suggest that relativization is but one of several resources that are more or less appropriate and more or less likely within a particular textual environment.

The next three chapters feature longitudinal studies of type of L2 instruction, each spanning the curricular length of a semester and focusing on vocabulary or grammar targets. It is noteworthy that all three studies exhibit a trend to deliver lengthy treatments and to allow for repeated and delayed assessment waves. That approach did not emerge until the late 1990s but is gaining importance in recent type-of-instruction studies, subtly pushing the domain towards a more longitudinal perspective (Ortega and Iberri-Shea, 2005). Another shared feature is that all three chapters offer rationales for curriculum-appropriate instruction which falls on the explicit end of the type-of-instruction continuum.

The studies reported in Chapters 8 and 9 were conducted in the same context investigated by Byrnes and Sinicrope (Chapter 7), and both focus on level 4 of that curriculum, where German students enroll in an advanced genre- and content-oriented course designed to foster advanced competencies beyond the three-year hallmark of college-level study. In Chapter 8, Sprang targets vocabulary instruction and draws on cognitive linguistics (Evans, Bergen, and Zinken, 2006). Specifically, the target of the study was vocabulary knowledge of verbs containing the German prefixes *be-* and *er-*. These prefixes combine with many roots to form many word families but are also informationally dense, conveying literal prototypical meanings as well as a number of figurative meanings that express subtle perspectives. Consider, for example:

> *gehen* ("go" or "walk")
> *begehen* ("moving through or along a path with a purpose")
> *ergehen* ("enact," "issue," "turn out with a goal or outcome")

In the example above, the meaning of *begehen* can be more literal, as in the phrase *den Weg begehen* ("to travel the path of . . ." or "to embark on . . ."), where a physical path is named (*Weg*, "road") or more metaphorical, as in the phrase *den Tag begehen* ("spend the day"), where the path is temporal (*Tag*, "day") and has an additional public and celebratory dimension. Similarly, the meaning of *ergehen* can be more literal, as in *ein Gesetz ergeht* ("a law goes out = is issued/promulgated"), but it can also be more metaphorical, as in the expression *jemandem gut/schlecht ergangen sein* ("things went well or bad for someone"). In the beginning of the semester, the advanced (post-third-year) students investigated by Sprang gave no indication that they were aware of any of the subtle meanings contributed by the two prefixes, even though they were able to loosely guess, on the basis of context clues, the meaning of some of the prefixed verbs that appeared in classroom materials.

Sprang tracked the learning experienced by two advanced L2 German learners in the group, who (as part of the regular curricular focus) encountered these forms intensively and also participated in three sessions working with a concordancer to guess the meanings of prefixed verbs. One of the two focal participants received an additional 30 minutes of metalinguistic explanation about the abstract prototypical concepts the *be-* and *er-* prefixes can convey in German. This was done with the goal to guide her deduction of the word meanings during the concordancing activities. The other focal participant received no explicit instruction on the semantics of the prefixes and was simply asked to induce the meanings during the concordancing activities. The learner who engaged in guided deduction evinced remarkable improvements during tests and stimulated recall interviews on week 5 and 12 of the semester (one and eight weeks after the intensive exposure treatment, respectively). Sprang interprets these findings as suggestive that advanced vocabulary learning is a gradual process that takes time and necessitates more than sheer, even if meaningful, exposure to sophisticated vocabulary in context. Instead, she argues for a regime of such sustained exposure supplemented with explicit concept-based instruction.

In Chapter 9, Liamkina investigates whether meaning-oriented instruction on the semantics of the German Dative case can help college students develop their awareness as well as their ability to use accurately this complex aspect of German grammar. Liamkina notes that these advanced L2 German learners often underused the Dative and instead realized its meanings with prepositional phrases or the Accusative case. She speculates that this is perhaps primed by the influence of their L1, English, which encodes Dative meanings with a preposition *to* or *for.*

Ich habe *dem Polizisten* den Verdächtigen beschrieben
"I described the suspect *to the police officer*"

Ich habe *meiner Mutter* Blumen gekauft
"I bought flowers *for my mother*"

In order to describe (and then pedagogically make sense of) the subtle range of meanings that the use of the Dative opens up for language users, Liamkina drew on the theoretical framework of the concept-oriented approach (Bardovi-Harlig, 2006) and cognitive linguistics (Langacker, 1999) and developed four lessons on the semantics of the Dative. She then delivered the lessons over two weeks and captured the benefits of instruction via three tests administered over the semester: immediately before, immediately after, and two months after the instructional treatment. Test performances were triangulated with stimulated recalls and classroom writing assignments. The 12 students involved in the study began the semester with a mean accuracy level of 60 percent in their use of the Dative case, despite their advanced level of overall competence. By the end of the semester, the mean had risen to 84 percent accuracy. Liamkina traces these changes back to the students' participation in the four lessons on the semantics of the Dative as much as to their further sustained engagement with the abstract meanings of the Dative across other instructional activities throughout the entire semester. It is noteworthy that Liamkina sets her longitudinal perspective against a full curriculum-wide context (Byrnes *et al.*, 2006; see also Chapter 7 by Byrnes and Sinicrope, this volume) and argues strongly for an "ecological longitudinal" approach to investigating effects of instruction.

In Chapter 10, Källkvist reports on the third longitudinal instructional study in the collection. The goal of the study was to ascertain which of two different types of focus-on-formS activities, translation or fill-in-the-blank, would prove to be more beneficial as the sole practice format for an EFL college grammar course in Sweden. The interest in translation as a pedagogical activity to teach grammar may seem odd, particularly to readers in the United States, where it is often considered unfashionable to teach grammar, let alone to do so via translation. Källkvist is well aware of this bias and provides a well-researched argument in defense of translation as a pedagogical tool for L2 grammar learning, particularly at advanced levels.

As in the studies reported in the two previous chapters, the investigation spanned a semester, the curricular goals were given primary importance, and the researcher was the teacher. However, in this case the design chosen was a quantitative experiment rather than a mixed methods case study. Furthermore, the students were assigned to the translation or the fill-in-the-blank treatment through a matched-pair random technique. To our knowledge, Källkvist is the first L2 classroom study to use the technique of matched-pair random assignment to treatments; indeed, random assignment of any kind is a rare virtue in experimental classroom studies of L2 instruction. For example, Norris and Ortega (2000) found only 31 percent of 77 study reports reported random assignment. The careful design is also reflected in the fact that activities in both treatments were kept as parallel as possible. Thus, they spread for exactly the same period (15 90-minute lessons over a semester), involved the same seven target structures, and were carried out during class time adhering to the same format: pair or group work first, followed by whole-class teacher-led discussion of the exercise answers. Benefits were assessed for each treatment relative to each other and by comparison to a baseline group that received meaning-only focused instruction.

After inspecting the results across three different tests administered on week 1 and again on week 13 of the semester, Källkvist concludes that both translation and fill-in-the-gap resulted in similarly sized benefits, with only small differences slightly in favor of the translation practice, and that both were clearly superior to the meaning-focused comparison condition. That is, rather than type of instruction, it was the explicit practicing of grammar points that made a difference in this study. Källkvist is careful to caution that this conclusion can only be made with regard to test-like elicitation tasks rather than spontaneous ability for use. In the end, she encourages teachers of advanced grammar courses to combine L1–L2 translation exercises with fill-in-the-blank exercises in their day-to-day instructional practices, since both appear to be beneficial for the development of accuracy in structures where L1–L2 misleading similarities or large differences create difficulties, even for advanced L2 learners.

Broadening notions of language, investigating context

The next three chapters move readers towards considering more global aspects of advanced L2 development: pragmatic comprehension ability, awareness of socio-linguistic variation, and global oral proficiency and fluency. They also speak to whether these L2 dimensions may be learned as a by-product of learners' engagement in various contexts, be it the formal foreign language classroom or the study abroad context.

In Chapter 11, Taguchi reports on a descriptive-quantitative investigation that gauged the changes in advanced pragmatic comprehension ability that could be observed among 92 college-aged students of EFL as a by-product of their completing a summer course at their university in Japan. Taguchi notes it is theoretically interesting to study the developmental progression of L2 inferential abilities that develop (or do not develop) in foreign language contexts. It is well known that in such contexts importance is often placed on declarative knowledge (i.e., vocabulary and grammar), particularly throughout the six- or seven-year mandatory study of English that is the norm in many national school curricula, including Japan. Furthermore, it is also clear that foreign language settings afford little opportunity for exposure to natural L2 input, through which pragmatic knowledge and awareness can arguably develop best. Under such circumstances, will pragmatic competence develop simply as a by-product of regular instruction? And, if so, what will be the pace and nature of such development?

Taguchi makes the argument that pragmatic comprehension of implied meaning, and particularly of nonconventionalized implied meaning, is an area of proficiency that develops slowly and at rather advanced stages of acquisition. For example, a good degree of sophistication in the L2 is needed for learners to process the intended force of the answer given in the following exchange:

How do you like your new house?
Oh, I don't want to change a thing about it.

Adopting an information processing perspective that draws from that taken by Segalowitz (2003), Taguchi defines advancedness in the area of comprehension of implied pragmatic meaning as "rapid and accurate skill execution" (p. 205). She therefore argues that both accuracy and speed measures need to be taken into account in longitudinal descriptions of pragmatic development. Taguchi finds that the 92 EFL students improved in their ability to process implied meaning over a short period of seven weeks of (intensive but non-pragmatic) L2 instruction, and that changes were greater for the less difficult type of implicature (conventionalized indirect refusals) than for the more difficult one (nonconventionalized indirect opinions). These foreign language learners, however, changed more noticeably with regard to comprehension accuracy than speed of processing. Thus, the seven-week window into the development of advanced L2 pragmatic abilities that this study affords points at some universal as well as some contextual effects. Namely, the higher difficulty of nonconventional meanings can probably be assumed to hold for L2 pragmatic learning in general, whereas the uneven development of accuracy versus speed of pragmatic processing can be considered a distinguishing feature of how advanced pragmatic capacities develop in foreign language settings specifically.

Chapters 12 and 13 report on longitudinal case studies of the nature of language and culture learning that takes place in two different contexts for study abroad, involving three college students in France and two high school graduates in Sweden, respectively. Both studies adopt a qualitative case study methodology that aptly reveals the tremendous individual variation which can be expected in the development of advanced L2 capacities. Both examine nonlinguistic sources of influence that may help explain why, by the end of the study, some of the learners were seen to be well on their way to attaining advanced capacities, whereas others showed clear evidence of stabilization. Despite these similarities, the researchers differ greatly in their choice of both focus of inquiry and theoretical framework.

In Chapter 12 Kinginger and Blattner focus on awareness of sociolinguistic variation and adopt a sociocultural, participatory, and post-structuralist framework that draws from traditions presented in Lantolf and Thorne (2006) and Pavlenko and Blackledge (2004), among others. The researchers investigated how three college students negotiated access to and participation in meaningful and consequential social encounters (what Kinginger and Blattner call "histories of engagement") while they spent a semester in France. They also document how these experiences mediated the students' emerging awareness of sociolinguistic variation.

Kinginger and Blattner view language ability as "intimately and concretely tied to language use in social settings of seemingly infinite and unpredictable variety" (p. 224) and consider sociolinguistic awareness of register variation a hallmark of advancedness. An important contribution they make is their insistence that awareness data (rather than direct performance data via, for example, discourse analysis of the learners' L2 production) must be obtained. Their rationale is that register choices are mediated not only by first-order indexicality, that is, the encoding through language of various features of the social context, such as formality and so on, but also by second-order indexicality, or the constitution through language of speaker's identity. Therefore, L2 learners may be aware of form–context relationships and yet may hesitate to use such knowledge in their active repertoire because of what such choices would convey about alternative imagined, resisted, or rejected identities.

In order to tap sociolinguistic and sociopragmatic knowledge without demanding performance, Kinginger and Blattner develop and report on the use of a novel instrument, the Language Awareness Interview. In it they follow a complex scoring procedure upon eliciting comments that reveal learners' understanding (or lack thereof) of colloquial phrases such as the following:

Stimulus: Elle a une *floppée* de *moutards*. (She has a *ton* of *kids*.)
Learner comment: Somebody talking about mustard? I don't know what *floppée* is, though.

Based on the triangulated analysis of the three case studies, the researchers conclude that the learning that results from study abroad is varied and complex, and that it does not stem from the simple properties of a static context, a change in surrounding geography. Instead, language learning in the study abroad context is mediated by the students' histories of engagement, their perceptions of their abroad experiences, and in sum by "how they position themselves with respect to the people they meet and the activities that become available to them" (p. 241).

In Chapter 13, Spenader focuses on global oral proficiency and fluency and adopts a cross-cultural psychology and group relations framework. The theories developed by these disciplinary neighbors are seldom explored in L2 learning research, despite their wide acceptance among social psychologists since the 1980s. Particularly well-established models of acculturation have been developed by John Berry in Canada and Colleen Ward in New Zealand, both UK-trained psychologists (Berry, 2005; Ward, Bochner, and Furnham, 2001). Making this interdisciplinary link, Spenader investigated the global oral gains of two high school graduates who were absolute beginners when they embarked on a year-long residence abroad experience in Sweden. She further inquired into the process of adapting to life in the new culture and how this process impacts on language learning. In a modification of the cross-cultural adaptation model tradition, which typically relies on large-scale survey data alone, Spenader triangulates data from psychology questionnaires with detailed interviewing and observation as well as with proficiency and fluency measures.

Spenader documents good initial L2 gains but subsequent stagnation at the Intermediate–High level in one of the two focal participants, and remarkable and sustained gains for the other participant, who went from zero knowledge of Swedish to Superior after five months and to close to Distinguished after ten months of residence. The researcher links these patterns of language growth with the very different acculturative strategies and attitudes towards the host environment that the two adolescent students exhibited. She concludes that maximizing opportunities for language use is of the essence in the design of optimal study abroad experiences and that language students should be encouraged to study an L2 in an abroad context even without any prior knowledge of the L2, because evidently success of various degrees is possible.

The last empirical study in the collection offers a fascinating recount by Angelelli (Chapter 14) of her unique longitudinal, ethnographic approach to the development of authentic tests that can assess the advanced capacities of medical interpreters. Although the study lasted a long time indeed (22 months followed by another

15 months), it is not a traditional longitudinal study, in that the researcher did not intend to arrive at an understanding of the object of inquiry examined, medical interpreting abilities, from the perspective of *change over time* (Ortega and Iberri-Shea, 2005). We have included the study in this collection, however, for two important reasons. First, it offers an honest and powerful testimony of the demands created by prolonged engagement in a research site (as Harklau, Chapter 2, also describes). Second, and even more crucially, Angelelli's chapter, focusing as it does on the ethnographic understanding of linguistic, sociolinguistic, and interpreting competencies of medical interpreters in three target languages (Hmong, Spanish, and Cantonese), uncovers a number of dimensions of advancedness that are typically neglected in SLA research, and particularly in decontextualized approaches to the study of L2 advancedness.

Angelelli's novel "longitudinally driven and contextualized approach" (p. 264) to the development of authentic assessments offers readers important insights. First, the researcher's many-month engagement in non-participant observation across multiple sites revealed that one of the most central advanced capacities needed for medical interpretation is the ability to interpret utterances in and out the two codes involved (e.g., English and Spanish) by brokering the various speech communities involved in a given interaction (e.g., those of the health provider, the patient, and the interpreter herself). Hence, at the heart of advanced interpreting abilities in medical settings is versatile code-switching among diverse repertoires for language use, involving a number of formal and informal, technical and lay, urban and rural varieties of both codes. In addition, Angelelli explicates the thorough process of developing authentic assessment of capacities grounded in situated language use, which involved analyses of documents, focus group interviews, consultations with experts, and extended discourse analyses derived from 492 interpreting excerpts in the three languages combined. The complex and lengthy process resulted in a novel set of tests for medical interpreters of Cantonese, Hmong, and Spanish that are "strongly reflective of register variation" (p. 273). They measure language ability for bilingual medical settings in the areas of reading, listening, speaking, and interpreting, sampling across communicative events that the ethnographic approach has deemed typical in those settings, and making use of authentic discourse materials and semi-authentic scripted scenarios. Angelelli's unique ethnographic approach and her rich descriptions of the advanced capacities of the medical interpreters she painstakingly observed sets a model for other researchers who might want to engage in future longitudinal investigations of the gradual development of such interpreting abilities in medical settings.

Towards longitudinal investigations of advanced L2 capacities

Each of the 14 chapters we just introduced—whether theoretical, methodological, or empirical, and whether descriptive, quasi-experimental, qualitative, or quantitative—focuses on different selected phenomena of advanced learning and adopts a different long-term view of the study of second language and literacy development. Our authors explore an array of areas that are subsumed within the construct of "advancedness," and do so across a range of target languages, types of learning, and contexts where advanced language learning happens and through diverse epistemological lenses. We view the diversity of focus, scope, methodology, and theory reflected in the volume as a strength of the collection. By the same token, there are many other contexts, foci, and epistemologies that are not represented in the collection that would, presumably, contribute greatly to shaping longitudinal research programs on L2 advancedness.

We do hope, however, that the collection helps make the case that longitudinal designs can uniquely help researchers document the lengthy trajectories of adults who strive to become multicompetent and multicultural language users, thus capturing speakers' gradual pathways towards comfortable, competent, and dynamically evolving abilities to deploy sophisticated capacities for the use of two or more languages (including second, foreign, or heritage languages). Precisely because no single collection can be exhaustive, we not only underscore the dire need for longitudinal studies that can capture longer stretches of learners' developmental trajectories towards advancedness but invite readers to imagine new, exciting possibilities for future longitudinal research programs.

Note

We gratefully acknowledge a 2003 postdoctoral fellowship awarded by the Spencer Foundation and the National Academy of Education to Lourdes Ortega, which gave the initial thrust to embark on the exploration of longitudinal research in applied linguistics. The views expressed in this collection are not necessarily those of either supporting entity.

References

American Council for the Teaching of Foreign Languages (ACTFL). (1999). *Proficiency guidelines revised*. Yonkers, NY: Author.

Bardovi-Harlig, K. (1994). Reverse-order reports and the acquisition of tense: Beyond the principle of chronological order. *Language Learning, 44*, 243–282.

Bardovi-Harlig, K. (2006). One functional approach to second language acquisition: The concept-oriented approach. In B. VanPatten and J. Williams (Eds.), *Theories in second language acquisition: An introduction* (pp. 57–75). Mahwah, NJ: Lawrence Erlbaum.

Berman, R. A., and Nir-Sagiv, B. (2004). Linguistic indicators of inter-genre differentiation in later language development. *Journal of Child Language, 31*, 339–380.

Berry, J. W. (2005). Acculturation: Living successfully in two cultures. *International Journal of Intercultural Relations, 29*, 697–712.

Brown, G., Malmkjær, K., and Williams, J. (Eds.). (1996). *Performance and competence in second language acquisition*. New York: Cambridge University Press.

Byrnes, H. (Ed.). (2006a). *Advanced language learning: The contribution of Halliday and Vygotsky*. New York: Continuum.

Byrnes, H. (2006b). What kind of resource is language and why does it matter for advanced language learning? An introduction. In H. Byrnes (Ed.), *Advanced language learning: The contribution of Halliday and Vygotsky* (pp. 1–28). New York: Continuum.

Byrnes, H., Crane, C., Maxim, H. H., and Sprang, K. A. (2006). Taking text to task: Issues and choices in curriculum construction. *ITA. International Journal of Applied Linguistics, 19*(2), 85–110.

Carroll, J. B. (1967). Foreign language proficiency levels attained by language majors near graduation from college. *Foreign Language Annals, 1*, 131–151.

Duff, P. A. (1993). Syntax, semantics and SLA: The convergence of possessive and existential constructions. *Studies in Second Language Acquisition, 15*, 1–34.

Evans, V., Bergen, B. K., and Zinken, J. (Eds.). (2006). *The cognitive linguistics reader.* London: Equinox.

Hakuta, K. (1976). Becoming bilingual: A case study of a Japanese child learning English. *Language Learning, 26*, 321–351.

Han, Z.-H. (2005). Fossilization: Can grammaticality judgment be a reliable source of evidence? In Z.-H. Han and T. Odlin (Eds.), *Studies of fossilization in second language acquisition* (pp. 56–82). Clevedon, UK: Multilingual Matters.

Hatch, E., and Lazaraton, A. (1991). *The research manual: Design and statistics for applied linguistics.* New York: HarperCollins Pub/Newbury House.

Huebner, T. (1983). *A longitudinal analysis of the acquisition of English.* Ann Arbor, MI: Karoma.

Ioup, G., Boustagoui, E., Tigi, M., and Moselle, M. (1994). Reexamining the critical period hypothesis: A case of successful adult SLA in a naturalistic environment. *Studies in Second Language Acquisition, 16*, 73–98.

Jia, G., and Aaronson, D. (2003). A longitudinal study of Chinese children and adolescents learning English in the United States. *Applied Psycholinguistics, 24*, 131–161.

Keenan, E. L., and Comrie, B. (1977). Noun phrase accessibility and Universal Grammar. *Linguistic Inquiry, 8*, 63–99.

Klapper, J., and Rees, J. (2003). Reviewing the case for explicit grammar instruction in the university foreign language learning context. *Language Teaching Research, 7*, 285–314.

Kramsch, C. (2006). From communicative competence to symbolic competence. *Modern Language Journal, 90*, 249–252.

Langacker, R. (1999). *Grammar and conceptualization.* New York: Mouton de Gruyter.

Lantolf, J. P., and Thorne, S. L. (2006). *Sociocultural theory and the genesis of second language development.* New York: Oxford University Press.

Leki, I. (2003). Living through college literacy: Nursing in a second language. *Written Communication, 20*, 81–98.

Levorato, M. C., and Cacciari, C. (2002). The creation of new figurative expressions: Psycholinguistic evidence in Italian children, adolescents, and adults. *Journal of Child Language, 29*, 127–150.

Mackey, A., and Gass, S. M. (2005). *Second language research: Methodology and design.* Mahwah, NJ: Lawrence Erlbaum.

MacWhinney, B. (2000). *The CHILDES project: Tools for analyzing talk.* Vol. 1, *Transcription format and programs* (3rd ed.). Mahwah, NJ: Lawrence Erlbaum.

Marx, N. (2002). Never quite a "native speaker": Accent and identity in the L2—and the L1. *Canadian Modern Language Review, 59*, 364–281.

Mellow, J. D. (2006). The emergence of second language syntax: A case study of the acquisition of relative clauses. *Applied Linguistics, 27*, 645–670.

Mohan, B., and Beckett, G. (2001). A functional approach to research on content-based language learning: Recasts in causal explanations. *Canadian Modern Language Review, 58*, 133–155.

Myles, F., Hooper, J., and Mitchell, R. (1998). Rote or rule? Exploring the role of formulaic language in classroom foreign language learning. *Language Learning, 48*, 323–363.

Norris, J. M., and Ortega, L. (2000). Effectiveness of L2 instruction: A research synthesis and quantitative meta-analysis. *Language Learning, 50*, 417–528.

Ortega, L., and Iberri-Shea, G. (2005). Longitudinal research in SLA: Recent trends and future directions. *Annual Review of Applied Linguistics, 25*, 26–45.

Pavesi, M. (1986). Markedness, discoursal modes, and relative clause formation in a formal and informal context. *Studies in Second Language Acquisition, 8*, 38–55.

Pavlenko, A., and Blackledge, A. (Eds.). (2004). *Negotiation of identities in multilingual contexts.* Philadelphia, PA: Multilingual Matters.

Sasaki, M. (2004). A multiple-data analysis of the 3.5-year development of EFL student writers. *Language Learning, 54,* 525–582.

Sato, C. (1990). *The syntax of conversation in interlanguage development.* Tübingen: Gunter Narr.

Schmidt, R. (1983). Interaction, acculturation, and the acquisition of communicative competence. In N. Wolfson and E. Judd (Eds.), *Sociolinguistics and language acquisition* (pp. 137–174). Rowley, MA: Newbury House.

Schumann, J. (1978). Second language acquisition: The pidginization hypothesis. In E. Hatch (Ed.), *Second language acquisition: A book of readings* (pp. 256–271). Rowley, MA: Newbury House.

Segalowitz, N. (2003). Automaticity and second languages. In C. Doughty and M. H. Long (Eds.), *Handbook of second language acquisition* (pp. 382–408). Malden, MA: Blackwell.

Shohamy, E. (2006). Rethinking assessment for advanced language proficiency. In H. Byrnes, H. D. Weger-Guntharp, and K. Sprang (Eds.), *Educating for advanced foreign language capacities: Constructs, curriculum, instruction, assessment* (pp. 188–208). Washington, DC: Georgetown University Press.

Thomas, M. (2006). Research synthesis and historiography: The case of assessment of second language proficiency. In J. M. Norris and L. Ortega (Eds.), *Synthesizing research on language learning and teaching* (pp. 279–298). Philadelphia, PA: John Benjamins.

Ushioda, E. (2001). Language learning at university: Exploring the role of motivational thinking. In Z. Dörnyei and R. Schmidt (Eds.), *Motivation and second language acquisition* (pp. 93–125). Honolulu, HI: University of Hawai'i, Second Language Teaching and Curriculum Center.

Vavrus, J. (2002). Postcoloniality and English: Exploring language policy and the politics of development in Tanzania. *TESOL Quarterly, 36,* 373–398.

Ward, C., Bochner, S., and Furnham, A. (2001). *The psychology of culture shock.* London: Routledge.

Wells, B., Peppé, S., and Goulandris, N. (2004). Intonation development from five to thirteen. *Journal of Child Language, 31,* 749–778.

Young, C. H., Savola, K. L., and Phelps, E. (1991). *Inventory of longitudinal studies in the social sciences.* Newbury Park, CA: Sage.

Part I

Theoretical and methodological explorations

2 Developing qualitative longitudinal case studies of advanced language learners

Linda Harklau

Abstract

Case study methodology has often been considered a "weak sibling" (Yin, 2003) among social science research methods. Yet longitudinal case studies are among the earliest and most enduring forms of empirical first and second language acquisition research. They have proven to be theoretically generative and have had a significant impact on the development of the field. In this chapter, I first describe typical features of longitudinal case study such as naturalistic inquiry and intensive documentation of a small number of learners. I then elaborate arguments for why longitudinal case study can provide unique insights into the processes of advanced second language acquisition. In particular, I suggest that case studies are especially suited to showing how context shapes advanced language learning over time. Because of their intensive and iterative nature, case studies can detect recurring features of learners' social and institutional environments that influence what language is acquired. By documenting how individual learners negotiate meaning across social contexts, I suggest that case studies might contribute to a reconceptualization of the phenomenon of advanced language proficiency—not as a single target but as a repertoire of multiple styles and registers of language that vary according to individual background, context, and modality.

Introduction

As Yin (2003, p. xiii) notes, case study methodology has often been considered a "weak sibling" among social science research methods. Yet, longitudinal case studies are among the earliest and most enduring forms of first and second language acquisition research. Case studies have proven to be both empirically rich and theoretically generative in studies of second language acquisition (SLA). In fact, in a recent review of case study research in SLA, van Lier (2005) asserts that case studies have "helped to shape the entire field in quite substantial ways" (p. 198).

In this chapter, I briefly define and review the history of longitudinal case study approaches to research on SLA. I focus specifically on qualitative, naturalistic approaches to case study. Next, drawing on my own experience with longitudinal case study research and the published work of others, I reflect on the methodological strengths of ethnographic case study. I argue that longitudinal case study is a method especially suited to the study of advanced language learning because it can help us to develop new, more context-sensitive insights about the process and product of advanced language learning. Finally, I conclude with some observations on logistical issues encountered in longitudinal naturalistic case study research with L2 learners.

The precedent for qualitative case studies of SLA

Longitudinal case study was perhaps the first empirical methodology applied to the modern study of second language acquisition. Hakuta (1986, p. 3), for example, chronicles Werner Leopold's (1939) careful decade-long analysis of his daughter's bilingual acquisition of German and English. Hakuta's own early work (1976) emulated Leopold's, creating a detailed longitudinal case study of one Japanese L1 child learning English. In the 1980s he identified at least 20 other case study reports of the acquisition of two or more languages in childhood (Hakuta, 1986). Longitudinal, naturalistic case study of child and adolescent second language learners continues to be a popular research method. Some notable recent examples include Caldas and Caron-Caldas' (2002) study of their three children's French and English language use; Hawkins' (2005) year-long study of four English language learners in an American kindergarten; Jia and Aaronson's (2003) three-year-long study of L2 gains and L1 attrition among ten Chinese L1 children and adolescents; Kanno's (2003) study of Japanese adolescent sojourners in Canada and Japan; Lam's (2000) study of an adolescent learning English through international internet-based communication; Toohey's (2000) study of six children from kindergarten through second grade; and Valdés' (2001) study of Mexican-American adolescents in northern California.

While case studies focusing on childhood second language acquisition have predominated, longitudinal case studies focusing on adult learners have likewise proven to be theoretically generative. Schumann's (1978) case study of Alberto led him to develop the influential theory about pidginization in SLA. Schmidt's (1983) three-year-long study of Wes, a Japanese immigrant to Hawai'i, illustrated that learners can develop a considerable degree of communicative competence even with an incomplete and fossilized mastery of L2 grammar. Huebner's (1983) case study of Ge, a Hmong refugee, showed that learners' interlanguage systems did not develop linearly but rather exhibited signs of backtracking and reformulation of grammar rules. Influential naturalistic case studies of adult L2 learners in recent years include the European Science Foundation's (ESF) massive (two and a half years) study of adult language learners (Perdue and European Science Foundation, 1993a, 1993b), including Broeder's (1991) follow-up examination of untutored adult SLA of Dutch, Norton's (2000) study of women immigrants in Canada, and Leki's (1999, 2001) five-year-long study of nonnative English speaking students' experiences with American academic writing in university settings.

While longitudinal case studies of L2 learners can take the form of a time series of decontextualized language production data sets (see, e.g., Regan, 2004; Zhang, 2004), most case study research in SLA has incorporated a naturalistic approach to data collection (Johnson, 1991), linking acquisition phenomena to the context in which they occur. My own case study research (Harklau, 1994a, 2000), for example, has taken an ethnographic orientation (Merriam, 1998, pp. 34–35), looking at English learners as participants in and products of the cultural context of US secondary schools.

Longitudinal case study research in SLA has taken a number of forms. Some, like Schumann (1978), Schmidt (1983), Huebner (1983), and Lam (2000), have focused intensively on single cases. Others have taken a self-case study or diary approach (typically involving a co-investigator) such as Schmidt's account of learning Portuguese in Brazil (Schmidt and Frota, 1986), Carson's (Carson and Longhini, 2002) self-study of learning strategies while learning Spanish in Argentina, Schultz' (Schultz and Elliott, 2000) account of learning Spanish in Colombia, and Grabe's (Grabe and Stoller, 1997) account of Portuguese reading and vocabulary development in Brazil. Recent work has tended to incorporate multiple case studies in the same setting. For example, I have conducted two longitudinal studies of multiple focal English learners in US high school and college settings (Harklau, 1994a, 2000). Toohey (2000) has traced the early experiences of multiple case studies of immigrant children in elementary school. Other examples include Dagenais and Day's (1998) work with trilingual children in a Canadian immersion program and Norton's (2000) study of Canadian immigrant women and identity. The ESF study (Broeder, 1991; Perdue and European Science Foundation, 1993b) not only collected naturalistic and elicited data from multiple cases, but collected it across several native language/ target language groups. Miles and Huberman (1994, p. 29, 172) and Merriam (1998, pp. 40, 195) point out that multiple case designs strengthen studies by creating potential for cross-case analysis and the identification of trends or patterns that transcend individual cases.

Defining features of qualitative case study

Case study methods have a number of champions among social and behavioral science researchers. Prominent contemporary advocates include Dyson and Genishi (2005), Gillham (2000), Hammersley, Gomm, and Foster (2000), Merriam (1998), Ragin and Becker (1992), Stake (2000), and Yin (2003). (In applied linguistics, the first book-length treatment on the subject appeared at the time the present collection was going to press: Duff, 2008.) Some scholars, such as Merriam (1998) and Stake (2000), define case study in terms of its unit of analysis—one case—more than any particular methodology. In fact, as Stake (2000) points out, not all case studies are even identified as such. Other case study methodologists, such as Yin (2003), argue that case study is defined by its process, a distinct form of empirical inquiry that "investigates a contemporary phenomenon within its real-life context" when contextual conditions are believed to be important to the object of study. Hammersley and Gomm (2000) likewise distinguish case study methods from other forms of inquiry along two dimensions. First, case studies can be differentiated from survey methods by the smaller number of subjects and more detailed information collected on each case. Second, they can be distinguished from experimental methods by their naturalistic orientation. The "case" in case studies may be an individual, but may also be "a group, a place, or an activity, or some combination of those units" (Dyson and Genishi, 2005).

When data are collected in "real-time" (as opposed to retrospective accounts), they are almost necessarily longitudinal in nature. Although there is no consensus about the minimum length for a qualitative study to be considered longitudinal (Saldana, 2003, p. 3), the *Inventory of longitudinal studies in the social sciences* (Young, Savola, and Phelps, 1991) uses one year as its benchmark. In ethnographic and other qualitative approaches, the purpose is to tie language acquisition and production to the contexts in which they took place, and thus to show the effects of context in shaping the process of language acquisition and the nature of language proficiency that is ultimately attained.

While qualitative case studies may differ widely in theoretical orientations and populations, they have in common the naturalistic, long-term, intensive documentation of processes of second language acquisition in a small number of language learners in context. Typically naturalistic forms of case study inquiry rely on at least three sources of data. Perhaps the most prominent form of data is repeated naturalistic participant observation. In the case of L2 learners, these data serve as a record of the characteristics of learners' spoken language input and interactions as well as of the sociocultural and institutional contexts in which they occur. These interactions might also be audio- or video-recorded. Another typical data source is samples of written sources of linguistic input and output. A third is interviews that serve as a means of eliciting learner perspectives on their own processes of acquisition. SLA researchers often supplement these sources with learner diaries or journals (e.g., Carson and Longhini, 2002; Norton, 2000; Schmidt and Frota, 1986). Yin (2003) suggests that case study design demands that these sources of data be triangulated or checked against each other.

Methodological strengths of longitudinal case study

One often cited reason for conducting case study research in SLA is to focus on the means to language proficiency rather than its endpoint, on what Saldana (2003, p. 7) terms "the from-through" instead of the "from-to." "From-to" studies, including cross-sectional work and even some longitudinal studies that take samples at discrete points in time, may not reveal *processes* of learning. For example, while the thrust of much early cross-sectional work in SLA was to develop a relatively incremental and fixed order of acquisition for morphosyntax in L2, case studies of learners by researchers such as Fillmore (1976), Hakuta (1976), and Huebner (1983) were able to show that learners in fact relied extensively on prefabricated patterns of utterances in their early production that could make a syntactic feature look acquired when in fact it was not yet an analyzed part of the learner's syntactic system. In other words, we need to look at the full sweep of the journey across time and not just a few snapshots along the way to truly understand second language acquisition.

For researchers taking interpretive approaches, another reason to use case studies is to carefully document the interaction of individual and context and to document how language learning is mediated by participants' understandings of and interactions with context over time. Of course, "context" can be defined in a number of ways (Goodwin and Duranti, 1992; Tarone, 2000), from discourse context (e.g., Han, 2000; Huebner, 1983; Toohey, 2000), to classroom and institutional context (e.g., Harklau, 2000; Toohey, 2000), to broader community, national, economic, and sociopolitical contexts (e.g., Kanno, 2003; Norton, 2000). Within these contexts, case studies offer the advantage of access to the frequently overlooked perceptions, beliefs, and attitudes of learners themselves (Kanno, 2003). As Carson and Longhini (2002) note, these perspectives are not easily gotten at through observation or production data alone.

Because of their iterative, longitudinal nature, case studies are especially well suited to detecting recurring features of social and institutional contexts that shape the nature of language that is acquired. For example, in one study (Harklau, 1994a, 1994b) I found that a US high school's ability tracking system created vastly different English language learning environments for immigrant students. Learners in high track classes interacted extensively with other students and the teacher through both talk and text, while students in lower tracks had much more limited and mechanistic experiences with English. Had I observed these differences in a single class, I might have attributed these differences to variability in individual teaching style or curricula, but longitudinal observations provided a clear pattern. Zentella's (1997) decades-long study of one Puerto Rican community in New York was able to illustrate contextual influences on processes of generational language shift and the acquisition and use of multiple dialects and registers of English and Spanish. Longitudinal case studies are also particularly noteworthy in their ability to document how changing contexts can change the nature of the learning experience (Harklau, 2000; Kanno, 2003; Norton, 2000).

The inductive nature of qualitative case study research also opens up possibilities to be surprised and to generate new theory about SLA. For example, when I began studying English language learners in a US high school, I had little awareness of ability grouping and could not have predicted that it could be an explanatory mechanism for SLA. It was the iterative process of observation, interviews, and looking at learners' spoken and written language production that enabled me to see that this was a significant factor in language development. The longitudinal nature of qualitative case studies also makes it a particularly forgiving method, allowing a researcher to change directions and test out new theories while still in the midst of data collection. So when I determined that ability tracking figured prominently in case study students' experiences, I had time to hone data collection to investigate the issue more intensively in subsequent work.

The iterative nature of longitudinal case study work provides a researcher with an opportunity to become part of the research sites and participants' lives that would otherwise be unlikely. It is perhaps as close to eliminating the observer's paradox that one is ever likely to come. The routine of regular observations and interviews leads to familiarity and a level of comfort with the researcher's presence. In my research in US secondary schools, school personnel start to recognize me and treat me on a par with other regular school visitors. They allow me an insider's freedom of movement in the school. Participants become quite accustomed to my visits, even anticipating my questions and helping with the research. They invite me to events outside of the research site—their homes, their weddings, and their graduations. In this sense naturalistic longitudinal work carries with it momentum that allows the researcher to become part of the research setting and makes data collection easier as it goes along.

The need for case studies of advanced second language acquisition

As van Lier (2005) notes, while existing case studies have shown that second language learning is a protracted process, most case studies have focused only on the initial stages of learning. Little work thus far has examined the equally crucial processes of advanced language learning. Case study, as a contextually dependent and naturalistic form of inquiry, is especially suited to this work because of the nature of advanced language acquisition.

There has been a tendency in SLA research to define target language proficiency in a relatively circumscribed way in terms of morphosyntax and phonology that are universally acquired by first language learners. Yet this approach fails us in studying advanced L2 learning in at least two ways. First, we know that the advanced stages of even first language acquisition are highly variable and heavily influenced by social context. Nippold (1998, p. 3), for example, notes that one of the most distinctive features of advanced first language acquisition in older children and adolescents is differential exposure to language domains depending on individual and social factors, and thus greater individual variation in language acquired. Likewise, Hoyle and Adger (1998, p. 7) point out that a central feature of first language development in later childhood and adolescence is the mastery of a variable range of registers. Advanced proficiency further demands the pragmatic competence to know when to shift among registers according to both social setting—e.g., an academic class discussion versus talk among friends—and modality—e.g., spoken language versus written language. So while the basic morphosyntax and phonology that have been the major focus of the field are necessary components of SLA, they are definitely not sufficient to be considered proficient in any given language domain. In fact, one may fossilize in morphosyntactic development but at the same time grow quite proficient in other ways. Ward (1997) provides the example of the Secretary General of the United Nations giving a lecture at his college and speaking "with charm and wit about what he called the 'United Nation.'"

Research suggests that both first (Nippold, 1998, p. 4) and second (Urquhart and Weir, 1998, p. 24) language learners acquire most of their knowledge of advanced lexical and grammatical patterns from written language. Tarone and Bigelow (2005) further suggest that experiences with alphabetic literacy also differentiate learners' ability to perceive and segment sounds in spoken language. Because exposure to written language is differentiated by social factors such as class, gender, and level of formal education, the nature of advanced language proficiency is inextricably linked to social factors and therefore necessarily variable. As Cook (2002) notes, "Some use the language for comparatively simple daily exchanges such as commuting to work. Some lead their entire lives through the second language . . . Hence the concept of a complete knowledge of a language is meaningless: competence is whatever it is" (p. 10). To illustrate, an immigrant learning English in a US high school learns more and different things about English than a peer who drops out of school and works as an unskilled laborer. Nevertheless, they could both arguably be classified as advanced language learners. In all, then, the study of advanced SLA demands that we move away from monolithic and circumscribed notions of language proficiency towards a conceptualization of proficiency as a repertoire of multiple styles and registers that vary according to individual background, social context, and modality (see, e.g., Tarone, 2000). Case study is a method ideally suited to exploring and theorizing this variability.

Second, by viewing advanced language learners as simply "incomplete versions of some complete final state" of monolingual-like competence (Cook, 2002, p. 10), we neglect the fact that the linguistic competence of multilinguals is, if anything, even more complex and varied than that of monolinguals. Cook and others (see, e.g., Firth and Wagner, 1997) argue persuasively that because the minds, languages, and lives of multilinguals are different from those of monolinguals, it is not appropriate to gauge multilinguals' linguistic performances against that of monolingual native speakers of a language. Cook concludes that, "In the absence of the native speaker, there is no single uniform criterion against which L2 users can be measured" (p. 10). Naturalistic case study provides an especially useful tool to explore advanced language learning as developing multicompetence, where a one-way relation of language dominance and transfer becomes an interrelationship and ecology (Haugen, 1987; Haugen, Eliasson, and Jahr, 1997) of language proficiencies and where issues of communicative competence are superseded by issues of code choice.

Methodological challenges of longitudinal case study

While case study offers many strengths for the study of advanced second language acquisition, it also undoubtedly has some drawbacks as well. It has not been common in SLA to have forthright discussions about the personal and professional challenges presented by various approaches to inquiry (see Schachter and Gass, 1996; Spada, 2005 for notable exceptions). There is a common tendency to make method narratives as impersonal and "clean" as possible in published research reports. This tendency may be amplified in reports using qualitative case study given the method's already vulnerable status in a field dominated by post-positivistic and experimental orientations. It must nonetheless be acknowledged that there are some significant methodological and logistical issues to be considered when undertaking longitudinal case study research.

For one thing, the structure of North American academia renders it all but impossible to undertake longitudinal research early in one's career. The tenure clock implicitly rewards short-term research that can quickly yield publications. Even post-tenure, review and merit systems operate on a yearly cycle that provides little incentive to undertake long-term projects without immediate publication potential. Often researchers who conduct longitudinal research do so while at the same time maintaining work on other shorter-term projects. However, the researcher's divided attention means that most longitudinal work is the product of compromises in the amount or depth of data collected at any given point. Given this logistical problem of time and resources, it is probably not coincidental that many longitudinal case studies have featured convenience samples such as the researchers' own family members—or even the ultimate convenience sample, the researchers themselves. Because of the relative rarity of true longitudinal social science research, institutional human subjects review boards may also find longitudinal projects unfamiliar and therefore problematic. The board at my institution, for example, has an arbitrarily set limit of five years for the conduct of any research study. Beyond that, a study must undergo the same lengthy and painstaking process of review and approval that it did initially, thus creating a significant disincentive for longer projects.

Longitudinal case study also presents logistical challenges in terms of managing an uneven workload over the course of the study. Even though many case study research reports portray the process as constant or iterative, in practice I suspect that is not most researchers' experience. For one thing, the start-up and wrap-up phases of longitudinal case study are inevitably more intensive. At the beginning of a project, the process of participant selection and recruitment is time-consuming and often involves multiple levels of review and permissions from the researcher's university, outside agencies, and participants. Perdue (and European Science Foundation, 1993a), for example, notes ESF project researchers had to devote a substantial amount of time to becoming familiar and trusted figures in the social networks of immigrant communities before they could recruit participants.

After initial recruitment, long-term case studies tend to fall into a routine, but I have nevertheless come to expect the unexpected—incidents that suddenly demand a great deal of time and attention. For example, on one occasion a participant in my research failed a course and jeopardized her high school graduation. As her school-designated "advocate," I was abruptly summoned to the school to represent her interests in an emotionally charged, high-stakes meeting with her mother, counselor, and teachers to resolve the problem. This is not work for those with inflexible schedules (or temperaments).

A related and seldom-discussed issue in longitudinal naturalistic research is data "messiness." The vicissitudes of case study subjects' personal lives often trump a researcher's data collection schedule, leaving data that have gaps and irregularities. For example, one of my research participants became ill while visiting family in Mexico. She was hospitalized there for two months and, while I was able to interview her about her experiences soon after her return, her absence nevertheless constitutes a hole in the data. Likewise, Lam (2000) indicates that in her case study of a Chinese-American youth, some of the participant's most formative moments as an English learner actually took place during a six-month period while she was away, leading her to document the changes she observed upon her return. The longitudinal aspect of case study tends to compensate for these sorts of lacunae, however, and the lengthier the study, the less significant they become.

Case study data also tend to be messy in terms of research settings. In order to keep participants engaged in long-term data collection, the researcher often has to be flexible about the time and places they work with case studies. Huebner (1983), for example, describes meeting Ge in his home, having a beer at his kitchen table while family members and friends came and went. He also describes driving him to social service agency appointments and even teaching him to drive. In my own work, I have met with participants not only at their schools but also in their homes, at libraries, college dormitories, coffee shops, shopping malls, and playgrounds.

Another logistical challenge is the negotiation of personal relationships between the researcher and researched. Because of the long-term one-to-one contact between case study participants and researchers, it is a form of research especially subject to the vagaries of interpersonal dynamics. Subjects may initially agree to participate because of some extrinsic motivation or reward, but ultimately whether they continue to participate has just as much to do with the personal relationships built and sustained over the course of the study. Perdue (and European Science Foundation, 1993a), for example, notes that only half of the ESF study participants were compensated and that payment seemed to have little effect on whether participants stayed with the study. Like anyone else, case study participants differ as individuals in their gregariousness and openness. Some may freely share details about their lives, while others never become entirely comfortable in the presence of a researcher. Because of the intensive nature of the relationship, a researcher often gains insight not only into second language learning, but also into participants' family, friends, work, and futures. Conversely, researchers may find that they must be willing to step out of the researcher/clinician persona and volunteer relevant aspects of their own personal lives in interactions with participants. Case study individuals also vary in their willingness to discuss aspects of the sociocultural, economic, and political contexts in which they are learning language. It may be painful, for example, for someone to relate incidents of ethnic harassment but nevertheless vitally important to documenting learners' motivation and attitudes about the target language. Asking the learner to reflect on the process of language learning may actually exacerbate negative affect or culture shock (Perdue and European Science Foundation, 1993a). Individual differences and variations in interpersonal relationships among researcher and researched thus inevitably affect the scope and strength of case study data and demand especially careful analytic attention when working across cases.

Attrition also poses special challenges in longitudinal case study research designs. Because of their reliance on intensive, long-term analysis of a handful of cases, every lost participant presents a potential threat to the ultimate validity and viability of the study. Furthermore, case study research on immigrants may be particularly subject to attrition because of the "fragile" (Perdue and European Science Foundation, 1993a, p. 44) and transient nature of immigrant communities. Researchers tend to address this problem by including extra cases going into a study. However, this practice renders the initial stages of a project very demanding. Perdue (and European Science Foundation, 1993a), for example, notes that the dropout rate on the ESF study was lower than expected, leaving researchers with a considerable body of data that was not used in the final analysis. Furthermore, because the researcher–researched relationship in longitudinal case study is fairly intimate on an interpersonal level, participants who wish to drop out of a study may be reluctant to inform the researcher directly and instead opt for less face-threatening but more ambiguous strategies such as postponing meetings. For this reason, many longitudinal qualitative researchers suggest that consent to participate does not end with the signing of one letter but is an ongoing and never-ending process.

While longitudinal inductive case study presents particular methodological strengths and opportunities for theory-building about advanced second language acquisition, it also presents unique challenges. For one, case studies of advanced language learners can generate enormous and almost unmanageable bodies of data over time. Even in a modest year-long study, I collected over 5000 pages of students' written language samples alone, to say nothing of interview transcripts and observational fieldnotes. Larger-scale multi-site projects such as the ESF study have generated upwards of 18,000 pages of transcription (Feldweg, 1993), rendering the logistics of data storage and retrieval a laborious and time-consuming process.

Another challenge in case studies of advanced language acquisition lies in documenting low incidence structures and lexical items that are not easily observed naturalistically. For this reason, many researchers who study advanced learners incorporate some form of elicitation task such as diary or other introspective reports (see, e.g., Carson and Longhini, 2002; Norton, 2000), retrospective protocols (see, e.g., Faerch and Kasper, 1987; Gass and Mackey, 2000), or elicitation or role-playing exercises (Perdue and European Science Foundation, 1993a). Furthermore, the nature of advanced learners' interactions with written texts, be it a literature text or email, are not easily captured by traditional naturalistic methodologies such as observation or videotape. This may likewise demand the inclusion of more elicit-ation, text analysis (see, e.g., Schleppegrell, 2004), retrospective protocols, and the like in order to address the full range of modalities, genres, and registers produced by the learner in a given context.

Challenges to the legitimacy of case study

In a field that has historically been dominated by broader survey and experimental approaches, qualitative case study may not be recognized as a legitimate and rigor-ous research methodology. Case study has sometimes been criticized as unscientific. However, while scientific research has been popularly associated with broader experimental and quasi-experimental methods, in fact particularistic descriptive work is a long-standing and widely accepted research method across the biological and social sciences. Case study is a typical method, for example, for biologists seeking to describe aspects of an ecosystem, changes in the system over time, or the role of a specific organism within the system. It is also widely employed in medicine and psychiatry to trace epidemiology and progression of diseases and treatments. Nevertheless, there is a stigma attached to case study. Perhaps one reason is that the label "case study" is often used incorrectly or imprecisely (Yin, 2003, p. xii) as a catch-all category for research that is clearly not experimental (Merriam, 1998, p. 43) or as a means of legitimizing small-scale pilot studies. How-ever, case study research is—or should be—subject to the same standards for scholarly rigor that characterize other qualitative, interpretivist work in the social and behavioral sciences.

A related issue is the field's unfamiliarity with how researcher subjectivity figures into qualitative, interpretivist research approaches. Case study researchers inevitably influence the phenomena we are investigating. We begin with a certain worldview and preconceptions and we shape and narrow the scope of inquiry over the course of data collection, directing attention to some facets of advanced language learning while neglecting others. It is a precept of interpretivist qualitative approaches that the researcher is the instrument of research and thus the researcher's subjectivity is considered a given in such approaches. However, it is worth emphasizing here that the researcher's own background and interests are pivotal factors in both lan-guage production observed and even more broadly in the shaping of case studies' experiences with the language. As Dyson and Genishi (2005) observe, "cases are constructed, not found" (p. 2).

A final challenge to the legitimacy of case study as a research methodology is the issue of generalizability of findings. Over the years there has been, and no doubt will continue to be, a debate among case study researchers regarding if and how case studies "count" as generalizable research (Dyson and Genishi, 2005). Some maintain that case studies are not designed to produce scientific generalizations (Lincoln and Guba, 1985). Indeed, they suggest that seeking to do so misses the main point of doing case study, which is to gain insight into particularistic, individual human experience. Others suggest that case study produces generalizations, but generalizations of a different order or kind than large-scale survey or experimental research (Hammersley, Gomm, and Foster, 2000). This issue remains to be addressed in the field of second language acquisition.

In spite of these challenges, my own experience confirms van Lier's (2005) faith in the theoretically generative nature of longitudinal case study research in our field. As I have argued here, in spite of its flaws, longitudinal case studies hold the potential to bring us new conceptualizations of the nature of advanced language learning. I believe such case studies will have broad implications for the field, problematizing views of advanced language proficiency as a singular and autonomous entity that can be defined independent of its social context and promoting more context-sensitive definitions of advanced proficiency.

References

Broeder, P. (1991). *Talking about people: A multiple case study on adult language acquisition.* Amsterdam/Berwyn, PA: Swets and Zeitlinger.

Caldas, S. J., and Caron-Caldas, S. (2002). A sociolinguistic analysis of the language preferences of adolescent bilinguals: Shifting allegiances and developing identities. *Applied Linguistics, 23*, 490–514.

Carson, J. G., and Longhini, A. (2002). Focusing on learning styles and strategies: A diary study in an immersion setting. *Language Learning, 52*, 401–439.

Cook, V. (2002). Background to the L2 user. In V. Cook (Ed.), *Portraits of the L2 user* (pp. 1–28). Clevedon, UK: Multilingual Matters.

Dagenais, D., and Day, E. (1998). Classroom language experiences of trilingual children in French immersion. *Canadian Modern Language Review, 54*, 376–393.

Duff, P. A. (2008). *Case study research in applied linguistics.* New York: Routledge.

Dyson, A. H., and Genishi, C. (2005). *On the case: Approaches to language and literacy research.* New York: Teachers College Press and National Conference on Research in Language and Literacy.

Faerch, C., and Kasper, G. (Eds.). (1987). *Introspection in second language research.* Clevedon, UK: Multilingual Matters.

Feldweg, H. (1993). Transcription, storage and retrieval of data. In C. Perdue and European Science Foundation (Eds.), *Adult language acquisition: Cross-linguistic perspectives.* Vol. 1, *Field methods* (pp. 108–130). New York: Cambridge University Press.

Fillmore, L. W. (1976). The second time around: Cognitive and social strategies in second language acquisition. Unpublished Doctoral Dissertation, Stanford University, Palo Alto.

Firth, A., and Wagner, J. (1997). On discourse, communication, and (some) fundamental concepts in SLA research. *Modern Language Journal, 81*, 285–300.

Gass, S. M., and Mackey, A. (2000). *Stimulated recall methodology in second language research.* Mahwah, NJ: Lawrence Erlbaum.

Gillham, B. (2000). *Case study research methods.* New York: Continuum.

Goodwin, C., and Duranti, A. (1992). Rethinking context: An introduction. In A. Duranti and C. Goodwin (Eds.), *Rethinking context: Language as an interactive phenomenon* (pp. 1–42). New York: Cambridge University Press.

Grabe, W., and Stoller, F. L. (1997). Reading and vocabulary development in a second language: A case study. In J. Coady and T. Huckin (Eds.), *Second language vocabulary acquisition: A rationale for pedagogy* (pp. 98–122). New York: Cambridge University Press.

Hakuta, K. (1976). A case study of a Japanese child learning English as a Second Language. *Language Learning, 26*, 321–351.

Hakuta, K. (1986). *Mirror of language: The debate on bilingualism.* New York: Basic Books.

Hammersley, M., and Gomm, R. (2000). Introduction. In R. Gomm, M. Hammersley, and P. Foster (Eds.), *Case study method* (pp. 1–16). Thousand Oaks, CA: Sage.

Hammersley, M., Gomm, R., and Foster, P. (2000). Case study and theory. In R. Gomm, M. Hammersley, and P. Foster (Eds.), *Case study method* (pp. 234–258). Thousand Oaks, CA: Sage.

Han, Z. H. (2000). Persistence of the implicit influence of NL: The case of the pseudo-passive. *Applied Linguistics, 21*, 55–82.

Harklau, L. (1994a). ESL and mainstream classes: Contrasting second language learning contexts. *TESOL Quarterly, 28*, 241–272.

Harklau, L. (1994b). Tracking and linguistic minority students: Consequences of ability grouping for second language learners. *Linguistics and Education, 6*, 221–248.

Harklau, L. (2000). From the "good kids" to the "worst": Representations of English language learners across educational settings. *TESOL Quarterly, 34*, 35–67.

Haugen, E. I. (1987). *Blessings of Babel: Bilingualism and language planning: Problems and pleasures.* Berlin/New York: Mouton de Gruyter.

Haugen, E. I., Eliasson, S., and Jahr, E. H. (1997). *Language and its ecology: Essays in memory of Einar Haugen.* Berlin/New York: Mouton de Gruyter.

Hawkins, M. R. (2005). Becoming a student: Identity work and academic literacies in early schooling. *TESOL Quarterly, 39*, 59–82.

Hoyle, S. M., and Adger, C. T. (1998). Introduction. In S. M. Hoyle and C. T. Adger (Eds.), *Kids talk: Strategic language use in later childhood* (pp. 3–21). New York: Oxford University Press.

Huebner, T. (1983). *A longitudinal analysis of the acquisition of English.* Ann Arbor, MI: Karoma.

Jia, G., and Aaronson, D. (2003). A longitudinal study of Chinese children and adolescents learning English in the United States. *Applied Psycholinguistics, 24*, 131–161.

Johnson, D. M. (1991). *Approaches to research in second language learning.* New York: Longman.

Kanno, Y. (2003). *Negotiating bilingual and bicultural identities: Japanese returnees betwixt two worlds.* Mahwah, NJ: Lawrence Erlbaum.

Lam, W. S. E. (2000). L2 literacy and the design of the self: A case study of a teenager writing on the internet. *TESOL Quarterly, 34*, 457–482.

Leki, I. (1999). "Pretty much I screwed up": Ill-served needs of a permanent resident. In L. Harklau, K. Losey, and M. Siegal (Eds.), *Generation 1.5 meets college composition: Issues in the teaching of writing to US-educated learners of English as a second language* (pp. 17–43). Mahwah, NJ: Lawrence Erlbaum.

Leki, I. (2001). "A narrow thinking system": Nonnative-English-speaking students in group projects across the curriculum. *TESOL Quarterly, 35*, 39–67.

Leopold, W. F. (1939). *Speech development of a bilingual child: A linguist's record.* Evanston, IL: Northwestern University.

Lincoln, Y. S., and Guba, E. G. (1985). *Naturalistic inquiry.* Beverly Hills, CA: Sage.

Merriam, S. B. (1998). *Qualitative research and case study applications in education* (2nd ed.). San Francisco: Jossey-Bass.

Miles, M. B., and Huberman, A. M. (1994). *Qualitative data analysis: An expanded sourcebook* (2nd ed.). Thousand Oaks, CA: Sage.

Nippold, M. A. (1998). *Later language development: The school-age and adolescent years* (2nd ed.). Austin, TX: Pro-Ed.

Norton, B. (2000). *Identity and language learning: Social processes and educational practice.* New York: Pearson Education Limited.

Perdue, C., and European Science Foundation (Eds.). (1993a). *Adult language acquisition: Cross-linguistic perspectives.* Vol. 1, *Field methods.* New York: Cambridge University Press.

Perdue, C., and European Science Foundation. (Eds.). (1993b). *Adult language acquisition: Cross-linguistic perspectives.* Vol. 2, *The results.* New York: Cambridge University Press.

Ragin, C. C., and Becker, H. S. (Eds.) (1992). *What is a case? Exploring the foundations of social inquiry.* New York: Cambridge University Press.

Regan, V. (2004). The relationship between the group and the individual and the acquisition of native speaker variation patterns: A preliminary study. *IRAL: International Review of Applied Linguistics in Language Teaching, 42,* 335–349.

Saldana, J. (2003). *Longitudinal qualitative research: Analyzing change through time.* Walnut Creek, CA: AltaMira Press.

Schachter, J., and Gass, S. M. (1996). *Second language classroom research: Issues and opportunities.* Mahwah, NJ: Lawrence Erlbaum.

Schleppegrell, M. J. (2004). *The language of schooling: A functional linguistics perspective.* Mahwah, NJ: Lawrence Erlbaum.

Schmidt, R. W. (1983). Interaction, acculturation, and the acquisition of communicative competence: A case study of an adult. In N. Wolfson and E. Judd (Eds.), *Sociolinguistics and language acquisition* (pp. 137–174). Rowley, MA: Newbury House.

Schmidt, R. W., and Frota, S. N. (1986). Developing basic conversational ability in a second language: A case study of an adult learner of Portuguese. In R. Day (Ed.), *"Talking to learn": Conversation in second language acquisition* (pp. 237–326). Rowley, MA: Newbury House.

Schultz, R. A., and Elliott, P. (2000). Learning Spanish as an older adult. *Hispania, 83,* 107–119.

Schumann, J. (1978). Second language acquisition: The pidginization hypothesis. In E. Hatch (Ed.), *Second language acquisition: A book of readings* (pp. 256–271). Rowley, MA: Newbury House.

Spada, N. (2005). Conditions and challenges in developing school-based SLA research programs. *Modern Language Journal, 89,* 328–338.

Stake, R. E. (2000). Case studies. In N. K. Denzin and Y. S. Lincoln (Eds.), *Handbook of qualitative research* (2nd ed., pp. 435–454). Thousand Oaks, CA: Sage.

Tarone, E. (2000). Still wrestling with "context" in interlanguage theory. *Annual Review of Applied Linguistics, 20,* 182–198.

Tarone, E., and Bigelow, M. (2005). Impact of literacy on oral language processing: Implications for second language acquisition research. *Annual Review of Applied Linguistics, 25,* 77–97.

Toohey, K. (2000). *Learning English at school: Identity, social relations, and classroom practice.* Clevedon, UK: Multilingual Matters.

Urquhart, A. H., and Weir, C. J. (1998). *Reading in a second language: Process, product, and practice.* New York: Longman.

Valdés, G. (2001). *Learning and not learning English: Latino students in American schools.* Vol. 27. New York: Teachers College Press.

van Lier, L. (2005). Case study. In E. Hinkel (Ed.), *Handbook of research in second language teaching and learning* (pp. 195–208). Mahwah, NJ: Lawrence Erlbaum.

Ward, M. (1997). Myths about college English as a Second Language. *Chronicle of Higher Education, 44* (5, September 26), B8.

Yin, R. K. (2003). *Case study research: Design and methods* (3rd ed.). Thousand Oaks, CA: Sage.

Young, C. H., Savola, K. L., and Phelps, E. (1991). *Inventory of longitudinal studies in the social sciences.* Newbury Park, CA: Sage.

Zentella, A. C. (1997). *Growing up bilingual: Puerto Rican children in New York.* Malden, MA: Blackwell.

Zhang, Y. (2004). Processing constraints, categorical analysis, and the second language acquisition of the Chinese adjective suffix. *Language Learning, 54,* 437–469.

3 Systemic Functional Linguistic explorations into the longitudinal study of advanced capacities

The case of Spanish heritage language learners

Mariana Achugar and M. Cecilia Colombi

Abstract

Systemic Functional Linguistics (SFL) (Halliday 1978, 1994; Halliday and Matthiessen, 2004; Martin and Rose, 2003; among others) is a social theory of language that provides researchers with unique constructs, tools, and insights for the study of advanced L2 capacities. In addition, SFL is particularly well suited to provide theoretical guidance in longitudinal investigations of L2 development. In this chapter, we discuss SFL principles, highlighting their relevance for the longitudinal study of advanced L2 capacities. We also illustrate these principles with data and findings from our longitudinal research program involving Spanish heritage language learners in US higher education contexts. SFL theory situates language development in its sociohistorical context linking patterns of language use to particular culturally relevant situations. In academic contexts language is used to display information using technical lexicon, with high degrees of structure and with an authoritative stance (Martin, 1993; Schleppegrell, 2004). Therefore, in this framework language development demands longitudinal measures that gauge the control users develop over time of particular lexico-grammatical patterns (e.g., grammatical metaphor, lexical density, grammatical complexity, clause combining and engagement) that index an academic context. The discussion will be fleshed out with examples from two studies in which we tracked oral and written development of Spanish in heritage speakers who are using Spanish in academic and professional contexts in the US. From this perspective, advanced language development was defined as changes that develop gradually over time in relation to academic contexts where there are institutionalized ways of using language that characterize disciplinary discourse communities.

Introduction

Systemic Functional Linguistics (SFL) is a social theory of language originally developed by Australia-based linguist Michael Halliday (1993, 1998, 2004; Halliday and Mathiessen, 1999) and expanded in the last two decades through the work of many scholars in Australia (Christie, 2002a, 2002b; Hasan and Martin, 1989; Martin, 1992; Painter, 1989), North America (Byrnes, 2006; Lemke, 1988, 1990, 1998; Mohan, 1986, 1997; Mohan and Huxur, 2001; Schleppegrell, 2004; Schleppegrell and Colombi, 2002), Latin America (Bolivar, 1994; Ghio and Fernández, 2005; Menéndez, 1993), and Europe (Coffin, 1997; Hunston and Thompson, 2000; Kress, 1994; Kress and Van Leeuwen, 2001). The theory situates language development in its sociohistorical context, linking patterns of language use to particular, culturally relevant situations. Thus, for example, it is through language use that the child is socialized into her culture:

> In the development of the child as a social being, language has the central role. Language is the main channel through which the patterns of living are transmitted to him, through which he learns to act as a member of a "society"—in and through the various social groups, the family, the neighbourhood, and so on—and to adopt its "culture", its mode of thought and action, its beliefs and its values.
>
> (Halliday, 1978, p. 9)

Developing language, then, means developing as a member of a cultural group (Painter, 1991, p. 44). It follows that longitudinal studies from an SFL perspective focus on language development as an intersubjective process that unfolds in particular social contexts. In the longitudinal study of first language (L1) acquisition from an SFL perspective, the focus is on how language plays a crucial role in the development of the child as a social being. In bilingual and second language (L2) development, too, the social practices individuals participate in are thought to shape the types of language they develop. Variability is also a central dimension of the framework. Since language varies according to its users' social positioning (e.g., social status, gender, regional origin) and according to its uses in different social contexts (i.e., registers), there are individual differences in the type of linguistic resources different people develop. Accordingly, language learning is a social process not only in terms of *what* is learned but also because of *how* it is learned (Derewianka, 1995).

Because of this capacity to address what language is and how it is learned in social as well as linguistic terms, the SFL framework provides researchers with unique constructs, tools, and insights for the study of advanced L2 capacities. As a theoretical framework that offers its own specific analytical apparatus, it allows for the explanation and operationalization of a fundamental relationship between language use and context. Within the SFL perspective, advanced language abilities are inherently developed over longer periods of time; at its core, development is an expansion and/or refinement of domains of language use.

In this chapter, we first discuss SFL principles, highlighting their relevance for the longitudinal study of advanced L2 capacities. We then focus on how change and time scales are conceptualized in SFL theory, presenting particular moments of language development and the semiotic resources associated with each of them. We also offer a brief review of the studies of L1 and L2 development using an SLF framework. In the second half of the chapter, we present a more detailed description of two projects investigating Spanish heritage language development in the United States.

Language and learning in SFL theory

We begin by presenting four crucial constructs embedded in SFL understandings of language and language learning: culture, social action, meaning, and semiotic activity.

Language is part of culture. The linguistic system is constituted by culture and in turn helps to reproduce and transform culture. Language choices are determined by context, but language also affects context. Because language "means" in a social context from a SFL perspective, it is analyzed in relation to its social use and function, a focus that inherently involves variation and a certain ethnographic orientation (see Harklau, Chapter 2, this volume).

Language is a form of social action. Language use in social contexts always achieves social purposes. To attain them, language users make choices from the repertoire of possibilities available to them in the language system. Put differently, context influences the type of language used, and users further shape the type of language used in different contexts. The system constrains the possible choices and is changed by the choices speakers make. The actual language that occurs in a particular setting is therefore probabilistic; that is, in certain contexts users tend to make certain choices. SFL models language and social context as semiotic systems in a relationship of realization with one another. This realization entails that language construes, is construed by, and (over time) reconstrues social context (Martin, 1997, p. 4).

Grammar is meaning. SFL takes a semantic perspective on grammar. That implies that meaning and form are not separated, but stand in a dialectic relation to each other. Meanings do not exist before the wordings that realize them (Hasan and Martin, 1989). The three major types of meaning that organize this grammar are: ideational (grammar as a representation and logical organization of human experience), interpersonal (grammar as an enactment of interpersonal relationships), and textual (grammar as discourse). Thus, grammar as a semiotic mode of activity models the material mode while being itself a component of what it is modeling (Halliday, 1998, p. 186).

Learning is a language-based semiotic activity. While SFL recognizes the importance of diverse semiotic systems for human experience (e.g., gestures), it gives priority to language. That central role of language pertains not only to meaning-making in general but to learning, particularly to what is called schooled learning, a critical context for attaining advanced levels of language use. Within Halliday's (1993) language-based theory of learning, learning of any subject matter is ultimately linguistic in nature: it is an expansion of meaning-making resources where grammar plays a central role. Accordingly, a natural language embodies in its grammar a theory of human experience (Halliday, 1998, p. 194). In our daily life, we work with a common-sense theory, what Halliday refers to as congruent semiosis, which privileges the dynamic flow of human experience; however, in more public and particularly in academic settings (the settings that we associate with advanced levels of language use), a more abstract or incongruent semiosis construes experiences in terms of objects, both real and conceptual, which allow us to reorganize and control our environment. For example, when talking about the past we tend to construct meanings in terms of the human participants involved ("George Bush started the second war between Iraq and the US"); but when we construct this event as part of the discourse of the discipline of history, it acquires a new meaning that highlights the historical forces instead of the human participants ("The war between Iraq and the US resulted from the confluence of economic and political forces").

Change and time scales in SFL theory

Language change can be described from different time scales. According to Halliday and Matthiessen (1999), there are three major types of processes by which meanings are created, transmitted, extended, and changed. They are depicted in Figure 1.

Phylogenesis refers to long-term change in the cultural context. For example, over time the scientific community has developed more abstract ways of making meanings to construct its understanding of reality (see Halliday's [1993, 1998] analysis of the development of grammatical metaphor in scientific discourse). This type of development of the meaning-making system sets the context against which medium-term change, as represented in individual development or *ontogenesis*, takes place. Therefore, the individual learner's development is not best understood as an unfolding, pre-set program but as a sociogenetic phenomenon, in which interaction plays a decisive role (Hasan and Perrett, 1994). Culture, society, and its institutions (e.g., school) influence *what* linguistic resources learners develop and *how* they develop them. Finally, *logogenesis* comprises short-term change, such as that found in the unfolding of a text. As stated, the ability to transform concrete into abstract representations within a text (for example, via nominalizations, as in "The participants <u>discussed</u> (verb) the events" > "The <u>discussion</u> (noun) became heated") is a particularly important meaning-making resource within certain kinds of texts.

In sum, phylogenesis provides the environment for ontogenesis, which in turn provides the environment for logogenesis. In other words, the stage a culture has reached in its evolution provides the social context for the linguistic development of the individual, and the stage this development has reached in the individual provides resources for the instantiation of the texts. Conversely, logogenesis provides the material for phylogenesis. That is, texts provide the means through which individuals interact to learn the system, and it is through the heteroglossic aggregation of individual (always already social) systems that the semiotic trajectory of a culture evolves.

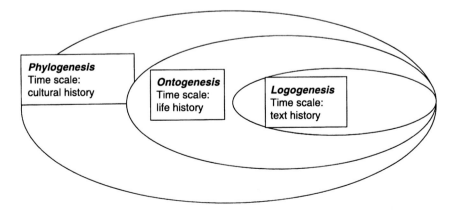

Figure 1 Types of change (based on Martin, 1997).

Ontogenetic moments and lexicogrammatical and discourse-semantic resources

SFL studies on language development (Halliday, 1993, 1998, 2004; see also Christie, 2002b, among others), have described the ontogenesis of language development from a toddler's protolanguage all the way to advanced language capacities (particularly academic language) as a movement marked by three main periods of language development or ontogenetic moments. They are schematically represented in Figure 2.

The first moment of development, interpersonal language, refers to early development from a protolanguage to a particular language and represents experience in mostly congruent form. The child is able to make grammatical generalizations, that is, she or he can move from the individual to the class category (e.g., dog > animal). The second moment develops during the elementary school years and characterizes the basic literacy of adolescents and young adults. It results from a progression from common sense to abstractness and consists of the ability to express abstraction in analysis, synthesis, and argumentation through new lexicogrammatical features. Finally, a third moment results from changes from nonspecialized to technical language (Halliday and Matthiessen, 1999, p. 618; Halliday, 1998; Christie, 2002a) and is characterized by "grammatical metaphor" (GM). Referring to various grammatically and semantically incongruent choices, grammatical metaphor is among the central features of advanced language use (see e.g., Halliday 1993, 1994, 1998). Illustrations of GM are italicized in the following example:

> Peor aún es la *emigración* masiva del campo a las ciudades, el *abandono* de las granjas *invadidas* por la sal de las *filtraciones* oceánicas, la *usurpación* económica de pueblos enteros por los traficantes de drogas *disfrazados* de hacendados, y la *contaminación* de la carne de las aves y los seres humanos por los plaguicidas y herbicidas tóxicos.
>
> (T. #10)

The word class is a noun but the meaning is an action in "*emigración*," "*usurpación*," "*contaminación*," or the word class is an adjective but the meaning is an action or a state in "*invadidas*," "*disfrazados*." Rather than nouns or adjectives, a more congruent or transparent choice would be for actions to be encoded as verbs.

The development of advanced language capacities, then, is conceptualized in ontogenesis as a movement from congruent, oral, interpersonal registers towards incongruent, written, academic registers. This movement can be tracked by charting the lexico-grammatical and discourse-semantic features of the texts a language user produces over time, among them grammatical metaphor, grammatical intricacy, lexical density, clause-combining resources, and metadiscourse choices denoting

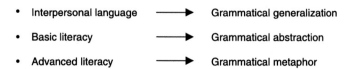

Figure 2 Ontogenetic moments of language development (adapted from Halliday, 1993, and Christie, 2002b).

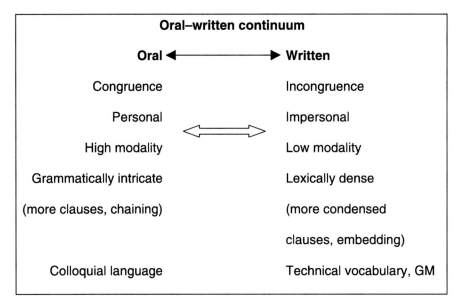

Figure 3 Some key lexicogrammatical and discourse-semantic features along the oral–written semiosis continuum (adapted from Halliday, 1985).

interpersonal stance, such as attitude, engagement, modality, and graduation (appraisal). In other words, SFL adds to the typical discussion of an oral–literate continuum an elaborate theoretical context, an elaborate set of concepts, and, by extension, an elaborate set of analytical tools. Figure 3 provides a summary of this development within the oral–written continuum.

As Figure 3 makes clear, in the SFL framework (Halliday, 1994; Martin, 1985, 1992) academic language is viewed as substantively differing from interactional registers, both in terms of its grammar and in terms of its discourse structure (Ravelli and Ellis, 2004; Schleppegrell, 2004; Schleppegrell and Colombi, 2002; Valdés and Geoffrion-Vinci, 1998; Ventola and Mauranen, 1996). Halliday (1994, p. 352) describes the "written language as more complex by being lexically dense: it packs a large number of lexical items into each clause [crystalline]; whereas spoken language becomes complex by being grammatically intricate: it builds up elaborate clause complexes out of parataxis and hypotaxis [choreographic]" (see also Halliday, 1985).

In addition, because in learning a language we learn to become members of particular social groups, a growing area of interest within SFL is the exploration of discourse-semantic resources as a way of indicating emerging and, ultimately, full membership in a group.

Longitudinal SFL studies of first and second language development

Consistent with the theoretical framework presented in the previous sections, SFL studies of language development favor analyses that relate text and grammar to the examination of meaning. Such studies combine qualitative and quantitative methods

Table 1 Four SFL longitudinal case studies of first language development at various ages

	Participant	Age	Length of study	Focus
Halliday (1973)	Researcher's son acquiring L1 English	9 months to 19 months	10 months	Functions of language, socialization
Painter (1999)	One child learning English as L1	2;6 to 5;0 years	Two and a half years	Language as tool for learning about the world
Torr (1997)	Researcher's daughter learning L1 English	2;6 to 4;3 years	21 months	Replication of Halliday (1973), modality
Derewianka (1995)	Researcher's son learning to write in L1 English	Childhood through adolescence	Several years	Grammatical metaphor

with descriptive analysis in two major areas: L1 learning of children and L1 and L2 development in educational contexts. While the latter are of particular interest here, longitudinal studies of young children, usually case studies, can also inform the work of L2 researchers: they strongly emphasize the importance of interpersonal meanings in the emergence of language and learners' active roles in the process of language development. Table 1 outlines four of these studies.

Within educational contexts with both L1 and L2 students, SFL work has been motivated by the recognition that schooling involves a process whereby students develop control over the types of texts (spoken and written) that are relevant to their educational and professional needs, especially those texts that are considered power-ful in society. Thus, SFL research has sought to make explicit the ways in which language is used in these "powerful contexts" and to enhance the opportunity of learners, most particularly disadvantaged learners, to interact and act in society by extending their linguistic repertoire (Christie, 2002a; Coffin, 1997; Hasan and Williams, 1996; Martin 1985, 1992; Rothery, 1996; Unsworth, 2000) toward the "language of schooling" (Schleppegrell, 2004). When students learn different subject areas, they learn particular ways of using language to construct knowledge. These ways have evolved in line with the interests of a particular scholarly community and go beyond the technical vocabulary that we typically associate with academic discip-lines. They also involve ways of constructing different social roles (e.g., experts vs. novices) and types of participation (e.g., full participation vs. peripheral participation) within these communities. Table 2 synthesizes some of the longitudinal SFL studies that focus on first and second language development in the educational context.

Collectively, these studies point to a clear line of development from a more con-gruent to more incongruent forms and more concrete to more abstract forms of meaning-making, marked by the development of particular linguistic resources (e.g. grammatical metaphor, grammatical intricacy, lexical density, technical vocabulary). While these features in and of themselves are not new in the discussion of advanced language abilities, the particular contributions that SFL makes are unique. SFL offers a clear way of modeling the relation of language and context with a strong meaning focus, a well-theorized and coherent way of addressing variation, change,

Table 2 Longitudinal SFL studies of L1 and L2 language development in educational contexts

	Participants	*Age/context*	*Length of study*	*Focus*
Christie (2002a, 2002b)	Middle and high school students	Adolescents/L1 (English) academic development, Australia	Several years (in progress)	Generalizations, abstractions, argument and reflection
Dubcovsky (2003)	Twenty-seven 4th and 5th grade students	9- to 11-year-old/bilingual program Spanish and English, US	Two academic years	Incipient academic writing development, focusing on the frequent use of "decir" and "cuando"
Go (2003)	Six 5th and 6th grade students	10- to 12-year-old Chinese and Vietnamese students learning English in the US	One academic year	Logical organization, complexity, genre, writing
Oteiza (2005)	Thirty college students	Heritage Spanish students in the US	One semester	Logical organization, writing
Woodward-Kron (2002)	Six undergraduate college students	Young adults, Australia	First- and third-year texts	Lexical density and technicality, abstraction, grammatical metaphor, projection, logical organization of written texts

and development, and an elaborate and nuanced conceptual apparatus that is able to capture development as an expansion of resources that allow choices within particular contexts of language use. Of interest in this context is the fact that this framework enables a particularly fruitful investigation of the ontogenic progression towards advancedness in academic language and written registers.

In the remainder of the chapter, we turn to two applications of SFL theory with a learner group that has been of particular interest to us—namely, college-age heritage Spanish speakers who not only need to expand their control over a range of oral and written academic registers but, just as importantly, need to negotiate, construct, and index new identities as members of the academic community.

The challenge of meaning in academic contexts for heritage speakers of Spanish and second language learners

Heritage speakers of Spanish in the US constitute an important student population with linguistic and educational needs (Colombi, 2002, 2006). They also present interesting challenges for the field of applied linguistics (Valdés, 2005), and provide an example of learners who exemplify issues of advancedness and the development of academic language capacities and identities.

These speakers' use of Spanish is usually limited to the home or familiar domains, although it should be noted that this situation has recently begun to change in the United States with the increase in the Spanish-speaking population and the economic advance of Spanish-speaking communities. As a result, they have developed language in informal contexts (that is, in restricted domains of use), and, by and large, have not used Spanish in situations where language is utilized to construct knowledge or negotiate the ways of being a member of a professional community. This, in turn, translates to not having the linguistic resources to respond appropriately to the demands of academic contexts. It is in this sense that heritage learners are similar to advanced L2 learners, since they both lack experience in the use of language in an academic context and have to expand their meaning-making resources to incorporate ways of using language in more specialized and abstract forms.

In the sections that follow, we describe our own longitudinal work within the SFL framework with heritage speakers who are using Spanish in academic and professional contexts in the US. The first study tracks the development of academic registers in oral and written language. The second investigates the development of academic identities.

The development of academic registers: Colombi's project with Latino college students in California

In 1999–2000 I started a longitudinal study in the Program of Spanish for Native Speakers at my home institution in order to examine the extent to which Latino college students develop full control of literate academic language. Over a nine-month period (three academic quarters) I collected all the written texts of 30 students. During the academic year of 2003–2004, in a second phase, I collected both oral and written texts of students.[1] The SFL language-based analysis of these texts was intended not only to describe academic language development in Spanish but to contribute to a visible pedagogy, that is, an explicit way of teaching the key features of language use in order to contribute to curriculum development for Spanish as a heritage language.

The program from which the data are drawn uses a theme-based curriculum and process-oriented writing methodology (multiple version assignments, peer editing, tutors). The Latino participants in the study were born in the US or immigrated, principally from Mexico, as small children. Two-thirds are Mexican American, the others come from Central America (El Salvador, Guatemala, and Nicaragua) and South America, especially from Colombia, thus reflecting the make-up of the Latino population in California.

Analytical framework

Previous research on academic writing in English as a second language and in Spanish as a native language has demonstrated how second language writers of English and native speakers learning to write in academic Spanish often draw on informal, oral-like registers (e.g., Valdés and Geoffrion-Vinci, 1998). Therefore, I based the analysis of the texts on two theoretical concepts: **lexical density** and **grammatical complexity**. They are fundamental to the distinction between spoken and written texts (Halliday 1985, 1994, 2004). **Lexical density** of texts was calculated by the number of content carrying words or "lexical items" (nouns, adjectives, adverbs, and verbs) as a proportion of the total number of words in the text. According to Halliday (1985), we can establish a continuum between the lexis (content words) and the grammar (non-content words) of English (and Spanish), with the first being made up of open systems of words and the second of closed ones. High-frequency lexical items such as *gente, cosas, ser, estar* were not counted as content words, as they fall more towards the oral end of the continuum. **Grammatical intricacy** was calculated by counting the number of clauses (main, paratactic, hypotactic) as a proportion of clause complexes. Spoken language becomes more complex by building more elaborate clause complexes out of parataxis and hypotaxis. Thus, Halliday's distinction between paratactic clauses (coordinated and juxtaposed clauses), hypotactic clauses (non-restrictive relative clauses, adverbial subordination, noun clauses subordinated to perception and saying verbs), and embedded clauses (restrictive relative clauses and noun clauses) is crucial to understanding the difference between spoken and written language. In SFL theory, embedded clauses (but not hypotactic clauses) are thought to be part of a larger constituent at the discourse level and, therefore, help to make language more dense at the level of the noun group, while paratactic and hypotactic clauses help to make the discourse more dynamic and complex.

Rosa's and Roberto's nine-month development of grammatical intricacy and lexical density

In Colombi (2000, 2002, 2006) I focused on the text analysis of written texts, and I charted writers' movement in the direction of incorporating more formal written register features into their texts. Taking the notion of a developmental path from a more oral to a more written style as the point of departure (see Figure 3), I documented how two college-level bilingual students, Rosa and Roberto, both enrolled in the theme-based curriculum, moved along this path in terms of grammatical intricacy and lexical density, together with the nominal group complexity of their essays. Although there is much inter-learner variability, the results of the text analysis summarized in Table 3 show a common trajectory toward lexically more dense (a feature

Table 3 Rosa's and Roberto's grammatical development

	Lexical density	*Grammatical complexity*
Rosa		
#1	**43.2%** (297/688)	**2.45** (49/20)
#3	**50.8%** (387/762)	**1.48** (52/35)
Roberto		
#1	**44.9%** (222/494)	**2.10** (42/20)
#3	**45.9%** (350/762)	**1.81** (60/33)

that is typical of the written end of the continuum) and grammatically less intricate (a feature that characterizes the oral end of the continuum) language.

These quantitative findings converge with those reported in studies of first and second language development analysis that have been conducted from non-SFL perspectives (e.g., Conrad and Biber, 2001; Reynolds, 2005; among others). However, beyond such purely quantitative results, usually measured in terms of grammatical complexity (see Ortega, 2003; Wolfe-Quintero, Inagaki, and Kim, 1998), SFL can provide insights about discourse semantics and the development of the text. It does so by bringing a theoretically coherent perspective to the concepts of unit of analysis, clause types, and lexical density, which enables a deeper understanding of how a movement away from chaining of coordinated clauses and toward condensation of information in the clause is functional for the development of academic registers over time.

Lucía's nine-month development from clause-combining strategies to grammatical metaphor

In Colombi (2002; see also Schleppegrell and Colombi, 1997)[2] I focused on clause-combining strategies to show how paratactic and hypotactic combinations are more typical of oral language and how students' texts become more lexically dense over time, not by using a greater number of content words but by using fewer clauses and condensing the information in the noun group; that is, by processes of nominalization and grammatical metaphor (Halliday, 1985, 1993, 1994, 1998). The critical question, then, pertains to what discourse-organizational advantages students gain by choosing strategies of clause combining and lexical density (for an extensive discussion of this from the perspective of coherence and cohesion, see Ryshina-Pankova, 2006).

Excerpt 1 presents the introductory paragraph to Lucía's first essay.[3] Here, Lucía begins her discussion about the importance of diversity with a rhetorical question that is answered by a clause complex consisting of six clauses in which she chains her ideas and elaborates about the advantage of having a diverse culture.

As the detailed clause analysis in Table 4 indicates, she connects her ideas through a convoluted sequence of paratactic and hypotactic clauses that chain one idea to the other as if she were dialoging with herself.

The logic-semantic conjunctions used are characteristic of oral registers: adding information with the connector *y* ("and", expansion) and reasoning in favor of

---

Excerpt 1 Lucía's first essay (Introduction/first essay—first version)

Necesidades universales

¿Como seria el mundo si no existiera la diversidad? Primero que nada todas las personas serian iguales y crecerian con la misma ideologia, lo cual causaria la extincion de la misma cultura porque las personas no tendrian una alternativa para pensar o encontrar soluciones a sus problemas. Por esta razon, es importante conservar la diversidad, lo cual solamente puede lograrse con la existencia de varias culturas. Carlos Fuentes, el autor de "La hispanidad norteamericana," afirma que: "las culturas solo florecen en contacto con las demas, y perecen en el aislamiento" (378). Al igual que Fuentes, estoy de acuerdo que las culturas florecen cuando se comparten con otros pero esto solo se puede lograr a traves de la inmigracion.

Table 4 Clause analysis of Lucía's introduction in first essay

Clause	Type
¿Como seria el mundo si no existiera la diversidad?	Main
Primero que nada todas las personas serian iguales	Main
y crecerian con la misma ideologia	Paratactic
lo cual causaria la extincion de la misma cultura	Hypotactic
porque las personas no tendrian una alternativa	Hypotactic
para pensar	Hypotactic
o encontrar soluciones a sus problemas.	Hypotactic
Por esta razon, es importante conservar la diversidad	Main
lo cual solamente puede lograrse con la existencia de varias culturas.	Hypotactic
Carlos Fuentes, el autor de "La hispanidad norteamericana," afirma que	Main
"las culturas solo florecen en contacto con las demas, y perecen en el aislamiento" (378).	Paratactic
Al igual que Fuentes, estoy de acuerdo	Main
que las culturas florecen	Hypotactic
[cuando se comparten con otros]	Embedded
pero esto solo se puede lograr a traves de la inmigracion.	Paratactic

Lexical density = 3.5 (42/120)
Grammatical intricacy = 2.8 (14/5)

Excerpt 2 Lucía's last essay (Introduction/12th essay—nine months apart—first version)

Evolucion de la mujer durante y posteriormente la Revolucion Mexicana

La Revolucion Mexicana fue una lucha hacia la prosperidad del pais. Los revolucionarios esperaban obtener democracia, estabilidad economica y social, y principalmente la liberacion de un gobierno establecido por mas de tres decadas. Esta revolucion no fue en vano, puesto que trajo a la vida de muchos campesinos recursos para sobresalir tal como tierras que fueron repartidas despues de la disminucion de los latifundios. Sin embargo, algo inesperado fue el cambio en el rol de la mujer no solo durante la revolucion sino tambien despues la revolucion. A pesar de que la continua violencia y muertes de la revolucion afectaron la vida de los mexicanos, incluyendo a la mujer, fue esta negatividad que impulso un cambio social y psicologico en la mujer.

---

diversity through a causal relation with *porque* ("because"). She argues her thesis by connecting it with the previous clause complex with another connector of causality *por eso* ("for that reason"), a congruent (transparent) form of expressing causality that is present and visible. In other words, logico-semantic relationships are expressed through grammatical complexity at the clause complex level, that is, through grammatical intricacy. For example, the first clause complex (*Primero . . .*) in Table 4 consists of six clauses (four hypotactic, one paratactic, and a main clause).

By contrast, Excerpt 2, written nine months later, shows a movement similar to that of Rosa and Roberto in their later essays.

Namely, as Table 5 shows, grammatical intricacy has diminished from 2.8 to 1.6, and the clause complexes consist mostly of one clause or two clauses. By contrast,

Table 5 Clause analysis of Lucía's introduction in last essay

Clause	Type
La Revolucion Mexicana fue una lucha hacia la prosperidad del pais.	Main
Los revolucionarios esperaban obtener democracia, estabilidad economica y social, y principalmente la liberacion de un gobierno establecido por mas de tres decadas.	Main
Esta revolucion no fue en vano	Main
puesto que trajo a la vida de muchos campesinos recursos	Paratactic
para sobresalir tal como tierras	Hypotactic
[que fueron repartidas despues de la disminucion de los latifundios.]	Embedded
Sin embargo, algo inesperado fue el cambio en el rol de la mujer no solo durante la revolucion sino tambien despues la revolucion.	Main
A pesar de que la continua violencia y muertes de la revolucion afectaron la vida de los mexicanos, incluyendo a la mujer,	Hypotactic
fue esta negatividad	Main
[que impulso un cambio social y psicologico en la mujer.]	Embedded

Lexical density = 4.3 (58/132)
Grammatical intricacy = 1.6 (8/5)

density of information is now realized at the level of the noun group through the use of GM.

Table 6 presents the ideational (experiential and logical) grammatical metaphors Lucía uses in her introduction to the last essay.

At the functional level, the GMs, predominantly nominalizations, present the information in a more incongruent way, by removing the agents of the actions. Abstraction and objectification are achieved by reconstruing actions as objects through nouns, that is, in a semantic link where the process (verbs) simultaneously maintains the meaning of an action and of a noun. This nominalization of processes permits their being modified through prepositional phrases and embedded clauses, a possibility that packs information at the level of the noun group. For example in *la liberacion de un gobierno establecido por mas de tres decadas, liberación* maintains the idea of the process *liberar* and functions as a noun *liberación* at the same time, allowing for elaboration and modification through the prepositional phrase *de un gobierno establecido por más de tres decadas*, which in turn includes another GM in the adjectification of the process *establecido*, which has been classified by another prepositional phrase, *por más de tres decadas*. Functionally this GM is presenting the event *liberación* . . . in a more abstract way by not identifying the agents that cause the "liberation" or the time when it occurred. In the same way, *establecido* condensed more information by doing the same thing; that is, by obscuring the agents of the *gobierno*. In sum, in this last essay Lucía expresses her ideas in a more abstract and objective way that is typical of the written form, through the use of GM (see Colombi, 2006, for a detailed analysis of this feature in bilingual students' texts).

Table 6 Ideational Grammatical Metaphors presented in the introduction to Lucía's last essay

Ideational Grammatical Metaphors	Semantic juncture
Evolucion *de la mujer durante y posteriormente la Revolucion Mexicana*	Grammatical category = noun Semantic function = verb
una lucha *hacia la prosperidad del país*	Grammatical category = noun Semantic function = verb
obtener *democracia, estabilidad economica y social*	Grammatical category = noun Semantic function = verb
la liberacion *de un gobierno . . .*	Grammatical category = noun Semantic function = verb
. . . **establecido** *por mas de tres decadas*	Grammatical category = adjective Semantic function = verb
despues de la **disminucion** *de los latifundios*	Grammatical category = noun Semantic function = verb
el cambio *en el rol de la mujer*	Grammatical category = noun Semantic function = verb
la continua *violencia y muertes de la revolucion*	Grammatical category = adjective Semantic function = verb
esta **negatividad** *que impulso . . .*	Grammatical category = noun Semantic function = verb
. . . un **cambio** *social y psicologico en la mujer*	Grammatical category = noun Semantic function = verb

The development and indexing of academic identities: Achugar's study of bilingual speakers in the southwest of the United States

As already stated, SFL theory views development and language expertise in terms of practices that emerge in a particular social context. Individuals develop specialized ways of using language through active participation and engagement in a community; in turn this process enables them to participate in and become members of the community, by aligning themselves with the identities shaped by the community. Advancedness in this case is conceptualized as being affiliated and recognized as a full member of the academic community. Thus, the SFL framework can be applied to study not only the development of academic language, but also the forging of academic identities as indexed in expanding language choices. This can be done by centering analysis on the lexico-grammatical and discourse-semantic choices used for constructing and indexing this expert or authoritative identity through interpersonal meanings.

In an ongoing longitudinal study, I am currently exploring just this phenomenon in a bilingual creative writing graduate program in Southwest Texas. Following Butt (2004), I focused on two forms of change: change in the "profile of an acculturated community member" and change in "the meaning potential available to a community" (p. 229). Grammatical features, as meaning-making practices (Williams, 2004), are being tracked in order to understand how language is used in this academic setting to signal membership in this professional community. In addition, I am following the academic community over a three-year time period in order to establish benchmarks and language assessment procedures grounded in community-based norms and to capture the possibilities and values attached to certain ways of using language in the community.

Begun in 2004, the research includes a cohort of nine students who entered the Master of Fine Arts (MFA) program at that time and who are enrolled in the bilingual creative writing program. The group includes heritage learners of Spanish from the local community, English L2 learners from Latin America, and Spanish L2 learners from other areas of the US. Individual tracking of change and development over time is done through interviews every fall semester and will encompass their three-year stay in the program. The group was interviewed three times throughout their stay in the program. The data presented here are drawn from transcripts of in-depth interviews of members of the community, including professors and students, which were carried out by me in the spring of 2004, fall of 2004, and fall of 2005. Data from interviews are complemented by classroom observations, and video and written text samples of students.

Analytical framework

The students' responses have been analyzed by identifying changes in the use of interpersonal resources, such as attitude, engagement, modality, and graduation in terms of lexico-grammatical (e.g., modality, vocabulary) as well as discourse-semantic features (e.g., concession, projection). In SFL these interpersonal features of academic registers are part of the appraisal system (Martin and White, 2005), "an approach to exploring, describing and explaining the way language is used to evaluate, to adopt stances, to construct textual personas and to manage interpersonal positionings and relationships" (White, 2006). They have also been described in the literature in terms of evaluation, metadiscourse, and stance (e.g., Hyland, 2002, 2004).

This system is realized through interpersonal meaning choices at the lexico-grammatical and discourse-semantic level. *Attitudes* refer to positionings in which language users assess either positively or negatively people, places, things, and happenings realized mostly through vocabulary selection. *Engagement* is the positioning in relation to others; it implies an interaction with other communities, speakers, or responses to prior utterances realized through projection (heteroglossia), polarity (negation), and the logical organization of ideas (concession). The last type of positioning considered in appraisal is the intertextual: the endorsement or rejection of others' positions or prior utterances realized through *modality, graduation,* and *projection.* These discursive and lexico-grammatical features serve to project the persona of the language user as an authorized voice in the community, establishing his or her orientation towards the content/field signaling their attitudes and positions. Members of an academic community use language in particular ways to represent themselves and their work in the particular ways sanctioned by their discipline or "guild."

The appraisal system of experts and novices in this academic community

The analysis of the community's socio-semiotic potential has so far resulted in a detailed discourse analysis of professors' and students' responses to similar interview questions. Comparison has revealed considerable variation in terms of the resources apprentices and experts in the community use to signal their identity as members of the academy by engaging other voices to support theirs through heteroglossia; showing levels of certainty and probability of their representations through modality; and by evaluating other members of their community through evaluations that connote social value and appropriateness.

The following discussion draws on a comparison of two excerpts from interviews conducted during the first year with Professor Carlos Salinas and MFA student Marcelo, both answering the question, "What does it mean that the program is bilingual?" Excerpt 3, taken from the professor's response, comes after he mentions that, for him, the fact that the program is bilingual refers mostly to the possibility of being exposed to two or more literary traditions and worldviews. The underlined parts of the text signal the appraisal resources used by the professor.

Salinas uses certain linguistic resources, among them concession (conjunctions and continuatives like *pero* ["but"] *entonces* ["then"]) to establish a dialogue with his professional community and positions himself and his voice as a writer as the product of influences from other writers (García Márquez, Neruda, Faulkner, Hemingway, etc.). At the same time, he hedges his positioning through the use of modality, constructing a sense of the probability and necessity of this affiliation. For example, words like *siempre* ("always") convey degrees of importance and frequency of the affiliation with this "not so well known writer." As a result, Salinas presents himself as a member of the professional community who is part of a validated and recognized literary tradition but, within that community, established his individuality by highlighting his connection to the "less well known writer." Comparative structures and polarity raise the force of the affiliation to more avant-garde members in the profession, *no tan famoso como* ("not as famous as"). This grading of the positioning is established semantically through graduation, providing force through the use of intensifiers, *muy difícil* ("very difficult"), and attitudinal lexis, *por estos lados* ("around these parts of the world"). These resources represent more indirect ways of taking a stance or positioning oneself,[1] thus signaling a wide repertoire of linguistic resources to construct an authoritative identity.

Excerpt 3 Professor Salinas on interview question, "What does it mean that the program is bilingual?"

"[. . .] como escritor las voces que me formaron a mí fueron voces europeas, norteamericanas y latinoamericanas// . . . <u>entonces</u> mi escritor, dos de mis escritores favoritos son García Márquez umm y Neruda ./ <u>pero también</u> otro escritor <u>muy difícil</u> (. . .) que es un escritor <u>no tan famoso como</u> los otros por este lado, <u>pero siempre</u> yo he escuchado su voz y me ha formado como escritor, como Faulkner y Hemingway y Whitman . . ."
[As a writer the voices that shaped me were European, North American and Latin American// . . . then my writer, two of my favorite writers are García Márquez umm and Neruda,/ but also another writer, very difficult (. . .) who is a not so famous one around here, not as the other ones, but I have always heard his voice and he has shaped me as a writer, as much as Faulkner and Hemingway and Whitman . . .] (Professor Carlos Salinas, Heritage Speaker of Spanish)[5]

Excerpt 4 Marcelo on year-1 interview question "What does it mean that the program is bilingual?"

"[. . .] y el hecho de que se manejen los dos idiomas sin distinción <u>completamente</u>, a mi <u>me impresiona, me encanta</u>. O sea, si estás hablando en clase dices algo en español y alguien da la respuesta en inglés. De repente lees un texto de alguien en inglés y luego lo lees en español después o incluso las mezclas que hacen, del spanglish que en el mismo texto hay frases en inglés con frases en español, <u>eso es bien interesante</u> y <u>se me hace bien padre</u> que <u>se puede</u> manejar así, que <u>lo acepten</u> así que lo hagan así. . ." (Marcelo, student from El Paso-Juárez area, Fall 2004)

Excerpt 4, by contrast, illustrates the range of resources one of the students in this cohort, Marcelo, showed during the first year in the program, based on the first and second interview data. This response comes after he has described his decision to come to this program and his subsequent experiences in it.

Like the professor, Marcelo, too, makes particular linguistic choices that denote attitudes, point to sources, and give a certain graduation to the information. He constructs affect attitudes by presenting direct representations of his feelings towards the way bilingualism is instantiated in the community, *me impresiona* ("it impresses me"), *me encanta* ("I love it"). Some distance is expressed by presenting information as mere "facts" through the use of nominalizations and objectifying constructions, which hides the source of these interpretations. For example, expressions such as *el hecho de que se manejen los dos idiomas . . .* ("the fact that both languages are used") allow the author to present interpretations as given and then to intensify the force of the evaluation, *sin distinción completamente* ("totally indiscriminately"). Also, he reports events without citing the source and without modalization, which privileges only one interpretation: the author disappears and the source of the interpretation is left impersonal, using projections within the clause complex, *si estás hablando en clase dices algo en español . . .* ("if you are talking in class you say something in Spanish . . ."). At the same time, the student avoids making explicit references to others through the use of impersonal object pronouns that nominalize expressions such as *que lo acepten así que lo hagan así . . .* ("that they do it like that, that they accept it like that"). These impersonal references point to a heteroglossic text but one that, in contrast with Excerpt 3, which had explicitly positioned the author in relation to clear referents in the community, avoids signaling the other voice. Not surprisingly, Excerpt 4 defines bilingualism in local terms, as a concrete experience. By contrast, the professor's response had chosen a wider context of reference and situated his particular experience and meaning of bilingualism in the program in relation to the larger professional community.

Tracking change in the appraisal system resources over time: Marcelo's interview a year later

A year later, after Marcelo had participated in the community for some time, he was asked to define once more what the bilingualism of the program then meant to him. Part of his answer is shown in Excerpt 5.

Marcelo now uses an interpersonal grammatical metaphor, an incongruent linguistic choice, through which the opinion of the speaker is introduced via a clause complex instead of through the more congruent modalization, to begin his

Excerpt 5 Marcelo on year-2 interview question "How would you define the meaning of bilingualism in the program?"

"[. . .] *este. . . yo creo . . . que es . . . la . . . como la capacidad . . . la posibilidad de . . . agarrar lo mejor de los dos mundos y hacer algo interesante. Hubo una **chava** que leyó . . . no me acuerdo cómo se llamaba ni cómo se llamaba lo que escribió pero . . . que leyó el otro día en el café . . . durante la presentación de Rio Grande Review está en la publicación en el último . . . que habla de **eso** del bilingüismo . . .*" (Marcelo, student from El Paso-Juárez area, Fall 2005)

discussion of what bilingualism means in this context, *yo creo que . . .* ("I believe that . . ."). Through the use of a mental projection that evaluates the information that follows, he positions himself and presents a subjective evaluation as an authorized speaker. The next clause is another projection, but this time an attempt to cite another "published author" as a recognized voice and source in order to support his position. It is not completely successful because he neither remembers what this person actually said nor his name. By using indefinite nouns and lexical choices that have a colloquial connotation to refer to the source, he lowers the force of the evaluation: *chava* ("girl"), *eso* ("that"). Even so, this move signals an awareness of the resources available to present oneself as an authority and to be recognized as a member of this professional community. Another way to accomplish that goal is by making reference to practices that are typical of the profession (i.e., readings and publications).

Conclusion: SFL contributions to the longitudinal study of L2 capacities

In this chapter we have outlined and exemplified with research data the principles of SFL and the predictions it makes about longitudinal development toward the full range of meaning-making capacities that a language system affords its users. We conclude here with some reflections on the particular strengths that SFL as a framework offers to researchers interested in investigating the development of advanced language capacities and, most particularly, the capacities for meaning-making in academic contexts needed by heritage Spanish speakers and other language minority populations as they gain access and navigate higher education.

SFL identifies particular lexico-grammatical and discourse-semantic resources that serve as indices of language development over time (e.g., grammatical metaphor, grammatical intricacy, lexical density, modality, clause-combining resources). Language development can be seen from different but interrelated time scales: phylogenetic, ontogenetic, and logogenetic. From the ontogenetic perspective, there is a movement from subjective and congruent ways of making meaning to more objective and incongruent forms of semiosis. The ontogenic progression towards advancedness has been fruitfully investigated in academic language and written registers, both in terms of major moments that signal more academic language and also in terms of inter-learner variability. Indeed, variability is expected and theorized in SFL because the framework acknowledges that learning takes different paths depending on the different opportunities and particular experiences individuals have with language.

Inasmuch as SFL views language and context as co-constituted it enables a consideration of language development in the context of a particular culture. "Context" is understood on the level of the context of the situation where language is produced and also on the level of the larger cultural context that creates the conditions for what it is possible to do with language within a particular group (Butt, 2004).

Finally, in their desire to understand the development of individual learners, particularly toward advanced levels of ability, researchers should be able to benefit not only from the clear integration of language and context in the SFL framework, but also from its ability to index changes towards an expansion of the meaning-making resources of individuals. SFL findings of a longitudinal progression towards advancedness can be expected to offer clear analytical tools and detailed analyses that connect grammar and meanings. But because grammatical features are seen in relation to meaning-making practices in SFL (Williams, 2004), they allow researchers to go well beyond the study of linguistic development. Language development can be measured and described in terms of an expansion of the individual's meaning-making potential. It can also be described and measured in terms of an evolving membership in a particular social group. Thus, within this framework advancedness is the ability to make meanings valued and associated with a particular social group, not a neutral and context-free type of linguistic competence. In educational settings, in particular, it also means being affiliated and recognized as a full member of an academic or professional community.

Notes

1. I want to acknowledge the cooperation of my colleague, Francisco X. Alarcón, Director of Spanish for Native Speakers at UCD, in allowing me to visit and collect the texts from the Program of Spanish for Native Speakers during the year 1999–2000 and 2003–2004.
2. For a further explanation on the clause classification according to their semantic discourse properties, see Schleppegrell and Colombi (1997).
3. All students' names are pseudonyms. The students' essays correspond to the first version of three multiple version assignments and have been copied without any alteration.
4. These are less common ways of establishing authority than the ones commonly studied in the literature—projecting clauses and citations used to support one's argument and validate one's position.
5. All the names are pseudonyms.

References

Bolivar, A. (1994). *Discurso e interacción en el texto escrito.* Caracas: Universidad Central de Venezuela.

Butt, D. (2004). How our meanings change: School contexts and semantic evolution. In G. Williams and A. Lukin (Eds.), *The development of language: Functional perspectives on species and individuals* (pp. 217–240). London: Continuum.

Byrnes, H. (Ed.) (2006). *Advanced language learning: The contribution of Halliday and Vygotsky.* London: Continuum.

Christie, F. (2002a). *Classroom discourse analysis.* London: Continuum.

Christie, F. (2002b). The development of abstraction in adolescence in subject English. In M. J. Schleppegrell and M. C. Colombi (Eds.), *Developing advanced literacy in first and second languages* (pp. 45–66). Mahwah, NJ: Lawrence Erlbaum.

Coffin, C. (1997). Constructing and giving value to the past: An investigation into secondary school history. In F. Christie and J. R. Martin (Eds.), *Genre and institutions: Social processes in the workplace and school* (pp. 196–230). London: Cassell.

Colombi, M. C. (2000). En vías del desarrollo del lenguaje académico en español en hablantes nativos de español en los Estados Unidos. In A. Roca (Ed.), *Research on Spanish in the United States* (pp. 296–309). Somerville, MA: Cascadilla Press.

Colombi, M. C. (2002). Academic language development in Latino students' writing in Spanish. In M. J. Schleppegrell and M. C. Colombi (Eds.), *Developing advanced literacy in first and second languages* (pp. 67–86). Mahwah, NJ: Lawrence Erlbaum.

Colombi, M. C. (2006). Grammatical metaphor: Academic language development in Latino students in Spanish. In H. Byrnes (Ed.), *Advanced language learning: The contribution of Halliday and Vygotsky*. London: Continuum.

Conrad, S., and Biber, D. (2001). Multidimensional methodology and the dimensions of register variation in English. In S. Conrad and D. Biber (Eds.), *Variation in English: Multi-dimensional studies* (pp. 13–42). London: Longman.

Derewianka, B. (1995). Language development in the transition from childhood to adolescence: The role of grammatical metaphor. Unpublished Ph.D. dissertation, Macquarie University.

Dubcovsky, L. (2003). In search of incipient academic writing. Ph.D. dissertation, University of California, Davis.

Ghio, E,. and Fernández, M. D. (2005). *Manual de lingüística sistémico funcional*. Santa Fé, Argentina: Universidad Nacional del Litoral.

Go, A. (2003). The writing development of Chinese and Vietnamese newcomer students. Unpublished Ph.D. dissertation, University of California, Davis.

Halliday, M. A. K. (1973). *Explorations in the functions of language*. London: Edward Arnold.

Halliday, M. A. K. (1978). *Language as a social semiotic: The social interpretation of language and meaning*. London: Edward Arnold.

Halliday, M. A. K. (1985). *Spoken and written language*. Burwood, Australia: Deakin University.

Halliday, M. A. K. (1993). Language and the order of nature. In M. A. K. Halliday and J. R. Martin (Eds.), *Writing science: Literacy and discursive power* (pp. 106–123). Pittsburgh: University of Pittsburgh Press.

Halliday, M. A. K. (1994). *An introduction to functional grammar* (2nd ed.). London: Edward Arnold.

Halliday, M. A. K. (1998). Things and relations. In J. R. Martin and R. Veel (Eds.), *Reading science* (pp. 183–235). New York: Routledge.

Halliday, M. A. K. (2004). *The language of early childhood*, ed. J. Webster. Vol. 4. London: Continuum.

Halliday, M. A. K, and Matthiessen, C. (1999) *Construing experience through meaning: A language based approach to cognition*. London: Cassell.

Halliday, M. A. K. with Matthiessen, C. (2004). *An introduction to functional grammar* (3rd ed.). London: Edward Arnold.

Hasan, R., and Martin, J. R. (1989). Introduction. In R. Hasan and J. R. Martin (Eds.), *Language development: Learning language, learning culture* (pp. 1–17). Norwood, NJ: Ablex.

Hasan, R., and Perrett, G. (1994). Learning to function with the other tongue: A systemic functional perspective on second language teaching. In T. Odlin (Ed.), *Perspectives on pedagogical grammar* (pp. 179–226). Cambridge: Cambridge University Press.

Hasan, R., and Williams, G. (1996). *Literacy in society*. London: Longman.

Hunston, S., and Thompson, G. (2000). *Evaluation in text*. Oxford: Oxford University Press.

Hyland, K. (2002). Authority and invisibility: Authorial identity in academic writing. *Journal of Pragmatics*, *34*, 1091–1112.

Hyland, K. (2004). Disciplinary interactions: Metadiscourse in L2 postgraduate writing. *Journal of Second Language Writing, 13*, 133–151.

Kress, G. (1994). *Learning to write.* (2nd ed.). London: Routledge.

Kress, G., and Van Leeuwen, T. (2001). *Multimodal discourse.* London: Edward Arnold.

Lemke, J. (1988). Genres, semantics, and classroom education. *Linguistics and Education, 1*, 81–99.

Lemke, J. (1990). *Talking science: Language, learning and values.* Norwood, NJ: Ablex.

Lemke, J. (1998). Resources for attitudinal meaning: Evaluative orientations in text semantics. *Functions of Language, 5*, 33–56.

Martin, J. R. (1985). *Factual writing: Exploring and challenging social reality.* Geelong, Vic: Deakin University Press (republished by Oxford: Oxford University Press, 1989).

Martin, J. R. (1992). *English text: System and structure.* Philadelphia, PA: John Benjamins.

Martin, J. R. (1993). Genre and literacy: modelling context in educational linguistics. *Annual Review of Applied Linguistics: Issues in Teaching and Learning,* 13, 141–172.

Martin, J. R. (1997). Analyzing genre: Functional parameters. In F. Christie and J. R. Martin (Eds.), *Genre and institutions* (pp. 3–39). London: Continuum.

Martin, J. R., and Rose, D. (2003). *Working with discourse.* London: Continuum.

Martin, J. R., and White, P. R. R. (2005). *The language of evaluation: The appraisal framework.* New York: Palgrave Macmillan.

Menéndez, S. M. (1993). *Gramática textual.* Buenos Aires: Plus Ultra.

Mohan, B. A. (1986). *Language and content.* Reading, MA: Addison-Wesley.

Mohan, B. (1997). Language as a medium of learning: Academic reading and cause. *Ritsumeikan Educational Studies, 10*, 208–217.

Mohan, B., and Huxur, G. (2001). A functional approach to research on content-based language learning. *Canadian Modern Language Review, 58*, 133–155.

Ortega, L. (2003). Syntactic complexity measures and their relationship to L2 proficiency: A research synthesis of college-level L2 writing. *Applied Linguistics, 24*, 492–518.

Oteiza, T. (2005). Acquiring Spanish academic language in the US for bilingual heritage speakers: A case study of undergraduate students. Paper presented at 2005 Georgetown University Roundtable on Languages and Linguistics.

Painter, C. (1989). Learning language: A functional view of language development. In R. Hasan and J. R. Martin (Eds.) *Language development: Learning language, learning culture* (pp.18–65). Norwood, NJ: Ablex.

Painter, C. (1991). *Learning the mother tongue* (2nd ed.). Geelong: Deakin University Press.

Painter, C. (1999). *Learning language and learning through language in early childhood.* London: Continuum.

Ravelli, L., and Ellis, R. (Eds.) (2004). *Analyzing academic writing: Contextualized frameworks.* London: Continuum.

Reynolds, D. (2005). Linguistic correlates of second language literacy development: Evidence from middle-grade learners' essays. *Journal of Second Language Writing, 14*, 19–45.

Rothery, J. R. (1996). Making changes: Developing an educational linguistics. In R. Hasan and G. Williams (Eds.), *Literacy in society* (pp. 86–123). New York: Longman.

Ryshina-Pankova, M. (2006). Creating textual worlds in advanced L2 writing: The role of complex theme. In H. Byrnes (Ed.), *Advanced language learning: The contribution of Halliday and Vygotsky* (pp. 164–183). London: Continuum.

Schleppegrell, M. J. (2004). *The language of schooling.* Mahwah, NJ: Lawrence Erlbaum.

Schleppegrell, M. J., and Colombi, M. C. (1997). Text organization by bilingual writers. *Written Communication, 14*, 481–503.

Schleppegrell, M. J., and Colombi, M. C. (Eds.) (2002). *Developing advanced literacy in first and second languages.* Mahwah, NJ: Lawrence Erlbaum.

Torr, J. (1997). *From child tongue to mother tongue: A case study of language development in the first two and a half years*. Monographs in Systemic Linguistics. Nottingham: Nottingham University Press.

Unsworth, L. (Ed.) (2000). *Researching language in schools and communities: Functional linguistic perspectives*. Washington, DC: Cassell.

Valdés, G. (2005). Bilingualism, heritage language learners, and SLA research: Opportunities lost or seized?, *Modern Language Journal, 89*, 410–426.

Valdés, G., and Geoffrion-Vinci, M. (1998). Chicano Spanish: The problem of the "under-developed" code in bilingual repertoires. *Modern Language Journal, 82*, 473–501.

Ventola, E., and Mauranen, A. (Eds.) (1996). *Academic writing*. Amsterdam: John Benjamins.

White, P. R. R. The appraisal website. www.grammatics.com/appraisal/. Accessed March 6, 2006.

Williams, G. (2004). Ontogenesis and grammatics: Functions of metalanguage in pedagogical discourse. In G. Williams and A. Lukin (Eds.), *The development of language: Functional perspectives on species and individuals* (pp. 241–267). London: Continuum.

Wolfe-Quintero, K., Inagaki, S., and Kim, H.-Y. (1998). *Second language development in writing: Measures of fluency, accuracy and complexity*. Manoa: Second Language Teaching and Curriculum Center, University of Hawai'i.

Woodward-Kron, R. (2002). Disciplinary learning through writing: An investigation into the writing development of undergraduate education students. Unpublished Ph.D. dissertation, Faculty of Education, University of Wollongong, Australia.

4 Investigating learner language development with electronic longitudinal corpora

Theoretical and methodological issues

Florence Myles

Abstract

Recent theoretical developments in SLA leave us with a complex and sophisticated research agenda. Taking the example of just one framework, questions about the initial state of second language learners, as well as about their ultimate attainment, are giving rise to much research. We need to be able to study development as it takes place within individual learners, in order to be able to test current hypotheses. We can only say that development has stopped, or that it is taking place, by studying learners over long periods of time. Using cross-sectional data is not helpful, as we have no way of knowing whether or not the linguistic representations we are comparing across learners are in fact similar. Using longitudinal data is problematic, however. Datasets are very expensive to collect, and it can be extremely difficult practically to study learners over long periods of time. Because of this, it is now imperative that, given the enormous resource and logistical implications of collecting good-quality longitudinal corpora, we make them widely available to the research community. Different researchers can then work on them from different points of view. Additionally, for datasets to be truly representative of learner development, they must be of sufficient size. Finally, but very importantly, the research community must agree on conventions for transcribing, storing, and analyzing such data, and must make use of available software in order to analyze it. The SLA research community is far behind other fields in taking advantage of computerized tools in order to assist it in furthering its research agenda. This chapter will discuss the theoretical reasons underlying the need to collect and share good-quality longitudinal learner corpora. It will then explore the methodological issues arising, before presenting a large database of French learner language oral corpora, freely available to the research community on the internet. The possibilities offered by the computerized analysis of corpora will also be demonstrated through a range of examples.

Introduction

Recent theoretical developments in SLA leave us with a complex and sophisticated research agenda. Taking the example of just one framework, Universal Grammar, questions about the linguistic representations learners bring to the L2 learning task (that is, their initial state) as well as about whether learners can ever have mental representations which are the same as native speakers (that is, their ultimate attainment) are giving rise to much research. Such questions, however, are often investigated through the study of cross-sectional data, which is not ideal for that purpose. We need to be able to study development as it takes place within individual learners, in order to be able to test current hypotheses. It is no surprise, for example, that the most significant contribution to the discussion of ultimate attainment comes from the longitudinal study of Patty (Lardiere, 1998a, 1998b, 2000), a Chinese learner of English who was studied over a period of some 10 years, after 18 years or so of exposure to English. We can only say that development has stopped, or that it is taking place, by studying learners over long periods of time. Using cross-sectional data is not helpful, as we have no way of knowing whether or not the linguistic representations we are comparing across learners are in fact similar.

Using longitudinal data is challenging, however. Datasets are very expensive to collect, and it can be extremely difficult practically to study learners over long periods of time. Because of this, it is now imperative that, given the enormous resource and logistical implications of collecting good-quality longitudinal corpora, we make them widely available to the research community. Different researchers can then work on them from different points of view. Additionally, for datasets to be truly representative of learner development, they must be of sufficient size and go beyond a single learner. The case of Patty is one case in point: because it is the only longitudinal corpus of a learner after considerable exposure to the L2, it has been used extensively by its author and others in order to inform the end-state debate. But Patty might be atypical and cannot necessarily be readily compared to other learners, nor her behaviour generalized. This is, however, what has happened in the literature. Moreover, Patty only represents one language pair (Chinese–English), and we need evidence from other language pairs.

Finally, but very importantly, the sharing of datasets will mean that the research community must agree on conventions for transcribing, storing, and analyzing such data, which is to be welcomed. At present, there are nearly as many transcription conventions as there are L2 researchers! By making datasets available, researchers will also be able to make use of powerful software in order to analyze them. The SLA research community is far behind other fields in taking advantage of computerized tools in order to assist in furthering its research agenda.

In this chapter, I will first briefly discuss the theoretical reasons underlying the need to collect and share good-quality longitudinal learner corpora. I will then explore the methodological issues arising, before arguing the case for systematic sharing of longitudinal datasets. Finally, I will present a large database of French learner language oral corpora, freely available to the research community on the internet, and will demonstrate through a range of examples the possibilities offered by the computerized analysis of corpora.

The need for longitudinal L2 corpora

What kind of datasets do we need?

It seems rather self-evident that good-quality second language research is crucially dependent on good-quality datasets. But what is a good-quality dataset? Quite obviously, this will depend to some extent on individual researchers' agendas. In the context of documenting and analyzing learner development, especially at advanced levels, I would like to argue that the most suitable datasets are (a) oral, (b) longitudinal, (c) encompassing a sufficient number of learners, and finally (d) representing a wide range of language pairs.

First, I believe that oral datasets are better representatives of the linguistic system underlying learner productions, as they are relatively freer from monitoring processes characteristic of written language, given the pressures of online speech production.

Second, longitudinal data are more suitable than cross-sectional data, if we are to truly document development, which happens within individuals. As we know that there is huge variation in both the rate of acquisition and the ultimate attainment of second language learners, it is difficult to find homogeneous cross-sectional groups. This is not to say that cross-sectional data do not have their place in SLA studies: large numbers of learners at similar stages of development can be very useful in determining typical learner profiles (Pienemann, 1998, 2005). But if we are to analyze learner development over time, then we need to be able to document changes as they occur. This is particularly true in advanced learners, given the plateaus they might be experiencing in their development.

Third, sufficient numbers of learners need to be studied if we are to be able to generalize across learners. As I mentioned in the introduction, very often implications are drawn from the study of very small numbers of learners. The case of Patty is an interesting one: it has attracted huge international interest because it is the only corpus to my knowledge which studied a learner over a substantial period of time (some 18 years), thus allowing Lardiere (1998a, 1998b, 2000) to make claims about the end-state of SLA on the basis of reliable evidence that development had stopped. For obvious reasons, this is difficult to achieve: finding learners who not only are still engaged in L2 learning after this long, but who are also willing to take part in a study over such a long period, is not easy. Drawing generalizable conclusions on the basis of one learner, however, is problematic; Patty might be atypical, and she only represents one language pair. Having at our disposal longitudinal datasets of substantial numbers of learners is the only way to avoid these potential pitfalls.

Finally, we need to have a wide range of languages represented, from typologically unrelated families. In order to understand the role of transfer, for example, it is crucial that we investigate learners from a range of different L1s who are acquiring the same L2. At present, the datasets we have are predominantly of L2 English, and other languages are very unevenly represented.

Why do we need datasets?

The need for good datasets is now crucially important. The field of second language research is relatively new in its present form (mid-1970s onwards). Like any new field of research, it has been primarily engaged in its initial phase in hypothesis generation. This type of work is most effective through the careful analysis of development in small, and therefore manageable, groups of learners. It is now time, however, to test current hypotheses on larger groups of learners, in order to ensure reliability and validity of our conclusions. In first language acquisition, research started in the earlier part of the 20th century with longitudinal diary studies of individual children in order to carefully document development (Brown, 1973; Chamberlain and Chamberlain, 1904; Grégoire, 1937, 1947; Leopold, 1939, 1947, 1949a,

1949b), and has now graduated to working with large datasets, usually containing longitudinal data from a large number of children (see the CHILDES database for the impressive list of such datasets currently available to the L1 research community; http://childes.psy.cmu.edu). In second language acquisition research, by contrast, most of the literature still relies on the study of small cross-sectional corpora, and has hardly started sharing datasets yet.

Within the context of advanced learners, large datasets are probably even more important than with early-stage learners. Very often, linguistic structures which are of theoretical interest to researchers are difficult and therefore rare in learner productions, as they tend to avoid producing them. It is only by having large datasets at our disposal that we are likely to find enough occurrences of such structures to understand their development. For example, the placement of adverbs in the advanced L2 French of L1 English learners poses interesting theoretical questions. This property is supposedly linked in theoretical terms to the verb-raising parameter, operative in French but not in English, which underlies word order differences between the two languages. Other properties of this parameter (postverbal negation; subject–verb inversion in interrogatives) seem to be acquired long before adverb placement, which remains problematic in even very advanced learners. But adverbs are very rare in spontaneous L2 data, and often have to be elicited through specially designed tasks, which might promote monitoring. Large longitudinal datasets of advanced learners would allow tracing their appearance over time, and across learners. Similarly, other late acquired phenomena such as sociolinguistic competence, pragmatic competence, or idiomatic use of language need large datasets to investigate development over time (Dewaele, 2004; Guillot, 2005; Warga, 2007).

What corpora are available?

The need for corpora, preferably oral and longitudinal, is not currently met through the corpora actually available to the SLA research community, which has been rather slow in making use of new technologies to assist its research. There is an increasing number of electronic corpora available, but they remain primarily written, cross-sectional, and L2 English is nearly always the target language (see Aston, Bernardini, and Stewart, 2004; Granger, Hung, and Petch-Tyson, 2002). Moreover, hardly any of these corpora have been tagged (e.g., for parts of speech) to facilitate their exploitation, nor are they stored and managed according to discipline-agreed conventions, as is the case in L1 acquisition research. They are not usually freely available to other researchers, either, and therefore represent a limited resource to investigate L2 development.

Advantages and disadvantages of electronic L2 corpora

One of the main advantages of electronic corpora is undoubtedly their accessibility. Given the huge cost of gathering and transcribing good-quality longitudinal oral data, being able to share corpora within our research community is imperative. This is now very easy to do: digital sound files and transcripts can be stored and managed electronically and accessed via a website. This in turn allows different researchers and research groups to use the data to fulfill their particular research goals. Moreover, other researchers are able to add additional coding to the dataset, for example, for discourse analysis purposes or phonological analysis, thus enriching the dataset. Once this process of data-sharing is underway, it will also enable the research community to identify what further corpora are needed—for example, in terms of language pairs, elicitation tasks targeting specific linguistic structures, and so on—and to engage in a concerted effort to construct databases which meet its requirements.

Another indirect advantage of data-sharing is that it will encourage researchers to agree on common procedures for key analytical stages, such as transcription, tagging, and the format of corpora (i.e., the information we need about the level of learners, described in standardized ways, the elicitation tasks, and so on). It will also foster discussions about the most appropriate ways to transcribe oral learner data—no easy task.

Electronic corpora can present some disadvantages, however. For example, transcription conventions which have been designed within the context of a specific research agenda might not be so appropriate for another. However, the availability of sound files makes it easy for other researchers to amend the transcripts to suit their own purposes. Another potential disadvantage is the overconfidence in the software tools available. Taggers can make mistakes, for example, and their output needs to be checked carefully. Similarly, researchers can be tempted to run complex analyses on a set of data because the tools are available, rather than in order to give answers to a carefully constructed and theoretically well informed set of research questions. The tools we use must serve our own agendas, rather than dictate them. There is no doubt, however, that the advantages far outweigh the disadvantages. If data accessibility is undoubtedly extremely important, the most useful feature of electronic corpora is the possibility of using software to assist in their analysis. I will now turn to the tools currently available to do so.

What tools are available?

A comprehensive review of the different kind of tools currently available in corpus linguistics is offered by Hunston (2002). She categorizes the types of analyses which can be carried out on corpora as either "word-based" or "category-based."

Word-based methods typically involve the retrieval of words or strings of words within a corpus, through the use of concordancers such as WordSmith Tools (Scott, 1999), which can then perform a range of numerical and statistical calculations on the data (e.g., frequency; type/token ratios; key-word identification; comparison of corpora; mean length of utterance). These tools have been used by some L2 researchers interested in the acquisition of discrete words or collocations, as this is what they best lend themselves to (Aijmer, 2002; Flowerdew, 2004; Hasselgren, 2002; Lenko-Szymanska, 2004; Nesselhauf, 2004). However, as the majority of L2 studies to date have been concerned with the development of morphosyntax, concordancers have been largely ignored by L2 researchers.

Category-based methods involve the annotation of the data in terms of categories (e.g., parts of speech—POS, discourse features, errors, etc.), which can then be searched in the same way as with concordancers (e.g., all third person singular verbs, all prepositions, etc.). The corpus can be annotated manually or (semi-)automatically, depending on a range of factors, such as the level of detail required, the size of the corpus, and the software tools available (Hunston, 2002). POS taggers are some of the most common category-based tools, and they can reliably (with over 90 percent accuracy) tag native corpora. The CLAWS tagger for example (www.comp.lancs.ac.uk/computing/research/ucrel/claws/), has recently been used to tag the 100-million-word British National Corpus (www.natcorp.ox.ac.uk). Parsers can also be used on tagged corpora to label sentences, clauses, and phrases of different syntactic types, but their output still usually requires careful manual checking and editing by researchers.

Category-based tools have been little used in second language research, in spite of their obvious usefulness. Bar a few exceptions (Borin and Prütz, 2004; Housen, 2002; Tono, 2004), SLA researchers' use of new methodologies has remained rather unambitious, limiting itself to the use of concordancers in the context of rather descriptive and atheoretical studies (Myles, 2005). This is unlike the field of first language acquisition, which has been making extensive use of the CHILDES software tools, which include POS taggers for a range of languages, as well as powerful search mechanisms.

In the second part of this chapter I turn to the exemplification of the possibilities offered by the use of computerized methodologies for investigating learner development, through the description of FLLOC, a recent initiative which involved the construction and exploitation of a database of French L2 oral corpora using the CHILDES software (MacWhinney, 2000a, 2000b).

Using CHILDES for SLA research: the FLLOC case study

The French Learner Language Oral Corpora (FLLOC) is a large database of French learner language oral corpora, freely available to the research community on the internet.[1] The range of examples presented in what follows attests to the possibilities offered by the computerized analysis of corpora via CHILDES. Before presenting the case study database and how the software has been used to assist its analysis, I need to describe briefly the program it uses, as well as the reasons for our choice of the software.

Why CHILDES?

CHILDES was created in the early 1980s in order to assist first language acquisition research. It is the brainchild of Brian MacWhinney and his team (MacWhinney, 2000a, 2000b), and is now used as standard in that field. It consists of a large database, a transcription system, and a range of computer programs which can be run on the data, including taggers and sophisticated search tools.

The reasons for opting for this software when embarking on the construction of a French L2 oral database were many. After reviewing what was available, it became clear that no L2-specific software was available (previous attempts had been discontinued), and the CHILDES system presented many advantages. In particular, it is constantly updated and well supported, it offers a range of both word-based and category-based programs, and it includes taggers for 11 different languages, with more in preparation.[2] It is also relatively flexible, and allowed us to adapt it to our

SLA-specific needs (see Marsden *et al.*, 2003; Myles and Mitchell, 2004; Rule, 2004; Rule *et al.*, 2003). Additionally, it is free, and its policy of open access makes it very easy to share data. Indeed, all researchers using CHILDES to construct a corpus are meant to donate it to the database.

What does CHILDES consist of?

The CHILDES system is in three parts. First, there is a system of transcription conventions, CHAT, which must be adhered to in order to be able to run the programs on the data. Second, CHILDES comprises an impressive range of commands (currently 37), collectively called CLAN, which carry out a range of operations such as tagging, searching, counting, etc. A series of "switches" also allow the outputs to be presented in different ways (e.g., by frequency, alphabetically, etc.).

Finally, the database, TalkBank, contains a large number of corpora, primarily of children learning a wide range of L1s, but also some language disorder data, and a small but increasing number of L2 corpora.

The FLLOC database

The FLLOC database currently contains five oral corpora, with a sixth one in preparation, totaling approximately 1,350,000 words representing some 1375 sound files and corresponding transcripts, which have also been tagged for parts of speech. The database is freely available from the FLLOC website (www.flloc.soton.ac.uk), which also contains information about each of the corpora (e.g., tasks used, level of the learners, transcription conventions, etc.), as well as about the CHILDES tools and how to use them. A search facility allows us to locate files according to a range of criteria (e.g., a specific learner, or a task, or a year group, etc.).

Table 1 shows the five corpora comprising FLLOC. All corpora have been formatted according to the CHILDES system, and can be downloaded from the website. The corpora have been either collected by our research team or donated to us by SLA researchers in the United Kingdom and other countries in Europe, and represent instructed learners of French from complete beginners to final year undergraduates. The L1 of the learners is English in all corpora but one (where it is Dutch).

An additional longitudinal corpus of 30 instructed learners (age 16–18, L1 English) is currently being collected. The FLLOC database will then contain corpora from learners at all levels, from complete beginners to final year undergraduates.

The next sections describe how the CHILDES tools are used for transcription, tagging, and computerized analysis, and how they have been adapted to SLA-specific purposes in the context of the FLLOC database.

Transcription

Transcription conventions are described in detail in the CHAT manual available online from the CHILDES website (http://childes.psy.cmu.edu), or as a hard copy (MacWhinney, 2000b), and must be adhered to for the CLAN programs to work effectively on the data. All files must start with a *header*, which identifies the file for

Table 1 The five FLLOC corpora

Corpus	Description
Progression Corpus	60 learners in years 7, 8 and 9 in the UK; age 12–14. Beginners at outset of data collection; longitudinal over 2¼ years. Range of 1:1 narrative and interactive tasks, such as story retelling, information gap, structured conversation, etc.
	≃ 720,000 words, 650 transcripts and sound files, approximately 10 to 15 minutes each.
Linguistic Development Corpus	20 learners in each of years 9, 10 and 11 in the UK; age 14–16. Post-beginners; cross-sectional. Four 1:1 tasks each, some repeated from Progression project.
	≃ 214,000 words, 240 transcripts/sound files, around 10 to 15 minutes each.
Reading Corpus	34 learners, UK GCSE oral examination; age 16. Post-beginners; 26 native controls.
	≃ 41,400 words, 60 transcripts.
Salford Corpus	12 university undergraduate learners in the UK. Intermediate to advanced; longitudinal over 4 years. Narrative and interactive tasks.
	≃ 332,000 words, 300 transcripts and sound files; approximately 5 to 10 minutes each.
Brussels Corpus	125 Dutch learners of French; 18-year-olds. Intermediate. Narrative task.
	≃ 41,800 words, 125 transcripts.

retrieval purposes, and which contains any additional information the researcher might find useful. The header will allow the CLAN programs to carry out analyses on specific files or batches of files. After the header, CHAT files are organized in *tiers*, which are of two kinds: the *main* or *speaker tier*, which always starts with * and contains the language actually spoken by the participants, and *dependent tiers*, which always start with a % sign, and contain any additional coding of the data. Examples of such dependent tiers are the %pho tier, containing phonological coding, the %mor tier with morphosyntactic tagging (which will be described later), the %com tier adding any commentary (e.g., whispering, laughing, pointing to picture, etc.), the %err tier specifying errors, and so on. Some tiers are generated automatically (e.g., the %mor tier containing morphosyntactic tagging), and others manually (e.g., the %com tier). There can be as many dependent tiers as there are research agendas, and many more are outlined in the CHILDES manual. This allows researchers working on a shared corpus to add their own level of coding if they so wish; this additional coding can then be available to other researchers. The data do not become increasingly cluttered, as files can be viewed without all the dependent tiers. CLAN programs can then be run on any of the dependent tiers, allowing, for example, to search for specific morphosyntactic categories (e.g., all verbs in the infinitive, all instances of masculine determiners followed by a feminine noun, etc.). Figure 1 shows what a CHAT file looks like. The excerpt is a cartoon description from a second year

```
@Begin
@Languages:      fr
@Participants:   R02 Subject, NIB Investigator
@ID:        fr|fllocsalford|R02||female|||Subject|university year 2 pre-residence abroad|
@ID:        fr|fllocsalford|NIB|||||Investigator|
@Situation:      Cartoon Description
@Date: 01-DEC-1990
@Coder:              NIB, converter AMD SJR
*NIB:    d' accord je vais maintenant te montrer un dessin humoristique.
*NIB:    il y a neuf images.
*NIB:    ca finit ici.
*NIB:    j' aimerais que tu le regardes et que tu me le décrives.
*R02:    oh <il y a> [/] il y a un homme et une femme qui euh se discutent dans la rue.
*R02:    et parce que um l' homme a um volé beaucoup de l' argent de [//] d' la femme.
*R02:    et um il y a un [= l] autre homme qui [/] qui marche dans [/] euh dans la rue.
*R02:    et <la regarde> [//] les regarde um pour xxx pendant des temps.
*R02:    et <puis il> [/] (rire) puis um il um continue à marcher.
*R02:    um mais um l' homme et la femme <ils se dis> [//] ils se discutent plus.
*R02:    um et l' autr/e vieil [//] um vieux homme <la um la regar> [//] les regarde encore.
*R02:    et voit que um l' homme um <est [= l] en train de euhm um don> [//] est en train de donner un
         coup de main à la femme.
*R02:    et <la f(emme)> [/] um la femme euh elle tombe um par terre.
*R02:    um et <le vieil> [//] le vieux homme <il prit> [/] il prit <le l> [//] euh l' autre homme um par la
         main.
*R02:    et il [/] ils se mettent <à di> [//] à se discuter.
*R02:    um et puis um cet homme euh voulait donner un coup de main à cet vieux homme.
*R02:    um mais um le vieux homme tombe par terre.
*R02:    et il [/] um il frappe euh la fin.
*R02:    et <elle casse> [/] elle casse um la jambe 0[=! rire].
@End
```

Figure 1 A CHAT file

university student from the Salford Corpus; "NIB" is the researcher and "R02" the student. The details of the transcription conventions can be found in the CHILDES or FLLOC websites.

Tagging

CHILDES currently includes Part of Speech (POS) taggers (called MOR) for 11 languages. The French tagger was written by Christophe Parisse in 2001. Figure 2 shows an excerpt from the transcript in Figure 1 after tagging.

The tagging can be generated very quickly on large batches of files, in three simple stages. Computerized analyses of various kinds can then be run on the data, either on the learner tier or directly on the morphosyntactic output. I will now review briefly the kind of analyses which CLAN enables you to perform.

Computerized analyses

As I mentioned previously, there are two main types of computerized analyses (Hunston, 2002): word-based analyses (which enable frequency lists, the calculation of measures such as mean length of utterance and type/token ratio, and the search for words or strings of words) and category-based analyses (which enable tagging and searches for morphosyntactic categories or strings). I will now briefly demonstrate the kind of programs included in CLAN. There are 37 commands currently available, and I will only outline some of the more common ones.

```
*R02:    oh <il y a> [/] il y a un homme et une femme qui euh se discutent
         dans la rue .
%mor:    co:act|oh pro:subj|il&MASC&_3S pro:y|y v:poss|avoir&PRES&3SV det|un&MASC&SING
         n|homme&_MASC conj|et det|une&FEM&SING n|femme&_FEM pro:rel|qui co|euh
         pro:refl|se&3SP v|discuter-PRES&_3PV prep|dans det|la&FEM&SING n|rue&_FEM .
*R02:    et parce que um l' homme a um volé beaucoup de l' argent de [//] d' la femme .
%mor:    conj|et conj|parce conj|que co|um det|le&SING n|homme&_MASC v:poss|avoir&PRES&3SV
         co|um v:pp|voler&_MASC&_SING adv|beaucoup prep|de det|le&SING n|argent&_MASC
         prep|de det|la&FEM&SING n|femme&_FEM .
*R02:    et um il y a un [= l] autre homme qui [/] qui marche dans [/] euh dans la rue
%mor:    conj|et co|um pro:subj|il&MASC&_3S pro:y|y v:poss|avoir&PRES&3SV
         det|un&MASC&SING adj|autre n|homme&_MASC pro:rel|qui v|marcher-PRES&_3SV
         co|euh prep|dans det|la&FEM&SING n|rue&_FEM .
*R02:    et <la regarde> [//] les regarde um pour xxx pendant des temps .
%mor:    conj|et pro:obj|les&PL v|regarder-PRES&_3SV co|um prep|pour undef|xxx prep|pendant
         det|des&PL n|temps&_MASC&_SINGPL .
*R02:    et <puis il> [/] (rire) puis um il um continue à marcher .
%mor:    conj|et v:inf|rire adv|puis co|um pro:subj|il&MASC&_3S co|um v|continuer-PRES&_3SV
         prep|à v:inf|marcher&INTRANS .
*R02:    um mais um l' homme et la femme <ils se dis> [//] ils se discutent plus .
%mor:    co|um conj|mais co|um det|le&SING n|homme&_MASC conj|et det|la&FEM&SING
         n|femme&_FEM pro:subj|ils&MASC&_3P pro:refl|se&3SP v|discuter-PRES&_3PV
         adv:neg|plus .
*R02:    um et l' autr/e vieil [//] um vieux homme <la um la regar> [//] les regarde encore .
%mor:    co|um conj|et det|le&SING pro|autre&_SING co|um adj|vieux&MASC&_SINGPL
         n|homme&_MASC pro:obj|les&PL v|regarder-PRES&_3SV adv|encore .
```

Figure 2 Excerpt tagged for parts of speech with MOR

Word-based analyses

The FREQ command of CLAN can very quickly run frequency lists on individual files or on batches of files. These lists can be very useful in the context of longitudinal corpora, to measure the lexical richness of individual learners and its development over time, as well as for group comparisons—for example, between learners and native speakers performing the same task. At the end of each frequency list, the program also gives the type/token ratio. Table 2 shows the output of FREQ for the file we have looked at previously in Figures 1 and 2.

The TTR command produces a traditional type/token ratio on any file or sets of files. However, type/token ratios have been criticized for being dependent on the size of the text, in that larger samples, containing larger numbers of tokens, will give lower values for TTR and thus distort the results (Malvern and Richards, 2002; Malvern *et al.*, 2004). Therefore, CLAN now also incorporates more sophisticated measures of lexical diversity. For example, the VOCD command runs a new measure devised by Brian Richards and David Malvern called D and gives much more accurate measures of lexical richness, avoiding the inherent flaw in raw TTR alluded to above (Malvern *et al.*, 2004).

CLAN also incorporates the usual range of concordancing programmes which allow searching for words or strings of words. For example, a search using the command COMBO for the word *homme* in the transcript provided in Figure 1 gives the output shown in Figure 3. The output indicates the command and which files and speakers it has been run on, as well as the line where each occurrence can be found and the total number of occurrences.

Table 2 FREQ output for Learner *R02

24 um	3 y	1 discuter
14 et	2 casse	1 don
13 la	2 cet	1 encore
11 homme	2 coup	1 euhm
10 il	2 discutent	1 fin
6 de	2 donner	1 frappe
6 euh	2 en	1 jambe
6 femme	2 est	1 l
6 l'	2 les	1 marche
5 se	2 mais	1 marcher
5 à	2 prit	1 mettent
4 a	2 que	1 oh
4 le	2 rue	1 parce
4 un	2 terre	1 pendant
4 vieux	2 tombe	1 plus
3 autre	2 train	1 pour
3 dans	2 vieil	1 regar
3 elle	1 argent	1 rire
3 ils	1 beaucoup	1 temps
3 main	1 continue	1 une
3 par	1 d'	1 voit
3 puis	1 des	1 volé
3 qui	1 di	1 voulait
3 regarde	1 dis	

71 Total number of different word types used
214 Total number of words (tokens)
0.332 Type/token ratio

Category-based analyses

We have already briefly demonstrated the POS tagging of the data. Concordances can then be carried out directly on this morphosyntactic output. For example, all occurrences of adverbs can be found in a large corpus at the touch of a button, or all verbs in the imperfect, all prepositions, and so on. Figure 4 explains the command needed to run a search with COMBO for all instances of a masculine determiner followed by a feminine noun.

Figure 5 shows the output of such a command, with a file that comes from a 16-year-old performing a narrative task, after four and a half years of learning French. This learner produced seven instances of feminine nouns following a masculine determiner. Complementary searches enable to find all possible agreement combinations very quickly. We can run this analysis for the same learner over time, therefore establishing how her article system develops, or across large groups of learners at various stages of development. Doing both allows us not only to document developmental trends across proficiency levels, but also to study the developing system within individual learners. It is only with large longitudinal corpora that this is possible.

These examples should have sufficed to demonstrate the possibilities computerized analyses offer. They are as endless as the research hypotheses themselves, and they should enable us to test current hypotheses much more thoroughly than we have been able to in the past.

```
combo +t*R02 +s"homme" 02R2.cha
*****************************************
```

From file <02R2.cha>

*** File "02R2.cha": line 14.
*R02:   oh <il y a> [/] il y a un (1)homme et une femme qui euh se discutent
        dans la rue .

*** File "02R2.cha": line 16.
*R02:   et parce que um l' (1)homme a um volé beaucoup de l' argent de [//] d'
        la femme .

*** File "02R2.cha": line 18.
*R02:   et um il y a un [= l] autre (1)homme qui [/] qui marche dans [/] euh
        dans la rue .

*** File "02R2.cha": line 22.
*R02:   um mais um l' (1)homme et la femme <ils se dis> [//] ils se discutent
        plus .

*** File "02R2.cha": line 24.
*R02:   um et l' autr/e vieil [//] um vieux (1)homme <la um la regar> [//] les
        regarde encore .

*** File "02R2.cha": line 26.
*R02:   et voit que um l' (1)homme um <est [- l] en train de euhm um don> [//]
        est en train de donner un coup de main à la femme .

*** File "02R2.cha": line 29.
*R02:   um et <le vieil> [//] le vieux (1)homme <il prit> [/] il prit <le l>
        [//] euh l' autre (2)homme um par la main .

*** File "02R2.cha": line 32.
*R02:   um et puis um cet (1)homme euh voulait donner un coup de main à cet
        vieux (2)homme .

*** File "02R2.cha": line 34.
*R02:   um mais um le vieux (1)homme tombe par terre .

Strings matched 11 times

Figure 3 Lexical search for *homme* with COMBO

```
combo +t%mor +s"det*MASC*^n*FEM*" 47L11FLO.mor.pst
```

+t%mor:	indicates the tier the search is carried out on
*:	indicates any metacharacter (some symbols might follow the MASC code on the *mor* output)
MASC:	the code for masculine
^:	followed by
n:	the code for noun
FEM:	the code for feminine
47L11FLO.mor.pst:	the name of the file. '.mor.pst' is the file extension after it has been tagged.

Figure 4 COMBO command to search MOR tier

From file <47L11FLO.mor.pst>

*** File "47L11FLO.mor.pst": line 11.
*L47:   la famille en vacances euh le grand_mère et les enfants euh euh et
        le lac et la maison de Wales [/] Wales .
%mor: det|la&FEM&SING n|famille&_FEM prep:art|en n|vacance&_FEM-_PL co|euh
        (1)det|le&MASC&SING (1)n|grand_mère&_FEM conj|et det|les&PL adj|enfant&_PL co|euh
        co|euh conj|et det|le&MASC&SING n|lac&_MASC conj|et det|la&FEM&SING
        n|maison&_FEM prep|de n:prop|Wales .

*** File "47L11FLO.mor.pst": line 40.
*L47:   um le mère um regarder le magasin euh .
%mor: co|um (1)det|le&MASC&SING (1)n|mère&_FEM co|um v:inf|regarder det|le&MASC&SING
        n|magasin&_MASC co|euh .

*** File "47L11FLO.mor.pst": line 47.
*L47:   le grand_mère peint <le mons(tre)> [//] le monster@s:d du lac .
%mor: (1)det|le&MASC&SING (1)n|grand_mère&_FEM v|peindre&PRES&3SV
        det|le&MASC&SING n:eng|monster det|du&MASC&SING n|lac&_MASC .

*** File "47L11FLO.mor.pst": line 65.
*L47:   um le mère et les garçons um faire les courses regarder le magasin .
%mor: co|um (1)det|le&MASC&SING (1)n|mère&_FEM conj|et det|les&PL n|garçon&_MASC-_PL
        co|um v:mdl|ex|faire&INF det|les&PL n|course&_FEM-_PL v:inf|regarder
        det|le&MASC&SING
        n|magasin&_MASC .

*** File "47L11FLO.mor.pst": line 71.
*L47:   ok um le grand_mère peint le en xxx .
%mor: co|ok co|um (1)det|le&MASC&SING (1)n|grand_mère&_FEM v|peindre&PRES&3SV
        det|le&MASC&SING prep|en |xxx .

*** File "47L11FLO.mor.pst ": line 79.
*L47:   un bouée deux bouées um treize bouées et quatre bouées [?] .
%mor: (1)det|un&MASC&SING (1)n|bouée&_FEM num|deux n|bouée&_FEM-_PL co|um
        num|treize n|bouée&_FEM-_PL conj|et num|quatre n|bouée&_FEM-_PL .

*** File "47L11FLO.mor.pst ": line 136.
*L47:   <le famille> [/] um le famille [^ eng: how do you say leave] ?
%mor: co|um (1)det|le&MASC&SING (1)n|famille&_FEM ?

Strings matched 7 times

Figure 5 Output of COMBO search on MOR tier

Conclusion

Recent developments in SLA research have generated sophisticated hypotheses which require testing. In most cases, in order to test these hypotheses, large longitudinal corpora are essential to be confident that the conclusions reached can be generalizable. We now have the tools to share such corpora, and to assist our analyses in powerful ways. The SLA research community, however, has been rather slow in taking up this opportunity, and it is now imperative that researchers are trained in the use of these tools, in the same way that first language acquisition researchers routinely are. I hope to have demonstrated and illustrated effectively the advantages this would bring to the whole research community and particularly to those interested in the longitudinal study of advanced L2 capacities.

Notes

This chapter draws on recent articles by the author (Myles, 2005, 2007; Myles and Mitchell, 2004).

1. Thanks are due to the other members of the research team involved in the FLLOC project: Rosamond Mitchell, Sarah Rule, Emma Marsden, Mischa Tuffield, and Vladimir Mircevski.
2. The 11 languages are Cantonese, Chinese, Danish, Dutch, English, French, German, Hebrew, Italian, Japanese, and Spanish.

References

Aijmer, K. (2002). Modality in advanced Swedish learners' written interlanguage. In S. Granger, J. Hung, and S. Petch-Tyson (Eds.), *Computer learner corpora, second language acquisition and foreign language learning* (pp. 55–76). Philadelphia, PA: John Benjamins.

Aston, G., Bernardini, S., and Stewart, D. (2004). *Corpora and language learners.* Philadelphia, PA: John Benjamins.

Borin, L., and Prütz, K. (2004). New wine in old skins? A corpus investigation of L1 syntactic transfer in learner language. In G. Aston, S. Bernardini, and D. Stewart (Eds.), *Corpora and Language Learners* (pp. 67–87). Philadelphia, PA: John Benjamins.

Brown, R. (1973). *A first language: The early stages.* Cambridge, MA: Harvard University Press.

Chamberlain, A., and Chamberlain, I. (1904). Studies of a child. *Pedagogical Seminary, 11,* 264–291, 452–283.

Dewaele, J.-M. (2004). The acquisition of sociolinguistic competence in French as a foreign language: An overview. In F. Myles and R. Towell (Eds.), *The acquisition of French as a second language,* special issue of the *Journal of French Language Studies, 14*(3), 301–319.

Flowerdew, L. (2004). The problem–solution pattern in apprentice vs. professional technical writing: An application of appraisal theory. In G. Aston, S. Bernardini, and D. Stewart (Eds.), *Corpora and language learners* (pp. 125–135). Philadelphia, PA: John Benjamins.

Granger, S., Hung, J., and Petch-Tyson, S. (2002). *Computer learner corpora, second language acquisition and foreign language teaching.* Philadelphia, PA: John Benjamins.

Grégoire, A. (1937). *L'Apprentissage du langage.* Vol. 1. Paris: Droz.

Grégoire, A. (1947). *L'Apprentissage du langage.* Vol. 2. Paris: Droz.

Guillot, M.-N. (2005). Aspects of pragmatic development in advanced L2 oppositional talk: Turn-initial NS and NNS mais and but in contrast. Unpublished manuscript, Dubrovnik.

Hasselgren, A. (2002). Learner corpora and language testing: Smallwords as markers of learner fluency. In S. Granger, J. Hung, and S. Petch-Tyson (Eds.), *Computer learner corpora, second language acquisition and foreign language teaching* (pp. 143–173). Philadelphia, PA: John Benjamins.

Housen, A. (2002). A corpus-based study of the L2 acquisition of the English verb system. In S. Granger, J. Hung, and S. Petch-Tyson (Eds.), *Computer learner corpora, second language acquisition and foreign language learning* (pp. 77–116). Philadelphia, PA: John Benjamins.

Hunston, S. (2002). *Corpora in applied linguistics.* New York: Cambridge University Press.

Lardiere, D. (1998a). Case and Tense in the "fossilized" steady state. *Second Language Research, 14,* 1–26.

Lardiere, D. (1998b). Dissociating syntax from morphology in a divergent L2 end-state grammar. *Second Language Research, 14,* 359–375.

Lardiere, D. (2000). Mapping features to forms in second language acquisition. In J. Archibald (Ed.), *Second language acquisition and linguistic theory* (pp. 102–129). Malden, MA: Blackwell.

Lenko-Szymanska, A. (2004). Demonstratives as anaphora markings in advanced learners'

English. In G. Aston, S. Bernardini, and D. Stewart (Eds.), *Corpora and language learners* (pp. 89–107). Philadelphia, PA: John Benjamins.

Leopold, W. (1939). *Speech development of a bilingual child: A linguist's record. Vocabulary growth in the first two years.* Vol. 1, Evanston, IL: Northwestern University Press.

Leopold, W. (1947). *Speech development of a bilingual child: A linguist's record. Sound learning in the first two years.* Vol. 2, Evanston, IL: Northwestern University Press.

Leopold, W. (1949a). *Speech development of a bilingual child: A linguist's record. Diary from age two.* Vol. 4, Evanston, IL: Northwestern University Press.

Leopold, W. (1949b). *Speech development of a bilingual child: A linguist's record. Grammar and general problems in the first two years.* Vol. 3, Evanston, IL: Northwestern University Press.

MacWhinney, B. (2000a). *The CHILDES project: Tools for analyzing talk.* Vol. 2, *The database* (3rd ed.). Mahwah, NJ: Lawrence Erlbaum.

MacWhinney, B. (2000b). *The CHILDES project: Tools for analyzing talk.* Vol. 1, *Transcription format and programs* (3rd ed.). Mahwah, NJ: Lawrence Erlbaum.

Malvern, D., and Richards, B. (2002). Investigating accommodation in language proficiency interviews using a new measure of lexical diversity. *Language Testing, 19*, 85–104.

Malvern, D., Richards, B., Chipere, N., and Durán, P. (2004). *Lexical diversity and language development: Quantification and assessment.* Basingstoke, UK: Palgrave Macmillan.

Marsden, E., Myles, F., Rule, S., and Mitchell, R. (2003). Using CHILDES tools for researching second language acquisition. In S. Sarangi, and T. van Leeuwen (Eds.), *Applied linguistics and communities of practice* (pp. 98–113). London: British Association for Applied Linguistics/ Continuum.

Myles, F. (2005). Interlanguage corpora and second language acquisition research. *Second Language Research, 21*, 373–391.

Myles, F. (2007). Using electronic corpora in SLA research. In D. Ayoun (Ed.), *French applied linguistics* (pp. 377–400). Philadelphia, PA: John Benjamins.

Myles, F., and Mitchell, R. (2004). Using information technology to support empirical SLA research. *Journal of Applied Linguistics, 1*, 69–98.

Nesselhauf, N. (2004). How learner corpus analysis can contribute to language teaching: A study of support verb constructions. In G. Aston, S. Bernardini, and D. Stewart (Eds.), *Corpora and language learners* (pp. 109–124). Philadelphia, PA: John Benjamins.

Pienemann, M. (1998). Developmental dynamics in L1 and L2 acquisition: Processability theory and generative entrenchment. *Bilingualism: Language and Cognition, 1*(1), 1–20.

Pienemann, M. (Ed.). (2005). *Cross-linguistic aspects of processability theory.* Philadelphia, PA: John Benjamins.

Rule, S. (2004). French interlanguage corpora: recent developments. In F. Myles and R. Towell (Eds.), *The acquisition of French as a second language*, special issue of the *Journal of French Language Studies, 14*(3), 343–356.

Rule, S., Marsden, E., Myles, F., and Mitchell, R. (2003). Constructing a database of French interlanguage oral corpora. In D. Archer, R. Rayson, E. Wilson, and T. McEnery (Eds.), *Proceedings of the Corpus Linguistics 2003 Conference* (Vol. 16, pp. 669–677). University of Lancaster, UK: UCREL Technical Papers.

Scott, M. (1999). *WordSmith tools.* New York: Oxford University Press.

Tono, Y. (2004). Multiple comparisons of IL, L1 and TL corpora: The case of the L2 acquisition of verb subcategorisation patterns by Japanese learners of English. In G. Aston, S. Bernardini, and D. Stewart (Eds.), *Corpora and language learners* (pp. 45–66). Philadelphia, PA: John Benjamins.

Warga, M. (2007). French interlanguage pragmatics. In D. Ayoun (Ed.), *French applied linguistics* (pp. 171–207). Philadelphia, PA: John Benjamins.

5 Planning, collecting, exploring, and archiving longitudinal L2 data

Experiences from the P-MoLL project

Romuald Skiba, Norbert Dittmar, and Jana Bressem

Abstract

Drawing from our experience with the longitudinal project "P-MoLL" (Skiba and Dittmar, 1992), which was run at the Free University in Berlin from 1982 to 1992, in this chapter we offer an overview of the relevant theoretical and methodological steps necessary to carry out valid and representative investigations of this kind. Starting with the planning of data collection, we present problems of data design. Several data design issues are discussed and illustrated, including longitudinal aspects (length of target language contact), cross-individual exposure and input to learning (tempo of acquisition and intensity of contact) and cross-sectional characteristics (comparable data structures). We then turn to methods of data collection, preparation, and analysis. We also show the importance for the data to be properly described and safely stored in order to avoid the danger that language resources that are created with huge efforts end up in data cemeteries. We argue for the importance of longitudinal L2 studies that investigate the lengthy course of L2 development from early to advanced stages.

Introduction

Longitudinal study has long been considered essential for substantive work on the acquisition of a first language (L1). Leopold's (1939) decade-long study of the acquisition of English and German by his daughter is among the best known early examples for this approach. Some 30 years later, Brown (1973) completed sophisticated longitudinal studies that addressed various ages of L1 learners. Miller (1979) used dense time intervals as well as a broad variety of informal contexts in parent–child interaction to expand our understanding of the gradual development of a first language; and in the 1980s, a crosslinguistic dimension was added to the longitudinal study of L1 development under Slobin's direction (Slobin, 1985).

Longitudinal studies on second language (L2) acquisition, too, have been conducted for quite some time, with Leopold's work providing an example for that focus, as well. However, the majority of such investigations have been individual case studies whose findings were less conclusive and more suggestive of the issues that could be fruitfully pursued (for a review, see Harklau, Chapter 2, this volume). Only more recently has the field seen the emergence of a coordinated and broad-based approach to the longitudinal investigation of L2 learning that inherently foregrounds methodological issues. Perhaps the best known among these projects are those undertaken under the sponsorship of the European Science Foundation, reported on, among others, by Perdue (1993). As expected, these broad-based projects required in-depth consideration of the kinds of methodological and data management issues that are necessary for longitudinal research. Although these recommendations were well set forth in published form (e.g., Perdue, 1984), their influence on how second language learning is generally imagined and researched has been surprisingly limited. For example, two treatments of theory and methodology in language learning, each roughly a decade apart from the first publications on the ESF Project (Doughty and Long, 2003; Tarone, Gass, and Cohen, 1994), essentially make no mention of critically important issues raised by the longitudinal study of language acquisition.

Given that state of affairs, it is worth revisiting some of the key insights gained from that earlier work while expanding them in light of more recent developments in corpus linguistics. We do so in this chapter drawing from our experiences in the P-MoLL project (*Modalität im Längsschnitt von Lernervarietäten*—Modality in a Longitudinal Study of Learner Varieties). This was a longitudinal project we conducted in the late 1980s, which investigated the naturalistic acquisition of German by learners with L1 Polish and Italian from the time of their arrival in Germany until three years later (for details, see Dittmar *et al.*, 1990; Dittmar and Reich, 1993; Dittmar and Terborg, 1991; Skiba and Dittmar, 1992). In this chapter we draw on our experiences in that project in order to offer an overview of general aspects of the longitudinal study of L2 learning. We also provide practical suggestions for planning and carrying out longitudinal studies, with particular emphasis on the consideration of technical issues in the conduct of such research. In so doing, we offer considerations that build on advances in corpus linguistics and, more generally, advances in modern technology that enable advantageous ways of dealing with annotation, archiving, metadata organization, retrieval, and analysis of complex data, such as those required in longitudinal study.

We have chosen to treat at some length matters that might appear to be no more than "practical tips" of do's and don'ts that simple prudence in research practice would seem to call for. But they deserve scrupulous attention, precisely because considering them carefully in advance of longitudinal study and adhering to them in the collection and analysis of data can make the difference between valid, representative, and insightful research and mere language evidence from which it is difficult to draw conclusions. Because these issues, too, should be considered ahead of time to maximize the eventual usefulness of data, awareness of technological limitations and opportunities can no longer be relegated to optional status.

Let us begin with a brief outline of the P-MoLL study, since it provides the context within which our "on-the-ground" experiences were gained.

The P-MoLL project

The P-MoLL project (*Modalität von Lernervarietäten im Längsschnitt*) was run at the Free University of Berlin from 1987 to 1992.[1] It focused on a broad range of communicative tasks and documented the acquisition of words, syntactic, and semantic ways of expressing modality, both explicit and implicit, through data that came from

audio- and videotape recordings. The data pertained to 16 Polish informants
(seven female and nine male), as well as one female Italian informant. Comparison
data from native speakers of German and Polish were also recorded (for details, see
Dittmar *et al.*, 1990, pp. 139–141).

Participants were selected according to the following criteria: (1) identical number
of male and female participants, (2) age range between 20 and 40 years, (3) different
social background, and (4) no or little knowledge of German at the time of their
arrival. All 16 were naturalistic learners. At the beginning of the study they had been
in Berlin for between two to eight months. Taking a descriptive and explanatory
perspective, learners' L2 acquisition profile was related to their interactional profile.

The study adopted the notion of "cycles" that had previously been used in the
ESF-Project (see Perdue, 1984).[2] Cycles are characterized by a fixed sequence of
communicative genres that are elicited within a fixed time frame, in this case 12
months, and that are repeated in the same fashion in subsequent cycles. Table 1
details the wide variety of communicative genres that were elicited in each cycle,
together with the specific tasks that tapped each genre.

In the case of the P-MoLL project, a total of three cycles extended over three
years. Specifically, the study proceeded in two cycles with eight recordings and a third
cycle with five recordings. Six months after completion of the study, we conducted a
post-study monitoring data take. During the first two cycles each recording consisted
of five discourse types; these were "retaken" in the same sequence with similar topics
that fit the particular communicative genre. During the second cycle, the discourse
type of "wishes and intents" was added; otherwise, the second cycle was essentially
a repetition of the first. The linguistic tasks from both the first and second cycles
were repeated in the third cycle over a total of five recordings. In order to probe
acquisition of the lexicon, the additional discourse type of "describing" was introduced. Altogether the following discourse types were used (see Table 1 for further
details):

1. *Free conversation (K):* nonstructured conversation between native (NS) and nonnative
   speakers (NNS) holding equal social positions;
2. *Instruction (I):* different ways of modalizing instructions by NNS to the NS, using different
   speech acts (ten different verbal tasks);
3. *Narratives (E):* retelling, telling of personal experiences, reporting on the participants'
   migration story; eight different tasks with different temporal and modal means;
4. *Problem solving (P):* ten tasks for probing verbal ways (modalizations) of solving a variety of
   difficult problems;
5. *Attitudes and evaluations (M):* ten tasks that document attitudes and evaluation of different
   events in society;
6. *Wishes and ends (B):* three interactions in a travel agency and in a dating agency where the
   NNS takes the position of the agent;
7. *Descriptions (D):* six different descriptions, ranging from description of a painting to explication of a recipe.

To serve as a basis of comparison, each of the communicative tasks performed by the
learners was also completed by four native speakers of the target and of the source
languages.

With the Berlin P-MoLL project on the acquisition of German by Polish and

Table 1 Overview of the seven elicited communicative genres with alternative subtypes fitting the particular communicative functions. Abbreviations represent the original German codes

Discourse type						
K	*I*	*E*	*P*	*M*	*B*	*D*
Open topic; with little intervention by interviewer; everyday conversation	*Instructions on actions and behavior by informant*	*Narrations, reports*	*Explanation of a serious problem and its solution*	*Topic of interest to the participant who comments on it*	*Role plays; elicitation of desires and intentions*	*Descriptions*
Of particular interest during the recording was news about the job, the family, etc., as well as activities that are a central part of the informants' life (such as school, children . . .)	**ASB** Instruction on the prosecution of theft of an ashtray	**CCP/HAR** Retelling of a movie	**DIT** Theft of personal belongings	**AMT** Eviction of an underage person	**RSB (a)** Information on cheap vacation to London	**BBS** Description of a picture
	EIN Filling out an invitation form	**DST** Retelling of theft of a ashtray	**FAB** Sole survivor of an airplane crash in the jungle	**AUS** School with a high number of foreigners	**RSB (b)** Change of roles and different destinations	**BFG** Sequencing of ten pictures in order to tell a coherent story
	LMP Construction of a lamp	**ERL** Telling of a surprising or astonishing event	**FLU** Solving a riddle	**DAR** Theft because of hunger	**EHE** Informant consults a dating agency	**FKI** Cooking of Flaczki (a Polish meal)
	KFM Instruction on the use of a coffee machine	**GSI** Retelling a dangerous situation or accident	**GLB** No money for paying restaurant bill	**EID** Attitudes towards Germans, the country, and the language		**TRH** Imagining a dream house

Specific communicative tasks

KSP
Explanation of a card game

MEN
Explanation of a game

MFZ
Explanation and instruction on a game

PKT
Instruction on the construction of a box and its preparation for mailing

PST
Instructions on how to respond in a night-time burglary

SMO
Instructions on how to respond in case of a smog alarm

KIN
Telling of a childhood story

MIG
Telling of migration/travel to Berlin

PST
Retelling of a burglary at night

URL
Retelling of last/best vacation

HAB
Rescue of people from a burning house

INS
Rescue of children on an island

REN
Landlord expects actions that cannot be fulfilled

RFP
Flat tire and no help available

SAR
Working without permission, employer denies wage

VSR
Role play: informant is judge in child custody case

HUN
High number of dogs and possible threats arising from them

LAN
Attitudes towards Germany, Poland, and the country the participant wished to live in

OTR
Attitudes towards extramarital relations

POB
Obligations of rich Poles to take care of newcomers

VGE
Is murder justifiable?

WAN
Advertisement and presentation of goods seen as leading to theft

WDK
Making vodka

WHG
Furnishing an apartment, given a particular layout

Italian speakers we showed how communicative competence in an L2 can be investigated over time by comparing progress across communicative genres organized in three cycles. A discussion of the substantive findings of the P-MoLL project is beyond the scope of the present chapter (the interested reader is referred to the results available in Dittmar and Terborg, 1991; Dittmar and Reich, 1993; Schumacher and Skiba, 1992; Skiba and Dittmar, 1992; and, more recently, Ahrenholz, 1998; Dimroth, 2004; and Reich, 2004). By coming to grips with the challenges involved in this three-year-long project, however, we gained unique insights into what it takes to design and conduct longitudinal studies that enable linguistic sophistication and explanatory value. It is these insights that constitute our focus in the remainder of the chapter.

General aspects of longitudinal studies

Of the many issues that the longitudinal study of naturalistic L2 learning raises, we have chosen three that deserve particular attention: the scope of the "longitudinalness" of the study; characteristics of the participants that might support or jeopardize the goals of the study; and issues of representativeness, comparability, and validity.

What does "longitudinal" mean?

Decisions regarding the length of the study are driven by its goals. Thus, at the most global level, research goals influence the number of participants, the number of data takes, the nature and length of each session, and the intervals that are appropriate for developmental features to be investigated at a sufficient depth and breadth. In our experience, good decision-making requires the prior creation of a well-crafted written plan that spells out the research design along with its major research questions. While subsequent adjustments may well be necessary, that initial design specification is critical.

Length of stay in the target society is of crucial importance for L2 learning that involves residence in a second language context, necessitating careful selection of study participants. In turn, aspects of the research goals and characteristics of the participants will influence various project conventions. In any case, because "time is of the essence," all documents have to be directly or indirectly connected to aspects of time and timing. Table 2 represents the relation between the type of data and the time component.

Another key parameter in all SLA studies, but especially in longitudinal studies, is age. How it is conceptualized is by no means a straightforward matter (see Birdsong, 2005; Dimroth, 2004). As Eckert states, "Like gender, age correlates with variation by virtue of its social, not its biological status (although biology of course is part of the social construction of age and gender)" (1996, p. 152). With regard to longitudinal study of language development, Eckert adds:

> two kinds of re-study of the same community are possible: studies of age cohorts as they pass through time, and studies of life stages as they are occupied by successive age cohorts. Studies in real time can also either follow the same individuals (panel study) or they can collect samples of comparable but different individuals at successive points in time (trend studies). A trend study with an age-graded sample is the only kind that can

Table 2 Relation of type of data and the time component

Data type / Time	What to consider before you start? *T 0*	What to add to document? *T1-Tn*
Recording related metadata	Tape labeling conventions, media file formats and naming conventions	Recording medium, date, recorded persons, tape label
Time-free metadata	Staff questionnaire with conventions for assuring anonymity, participant's name, date and place of birth, sex, professional background, first contact with the L2	See Table 3
Time-sensitive metadata	Conventions for protocols and other metadata	Intensity of contact with the new language community, language knowledge (subjective)
Annotations/transcripts	File formats and naming conventions, annotation conventions and tools	Files and folders organization. controlled vocabularies (CVs) for annotation values
Lexical data	Compatibility of annotation formats and exploration tools	Word lists, annotation value lists

unequivocally show change in progress as it shows successive cohorts at each life stage. A panel study is the only kind that can unequivocally show change in the individual lifetime, as it sees the same people at different life stages.

(1996, p. 153)

In line with the interests of research that is focused on language development, and different from sociolinguistic aims of analysis, longitudinal studies of L2 learning are typically panel studies.

Finally, length of observation needs to be considered carefully. This requirement obtains not only because of the inherently longitudinal nature of language learning but because, as several analyses have indicated, the speed of the learning process can differ appreciably (see Klein and Dittmar, 1979; Klein and Perdue, 1997). This difference holds, although the inner structure of the L2 variety remains the same (see Klein and Dittmar, 1979; Skiba and Dittmar, 1992).

What does "cross-individual study" mean?

One expects participants to have different profiles in terms of age, sex, and educational background. In addition, they are likely to have different levels of language ability, different native languages, and different learning habits, styles, and abilities. All of these characteristics figure in the planning of a longitudinal study and may necessitate adjustments of research goals as well as study design. Often organizational and financial constraints and opportunities enter this decision-making process.

To summarize, longitudinal studies in L2 acquisition require the following considerations and conditions:

1. Participants should be observed in "real time," i.e., appropriate intervals have to be chosen according to the main research questions (children require a higher, adults a lower, density of intervals).
2. Assuring that participants stay in a longitudinal study is both essential for the study itself and a constant challenge. For that reason, starting out with twice the number of participants than originally planned is a good rule of thumb. For that reason also, researchers must continually motivate additional sessions in order to get the required amount of data, particularly in extended studies.
3. The representativeness of data obtained in the different sessions is influenced by numerous factors, among them stress, fatigue, a sense of well-being, and, last but not least, technical problems.
4. Linguistic validity is best ensured by considering the nature of the conditions that should obtain for eliciting the kinds of data that the study seeks. Obstacles notwithstanding, the intention is to obtain the most natural L2 data possible.
5. In addition to gathering language samples from the L2 learners, data should also be obtained under comparable conditions from native speakers of both the source and the target language. These elicitations allow for valid cross-linguistic comparison inasmuch as they permit the description and evaluation of learners' L2 in light of average source and target language competence.
6. Within a longitudinal study, both stable and variable factors of learning a second language should be defined (and then controlled) as narrowly and explicitly as possible.

What do "representative," "comparable," and "valid" mean?

A high level of comparability among the study participants is a key way to ensure the comparability of data from the oral and/or written texts produced by the learners. Simply put, data that have been collected under the same controlled conditions are more readily comparable. When a single, well-structured task as performed by different participants is well documented, it is possible to make valid statements about the similarities and differences in how the task was handled. Further descriptions can characterize both the linguistic structures and the strategies used. The explanatory power of such statements extends to variability of language use in one task type by different learners and to different communicative patterns that might apply to the performance of a given task.

However, single-task studies do just that: they reflect on a particular, perhaps even isolated aspect of the communicative competence of the learner. Therefore, a broad range of different communicative routines should be documented in order to facilitate valid inferences about learners' communicative abilities. At the very least, both monological and dialogical tasks that represent different communicative genres should be included (cf. Halliday, 1978, Chapter 3; Martin, 2001). But that step has consequences for the analysis: while a collection of heterogeneous text types enhances the quality of statements researchers can make about learners' L2 abilities, it simultaneously reduces the explanatory power of particular text-type characteristics. In other words, validity is itself a relational construct that can refer to different preferences and interests that are embedded in and arise from the research design. Findings are considered valid if they are based on representative and comparable data.

In light of such considerations, the following phenomena lend themselves to comparisons: (1) lists of lexical units constructed automatically from transcripts; (2) lists of grammatical and other functional coding, such as coding of case or information structure on the basis of annotations; and (3) opinions about learners' strategies, particularly as they relate to style and register, as compiled from quantitative and qualitative analyses.

Documentation of learner development requires attention to the following issues. In and of themselves text types, such as instructions or narratives, do not ensure data comparability. As Table 1 indicates (cf. also the last chapter of the P MoLL pro ject), a particular genre type can be elicited in conjunction with different communicative tasks. For that reason, communicative tasks often provide a particularly appropriate focus for elicitation. Also, because significantly unequal amounts of data can cause statistical problems, it is wise to specify time limits for the data take and, by implication, the recording of the data. Finally, as already stated, triangulation with data obtained from native speakers of both the L1 and L2 provides an additional basis for data comparison.

Planning and carrying out of a longitudinal study

It is a truism that linguistic analyses dramatically increase their meaningfulness when they are based on large databases. A good bit of the interest in corpus-based L2 acquisition research derives from that fact. Drawing on the tradition of corpus linguistics (cf. Biber and Conrad, 1998; Schwitalla and Wegstein, 2005), as well as empirical language research, corpus-based studies offer the following advantages: they define technical and conceptual standards for data storage (cf. Gibbon, Moore, and Winski, 1997); they structure and code both data and data analysis; they keep data and research results from physical decay; and they make them available to other research groups and research generations.

To achieve those goals, special care is required both for *data contents* (i.e., what is being recorded) and *data formats* (i.e., how the data are stored and processed). With regard to data content, longitudinal SLA studies will need to consider the following:

- Recording intervals have to be specified. There are no general criteria for doing so; instead, research foci and interests enter into the determination (e.g., comprehension vs. production, the nature of input; for examples, see Tomasello and Stahl, 2004).
- The learners themselves have to be specified in terms of characteristics that apply to the group.
- A broad variety of speech and communicative functions should be documented in order to ensure representativeness and comparability of the data.
- Sociopsychological information about the learners at different times of data collection should be documented, across the different participants and longitudinally for a particular participant. While the quality and character of the primary, linguistic data are crucial (as captured, for instance, in audio or video recordings), they should be augmented by information about the social and psychological circumstances of the learning process.

With regard to data format, points that deserve attention include:

- recording circumstances and devices (hardware, protocols, and other conventions)
- technical aspects of primary data storing (file formats, data management)

- annotation (transcription) of primary data (computer tools and file formats)
- metadata formats and tools
- aspects of data exploration (computer tools, file formats, and the structuring of data).

The following observations incorporate both of these aspects into practical advice during the implementation phases of a study: data collection, data segmentation, metadescription of the data, annotation/coding of the data, construction of the corpus, and data exploration. Each of these phases builds on the previous one but requires different data formats. For example, information about the date of the recording has to be noted on the recording tape as well as on all transcripts, media files, and metadata so that it can be considered during the exploration process.

Data collection: obtaining the raw data

Nothing is more crucial than the quality of the raw data (see in particular Labov, 1970). Where possible, we recommend video recordings for their ability to capture contextual information. Researchers should consider, as well, the possibilities and consequences of data compression to enable additional processing in the future (see Cholin, 2004). Raw data should also include written reports or reports recorded on tape, such as information about the informants and the situation of recording. This information is important both for analysis and for construction of the corpus. Unambiguous conventions for data labeling[3] and keeping records[1] will ease future work, as Myles (Chapter 4, this volume) also notes. For that reason, computer use should be considered early on. Likewise, decisions about recording formats, compression of data, data digitization, and storage space should be made prior to obtaining data.

Even so, surprises are inevitable. Among the most serious are participants leaving the project or losing interest, or computer files or recording tapes being damaged or destroyed. Backups and copies of recordings should therefore be part of study administration.

Data segmentation

Data segmentation is based on the research design drawn up at the beginning of the study. Not only will such information ease the actual recording; it will also ease future segmentation of the raw data. Together, the recording reports (*Abhörprotokoll*), the research design, and the examination of the raw data facilitate determining the relevant sequences of raw data, that is, their beginning and end. Irrelevant information (e.g., technical trouble during recordings) can be deleted or marked as such.

Regardless of which device was used for recording, the data can be digitized and saved as a computer file. Gradually, international standards for this important step are being developed (for an overview, see, for example, Wittenburg, Skiba, and Trilsbeek [2005]; and, for practical advice, see www.mpi.nl/corpus/a4guides). Digitization also enables structuring the raw data physically; for instance, by converting recorded data to computer files of a suitable size that can be used as units of analysis, a kind of data segmentation that, earlier on, had taken place during transcription. Conventions of data naming play an important role in this process.

Metadescription of the data

Beyond information about the participants in the communicative event that yields the data, metadata include birth date and place, date of arrival in the target society, and language competence at the time of arrival. Ideally this information should be collected during the first session. Two types of data can be distinguished: (a) *time-free metadata* and (b) *time-sensitive metadata*. For both types, computer-based tools exist that help store and manage all the data in a standardized and efficient way. Figures 1 and 2 illustrate how conventions for transcription headers can be used to keep track of time-free and time-sensitive metadata.

Time-free metadata, an example of which can be found in Table 3, are expected to stay valid for the time of the study. These data can contribute to the explanation of

> **File name: P-DS6E1.CCP**
> *L1: P*
> *L2: D*
> *INFORMANT: I=S(ascha) P10*
> TEST NUMBER: 6
> CYCLE: 1
> TEST NAME: CCP
> DATE OF RECORDING: 07.04.86
> PLACE OF RECORDING: seminar room, FU Berlin
> **RECORDING DEVICE: SONY TCM-600 B**
> **DEVICE USED FOR TRANSCRIPTION: SANYO TRC 8700**
> **TRANSCRIBED BY/AT: Lena, 08.04.87**
> **SIDE OF TAPE: 1**
> **VIDEO (Y/N): N**
> EXPERIMENTER: Lena
> LENGTH OF STAY AT THE TIME OF THE RECORDING: 7 Months

Figure 1 Example of header for transcriptions containing relevant information on the recording

> Informant (code)
> Protocol
>
> Name: Date: Time of recording:
> Recording device: Place:
> Persons present:
>
> If the learner learns German at a school:
>
>   (a) where
>   (b) since when
>   (c) how many hours a week
>   (d) which textbook
>
> Which lessons have been dealt with since the last interview?
> Personal learning impression
>
> Situation (food, drinks)
> Topics of conversation (striking features of the nonverbal aspects, such as gestures, facial expressions, shock)

Figure 2 Time-sensitive metadata (interview protocol)

Table 3 Time-free data: social data (first interview questionnaire, example from the P-MoLL project)

Introduction of the informants (first interview)

---

1. Biographical data / social data
1.1   Blinded name, number, and code
1.2   Sex
1.3   Date and place of birth
1.4   Last residence in Poland
1.5   Personal situation in Poland
1.6   Education
1.7   Training/work in Poland
1.8   Arrival in Berlin
1.9   Beginning of recordings
1.10 Language competence in German
1.11 Other languages

2. Initial situation in Berlin
2.1   Acquisition of German in school contexts (type, length, intensity of the course)
2.2   Assessment of language competence in German
2.3   Work (type, how many hours per week)
2.4   Personal situation/social contacts
2.5   Living arrangements

---

the learning results at different phases of the study. Depending on the nature of the study, such information might include first language dialect, particular aspects of their various socializations, and social milieu of current living conditions. Because recordings need to remain anonymous, time-free metadata should also provide information about reference to the participants according to the project conventions. Anonymity and confidentiality are subcomponents of larger ethical issues that must be scrupulously observed in human subject research such as longitudinal L2 studies. In many countries (e.g., the United States), such research falls under stringent guidelines prepared by institutional review boards. Among other aspects, these state the researchers' responsibilities toward the study participants at all phases of the study. Anyone contemplating longitudinal research (for that matter, any SLA research) should be thoroughly familiar with the stipulations of such guidelines and obtain the necessary research approvals. Only data that have been obtained in this fashion will qualify for inclusion in larger databases, such as those maintained by the Max-Planck-Institute or CHILDES.

Time-sensitive data, on the other hand, include information that changes over the period of the study and pertains, for example, to school, work, social/personal contacts, and changes in participants' private lives. Free conversations at the beginning of each recording session or questionnaires are good ways of obtaining this kind of information. Such continuing biographical updates by means of conversation, very much in the tradition of ethnographic research, simultaneously offer metacommunicative information while also providing naturally spoken data. At the same time, paper-based protocols created during free conversations continue to be a valid form of documentation.

As Figure 2 indicates, the first lines help to identify the informant, time, and

place of the recording and the presence of other persons. The second section speci-
fies the most important events and circumstances of the *personal present state* of the
learner, as it is embedded in its own "ecology." It documents occurring changes in
strategies and cognitive behavior towards the appropriation of the L2. The last
section focuses on the quality of the elicitation situation (formal and informal
aspects) and nonverbal behavior. Taken together, these metadata document the situational and nonverbal characteristics of the elicitation session and of the most
important changes in the ongoing learning process. Also of interest are technical and
recording-related metadata, e.g., information that reveals which tape (or part of a
tape) contains a particular recording. Such time-sensitive metadata help segment the
data and, in case of loss of computer files, save information via a master tape.

Annotation of data

Modern annotation tools for transcription, coding, and so on can greatly facilitate
direct access to the underlying media and thus profoundly influence the annotation
process and its end products. Starting with real (primary) data, the annotation process facilitates the coding of pronunciation and intonation; in that sense, modern
transcription can also be seen as a kind of annotation—an annotation of the data
stream (Bird and Liberman, 2001). We recommend computer programs that allow
direct integration of media and system-independent coding.[5] Another way to ensure
quality is through UNICODE-based character encoding and XML-based structures
(for details, see Skiba, 2006). An overview of the relevant computer programs and
their theoretical basis can be found in Dittmar (2004).

Exploration

All collected data are used for exploratory searches and comparisons at the data
analysis stage. Among the features available for comparative study are word lists or
collections of annotation categories that are assembled according to chronological
and inter-individual criteria. Computer use is almost indispensable at this stage,
though care has to be taken with regard to a program's ability to interpret various
data formats and with regard to compatibility between annotation files and analytical
tools. Therefore, import and export as well as convertibility of annotation files are
key features that need to be considered prior to data annotation.

Combining metadata and annotation searches expands the possibilities for data
exploration. For example, some programs (e.g., CLAN; see Myles, Chapter 4, this
volume) correlate length of stay with morphosyntactic variables, but only when
this kind of information is stored in the conventions chosen for file names. More
generally, adhering to data format standards at each stage of the study is of crucial importance, as is widely acknowledged by discussions found in the most
important coding manuals, including those produced in conjunction with CHILDES
(MacWhinney, 1995), ESF (Perdue, 1993a), and LIDES (Barnet *et al.*, 2000). An
alternative to existing norms are XML-based formats. These allow easier conversion
of data and are future-oriented (see Wittenburg, Skiba, and Trilsbeek, 2004).

Conclusion

In this chapter, we focused on the challenges posed by the need to study second language development longitudinally. We explored a number of research-methodological issues that follow from the challenges we grappled with in the original research design and completion of the longitudinal Berlin P-MoLL study. Reflecting developments since then, we also referred to technical issues that substantially contribute to researchers' ability to account for the long-term trajectories in L2 learning that learners follow. Although we may have emphasized demands of methodology and design, we would also like to note, based on our P-MoLL experiences, that it is imperative for SLA researchers interested in longitudinal research to document the verbal skills of learners across different communicative genres over time, and that it is imperative that they do so by closely linking language performance with insightful information about the personal and social conditions of individual learners.

While there can be no doubt that longitudinally oriented research will continue to be complex and, therefore, will continue to be relatively rare, developments in the field also justify the hope that, in the future, our understanding of the nature of language learning can build on the kind of sophisticated data gathering and data analysis that is possible with longitudinal study. In turn, such a research methodology is required if we are to capture what is "patterned and consistent" and what is "variant" in the development and use of language over time.

Notes

1. Supervised by Norbert Dittmar, the project was funded by the German Science Foundation (DFG).
2. The study also benefited from the conventions of data elicitation and transcription used in the ESF project.
3. See a model proposal on www.mpi.nl/corpus/a4guides/tapelabeling.pdf.
4. Valid and reliable sheets for coding have been developed for the former Heidelberg Project (Klein and Dittmar, 1979), the ESF Project (Perdue, 1984), and the so called RUSIL project (German-Israeli cooperation, see Dittmar, Spolsky, and Walters, 2002). Samples can be obtained from Norbert Dittmar at diso@zedat.fu-berlin.de.
5. Annotation systems such as CHAT, based on CLAN (cf. MacWhinney, 1995), are not flexible enough for all research purposes. A program like ELAN (Brugman and Russel, 2004) is designed for a free definition of coding features.

References

Ahrenholz, B. (1998). *Modalität und Diskurs: Instruktionen auf deutsch und italienisch. Eine Untersuchung zum Zweitspracherwerb und zur Textlinguistik.* Tübingen: Stauffenburg Verlag.

Barnet, R., Coda, E., Eppler, E., Forcadell, M., Gardner-Chloros, P., van Hout, R., Moyer, M., Torras, M., Turell, M., Sebba, M., Starren, M., and Wensing, S. (2000). The LIDES coding manual: A document for preparing and analyzing language interaction data. *International Journal of Bilingualism, 4,* special issue, 131–270.

Biber, D., and Conrad, S. (2001). Register variation: A corpus approach. In D. Schiffrin, D. Tannen, and H. Hamilton (Eds.), *The handbook of discourse analysis* (pp. 175–196). Malden, MA: Blackwell.

Bird, S., and Liberman, M. (2001). A formal framework for linguistic annotation. *Speech Communication 33,* 23–60.

Birdsong, D. (2005). Interpreting age effects in second language acquisition. In J. Kroll and A. DeGroot (Eds.), *Handbook of bilingualism: Psycholinguistic perspectives* (pp. 109–127). New York: Cambridge University Press.

Brown, R. (1973). *A first language: The early stages.* Boston, MA: Harvard University Press.

Brugman, H., and Russel, A. (2004). Annotating multi-media/multi-modal resources with ELAN. In X. Fátima Ferreira *et al.* (Eds.), *Proceedings of the 4th International Conference on Language Resources and Evaluation (LREC2004-Lisbon)* (pp. 2065–2068). Paris: ELRA— European Language Resources Association (CD-ROM).

Cholin, J. (2004). Video recording in the field. *Language Archives Newsletter, 4,* 5–8.

Dimroth, C. (2004). *Fokuspartikeln und Informationsgliederung im Deutschen.* Tübingen: Stauffenburg Verlag.

Dittmar, N. (2004). *Transkription. Ein Leitfaden mit Aufgaben für Studenten, Forscher und Laien.* 2nd ed. Qualitative Sozialforschung, Vol. 10. Wiesbaden: Verlag für Sozialwissenschaften.

Dittmar, N., and Reich, A. (Eds.) (1993). *Modality in language acquisition/Modalité et acquisition des langues.* New York: Mouton de Gruyter.

Dittmar, N., Reich, A., Schumacher, M., Skiba, R., and Terborg, H. (1990). Die Erlernung modaler Konzepte des Deutschen durch erwachsene polnische Migranten. Eine empirische Längsschnittstudie. *Info DaF, 17,* 125–172.

Dittmar, N., Spolsky, B., and Walters, J. (2002). *Convergence and divergence in second language acquisition and use: An examination of immigrant identities in Germany and Israel.* Final Scientific Report of the GIF—German–Israeli Foundation for Scientific Research and Development.

Dittmar, N., and Terborg, H. (1991). Modality and second language learning: a challenge for linguistic theory. In T. Huebner and C. A. Ferguson (Eds.), *Crosscurrents in second language acquisition and linguistic theories* (pp. 347–384). Philadelphia, PA: John Benjamins.

Doughty C., and Long, M. H. (Eds.) (2003). *The handbook of second language acquisition.* Malden, MA: Blackwell.

Eckert, P. (1996). Age as a sociolinguistic variable. In F. Coulmas (Ed.), *Handbook of sociolinguistics* (pp. 151–167). Oxford: Blackwell.

Gibbon, D., Moore, R., and Winski, R. (Eds.) (1997). *Handbook of standards and resources for spoken language systems.* New York: Mouton de Gruyter.

Halliday, M. A. K. (1978). *Language as a social semiotic: The social interpretation of language and meaning.* London: Edward Arnold.

Klein, W., and Dittmar, N. (1979). *Developing grammars: The acquisition of German syntax by foreign workers.* Berlin/Heidelberg: Springer.

Klein, W., and Perdue, C. (1997). The basic variety or: Couldn't natural languages be much simpler? *Second Language Research, 13,* 301–314.

Labov, W. (1970). The logic of nonstandard English. In J. E. Alatis (Ed.), *Linguistics and the teaching of standard English to speakers of other languages or dialects (Report of the Twentieth Annual Round Table Meeting on Linguistics and Language Studies* (pp. 1–43). Washington, DC: Georgetown University Press.

Leopold, W. F. (1939). *Speech development of a bilingual child: A linguist's record.* Evanston, IL: Northwestern University.

MacWhinney, B. (1995). *The CHILDES project: Tools for analyzing talk.* 2nd ed. Hillsdale, NJ: Lawrence Erlbaum.

Martin, J. R. (2001). Cohesion and texture. In D. Schiffrin, D. Tannen, and H. Hamilton (Eds.), *The handbook of discourse analysis* (pp. 35–53). Malden, MA: Blackwell.

Miller, M. (1979). *The logic of language development in early childhood.* Berlin: Springer.

Perdue, C. (1984). *Second language acquisition by adult immigrants. A field manual.* Rowley, MA: Newbury House.

Perdue, C. (1993). *Second language acquisition by adult immigrants,* 2 vols. New York: Cambridge University Press.

Reich, A. (2004). Lexikalische Schwierigkeiten in der exolingualen Kommunikation–Communication strategies revisited. Unpublished Ph.D. dissertation, Free University of Berlin (to be published by Stauffenburg Verlag).

Schumacher, M., and Skiba, R. (1992). Prädikative und modale Ausdrucksmittel in den Lernervarietäten einer polnischen Migrantin. Eine Longitudinalstudie. Part 2. *Linguistische Berichte, 142*, 451–475.

Schwitalla, J., and Wegstein, W. (Eds.) (2005). *Korpuslinguistik deutsch: synchron-diachron-kontrastiv. Würzburger Kolloquium 2003*. Tübingen: Niemeyer.

Skiba, R. (2006). Computer analysis. Corpus based language research. In U. Ammon, N. Dittmar, K. Mattheier, and P. Trudgill (Eds.), *Sociolinguistcs. An international handbook of the science of language and society*, Vol. 2 (pp. 1187–1196). New York: Mouton de Gruyter.

Skiba, R., and Dittmar, N. (1992). Pragmatic, semantic and syntactic constraints and grammaticalisation: A longitudinal perspective. *Studies in Second Language Acquisition, 14*, 323–349.

Slobin, D. (1985). *The crosslinguistic study of language acquisition*. Vols. 1–5. Hillsdale, NJ: Lawrence Erlbaum.

Tarone, E., Gass, S., and Cohen, A. (1994). *Research methodology in second-language acquisition*. Hillsdale, NJ: Lawrence Erlbaum.

Tomasello, M., and Stahl, D. (2004). Sampling children's spontaneous speech: How much is enough? *Journal of Child Language, 31*, 101–121.

Wittenburg, P., Skiba, R., and Trilsbeek, P. (2004). Technology and tools for language documentation. *Language Archives Newsletter, 5*, 3–4.

Wittenburg, P., Skiba, R., and Trilsbeek, P. (2005). The language archive at the MPI: Contents, tools, and technologies. *Language Archives Newsletter, 5*, 7–9.

6 Issues in the quantitative longitudinal measurement of second language progress in the study abroad context

Jonathan Rees and John Klapper

Abstract

Research into second language acquisition in a study abroad (SA) context is a complex and demanding activity, given the large number of variables involved, especially when a longitudinal perspective is adopted. Longitudinal studies in this field have consequently focused on the undergraduate experience of foreign language students in higher education, allowing for the systematic collation of data within a controlled SA framework. In this chapter, we detail the major longitudinal study types employed in this context. We compare and contrast the various existing SA designs and paradigms, showing similarities and differences in research methodology. We also examine the role played by national higher education culture, institutional culture, and second/foreign language learning culture in determining these differences in approach. We conclude with recommendations for improved quantitative longitudinal research of SA contexts in three areas: the basis of comparison used to evaluate the proficiency progress made by subjects, the legitimate employment of qualitative investigation methods within the longitudinal framework, and the level of statistical precision employed in the measurement and analysis of progress rates.

Introduction

Over the last 30 years, there has been a growing international research interest amongst applied linguists in the residence or study abroad (SA) component of higher education modern foreign language programs. Two principal reasons exist for this interest.

First, applied linguists have been eager to compare and contrast the process of second language acquisition in two theoretically very different learning contexts, i.e., the formal language-learning classroom at home and the naturalistic environment of the target language country. These contexts allow for detailed investigation of methodological issues in foreign language teaching (e.g., the value of a particular methodology in different contexts) and of aspects of foreign language development under different experimental conditions (e.g., the order and speed of acquisition of morphosyntactic features or the development of passive recognition and active use of lexical items). It should be noted, however, that in certain cases the two language learning contexts are not so distinct: some SA programs include a formal classroom-learning component in the target language country and some at home (AH) programs allow for quasi-immersion experiences within the institution or through contact with native speaker communities in the home country (this is particularly true in the USA).

Second, applied linguists in their role as academics and educationalists have been eager to substantiate their intuitive feeling that SA brings great educational benefits, not least in terms of strong linguistic gains for foreign language students. Before the 1970s no experimental work had been undertaken and the only evidence available for the importance of study abroad to the development of foreign language skills was the findings from Carroll's (1967) study showing "time spent abroad" as one of the two main predictors of proficiency levels in colleges/universities in the USA.

The substantiation of this claim is extremely important, in that greater mastery of a foreign language figures strongly in the thinking of many who study abroad, even for subject-specific reasons (e.g., a Chinese student studying civil engineering at a UK or US university). It is also important in the thinking of governments and higher education policy-makers who are constantly reviewing the cost–benefit ratio of allowing students to study abroad. In the UK alone, for example, approximately 12,000 students go abroad each year for study, work placement, or teaching (Coleman, 1996), a figure that excludes nonlanguage students opting to pursue part of their university studies in another country. Based on this figure we estimate that in terms of living expenses alone this costs a country like the United Kingdom something approaching $60 million per annum. Such considerations, allied to concerns about quality assurance, prompted the Higher Education Funding Council for England in recent times to invest a total of just over $1 million from its Fund for the Development of Teaching and Learning in three major pedagogical research projects looking at various aspects of preparation for and support of residence abroad.

In this chapter we seek to demonstrate that, despite the claims of some researchers, the case for strong foreign language proficiency gains during SA is far from proven and that there is a need for continuing quantitative longitudinal research. We first review the variety of SA studies undertaken, briefly discussing issues related to cross-sectional and subjective longitudinal research into holistic foreign language development. Having established the overall research context, we then move to our primary discussion, which focuses on the strengths and weaknesses of objective quantitative longitudinal studies, the most popular type of investigation into linguistic gains during SA. We present a classification for the main design genres for this category of study, analyzing pragmatic and theoretical reasons for differences in design. We then detail the ongoing challenges to quantitative longitudinal measurement in SA investigations, including the integration of qualitative methods into quantitative longitudinal research. We conclude by charting a path for the future development of quantitative longitudinal SA studies.

Overview of SA research

As a consequence of the recent growth in research interest in SA, there have been a significant number of studies in the 1990s and 2000s seeking to measure the effects of a period of SA. The majority of these have focused on the development of second/foreign language skills (e.g., Coleman, 1996), and are the subject of much of the discussion in this chapter. Other SA research foci have included: the development of "nonlinguistic" skills, such as the development of intercultural understanding (e.g.,

Williams, 2005), the change in perceptions brought about by a SA period (e.g., Stephenson, 1999), and the long-term career effects of a period of study or residence abroad (e.g., Alred and Byram, 2002).

Our analysis will address projects whose main focus has been the development of second/foreign language skills. These include studies involving measurement of the development of:

- syntactic, lexical, morphological, sociolinguistic, and sociopragmatic competence in the SA context
- global proficiency or the major modalities (we include in this category studies of fluency).

Studies in the first category have employed mainly production/corpus data (for a useful description, see Myles, 2005), while those in the second have drawn almost exclusively on task and test data. Figure 1 provides an overview of SA study types over the last 30 years.

As Figure 1 shows, a useful distinction can be drawn between studies examining the development of specific "atomized" aspects of the target language (often morphological, syntactical, or lexical) and those seeking to measure holistic language skills. This distinction does not always hold, in that some researchers seek to measure both discrete and holistic aspects of language development (e.g., Klapper and Rees,

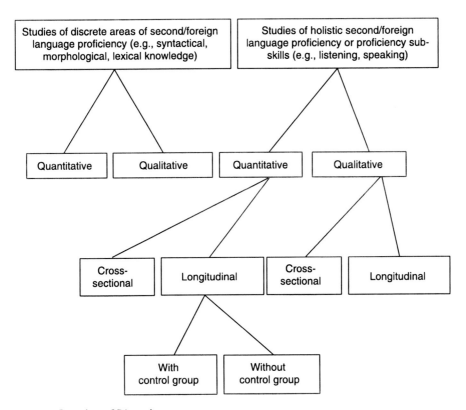

Figure 1 Overview of SA study types.

2003, 2004). In these cases, however, the researchers usually state their primary focus. Studies on both sides of the proficiency divide can be either quantitative or qualitative in nature. In general terms, the quantitative studies seek to measure the level of gains, whereas the qualitative studies attempt to investigate the factors producing or influencing those gains.

As indicated in the introduction, we wish to discuss in this chapter the more popular of these two research categories, the measurement of holistic language skills. By far the majority of studies here are quantitative and we shall focus on these in particular. Quantitative studies can be classified along two dimensions: "subjective" and "objective," "cross-sectional" and "longitudinal". Subjective types aim to measure foreign language development by drawing on assessment in the form of self-reporting data, interviews, surveys, and questionnaires (see Opper, Teichler, and Carlson, 1990; Teichler and Maiworm, 1997). They apply quantitative analysis techniques to attitudinal data. Objective types, on the other hand, employ test or task assessment instruments generating interval data which is then subjected to quantitative analysis. Cross-sectional studies rely on a single assessment, whereas longitudinal studies draw on a series of assessments. This second distinction between types is not always clear, with some studies taking a longitudinal perspective on certain elements of proficiency development and a cross-sectional view of others (e.g., Lafford, 1995).

Although our principal concern here will be with quantitative objective longitudinal studies of holistic foreign language development, in order to analyze the value of these it will be helpful first of all to briefly examine the strengths and weaknesses of some of the other popular types of investigation into holistic foreign language development, namely cross-sectional quantitative studies and subjective quantitative longitudinal studies.

Cross-sectional quantitative studies

Cross-sectional quantitative studies (depending on their scale) are easier to administer than longitudinal ones, in that they require limited assessment time and avoid the difficulties inherent in repeated measures testing—both in terms of statistical requirements and missing data problems (cf. our later discussion on observing statistical requirements). They provide a "quick" picture of student attainment without the long delays associated with full longitudinal studies. They fail, however, to compare group progress in any meaningful way, since they provide no baseline data (starting point) against which progress can be measured. Nor do they offer any information on differential individual progression, a growing area of interest in SA research.

Two main types have been attempted. The first involves the comparison of scores or grades for a group returning from a study abroad period (SA group) and a group that has remained at home (AH group). In this type of study, in contrast to longitudinal research, no pre-SA assessment is made and comparisons depend solely on post-SA results (e.g., Freed, Lazar, and So, 1998; Lafford, 1995). The data provided by this research appears to be valuable, generally reinforcing the view that those who undertake a SA period make greater gains in aspects of foreign language proficiency than those who stay at home. However, such data is not only limited in scope but it also has questionable validity owing to a failure on the part of the researchers to ensure that the gains made by the SA group are compared with gains from a group of similar prior ability and attainment level receiving equal foreign language exposure but in a different context.

Lafford's (1995) study is fairly typical in that she compares scores on a standardized oral proficiency test for three groups: one that went for a SA semester to Mexico ($n = 13$), one that spent a SA semester in Spain ($n = 16$), and one that completed all four semesters of Spanish study at the home university, Arizona State University ($n = 13$). The study illustrates the inherent problems of "comparative studies" of a cross-sectional nature, in which little consideration has been given to the comparability of groups, either in terms of their make-up or the experiences they are undergoing (the same criticism can be extended to some longitudinal studies, as well). In Lafford's study, the only similarity between groups is their internal heterogeneity. Commenting on the make-up of the groups in terms of their starting levels of Spanish proficiency, the author states that "as in most universities, the study abroad groups were heterogeneous . . ." She adds: "the control group evidenced this same type of heterogeneity . . ." (Lafford, 1995, p. 98). In effect, there is a complete lack of control in the study for ability levels, prior attainment, and aptitude. Nor is there any basis for comparison of time on task: the home control group spent four semesters on a non-intensive basis, whilst the two SA groups spent one semester on an intensive basis. Moreover, the Spain group received a repeated measures OPI (a longitudinal element), whilst the other two groups received only one administration.

The second type of cross-sectional study involves the comparison of scores/grades on a standardized proficiency test for different groups of students at various stages in their university career. Coleman (1996, 1998), in his European Language Proficiency Survey (ELPS), compares the proficiency level of students as measured by standardized C-tests in different year groups of undergraduate degrees. Using data from approximately 100 different institutions and covering a number of foreign languages (gathered at one point in time), Coleman seeks to map the average progression of subjects during residence abroad by comparing the scores of pre-SA cohorts with different post-SA cohorts.

Although this study is different from that of Lafford and is on a far larger scale, it is still subject to the same criticism—that is, that it fails "to compare like with like." Indeed, the study compares the performance on a C-test of cohorts of varied ability and attainment levels. Moreover, for each foreign language represented in the study (French, German, Spanish, Russian) there is a considerable difference in cohort size for each program year represented. For example, for French the total number of students in year 1 is 5115, while for year 3 (SA year) the number is only 772 (Coleman, 1996, p. 178). This large imbalance in sample sizes can only serve to compound any distortion produced by the cohort problem mentioned above.

Subjective quantitative longitudinal studies

There are few studies of significance in this category, although objective quantitative studies have sometimes incorporated a subjective quantitative element (e.g., Klapper and Rees, 2005). The major study is that of Teichler and colleagues, who investigated the SA experience of ERASMUS students[1] over the period 1988 to 1997 (see Teichler, 1991; and also Maiworm, Steube, and Teichler, 1991; Opper, Teichler, and Carlson, 1990; Teichler and Maiworm, 1997). Their study covers many aspects of SA, including the development of the main foreign language modalities and the acquisition of cultural, social, and current affairs knowledge of the host country. Progress in these areas is assessed through the administration of a questionnaire, requiring respondents to self-rate on Likert-scale-type items. With reference to foreign language development, subjects are asked to self-rate their pre- and post-SA proficiency for the four modalities both within the academic setting and outside the classroom. Importantly, the self-rating of the pre-SA proficiency is conducted "retrospectively," shortly after the study abroad period.

On the surface, such studies share many features in common with sociocultural qualitative investigations (to be discussed later), in that they draw on attitudinal introspective data. There are, however, major differences. Firstly, the main focus is the attempt to quantify the level of progress made by subjects, instead of investigating the causes of different behavior and performance. Secondly, the actual data gathering instruments (e.g., reports and questionnaires) are far more prescriptive than those generally employed in sociocultural studies, not allowing for wide-ranging introspective thought on the part of the respondent.

Overall such studies suffer from the same weaknesses as other types of SA inquiry. As Teichler and Maiworm (1997, p. 124) point out, their study allows for no comparison of performance with other groups: "Erasmus students' achievements should, in an ideal world, be compared with those of a control group." They also draw attention to the danger of self-rating data, conceding that "there is no doubt that self-ratings of achievement are subjective and on average somewhat too favourable" (p. 114). They even go so far as to suggest that students' self-ratings should be compared with objective achievement measures.

These weaknesses are to a certain extent counterbalanced by the large-scale research possibilities facilitated by such an approach. Indeed, the simplicity of the data gathering process (i.e., the administration of questionnaires) and the ease with which Likert scale data can be analyzed, allow for large sample research over a long period of time. Teichler and Maiworm (1997), for example, conducted a multi-year study involving more than 11,000 subjects over a period of six years.

Subjective quantitative studies have a role to play in SA research. They may, however, be better suited to the evaluation of the benefits of particular projects (as in the case of the investigation of the ERASMUS program) than to the detailed investigation of foreign language development during SA.

Longitudinal SA research genres: different approaches

As already noted, the most popular of SA study types is the quantitative longitudinal measurement of global foreign language proficiency or major language sub-skills (e.g., reading) development. These studies rely mainly on repeated measures assessment of subjects. Some are embedded in a broader research framework (e.g., Brecht, Davidson, and Ginsberg, 1993; Moehle, 1984; Rees and Klapper, 2005), in which study abroad is not the only focus. There are approximately 15 individual reported studies within this class of quantitative longitudinal studies. Some are European in origin (e.g., Dyson, 1988; Milton and Meara, 1995; Moehle and Raupach, 1983; Willis *et al.*, 1977), while others derive from the North American context (e.g., Brecht, Davidson, and Ginsberg, 1995; DeKeyser, 1991; Freed, 1995; Freed, Segalowitz, and

Dewey, 2004). It is to this type of study (quantitative, longitudinal) that we will turn our attention in the remaining sections of the chapter.

It is helpful to classify existing studies into three broad genres, each of which has merits as a pathway for the further development of longitudinal design. Table 1 shows the three main types of study employed to date to measure second language progress longitudinally during study abroad.

All three genres have similarities, relying upon the pre-/post-assessment of students pursuing a period of study abroad. In this sense, all three genres should be subject to a high degree of statistical scrutiny, associated with the use of tests/tasks in general and repeated measures assessment in particular (see later for detailed discussion).

The three genres, however, differ markedly in other ways. First, the term "longitudinal" applies in different ways to each. The short-stay genre focuses on a limited SA period (3–6 months) for a single sample, the longer-stay focuses on periods of 6–12 months for a single sample, and the "multi-year" on a limited SA period (3–6 months) for different samples over a number of years. This difference in study duration is further accentuated by the timing of the pre- and post-testing administrations, with some studies only completing the SA post-test several months after the SA period has been completed (e.g., Klapper and Rees, 2003).

Such differences in study duration reflect the range of practical experimental conditions faced by researchers at national and local levels. Researchers are limited by national educational cultural differences concerning the desired length of residence abroad. In general terms, institutions in the USA favor shorter "elective" SA stays (one semester or less), whilst UK institutions favor longer "mandatory" stays (6 or 12 months). Researchers also have to contend with local differences in institutional chronologies, with different institutions offering different windows of opportunity for repeated measures testing. They further encounter, at the local level, different

Table 1 Longitudinal study genres for foreign language learning progress within the SA context

Genre	Design	Examples
Short-stay	Pre/post with AH and SA control group(s)	Freed (1995)
		Freed, Segalowitz, and Dewey (2004)
	Groups matched by number of prior years of instruction, not by level	DeKeyser (1986, 1991)
Longer-stay	Single sample over whole program of study (time-series design)	Klapper and Rees (2003, 2004)
	Repeated measures testing including pre/post for SA	
	Subgroup analysis	
Multi-year study	Multiple samples over repeated SA experience	Brecht, Davidson, and Ginsberg (1993, 1995)
	Pre-/post-design	
	Multiple groups	
	Multiple years of study	

expressions of institutional research cultures, with some universities offering far more cross-faculty cooperation (essential for SA research) than others. All these differences influence the duration of SA research, either in terms of subjects' exposure to the foreign language or the intervals between testing.

Second, each genre offers a different basis for comparison of measured foreign language proficiency development. Early longitudinal studies, particularly in the short-stay genre (e.g., Dyson, 1988; Moehle, 1984; Willis *et al.*, 1977), have been criticized because they failed to put the reported proficiency gains in perspective, providing no basis of comparison that would allow for a meaningful evaluation of rate of progress. In other words, early longitudinal studies showed that students were making gains during the SA period, but failed to show whether these gains were significantly better or worse than the gains that students would have made if they had stayed at home and followed either a normal classroom-based program or an intensive immersion course. This search for a meaningful basis of comparison remains a key issue for all SA research into proficiency gains and we will return to it in more detail later (see also Rees and Klapper, 2005).

The short-stay genre seeks to address earlier shortcomings by providing a basis for comparison through the deployment of an AH group alongside the SA group. In certain cases, more than one control group is employed, with investigators including another AH group that follows a different type of foreign language course to that offered by the home institution (e.g., the summer intensive group in Freed, Segalowitz, and Dewey, 2004). The rationale for such a research design is that this kind of procedure allows for a direct evaluative comparison of the mean progress rates of the AH groups and the SA group. The longer-stay genre, on other hand, compares the progress data from the at-home phase of the degree program (typically the first two years of the course) with progress from the SA period for the same group. Meanwhile, the multi-year study provides another possibility for comparison, namely the year-on-year comparison of different samples experiencing the same type of SA experience.

All three types potentially offer useful data concerning progress rates. The short-stay and the longer-stay genres provide valuable comparative data on differential progress between the home and SA contexts, while the multi-year study affords insights into the stability of progress rates over SA—something not available in studies of the first two types.

Ongoing challenges to longitudinal measurement

Making meaningful comparisons

The differing approaches to the basis of comparison question owe more to the pragmatic empirical conditions faced by researchers from different countries than to major philosophical differences in position. For example, UK-based researchers, owing to foreign language education policies, do not have recourse to AH control groups, since, in the UK, study abroad is a quasi-obligatory feature of all foreign language undergraduate programs. US-based researchers, on the other hand, do have this opportunity, but with it comes the complex problem of properly matching groups for comparison purposes, a consideration which has received far too little attention in the studies published to date. North American researchers also have the opportunity to adopt a multi-year approach, since their higher education SA programs are more institutionally controlled than in the UK, where residence abroad is, in large part, an individual enterprise with far less structure, direction, and curricular consistency.

To date, however, research in each genre has suffered from design weaknesses. Although recent studies of the short-term type have sought to remedy the lack of control groups evident in earlier research, two weaknesses are still evident in such studies. First, the group sizes are extremely small in sampling terms. Second, there is a failure to recognize that there is a need for control groups(s) to be matched with the SA group with regard to academic (year of study, previous language level) and affective profile (motivational or aptitude level). Without this careful matching, the data obtained cannot answer the vital question: "What progress would the study abroad group have made if it had stayed at home?"

Freed, Segalowitz, and Dewey (2004), for example, report a short-term study in which the progress of a group studying French in a SA context is compared with that of an at-home (AH) group and a group following an intensive domestic immersion (IDI) program. The only matching criteria for the groups cited in the study are the following: all subjects were from the same institution and none of the subjects had ever studied abroad. The heterogeneity of the sample from which the three groups were taken is evident. The researchers state: "The academic majors of the participants spanned the social science, humanities, and science curriculum. Of the total group, only six students were enrolled in 1–5 French courses during the study period" (p. 280). Table 2 provides detail of the profile of each group in the study.

Longer-stay studies have also shown weaknesses in research design. Klapper and Rees (2003, 2004) sought to compare the progress of their cohort of undergraduate students during the AH formal classroom stage of their degree program with the progress made during the cohort's SA year. The testing intervals employed in the study, however, are subject to criticism. The cohort is assessed at three points: the start of the degree program (1 month), at the end of year 2 (20 months) and at the beginning of year 4 (36 months). The large gaps between testing mean that the comparison of progress between the initial stage of the degree and the SA period is problematic. More regular testing intervals would have provided a more accurate basis for comparison and would have allowed greater profiling of fluctuations in language development.

The multi-year genre also has its weaknesses. To provide the resources required to run such an ambitious research program, the involvement of a large organization is required. In the case of Brecht, Davidson, and Ginsberg (1993, 1995), the organization is the American Council of Teachers of Russian, which provides study abroad

Table 2 Sample groups employed in Freed, Segalowitz, and Dewey (2004)

Group	Sample size	Study period
Study abroad	$n = 8$	12 weeks
Control group (AH)	$n = 8$	12 weeks
Control group (IDI)	$n = 12$	7 weeks

courses in Russia. Unfortunately, this means that the yearly study sample is heterogeneous, being drawn from a large number of sending institutions with mixed intakes. The yearly SA sample includes undergraduates, postgraduates, and doctoral students. It includes language learners of vastly different competences and with different educational careers.

It appears that studies in all three genres have suffered from an inadequate basis for comparison. Researchers now need to make the issue of comparison central to their studies and to refine their procedures for obtaining meaningful data. Given the vast number of variables at play in this type of research, it is unlikely that any study will be able to secure genuine "control" groups, but researchers should at least attempt to make the best comparisons possible.

Recognizing different models of foreign language proficiency

Any researcher seeking to measure foreign language proficiency gains during SA through a longitudinal study faces one of the most intractable questions in applied linguistics, namely: "What constitutes foreign language proficiency?"

There exists a range of views about the nature of proficiency. At one end of this continuum, it is regarded as indivisible from a generic competence applicable to all skill areas (see Oller, 1979). At the other end, proficiency is thought to be composed of a number of interrelated competencies—for instance, sociocultural, pragmatic, discourse, textual, strategic, and fluency (see Bachman, 1990)—or of discrete areas of knowledge allied to the four basic language skills of listening, speaking, reading, and writing (see Carroll, 1968; Lado, 1961).

If the researcher tends to the view that proficiency is essentially indivisible and uses "integrative" tests for measurement purposes, then critics will claim that the study has failed to measure proficiency gains in other important aspects of proficiency (e.g., discourse competence or fluency in speaking). If, on the other hand, the researcher adopts an atomized view of proficiency, it will be pointed out that it is impractical to test all the different skill or competence areas involved in such models, since it would require a massive battery of tests and a large amount of intrusive testing time to adequately sample all the theoretical components of proficiency.

In practical terms, no longitudinal study will be able to measure all aspects of proficiency gains. It would be sensible, therefore, for researchers in the field to recognize that individual studies can only serve as providing one piece in the jigsaw.

With regard to design, the following guidelines would also seem appropriate:

- A minimum of two measures of proficiency should be used in any given study. This is helpful in two ways: firstly, where the researcher is investigating broad areas of competence, the use of multiple measures ensures a breadth of coverage; secondly, where the researcher is investigating a single aspect of proficiency whose construct is problematic (e.g., fluency), the use of two complementary measures ensures greater confidence in the study findings.
- Only assessment instruments which have been previously trialed and have some form of psychometric pedigree (in terms of reliability and validity data) should be employed; this does not exclude home-made tests, provided they are well constructed and have been fully piloted.

- Overgeneralized claims based on a small number of proficiency measures should be avoided.

Combining quantitative and qualitative SA research

Qualitative assessment, independent of quantitative measurement, has made a significant contribution to SA research in general and has often been employed for the investigation of factors deemed to be contributory to foreign language development, in particular. Pellegrino (1998), for example, examines the effect of student beliefs concerning foreign language learning on behavior during SA and the effect of beliefs about the value of the language learning classroom in the SA context. Other studies have focused on the nonlinguistic development of those studying abroad. Stephenson (1999), for example, investigates changes in participants' cultural perspectives and personal values.

Early qualitative studies of the SA experience, however, do not benefit from the same attention to research quality considerations highlighted in recent literature (Edge and Richards, 1998; Lazaraton, 2003; see also discussion in Pellegrino, 1998) and demonstrated in the latest studies (see Kinginger and Blattner, Chapter 12, and Spenader, Chapter 13, both this volume). These considerations include the following:

- clear warrant for line of inquiry
- correct framing of research questions
- representative sample selection
- appropriate length of fieldwork
- justification for selection of data for analysis
- legitimate interpretation of data.

Surprisingly, however, many of the early qualitative studies are readily and uncritically quoted in the SA literature. For example, Siegal's (1995) study is often cited as "evidence" of the gender effect on linguistic progress in the SA context. The study relies upon data from a very small sample of four Westerners learning Japanese in Japan. All four are women, allowing for no contrastive data with the male experience (a clear case of poor framing of essential research questions in qualitative research). The author then decides to limit her discussion to just two out of the four subjects (a clear case of inadequate sample size).

As already mentioned, qualitative methods of investigation have also been combined with longitudinal quantitative studies. They have served either as a means of investigating the findings of the quantitative study, or as a means of broadening the field of inquiry beyond the measurement of foreign language proficiency development. Many of these "integrated" investigations are subject to the same weaknesses evident in the early independent studies. For example, Polyani (1995), using introspective qualitative data (narrative journals), seeks to provide an explanation for the greater improvement by male students than their female counterparts on listening and speaking skills (as measured by Brecht, Davidson, and Ginsberg, 1993, 1995) during a Russian study abroad program for North American students. Polyani (1995) claims, on the basis of a highly selective analysis of the large body of data available, that "the women in the Living Abroad Programs are learning to negotiate treacherous waters based on gender-related behavior, which requires coping with severe gender problems" (p. 289). There is no presentation of a systematic analysis of the data available (journals from 160 students, and extensive journals from 80 students) in support of this claim. Instead, the author cites from a mere handful of journals. Such a selective use of introspective data suggests that idiographic data is being interpreted here in normative ways.

The same lack of a clear systematic analytical framework is evident in the qualitative investigation conducted by Brecht, Davidson, and Ginsberg (1995), incorporated into their quantitative longitudinal study measuring second language development. Using data derived from classroom observations, interviews, narrative journals, and oral journals, the researchers sought to investigate the value of formal classroom instruction during SA. Once again, however, there is little evidence of analytical rigor or a clear framework for the selection and interpretation of data. This is despite the clear recognition of these requirements in the text.

We believe that introspective qualitative methods of investigation can be usefully employed within longitudinal quantitative studies. Using such methods it is possible to generate data that, if systematically analyzed and properly interpreted, provide helpful insights into quantitative findings. Alternatively, qualitative data can be employed for individual case analysis, especially in the examination of exceptional individual performance, as highlighted by quantitative progress data. This is very much in keeping with a sociocultural perspective of second language acquisition, which conceives learners first and foremost as individuals (Lantolf, 2001, p. 155). An effective combination of the two research methodologies is highly desirable and beneficial, in that the quantitative longitudinal approach provides a framework for prolonged fieldwork, whilst the qualitative approach allows for a meaningful interpretation of otherwise sterile quantitative findings.

Observing statistical requirements

Rigor in statistical analysis is required, if we are to regard as credible the findings of quantitative longitudinal studies investigating foreign language improvement during study abroad. This rigor should be evident in a number of areas. We will focus on four in particular:

- the investigation of all testing/assessment instruments to ensure that they are reliable in measurement terms
- the careful calibration of tasks/tests to ensure an adequate scale of measurement and thus avoid the ceiling effect (i.e., lack of scope for the measurement of improved performance)
- the application of correct procedures when interpreting the statistical significance of gains in test scores obtained through repeated measures testing
- the treatment of missing values.

Studies to date in each longitudinal genre have shown weaknesses in at least one of the areas mentioned above. Many of the short-stay investigations have failed to address the issue of testing instrument reliability. Some researchers have constructed their own "home-made" testing instrument, with no reference to its consistency in measurement. Freed, Segalowitz, and Dewey (2004), for example, employ a six-component instrument for the measurement of fluency but fail to provide evidence of its reliability. DeKeyser (1991), in his investigation of the development of communication skills during SA, employs a grammar test and an oral test, without investigating the reliability of each measure. Other researchers have adopted testing instruments that have been subject to strong criticism for the same reason (e.g., the use of the ACTFL/ILR Oral Proficiency Interview).

Still others have attempted to employ language tasks rather than language tests and thus avoid the requirement for a clear statement of measurement reliability. The tasks, however, are tests in all but name and fit well with Cronbach's (1971) definition of a test as "a systematic procedure for observing a person's behaviour and describing it with the aid of a numerical scale or category system."

This point is of importance when discussing the issue of test calibration. Early studies (e.g., Freed, 1990; Hart, Lapkin, and Swain, 1994), particularly of the short-stay genre, have been criticized by subsequent researchers for their lack of control with regard to the potential for a ceiling effect produced by the test employed in their study. This criticism relates to investigators' failure to refine their tests using performance data from subjects with a similar level of attainment and ability in a trial administration of the test items. Such a criticism, however, applies just as much to the employment of untrialed tasks as it does to tests (see Cronbach's definition above). DeKeyser (1991), in his comparative study of a very small SA group of North American students in Spain (n = 7) and a very small AH group (n = 5) at a university in the USA, employs as part of his assessment battery a picture description task. There is no information given in the study on the reliability of the task or on whether it had been trialed and refined in any way.

The employment of trialed tests such as the ELPS C-test (used by Klapper and Rees, 2003, 2004) and the OPI (in its standardized form) provide the best way of ensuring avoidance of the ceiling effect in longitudinal studies. They provide clear "benchmark" data through their trialing and previous administrations with similar samples. If tasks are to be employed in the pursuit of the measurement of proficiency sub-skill improvement, then far more rigor is required with regard to the trialing and calibration of these tasks.

Repeated measures (RM) assessment is integral to longitudinal studies of foreign language improvement and usually takes the form of a pre-/post-test design, with subjects being assessed before and after the treatment or experiment period. In a lengthy study the number of assessments may reach as many as four or five. Numerous researchers in all three longitudinal genres have employed the score data collated from RM assessment to test for a statistically significant difference in mean scores between assessments. This has been done either through the use of independent t-tests (where one assessment has been repeated with the same sample) or through an ANOVA procedure (where there has been more than one repeated measurement for the same sample). Findings have been reported from these procedures to provide support (or counter-evidence) for the belief that SA brings statistically significant gains in test/task scores.

In most cases, however, greater caution should have been exercised in the reporting of these findings, since RM data violates an underlying assumption of ANOVA, namely that all observations are independent. Simple *post hoc* tests for ANOVA are not appropriate to RM data. Various methods have been devised to correct the overgenerous significance values produced for multiple *post hoc* tests on RM data. These methods, whose merits are themselves the subject of some debate, are now becoming more widely known in the field and are discussed in a separate paper (White and Rees, forthcoming).

Another statistical challenge inherent in longitudinal SA studies is that of the treatment of missing values. In most studies, data is not available for some subjects who fail to complete one or more of the experimental assessments (we may refer to this as sample attrition rate). This problem is particularly acute where the original sample size is small or where attrition affects one group more severely than another in a comparative study (e.g., a study with a control group). In some cases, the attrition rate may exceed 30 percent of the original sample, where students change courses or are simply unavailable for their assessments as a result of illness or other circumstances.

Different solutions have been proposed to this major problem for longitudinal research design and these too are discussed with reference to the SA context in White and Rees (forthcoming). Rather surprisingly, there has been little or no discussion of the issue in the SA literature, and researchers have been slow to provide a clear rationale for adopting a particular approach to the treatment of missing values.

Conclusion

Some leading researchers in the SA field (e.g., Coleman, 1998; Freed, 1998, 1999) have suggested that there is a sufficient body of research evidence to show that residence abroad brings strong second/foreign language holistic proficiency gains. They cite (mainly) the findings from the cohort of quantitative longitudinal studies as their principal justification for this claim. Freed (1999) states that "the results of studies based exclusively on test scores support our faith in the study abroad experience to improve specific language skills, particularly along the oral–aural continuum" (p. 20). They consequently suggest that SA research should now focus on other issues, such as the explanation of the processes determining second language improvement during SA, the description of SA-related factors contributing to success or failure, and the optimum length of residence abroad.

This chapter has shown that quantitative longitudinal studies fall into one of three categories, reflecting differing national contexts. Each study is limited both by local experimental conditions (subject availability, assessment time, institutional chronology) and theoretical parameters (operational definition of proficiency). This variety of approach is nonproblematic in itself, in that it elicits useful data concerning a number of differing contexts, thus providing a more comprehensive picture of the linguistic benefits of study abroad. It is, however, questionable whether the longitudinal studies that have been conducted hitherto are sufficiently robust in research design terms to support the view that the case for strong foreign language proficiency gains during SA is already proven. Our discussion has shown that longitudinal research in this area is embryonic and underdeveloped and that many, if not all, of the studies to date suffer from weaknesses, which would attract justifiable criticism in other areas of applied linguistics quantitative research.

We conclude that in the research design of future quantitative longitudinal studies into second language gains during SA, particular attention should be paid to *three* specific areas: the basis of comparison used to evaluate the proficiency progress made by subjects; the legitimate employment of qualitative investigation methods within the longitudinal framework; and the level of statistical precision employed in the measurement and analysis of progress rates. Addressing these three issues will provide us with a much more accurate and meaningful picture of foreign language gains during study abroad.

Note

1. The ERASMUS (European Community Action Scheme for the Mobility of University Students) program was founded by the European Community in 1987 and since then offers within-Europe study-abroad opportunities to European university students for periods that range between three and twelve months. For information, see http://ec.europa.eu/education/programmes/socrates/erasmus/what_en.html.

References

Alred, G., and Byram, M. (2002). Becoming an intercultural mediator: A longitudinal study of residence abroad. *Journal of Multilingual and Multicultural Development, 23*, 339–352.

Bachman, L. F. (1990). *Fundamental considerations in language testing.* New York: Oxford University Press.

Brecht, R., Davidson, D., and Ginsberg, R. (1993). *Predictors of foreign language gain during study abroad.* Washington, DC: National Foreign Language Center.

Brecht, R., Davidson, D., and Ginsberg, R. (1995). Predicting and measuring foreign language gains in study abroad settings. In B. Freed (Ed.), *Second language acquisition in a study abroad context* (pp. 37–66). Philadelphia, PA: John Benjamins.

Carroll, J. B. (1967). Foreign language proficiency levels attained by language majors near graduation from college. *Foreign Language Annals, 1*, 131–151.

Carroll, J. B. (1968). The psychology of language testing. In A. Davies (Ed.), *Language Testing Symposium: A psycholinguistic perspective* (pp. 46–69). New York: Oxford University Press.

Coleman, J. A. (1996). *Studying languages. A survey of British and European students. The proficiency, background, attitudes and motivations of students of foreign languages in the United Kingdom and Europe.* London: Centre for Information on Language Teaching and Research.

Coleman, J. A. (1998). Language learning and study abroad: The European perspective. *Frontiers. The Interdisciplinary Journal of Study Abroad, 4*, 167–203. Accessed online on January 4, 2006 at www.frontiersjournal.com/issues/vol4/index.htm.

Cronbach, L. J. (1971). Test validation. In R. L. Thorndike (Ed.), *Educational measurement* (2nd ed.). Washington, DC: American Council on Education.

DeKeyser, R. (1986). From learning to acquisition? Foreign language development in a US classroom and during a semester abroad. Unpublished doctoral dissertation, Stanford University.

DeKeyser, R. (1991). Foreign language development during a semester abroad. In B. Freed (Ed.), *Foreign language acquisition research and the classroom* (pp. 104–119). Lexington, MA: D. C. Heath.

Dyson, P. (1988). *The effect on linguistic competence of the year spent abroad by students studying French, German and Spanish at degree level. Report for the Central Bureau for Educational Visits and Exchanges.* New York: Oxford University Language Teaching Centre.

Edge, J., and Richards, K. (1998). May I see your warrant, please? Justifying outcomes in qualitative research. *Applied Linguistics, 19*, 334–356.

Freed, B. (1990). Language learning in a study abroad context: The effects of interactive and non-interactive out-of-class contact on grammatical achievement and oral proficiency. In J. Atlatis (Ed.), *Linguistics, language teaching and language acquisition: The interdependence of theory, practice and research* (pp. 459–477). Washington, DC: Georgetown University Press.

Freed, B. (1995). What makes us think that students who study abroad become fluent? Language learning and study abroad. In B. Freed (Ed.), *Second language acquisition in a study abroad context* (pp. 123–148). Philadelphia, PA: John Benjamins.

Freed, B. (1998). An overview of research in language learning in a study abroad setting. *Frontiers. The Interdisciplinary Journal of Study Abroad, 4*, 31–60.

Freed, B. (1999). Retrospective views from the president's commission on foreign language and international studies and prospects for the future: study abroad and language learning. Accessed online on January 4, 2006 at http://language.stanford.edu/about/conference papers/freedpaper.html.

Freed, B., Lazar, N., and So, S. (1998). Fluency in writing: Are there differences between students who have studied abroad and those who have not? Paper delivered at the Annual Meeting of the Modern Language Association, San Francisco, CA.

Freed, B., Segalowitz, N., and Dewey P. (2004). Context of learning and second language fluency in French. *Studies in Second Language Acquisition, 26*, 275–301.

Hart, D. S., Lapkin, S., and Swain, M. (1994). *Impact of a six month bilingual exchange program: Attitudes and achievement.* Report to the Department of the Secretary of State. Toronto: OISE Modern Language Centre.

Klapper, J., and Rees, J. (2003). Reviewing the case for explicit grammar instruction in the university foreign language learning context. *Language Teaching Research, 7*, 285–314.

Klapper, J., and Rees, J. (2004). Marks, get set, go: An evaluation of entry levels and progress rates on a university foreign language programme. *Assessment and Evaluation in Higher Education, 29*, 21–39.

Lado, R. (1961). *Language testing.* New York: McGraw-Hill.

Lafford, B. (1995). Getting into, through, and out of a situation: A comparison of communicative strategies used by students studying Spanish abroad and "at home." In B. Freed (Ed.), *Second language acquisition in a study abroad context* (pp. 97–121). Philadelphia, PA: John Benjamins.

Lantolf, J. (2001). (S)econd (L)anguage (A)ctivity theory: Understanding second language learners as people. In M. Breen (Ed.), *Learner contributions to language learning* (pp. 140–158). New York: Longman.

Lazaraton, A. (2003). Evaluative criteria for qualitative research in applied linguistics: Whose criteria and whose research? *Modern Language Journal, 87*, 1–12.

Maiworm, F., Steube, W., and Teichler, U. (1991). *Learning in Europe. The ERASMUS experience: A survey of the 1988–89 ERASMUS students.* London: Jessica Kingsley.

Milton, J., and Meara, P. (1995). How periods abroad affect vocabulary growth in a foreign language. *ITL: Review of Applied Linguistics, 107/108*, 17–34.

Moehle, D. (1984). A comparison of the second language speech production of different native speakers. In H. W. Dechert, D. Moehle, and M. Raupach (Eds.), *Second language productions* (pp. 26–49). Tübingen: Gunter Narr.

Moehle, D., and Raupach, M. (1983). *Planen in der Fremdsprache.* Frankfurt: Peter Lang.

Myles, F. (2005). Interlanguage corpora and second language acquisition research. *Second Language Research, 21*, 373–391.

Oller, J. W., Jr. (1979). *Language tests at school: A pragmatic approach.* New York: Longman.

Opper, S., Teichler, U., and Carlson, J. (Eds.). (1990). *Impact of study abroad programmes on students and graduates.* London: Jessica Kingsley.

Pellegrino, V. (1998). Student perspectives on language learning in a study abroad context. *Frontiers. The Interdisciplinary Journal of Study Abroad, 4*, 91–120.

Polyani, L. (1995). Language learning and living abroad. In B. Freed (Ed.), *Second language acquisition in a study abroad context* (pp. 271–291). Philadelphia, PA: John Benjamins.

Rees, J., and Klapper, J. (2005). Researching the benefits of residence abroad for students of modern foreign languages. In M. Tight (Ed.), *International perspectives on higher education research* (pp. 67–98). New York: Elsevier.

Siegal, M. (1995). Individual differences in study abroad: Women learning Japanese in Japan. In B. Freed (Ed.), *Second language acquisition in a study abroad context* (pp. 225–243). Philadelphia, PA: John Benjamins.

Stephenson, S. (1999). Study abroad as a transformational experience and its effect upon study abroad students and host nationals in Santiago, Chile. *Frontiers. The Interdisciplinary Journal of Study Abroad, 4*, 1–38. Accessed online on January 4, 2006 at www.frontiersjournal.com/issues/vol5/index.htm.

Teichler, U. (1991). *Experiences of ERASMUS students: Select findings of the 1988/89 survey.* Kassel: Gesamthochschule Kassel.

Teichler, U., and Maiworm, F. (1997). *The Erasmus experience: Major findings of the ERASMUS evaluation research.* Luxembourg: Office for Official Publications of the European Communities.

White, A., and Rees, J. (forthcoming). Theoretical considerations and practical issues in longitudinal measurement in applied linguistics.

Williams, T. R. (2005). Exploring the impact of study abroad on students' communication skills, adaptability and sensitivity. *Journal of Studies in Intercultural Education, 9*, 356–371.

Willis, F., Doble, G., Snakarayya, U., and Smithers, U. (1977). *Residence abroad and the student of modern languages: A preliminary study.* Bradford: University of Bradford Modern Languages Centre.

Part II

Empirical investigations

7 Advancedness and the development of relativization in L2 German

A curriculum-based longitudinal study

Heidi Byrnes and Castle Sinicrope

Abstract

In this chapter we report on a descriptive longitudinal investigation of the L2 German relative clauses produced by 23 students. As they progressed along the entire undergraduate sequence, each student engaged in a key writing event at the end of each of four curricular levels, resulting in a longitudinal corpus of 54,322 words that contained 454 relative clauses. Only weak support was found for an implicationally constrained development of relativization along the Noun Phrase Accessibility Hierarchy proposed by Keenan and Comrie (1977) and so often used in previous SLA research. Instead, the implicational scaling findings yielded gaps in the predicted sequences that affected between 20 percent and 30 percent of the sample at each level. It was also found that the full range of relative clause types had emerged already at the end of Level 2 for some students and that relativization progressed through Levels 3 and 4 towards an intensification of su relativization and a reduction of the range and complexity of more marked types, coupled with a steady increase in overall frequency of relativization. The findings challenge the commonly accepted assumption that emergence and use of the most marked relative clauses can be usefully considered a sign of advancedness. In addition, they extend Pavesi's (1986) claim about the superiority of instruction over naturalistic acquisition for ultimate attainment of L2 relative clauses.

Introduction

In their survey of recent research articles in second language acquisition (SLA) with a longitudinal methodology, Ortega and Iberri-Shea (2005) offer critical reflections on the methodology as well as suggestions for its improvement in light of the special opportunities and challenges it presents for the study of L2 development, particularly instructed L2 development. The trends the researchers identified, along with the unresolved issues, provide something like a contrastive analysis between prevailing, primarily cross-sectional SLA research traditions and outstanding characteristics of longitudinal studies, along with a framework for situating diverse kinds of longitudinal studies and their findings. In this chapter we make use of these perspectives and discuss the longitudinal development of advanced L2 German ability with an emphasis on relativization. We begin with a critical review of extant research on the development of relativization strategies by L2 learners, followed by a characterization of the curricular context that defines this study on language development in the German Department at Georgetown University. We then offer the findings of the study in the following progression. First, we present findings from an analysis of the longitudinal development of relativization in 76 texts written by 23 students in light of Keenan and Comrie's (1977) Noun Phrase Accessibility Hierarchy (NPAH). The findings are initially presented in categories that have been accepted practice in cross-sectional relativization studies but corroborate as well other researchers' suggestions for change. Subsequently, we take a fine-grained longitudinal perspective on the data by providing a detailed analysis of the use of relativization by two of the student writers. We conclude by exploring possible implications of the study's longitudinalness for an understanding of the nature of L2 development and, more generally, for future SLA research. This includes the possibility of reconceptualizing the nature of relativization and its development and use in learner language as reflecting the intersection of formal syntactic and textual meaning-oriented aspects.

Relativization and instructed L2 development

The theoretical paradigms that have guided past studies of second language (L2) relativization center around the notion of predictiveness in terms of presumed processing difficulty and a hierarchy of accessibility. These frameworks are either psycholinguistically driven, that is, they are concerned with working memory and processing constraints, or they are derived from a crosslinguistic, universally oriented paradigm that builds on learners' posited internal representation of language. While early studies examined the potential role of L1 transfer and interference, later studies focused on testing the predictive value of a hypothesized universal order of difficulty.

Three hypotheses have gained particular prominence for addressing presumed factors of difficulty in the acquisition of relativization: Sheldon's (1974) Parallel Function Hypothesis, Kuno's (1974) Perceptual Difficulty Hypothesis, and Keenan and Comrie's (1977) Noun Phrase Accessibility Hierarchy (NPAH). This last one was investigated in the present study because it is the framework most frequently employed in L2 studies (e.g., Doughty, 1991; Gass, 1979). Not only does the NPAH make particularly strong theoretical claims, it also has noteworthy affinities to other important theories in SLA, among them Pienemann's (1998) processability theory. Finally, it has also led to pedagogical recommendations for how relativization might most appropriately be taught (Gass, 1982).

The NPAH posits a universal ordering of relative clause types based on typological markedness, where the presence of some structures (more marked) implies the presence of others (less marked) but not vice versa. Specifically, relative clauses containing subject (su) pronouns are presented as the most accessible universally, followed by direct object (DO), indirect object (IO), objects of preposition (OPREP), possessive (GEN), and object of a comparison (OCOMP), respectively. Furthermore, if a language can relativize on a given position on the hierarchy, e.g., object of a preposition, it can also relativize on all the higher positions (indirect object, direct object, and subject) but not necessarily the lower positions (genitive, object of comparison). The hierarchy is illustrated in Table 1 for both English and German.

When applied to L2 acquisition, the NPAH framework proposes an implicational hierarchy in acquisition from least to most marked structures; for the development of relative clauses in L2 learners, this translates into a predicted learning progression

Table 1 The NPAH illustrated in English and German

Clause type	English example	German example
SU	The ring *that is missing* was mother's	Der Ring, *der fehlt*, gehörte meiner Mutter
DO	The ring *that I'm describing* is a small gold one	Der Ring, *den ich beschreibe*, ist ein kleiner goldener
IO	The person *that I loaned the ring to* may have lost it	Die Person, *der ich den Ring geliehen habe*, hat ihn vielleicht verloren
OPREP	The small case *in which she kept the ring* was black	Das kleine Kästchen, *in dem sie den Ring aufbewahrte*, war schwarz
GEN	Another case *whose contents are unknown* is also missing	Ein weiteres Kästchen, *dessen Inhalt unbekannt ist*, fehlt auch
OCOMP	There is nothing *that this ring is less important than* right now	[Not possible]

Note: The English examples are taken from Yule (1998, p. 261); German examples are close translations.

from most to least accessible types: SU > DO > IO > OPREP > GEN > OCOMP. SLA researchers who have adopted this framework argue that the acquisition of a particular position on the hierarchy implies acquisition of all implicated positions. For example, within a strict interpretation of the NPAH, if students can successfully form OPREP relative clauses, they are also capable of producing IO, DO, and SU relative clauses. No direct claims are made about the length of time necessary for learners to develop the ability to form relativizations at the lower end of the hierarchy, but an implied theoretical assumption is that these more marked forms are late-emerging and therefore may be interpreted as a sign of advancedness.

Relativization in German: a contrastive summary

As Table 1 shows, relativization strategies in English and German are quite similar in many respects. German relativizers fulfill the same functions as their English counterparts. They can function as subjects (SU), direct objects (DO), indirect objects (IO), objects of prepositions (OPREP), and possessives (GEN), although, in contrast with English, they cannot function as objects of comparison (OCOMP). Similarities extend as well to the position of relative clauses within a sentence. They always occur to the right of the antecedent. Many relative clauses indeed occur in sentence-final position; however, depending on context, content, and type of relative clause, they may also be center-embedded. Also like English, German relativization can refer both to an antecedent NP and to an entire proposition. Finally, neither language allows resumptive pronouns (for example, *The ring that I'm describing *it* is a small gold one).

These similarities notwithstanding, several features of the German language add considerable complexity to the task that L2 learners face when they attempt relativization in German. In the realm of differences and challenges, one important feature is the fact that German relative pronouns agree with the antecedents in number and gender while observing obligatory case markings according to the relativizer's

function in the dependent clause. This is shown in illustration (1), where the antecedent *keinen Teil* ("no part") is a masculine singular noun and the relative pronoun
referring to it, *den*, is marked for masculine and singular as well as for accusative
because it is the direct object of the verb phrase *unerforscht verließ* ("left unexplored")
in the subordinated clause:[1]

> (1)   Es gab keinen Teil des Umgebungswaldes, *den Herr Sommer unerforscht verließ.*
>   There was no part of the surrounding forest **that Mr. Sommer left unexplored**.

Because, besides few generalizations, German noun gender assignments appear to
be highly idiosyncratic, errors in relativization often hinge just as much on that factor
than on functional relationships. Furthermore, although nearly all German nouns
have unique gender assignments, blended gender/number/case-marking forms show
a high level of syncretism, that can translate into learning difficulties, particularly
with definite and indefinite articles for masculine and neuter nouns.

More important for relativization per se are the following observations. Because
certain German verbs have fixed case requirements (e.g., "dative verbs" such as *helfen,
folgen, danken* or "to help," "to follow," "to thank"), these govern the function of the
relativizer, which then shows appropriate case markings. In illustration (1), for
instance, *den* is in the accusative case because the verb phrase in the relative clause
("to leave unexplored") requires such a case. In addition, as all dependent clauses,
German relative clauses are characterized by a "verb-last" position, which places the
finite verb at the end of the clause. This contrasts with the verb-second rule of
German main or independent clauses. German, unlike English, does not differentiate between animate and inanimate antecedents (that is, there is no analogous alter-
nation as in the English *who* and *which*). Finally, unlike English, German cannot drop
the relativizer (such deletions are a frequent focus of English-focused relativization
studies).

It is important to note that the present study focuses on the development of
complexity (operationalized via markedness in the NPAH framework) in relativization, rather than accuracy. Thus, although the challenges described in this section
tend to be long-lasting even for advanced learners when the attainment of accurate
performance levels is a pedagogical goal, none of these so-called errors were counted
as counter-evidence for students' use of relativizing structures in the present study.
More details will be given on this issue in the section on data coding.

Approaches to the study of L2 relativization and their findings

Most studies of L2 relative clauses have pursued the idea that relativization is a
"difficult" and late-acquired phenomenon. Both descriptive and instructional studies
have focused on the question of whether the full relativization options of an L2 can
be acquired by (or taught to) L2 learners. Of particular interest for instructional
arguments is Pavesi's (1986) comparison of instructed and naturalistic settings inasmuch as it demonstrated that the formal context of instructed learning may promote
the acquisition of more marked relative clause types, though it does not affect the
order of emerging relative clause types.

Also, most research has focused on relative clause development of instructed

English as a second language (ESL) learners, many of whom combined the naturalistic acquisition experience of living in an English-speaking country with instruction in ESL courses. Considerably fewer in number, non-English language studies published in the 1980s pertain to a diversity of languages, among them Chinese, French, German, Portuguese, and Swedish (Hawkins, 1989; Hyltenstam, 1984, 1987; Tarallo and Myhill, 1983). More recently, Ortega (2000) offered an investigation of the development of relativization by instructed Spanish as a foreign language learner, drawing on written longitudinal data collected over the span of one semester.

With some exceptions (Gass, 1980; Ortega, 2000; Schachter, 1974), relativization studies rely mostly on experimental data elicitation and use a combination of grammaticality judgments, sentence combinations, and fill-in-the-blank questions. Building on the seminal research by Gass (1979) and Schachter (1974) with ESL learners, studies follow a nearly canonical set of research questions based on difficulties experienced by these learners, such as resumptive pronouns, relativizer deletion, preposition stranding, and preposition deletion. The most frequently targeted level of language ability is the intermediate to advanced level, which in the ESL studies is typically determined by enrollment in particular classes or by pre-test results. For the instructional intervention studies, this allows the researchers to instruct subjects on a particular type of relative clause (often the more marked OPREP) and then observe their performance on instructed and non-instructed relative clause types. Although these studies include pre- and post-tests, they are designed as short-term, delimited interventions that are presumed to lead to immediately measurable changes, with a pre-test-to-post-test span ranging from two days (Eckman, Bell, and Nelson, 1988) to two and a half weeks (Doughty, 1991).

Overall, the studies have lent mixed support to the NPAH as a predictor of difficulty in L2 relative clause acquisition. Suggested explanations for these mixed results range from the need to take a multi- rather than a single-factor approach (e.g., Gass, 1980), to the possibility that "lexical salience, surface structure (dis)similarity, and interface with L2 knowledge of other subsystems" might need to be considered in order to account for the observed phenomena (Ortega, 2000, p. 306).

Despite persistent interest in instructed learners and issues of optimal instruction for relativization (e.g., Doughty, 1991; Eckman, Bell, and Nelson, 1988), none of the accumulated research studies appear to refer in any meaningful fashion to the instructional context. Instead, they merely evaluate learner's relativization abilities at the time of the research study. In the present study, we purposefully integrate the investigation of relative clause development into the larger curricular and pedagogical context of the students' L2 development.

The curricular context of the study

As Ortega and Iberri-Shea (2005) rightly point out, the issue of "time" is by no means a straightforward matter in the longitudinal investigation of instructed L2 development. In the context of this study of adult instructed learners, time is initially understood as institutional, rather than biological, and the time length of investigation is thus framed within the standard four-year bachelor degree program of US institutions of higher education. However, reflecting its emphasis on instructed L2 development and, by implication, the outcomes of teaching and learning, the study additionally and uniquely states time in terms of a highly elaborated curricular progression that has imagined and specified learning goals for an entire four-year undergraduate sequence rather than, as is customary, for the first few semesters of language instruction.

That curriculum, first put in place over a three-year period between 1997 and 2000 at Georgetown University German department and entitled "Developing multiple literacies," had two interrelated goals and implementational characteristics that are relevant to the study (see *Developing Multiple Literacies*, n.d.). On the content side, it sought to create a programmatic framework that would enable learners, even those who might only be starting their study of German, to attain "advanced" forms of L2 literacy. On the programmatic side, it endeavored to overcome the customary split between largely content-indifferent language courses ("the language sequence/ language requirement") and language-indifferent content courses ("the upper level courses"). The result is a genre-based curriculum that integrates the acquisition of substantive content with the acquisition of German throughout the entire four-year college program.[2]

The choice of genre was motivated both theoretically and pedagogically (see Byrnes and Sprang, 2004). In order to foreground L2 literacy and the semiotic relationship between culture and language, the curriculum project turned to Systemic Functional Linguistics (SFL) in the Hallidayan vein because of its meaning-orientation that focuses on oral and written texts produced in a particular context of situation within a larger context of culture as the locus of human meaning-making. In particular, its genre approach (see Martin, 2000, from among a prolific list of publications on this orientation) offered a way of constructing a curricular progression that, in line with Stenhouse's (1975) understanding of curriculum, would lay out essential educational principles in a way that makes them available for public scrutiny, first department-internal public scrutiny and, subsequently, profession-wide scrutiny.

In the process of appropriating SFL for its literacy-oriented goals, the department extended previous work, both that arising from the Australian SFL context and that informed by SLA research and pedagogy. It did so by refashioning the ubiquitous notion of "task" from primarily oral communicative activity intended to create an "authentic, real world" in the language classroom (most commonly at the intermediate level) into genre-based tasks. This way of conceptualizing task would bring the vastly larger and more challenging imagined and construed worlds of oral and written texts into classrooms in order to facilitate language development to upper levels of ability. In a genre-based conceptualization textual worlds stand in no opposition to the "real" world of communicative interactions; instead, they are at the heart of human ways of creating any language-based meaning and of going about knowing in the world through language (for an excellent discussion of the critical role of construal for human meaning-making, see Halliday, 1996). Finally, under this reconceptualization of tasks, the curriculum includes both oral and written genres right from the start. It further arranges them in a developmentally motivated fashion that moves from the primary discourses of familial and quotidian life to the secondary discourses of public life, including institutions and professions, and it explicitly uses their different forms of meaning-making as the basis of pedagogical practice. By adopting such a radically transformed notion of task the department was able to envision an articulated curriculum that could be projected to lead to advanced levels of ability. (From the SFL side of these issues, see Halliday, 1993, 2002, and Schleppegrell, 2004; for some of the consequences of this move within the *Developing Multiple Literacies* curriculum, see Byrnes 2001, 2002, 2005; Byrnes and Sprang, 2004; Byrnes *et al.*, 2006; and Crane 2006.)

Structurally, the curriculum proceeds through five levels, with Levels 1–3 constituting a required sequence of courses, and Levels 4 and 5 offering an increasingly broader array of content and course options. Table 2 provides an overview; full additional details of level-specific instructional and learning goals can be found in the website (*Developing Multiple Literacies*, n.d.). The longitudinal analyses presented in this chapter span Levels 1 through 4.

Internally, the curriculum's focus on text and genre has been expressed in various ways that continue to evolve. Two are of particular interest in this study. The first is the notion of a developmental trajectory from the interactive and overt dialogism of conversations to the covert dialogism of written language to learners' metalinguistic awareness of a dialogism between their own language use and the entire language system (see Wertsch, 2006 who builds on Bakhtin's notion of individual utterances being in dialogue with the language system, itself understood as a

Table 2 Curricular sequence of courses in the "Developing multiple literacies" curriculum at Georgetown German Department

---

A. Sequenced Courses

Level 1—Contemporary Germany ("Basic")
Introductory German I and II: (2-semester sequence: 3 credits each) OR
Intensive Basic German: (1-semester course: 6 credits)
The themes for this level are coordinated with the textbook *Kontakte* (Terrell *et al.*, 2005). A significant amount of authentic outside material is incorporated in order to provide a discourse and literacy focus even at this level. This is the only level that uses a textbook.

Level 2—Experiencing the German-speaking World ("Intermediate")
Intermediate German I and II: (2-semester sequence: 3 credits each) OR
Intensive Intermediate German: (1-semester course: 6 credits)

Level 3—German Stories and Histories ("High Intermediate–Advanced")
Advanced German I and II: (2-semester sequence: 3 credits each) OR
Intensive Advanced German: (1-semester course: 6 credits)
Overview of developments in Germany from 1945 to present.

B. Non-sequenced Courses ("Advanced")

Level 4
One 4-credit course ("Text in Context") plus five additional 3-credit courses with similar language acquisition goals (though different emphases).

Level 5
Along with exploring topics in 18th- through 20th-century German studies and selected topics in German linguistics, these courses aim to develop high levels of sensitivity, reflectivity, and interpretive abilities directed toward other and self in a cultural context, and the ability to function in the German language in various forms of elaborated secondary discourse with a high level of accuracy, fluency, and complexity of language use in a variety of contexts.

Note: As indicated, Levels 1–3 are offered either as regular non-intensive or as intensive sequences. A three-credit non-intensive course has approximately 42, a six-credit intensive course about 85 contact hours per semester.

generalized collective dialogue). The second emphasizes the link between genre and narrativity in order to highlight "central characteristics of cohesive and coherent texts and for making learners aware of the shift in semiotic practices that accompanies the shift from telling private stories to presenting public (hi)stories" (quoted from a curricular document on writing development; see *Developing Multiple Literacies*, n.d.).

Writing in the curriculum and prototypical performance writing tasks

Within this programmatic context and educational vision, writing development became a privileged site for pedagogical action and for examining learning outcomes. Therefore, in the initial three years of development of the curriculum both the envisioned curricular progression and the supporting pedagogical action were most extensively laid out in the context of writing development. Within the larger framework of genre-based tasks toward advanced literacy, the writing done in this curricular context is characterized by a tripartite division into: "task," understood in terms of the textual genre students are to produce; "content," in terms of the major content areas they should address; and "language features," broken down into discourse-level, sentence-level, and lexicogrammatical features (see Byrnes, 2002). Because these three aspects are completely integrated, teachers and learners alike have found useful the metaphors of "breadth" of obligatory and optional genre moves for better conceptualizing task, of "depth" of information for addressing content issues, and of "quality" for judging the nature of the formal features of language. In fact, these notions might be said to express, at a general level, the meta-awareness about genre-based writing that all actors in the program have developed.

The special position of writing in our curricular thinking led to the establishment of end-of-semester prototypical writing tasks for each level (henceforth called "prototypical performance writing tasks" or PPTs) through which the attainment of curricular goals could be evaluated. Typically, writing tasks are assigned at the end of a thematic unit after in-depth engagement with various texts at all levels of the language system, from text organization to diverse lexicogrammatical features, to semantic fields for enhancing the acquisition of thematically organized vocabulary. Because the task is done at home without time pressure, the conditions for writing would seem to offer an ideal situation for yielding language "performance" that approximates learners' "competence," to use Ellis's (2005) characterization of the relationship between planning, task, and quality of language. Thus, faculty created a PPT for each level in order to ascertain whether students do indeed attain the stated writing goals—for each curricular level and for the curriculum as a whole. An overview of the PPTs for Levels 1–4 is provided in the Appendix.

Each PPT was intended to be a key writing event at the end of curricular Levels 1–3 and the Level 4 course "Text in Context." It is designed to afford students the opportunity to use the content and language developmental features that typify the curricular level beyond the diversity of individual genres and themes that otherwise characterize a course, and also to set up a likelihood, though by no means certainty, that they would in fact do so. Viewing the four PPTs as a series, faculty can monitor articulation of learning goals across the curricular levels. By extension, by analyzing students' actual performances across levels, they can assess the extent to which learners reach level-specific and, indirectly, long-term programmatic goals, even under the conditions of genre-induced and, importantly, intended differences in the nature of the writing tasks. Such evidence can inform on the need for adjustments in learning goals, the curriculum, materials, and pedagogy, thereby setting in motion the washback effect of assessment. In short, the PPTs are conceived of as central markers for tracing and monitoring language development in the program and for individual learners traversing the curriculum.

The PPT corpus

It soon became clear that a focus on writing would enable the department to gather evidence of student learning as part of its regular educational activities. Consequently, the department (including faculty, teaching assistants, and even undergraduate student researchers) embarked on a collectively owned, large-scale study of the curriculum, with a natural focus on writing.[3]

Rather than random or targeted sampling, exhaustive sampling of the entire population was the approach adopted. Thus, the entire population of students enrolled in the German department at Georgetown University was invited to participate in various components of the overall study. The most important research effort and the one from which this chapter draws its data, was the systematic collection of the aforementioned PPTs, between spring 2001 and spring 2004, from all students at the end of instructional Levels 1, 2, 3, and "*Text in Context*" who consented to participate in the study.[1] PPTs from a total of 329 students were obtained over the three years of data collection, giving a corpus with a total word count of 212,796 words. Table 3 displays the number of prototypical performance writing task samples collected by level and task type in the full curricular study.

To date the considerable data referenced in Table 3 have been analyzed primarily in order to characterize the development of syntactic complexity within the curriculum (see Byrnes *et al.*, 2005; and particularly Maxim, 2005, and Norris, 2005).

More important for this chapter, by tracing students who had completed a minimum of three consecutive curricular levels, a subcohort of 23 students, the so-called longitudinals, was identified; they had completed either Levels 1–3 (n = 9), Levels 2–4 (n = 7), or Levels 1–4 (n = 7). These 23 students produced 76 PPTs available for the longitudinal study of the development of relativization, the focus of this chapter.[5]

Table 3 Prototypical Performance Writing Task (PPT) samples collected in the overall curricular study

n	PPT
Level 1	98
Level 2	100
Level 3	77
Level 4	54
Total samples	**329**
Total words	**212,796**

Its total word count is 54,322 words. Tables 4 and 5 summarize the data for the present longitudinal study.

Research questions

The following research questions are addressed in the present study:

1. Does the frequency of relative clause use change for the groups as they progress through the four curricular levels?
2. Does the complexity of relative clauses, as measured by length (mean number of words) and position (e.g., center embedding), change?
3. Does a claimed implicational hierarchy provide explanatory value for the data?
4. Within the framework of the NPAH, what types of relativization are produced by individual learners as they traverse consecutive curricular levels?

Analysis

Data coding

All longitudinal writing samples produced by the 23 students ($k = 76$) were transcribed and first segmented into T-units. Subsequently, each identified clause was classified as independent or dependent and assigned to a clause type (e.g., adverbial, nominal, relative, infinitival, elided, and so on). The analyses then focused on relative clauses exclusively.

Only those relative clauses included in the categories of the NPAH are reported on in this chapter. Hence, relative clauses that had an entire proposition as their antecedent were not coded. Also, relative clauses whose relativizer was elided between multiple verbs were analyzed exactly once, although they do constitute a more complex occurrence of relativization. Because the present study pursues only occurrence-related descriptive goals at this point, "recognizability" as intended

Table 4 Participant sample size by level for the longitudinal PPT data (total $n = 23$)

Type of longitudinal	Level 1	Level 2	Level 3	Level 4
Levels 1–3	9	9	9	
Levels 2–4		7	7	7
Levels 1–4	7	7	7	7
Total *n* by level	**16**	**23**	**23**	**14**

Table 5 Corpus size for the longitudinal PPT data by level

Type of longitudinal	Level 1	Level 2	Level 3	Level 4	Total
Levels 1–3	3590	5328	6016		14,934
Levels 2–4		4306	5308	8133	17,747
Levels 1–4	2931	4448	4960	9302	21,641
Total word count	**6521**	**14,082**	**16,284**	**17,435**	**54,322**

relativizations rather than accuracy-related issues became the primary coding criterion, notwithstanding non-targetlike suppliance in areas such as inflected elements involving the relativizer or even in choice of relativizer. An illustration of unsuccessful inflection is given in (2), where the writer supplied the relative pronoun in the nominative case (*der*) where the accusative case is required by the verb (*sah*, past tense of *sehen*, "to see"). Nevertheless, the relative clause was counted as DO:

(2) Du bist der Junge, *der ich in dem Sturm sah*
     You are the boy **who (whom)** *I saw in the storm.*

An example of non-targetlike choice of relativizer is provided in (3). Here the student supplied a plural dative definite article (*den*) rather than a plural dative relativizer (*denen*), but the clause was nevertheless counted as an IO relative clause:

(3) Ein funktionierender Rechtsstaat, offene Gesellschaft und die Achtung der Menschenrechte sind die Anforderungen, **den** *die Beitrittskandidaten* **entsprechen** *müssen.*
     A functioning constitutional state, an open society, and attention to human rights are the requirements **that** *the candidate countries for accession to the European Union must* **meet.**

In addition to identifying all relative clauses and tallying them by NPAH type, clause length in words was calculated by counting the number of orthographic words in each relative clause, including the relative pronoun and other embedded clauses within it, if any. Finally, the number of center-embedded relative clauses was calculated relative to the overall number of relative clauses for each level. These two additional figures provide a foundation for evaluating claims about the relationship between processing constraints and advancedness.

Intercoder reliability

Intercoder reliability (ICR) figures were calculated for all phases of data analysis as simple percent agreement (that is, total coding decisions minus discrepancies divided by the total coding decisions). Table 6 displays mean values for the reliability coefficients for the reliability of codings. They were calculated on the full curricular study sample (see Table 3). Reliability figures for the identification and coding of all dependent clauses, including the relative clauses used in this study, ranged from a lowest of .88 and a highest of .92 by level, with an average intercoder reliability of .90 (a total of 9770 dependent clauses were coded in these analyses, resulting in 996 discrepancies). For this initial clause coding phase, 260 out of 339 files (or 77 percent)

Table 6 Intercoder reliability summary

Coding phenomenon	Mean intercoder reliability	Double-coded
Dependent clauses	0.90	77%
Relative clause types	0.96	100%
Length of relative clause	0.96	100%

were double coded. During the coding phase of the longitudinal data by NPAH type, all 76 files (or 100 percent) were double coded. The resulting reliability ranged from a lowest of .91 and a highest of .99 by level, with an average intercoder reliability of .96 (that is, a total of 454 relative clauses were classified, resulting in 20 discrepancies). Lastly, an analysis of clause word length yielded an intercoder reliability between .93 and .97 by level, averaging .96, with 100 percent of the files double coded (454 relative clauses, 21 discrepancies). Any discrepancies in the coding of longitudinal data were subsequently solved by discussion and agreement.

Results

Research Question 1: Frequency of relative clause use by groups across curricular levels

As Figure 1 shows, 23 relative clauses were found in the Level 1 data, which comprised the performance of 16 students in total (see Table 4). This is a very small incidence of overall relativization. It amounts to only 7 percent of all the subordinate clauses produced at this level and translates into 2.5 relatives per learner (this average takes into account that only nine learners at Level 1 actually produced relative clauses; see Figure 5). DO relative clause types have the highest frequency of suppliance: 12 tokens contributed by six different students at Level 1. This is closely followed by SU types, which amounted to a total of 9 tokens contributed by seven different students.

Only two OPREP tokens occur in the Level 1 data, each contributed by a different student. However, in light of NPAH claims, the occurrence of OPREP is noteworthy. Already in Level 1, two students may have reached a supposedly advanced OPREP stage in a non-experimental environment. Also noteworthy is the fact that no IO types are attested, even for the two students who were able to produce the supposedly more marked OPREP. This amounts to an empirical gap in the posited acquisitional implicational hierarchy.

Figure 2 shows a dramatic increase in relative clause production for the Level 2 data, which contain almost five times more relative clauses than the Level 1 data. The total number of 110 relative clauses account for 11 percent of all subordination

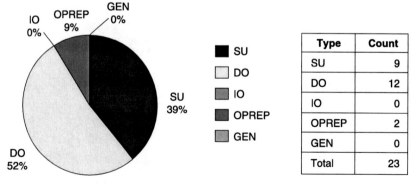

Figure 1 Distribution of relative clause types in Level 1

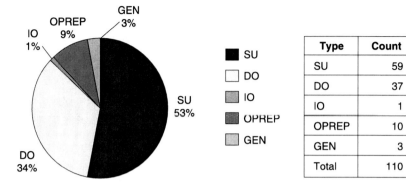

Figure 2 Distribution of relative clause types in Level 2

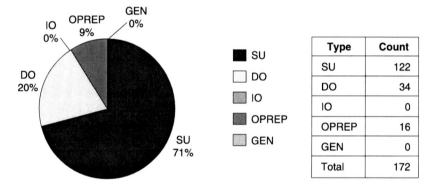

Figure 3 Distribution of relative clause types in Level 3

at this level. Now all learners but one (out of 23) produce relativization, with an average of almost 5 relative clauses per student.

The full range of relative types is attested at Level 2, although differences in frequency of suppliance are pronounced according to type. SU relative clauses are most frequent and are produced by all learners but two. Put differently, 91 percent of Level 2 writers produced SU. The second most frequent type is DO clauses, which are produced also by 17 students or 74 percent of Level 2 writers. Assuming that DO relative constructions are cognitively more complex or, conversely, that SU relativizations are cognitively and formally more accessible, this result readily fits into the projections of the NPAH. There are 10 OPREP relative clauses, produced by eight different learners. While this type of relative clause is clearly much less frequent than SU and DO, its suppliance is now more widespread than at Level 1. The IO and GEN types are extremely infrequent, with only one and three students, respectively, producing 1 token of either one. It is noteworthy that the 3 GEN tokens at Level 2 are the only three instances of this most marked type of relativization in the entire longitudinal corpus. That is, GEN appears only at Level 2 in the data.

Figure 3 shows yet another increase in overall relative clause frequency at Level 3. At this level all but one learner (or 22 of 23) uses relativization of some kind, with an average of over 7 relative clauses by learner. Relative clauses now account for

18 percent of all the subordination used by these 23 students. However, the complexity and range of relative types employed by the 23 Level 3 writers appears to suffer when compared to the previous Level 2. The number of DO in these data remains similar to that of Level 2 (37 and 34 tokens, respectively), but in fact there is a reduction in the number of different students that contribute the more marked DO relative clauses to the analyses, from 17 in Level 2 to 10 in Level 3. Likewise, the frequency of OPREP suppliance grows only slightly, from 10 tokens produced by eight different writers at Level 2 to 16 tokens contributed by 10 different writers at Level 3. Two types of relative clauses, IO and GEN, are entirely absent in the Level 3 data. Thus, the increase in overall relative production at Level 3 is largely attributable to the more abundant suppliance of SU relative clauses. These least marked clauses are now double the number that was found in Level 2 and are used by all but one Level 3 learner.

Finally, as Figure 4 shows, the data in Level 4 appear to intensify the pattern already observed for Level 3 of polarization towards suppliance of mostly SU relative clause types and reduction of variation and complexity of types produced. Relative clauses account for 20 percent of all subordination produced at Level 4 and are produced on the PPTs at an average of over 13 relative clauses per writer. All writers but one produced at least some relativization. However, only seven learners (or half of the 14 in the Level 4 sample) used DO relative clauses, and they did so at a moderate average rate of 2.5 per writer. The OPREP suppliance rate remains stable and small, with only 12 tokens contributed by only seven learners at this most advanced curricular level. Once more, GEN relative clauses are absent and there are only two examples of IOs, each produced by a different student.

To sum up, the frequency of relative clause use in these samples representing the four-year curriculum showed a steady increase in the overall frequency of use of relativization, as is summarized in Table 7. However, as presented in more detail in Figures 1 through 4, the data also revealed changes in distribution of typological markedness that seem contrary to at least some of the stronger (and yet frequent) interpretations—in SLA research, that cognitive accessibility of a particular phenomenon can be meaningfully correlated with use and with advancedness.

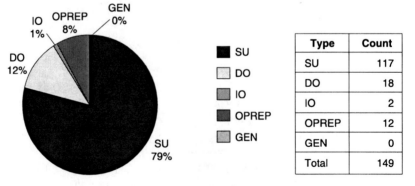

Figure 4 Distribution of relative clause types in Level 4

Research Question 2: Complexity measured by length and position of relative clauses

Clause complexification can usefully be investigated in terms of length of relative clause and degree of embeddedness (that is, whether they appear in final or center positions in the matrix clause). The findings for length are presented in Table 8.

Although the data reveal a steady increase in average length, they also show an increase in standard deviation. Indeed, the range of the length of relative clauses grows from a minimum of 3 and a maximum of 7 words in Level 1 to a minimum of 2 and a maximum of 21 words in Level 4. Thus, although students produce on average slightly but steadily longer relative clauses as they progress through the curriculum, learner performance becomes less and less predictable or more variable at higher levels.

As for relative clause position, Table 9 shows no overall growth in percent of center-embedding relative clauses across the levels; a strict interpretation of the data might even note a seeming "loss" in that capacity. However, a more contextual analysis reveals countervailing evidence. Center-embedded Level 1 clauses are short

Table 7 Frequency use of relative clauses across the four-year curricular sequence

Level	Total RC	% writers	Average RC use	% Total subordination
1	23	56% (9/16)	2.5	7%
2	110	95% (22/23)	5	11%
3	172	95% (22/23)	7	18%
4	149	93% (13/14)	13	20%

Table 8 Relative clause length and standard deviation by level

Level	n	k	Average length of relative clause (words)	Standard deviation	Range (words)
1	16	23	4.35	1.03	3–7
2	23	110	5.31	1.85	2–13
3	23	172	6.26	2.69	2–15
4	14	149	6.72	3.02	2–21

Note
n = number of learners; k = number of relative clauses.

Table 9 Percent of center-embedded relative clauses by level

Level	Total RC	Embedded RC	% embedded
1	23	5 (22%)	22%
2	110	16 (15%)	15%
3	172	30 (17%)	17%
4	149	26 (17%)	17%

elaborations of three to five words on a noun phrase in the matrix sentence, as in illustration (4):

(4)   Der alte Mann, ***der sehr nett war***, sag mir dass ich geradeaus gehen müsste bis ich das Krankenhaus auf dem linken Seite sah.
The old man, ***who was very nice,*** told me that I had to go straight until I saw the hospital on the left.

In Level 4, however, they range from even shorter two-word modifications to more complex relative clauses of 11 words, as illustrated in (5):

(5)   Der wichtigste Faktor, ***der eine politische Vertiefung der EU ähnlich zum amerikanischen Integrationsprozess entgegenwirkt***, ist die Identität.
The most important factor ***that counteracts a political deepening of the EU similar to the American process of integration*** is identity.

In sum, the analysis of relative clause length is only suggestive of largely variable but overall positive increases in relative clause length, whereas position of relative clause sheds little light on developmental progression.

Research Question 3: Implicational scales by level

It should be clear from the presentation of findings in Figures 1 through 4 that the instances of IO and GEN relative clause types were extremely rare in the data across all levels (there were only 3 tokens of each total). Following the NPAH predictions, GEN is expected to be the most marked and therefore least frequent and latest. This fits well with the present data. However, IO is posited to be less marked than OPREP, and the total of 40 OPREP tokens in the corpus stand in stark contrast to the 3 IO tokens. Thus, the results for IO challenge the theoretical predictions in the NPAH framework. Similar observations have been reported by Hyltenstam (1984) for Swedish, Pavesi (1986) for English, and Ortega (2000) for Spanish relative clauses. All three researchers report that IO and OPREP were reversible in their implicational data. Therefore, an alternative data-driven implicational relationship was tested for the present German learners, where the positions of OPREP and IO were reversed, yielding the following sequence: SU > DO > OPREP > IO > GEN. This change resulted in Guttman scaling coefficients of reproducibility and scalability that were more satisfactory than those obtained when the original implicational scale proposed by Keenan and Comrie (1977) (that is, SU > DO > IO > OPREP > GEN) was employed.[6] Consequently, we present the data using this data-adjusted implicational hierarchy.

As Figure 5 shows, seven students (44 percent) at Level 1 did not engage in relativization in the PPT, which involved writing a letter to a friend (see Appendix). Six students (38 percent) exhibited relative clause production that follows the implicational pattern of the revised NPAH, and three (19 percent) produced the more marked types of DO or OPREP without instances of implicated levels.

Looking at the Level 2 data in Figure 6, 15 learners (65 percent) fitted the implicational predictions for acquisition of relativization, and only one learner

Student	SU	DO	OPREP	IO	GEN
3110	+	+	+	-	-
0098	+	+	-	-	-
1094	+	+	-	-	-
1096	+	+	-	-	-
3111	+	+	-	-	-
1097	+	-	-	-	-
2090	-	(+)	-	-	-
2113	-	(+)	-	-	-
2095	-	-	(+)	-	-
0119	-	-	-	-	-
2086	-	-	-	-	-
2098	-	-	-	-	-
2106	-	-	-	-	-
3095	-	-	-	-	-
3112	-	-	-	-	-
3113	-	-	-	-	-

Figure 5 Implicational scales for Level 1 (*n* = 16)

Note: Coefficient of reproducibility: 0.96; Coefficient of scalability: 0.95.

Student	SU	DO	OPREP	IO	GEN
1096	+	+	+	(-)	+
2095	+	+	+	(-)	+
0098	+	+	+	-	-
1097	+	+	+	-	-
2096	+	+	+	-	-
3111	+	+	+	-	-
0119	+	+	-	(+)	-
0122	+	+	-	-	-
1117	+	+	-	-	-
2075	+	+	-	-	-
2080	+	+	-	-	-
2098	+	+	-	-	-
3030	+	+	-	-	-
3095	+	+	-	-	-
3110	+	+	-	-	-
3112	+	+	-	-	-
1094	+	-	(+)	-	-
2106	+	-	(+)	-	-
2113	+	-	-	-	(+)
2086	+	-	-	-	-
3005	+	-	-	-	-
3072	-	(+)	-	-	-
3113	-	-	-	-	-

Figure 6 Implicational scales for Level 2 (*n* = 23)

Note: Coefficient of reproducibility: 0.94; Coefficient of scalability: 0.65.

(4 percent) did not engage in relativization in the PPT, which at this level involved writing an alternative ending to a novel they had read (see Appendix). However, seven learners (31 percent) produced at least one clause type that falls outside the implicated hierarchy levels, suggesting that they might have skipped a type (and, in the case of learner 2113, the whole hierarchy!).

Similarly, Figure 7 shows that 17 students (74 percent) at Level 3 fitted the NPAH pattern, and only one student (4 percent) did not produce relative clauses at all (a different one from Level 2). Once again, however, several students produced relative clause types that are one stage beyond the highest implicated level (and, in the case of learner 0119, two gaps are noted). Specifically, five writers (22 percent) skipped an implicationally related type on this level's PPT writing, which involved a journalistic treatment of the reading "At home in Germany? Portrait of a Vietnamese family" (see Appendix). Strikingly, all of these five writers produced only su and oprep without any use of do types.

Referring to Level 4 data, Figure 8 once more shows that the majority of students (nine, or 64 percent) exhibit the predicted implicational relation and only one (7 percent) does not produce relativization on the PPT at this level, which involved writing a speech on the topic of "The constitution of the EU and the US: Possible comparisons and lessons," to be delivered before a German Rotary Club audience (see Appendix). Once again, several learners (four, or 29 percent) skipped levels of the hierarchy; two of these cases show multiple gaps in the theoretically predicted implicational relationship: Student 2098 produced su, oprep, and io, but not do

Code	SU	DO	OPREP	IO	GEN
1094	+	+	+	-	-
1096	+	+	+	-	-
2106	+	+	+	-	-
3111	+	+	+	-	-
3113	+	+	+	-	-
0098	+	+	-	-	-
0122	+	+	-	-	-
2075	+	+	-	-	-
2080	+	+	-	-	-
2095	+	+	-	-	-
3005	+	+	-	-	-
3110	+	+	-	-	-
3112	+	+	-	-	-
0119	+	-	(+)	-	(+)
1117	+	-	(+)	-	-
2113	+	-	(+)	-	-
3030	+	-	(+)	-	-
3095	+	-	(+)	-	-
1097	+	-	-	-	-
2086	+	-	-	-	-
2096	+	-	-	-	-
3072	+	-	-	-	-
2098	-	-	-	-	-

Figure 7 Implicational scales for Level 3 (*n* = 23)

Note: Coefficient of reproducibility: 0.90; Coefficient of scalability: 0.74.

Student	SU	DO	OPREP	GEN	IO
0122	+	+	+	-	-
1096	+	+	+	-	-
1097	+	+	+	-	-
2095	+	+	+	-	-
2080	+	+	-	-	-
3005	+	+	-	-	-
3030	+	+	-	-	-
2098	+	-	(+)	-	(+)
0098	+	-	(+)	-	-
2106	+	-	(+)	-	-
2086	+	-	-	-	(+)
1117	+	-	-	-	-
2075	+	-	-	-	-
3072	-	-	-	-	-

Figure 8 Implicational scales for Level 4 (*n* = 14)

Note: Coefficient of reproducibility: 0.93; Coefficient of scalability: 0.71.

and GEN; Student 2086 produced only tokens of the most (IO) and least (SU) marked types.

In sum, gaps in the predicted implicational quality of relative clause development were observed at all four levels, and they affected roughly between 20 percent and 30 percent of the sample at each level. The gaps came about as a result of skipping one implicationally related type, although in one case at each level it also involved skipping more than one type (Student 2095 at Level 1; Student 2113 at Level 2; Student 0119 at Level 3; and Student 2098 at Level 4). The most frequent case of evidence against the NPAH predictions for L2 development was found in learners who would produce OPREP without DO relative clauses, something that happened for eight students located at Levels 3 or 4.

Research Question 4: Longitudinal development of relativization by individuals

Given the weak support for implicational patterns of relativization found for research questions 1 through 3, the unique opportunity of longitudinal study to trace individual learner behavior becomes all the more important. Figure 9 shows the relative clause types produced over time by the seven learners for whom written samples were available from Level 1 all the way to Level 4; Figure 10 presents the same information for the nine students who contributed data from Levels 1 through 3; and Figure 11 offers yet the same information for the seven students whose writing represents a progression from Levels 2 through 4.

For reasons of space, two individual data sets are highlighted here to illustrate the general pattern. We look first at Student 2095, who by Level 4 was producing SU, DO, and OPREP and therefore had "acquired" relativization to a high level (only four students at Level 4 exhibited this pattern, which conforms to the NPAH pattern once IO and OPREP are reversed; see Figure 8). We then look at Student 2075, who at Level 4 had managed to produce only SU types in his writing.

Student 2095 (see Figure 9) uses typologically marked, "advanced" relative clauses in Levels 1 and 2. At Level 1, the "advanced" type OPREP constituted the single instance of relative clause used by this learner. Relative clause use went up to 11 tokens at Level 2, comprising the entire range of relative types except for IO (which creates a gap in the implicational hierarchy for this learner profile). As he moved along the four-year curriculum, this student produced another 11 relative clauses at Level 3, and another 14 at Level 4. However, there is a lack of more marked relative clause types at these two more advanced curricular levels (although eventually OPREP does reappear at Level 4).

This writer clearly produces some longer relative clause types in Levels 2, 3, and 4. Example 6 is written at Level 2; Example 7 comes from his Level 4 writing.

(6)   Seine Streifzüge waren etwas, *die ich erkläen nicht konnte*. [Level 2; 5 words long]
      His aimless wanderings were something *that I could not explain.*

(7)   Die Schwierigkeit hier ist nämlich das Fehlen von einer vereinheitlichten Perspektive, *die die Ziele beider Läder vermitteln känte*. [Level 4; 7 words long]
      Of course, the difficulty here is the lack of a unified perspective *that could communicate the goals of both countries.*

Student		SU	DO	OPREP	IO	GEN
0098	Level 1	+	+	-	-	-
	Level 2	+	+	+	-	-
	Level 3	+	+	-	-	-
	Level 4	+	-	+	-	-
1096	Level 1	+	+	-	-	-
	Level 2	+	+	+	-	+
	Level 3	+	+	+	-	-
	Level 4	+	+	+	-	-
1097	Level 1	+	-	-	-	-
	Level 2	+	+	+	-	-
	Level 3	+	-	-	-	-
	Level 4	+	+	+	-	-
2086	Level 1	-	-	-	-	-
	Level 2	+	-	-	-	-
	Level 3	+	-	-	-	-
	Level 4	+	-	-	-	+
2095	Level 1	-	-	+	-	-
	Level 2	+	+	+	-	+
	Level 3	+	+	-	-	-
	Level 4	+	+	+	-	-
2098	Level 1	-	-	-	-	-
	Level 2	+	+	-	-	-
	Level 3	-	-	-	-	-
	Level 4	+	-	+	-	+
2106	Level 1	-	-	-	-	-
	Level 2	+	-	+	-	-
	Level 3	+	+	+	-	-
	Level 4	+	-	+	-	-

Figure 9 Longitudinal individual data for Levels 1 through 4 ($n = 7$)

Student		SU	DO	OPREP	IO	GEN
0119	Level 1	-	-	-	-	-
	Level 2	+	+	-	+	-
	Level 3	+	-	+	-	+
1094	Level 1	+	+	-	-	-
	Level 2	+	-	+	-	-
	Level 3	+	+	+	-	-
2096	Level 1	-	+	-	-	-
	Level 2	+	+	+	-	-
	Level 3	+	-	-	-	-
2113	Level 1	-	+	-	-	-
	Level 2	+	-	-	-	+
	Level 3	+	-	+	-	-
3095	Level 1	-	-	-	-	-
	Level 2	+	+	-	-	-
	Level 3	+	-	+	-	-
3110	Level 1	+	+	+	-	-
	Level 2	+	+	-	-	-
	Level 3	+	+	-	-	-
3111	Level 1	+	+	-	-	-
	Level 2	+	+	+	-	-
	Level 3	+	+	+	-	-
3112	Level 1	-	-	-	-	-
	Level 2	+	+	-	-	-
	Level 3	+	+	-	-	-
3113	Level 1	-	-	-	-	-
	Level 2	-	-	-	-	-
	Level 3	+	+	+	-	-

Figure 10 Longitudinal individual data for Levels 1 through 3 ($n = 9$)

Nevertheless, his average length does not increase significantly across curricular levels and it matches the overall averages for the 23-student data pool (see Table 8). This can be seen in Table 10, which describes both the average and range of length for the relative clauses supplied by Student 2095 at each curricular level.

Thus, despite the fact that this student can be placed at the OPREP acquisition stage by Level 4, other analytical categories would describe Student 2095 as average. It is interesting, however, to compare over time the amount of subordination employed by this learner vis-à-vis the percentage of it involving relative clauses. The figures are shown in Table 11.

When comparing relativization with overall amount of subordination, it turns out that, together with relative clause use, overall subordinate clause use increased dramatically for this learner at Level 2, whereas in Level 3 amount of subordination and relativization grew slightly only, and in Level 4 relative clause use increased despite a decrease in the overall amount of subordination.

In sum, the patterns for Student 2095 suggest a learner who relies heavily on the more accessible SU and DO types (with merely four tokens involving other types in all four levels combined) but experiments with subordination in general and with

Student		SU	DO	OPREP	IO	GEN
0122	Level 2	+	+	-	-	-
	Level 3	+	+	-	-	-
	Level 4	+	+	+	-	-
1117	Level 2	+	+	-	-	-
	Level 3	+	-	+	-	-
	Level 4	+	-	-	-	-
2075	Level 2	+	+	-	-	-
	Level 3	+	+	-	-	-
	Level 4	+	-	-	-	-
2080	Level 2	+	+	-	-	-
	Level 3	+	+	-	-	-
	Level 4	+	+	-	-	-
3005	Level 2	+	-	-	-	-
	Level 3	+	+	-	-	-
	Level 4	+	+	-	-	-
3030	Level 2	+	+	-	-	-
	Level 3	+	-	+	-	-
	Level 4	+	+	-	-	-
3072	Level 2	-	+	-	-	-
	Level 3	+	-	-	-	-
	Level 4	-	-	-	-	-

Figure 11 Longitudinal individual data for Levels 2 through 4 ($n = 7$)

Table 10 Relative clause length and range of length for Student 2095

Level	k	Average length	Minimum–maximum
1	1	5	—
2	11	5.64	4–11
3	11	6.91	3–12
4	14	6.57	3–10

Table 11 Overall subordination vis-à-vis relativization for Student 2095

Level	Total RC	Subordinate clauses	Relative clauses
1	1	21%	3%
2	11	40%	20%
3	11	42%	22%
4	14	36%	24%

relativization in particular, most noticeably at the intermediate Level 2, and achieves productive control of OPREP relativization by Level 4.

By comparison, Student 2075 (see Figure 11) presents yet another puzzling picture in terms of the NPAH or simple notions of development. This learner started off using six SU and DO relative clauses at Level 2. He was more conservative than Student 2095, as he did not use any more marked types to start with. Indeed, on

Table 12 Relative clause length and range of length for Student 2075

Level	k	Average length	Minimum–maximum
2	6	4.83	3–6
3	9	8.22	3–14
4	4	9.50	8–13

PPTs that reflected what he had achieved at three junctures on the equivalent of three years of instruction, the most marked relative clause Student 2075 ever produced was DO. In Level 3, he used nine relative clauses, but there is no expansion of types. Oddly, at the most advanced level in the curriculum, he produces less marked types and fewer relative clauses: only four SU tokens.

And yet, designation of this student's relative clause production as below average can be challenged. Although he uses only four to nine relative clauses per level, Table 12 shows that their average length is above the group average for Levels 2, 3, and 4. Furthermore, the Level 3 range reveals that Student 2075 varies length by a maximum of 11 words, whereas by Level 4 the four relative clauses exhibit a length that is both high and quite stable (from 8 to 13 words).

A representative comparison between Level 2 and Level 4 writing by Student 2075 is provided in (8) and (9):

(8) Ich bin auf einen Baum geklettert, ***der neben das Ufer stand***, so ich Herrn Sommer besser anschauen könnte. [Level 2; 5 words long]
I climbed up a tree ***that stood next to the bank*** so that I could see Herr Sommer better.

(9) Amerikaner haben eine schlechte Reputation, ***die tier unsere Gierigkeit fü Geld und Reichtum spricht.*** [Level 4; 9 words long]
Americans have a bad reputation ***that speaks about our greediness for money and affluence.***

Perhaps this writer could therefore be characterized as having a better awareness than Student 2095 of when and how to use relative clauses to suit his purposes. After all, use of relative clauses, as contrasted with adverbial clauses, constitutes an "investment" in syntactic complexity that correlates with meaning density as compared with meaning extension: when he uses relative clauses at more advanced levels they tend consistently to be longer, presumably adding dense meaning specification to the noun being modified. By contrast, amount of relativization in relation to overall subordination, as shown in Table 13, would seem to reconfirm that Student 2075's relative clause development is below average: despite an increase in relative

Table 13 Overall subordination vis-à-vis relativization for Student 2075

Level	Total RC	Subordinate clauses	Relative clauses
2	6	42%	10%
3	9	48%	17%
4	4	40%	8%

clause production between Level 2 and Level 3, Student 2075 uses only four relative clauses, 8 percent of all subordinate clauses, in Level 4.

Recapitulation of findings

The present study offered several important findings. First, overall frequency of relative clause use supports the prediction that relativization is a feature of inter-language that is used only minimally at lower levels and steadily increases over time. For the groups and for individuals, the greatest increases in frequency of use occurred from Level 1 to Level 2 (when absolute frequency grew by five times) and from Level 2 to 3 (when the proportion of relativization to overall subordination goes up from 11 percent to 18 percent). Although absolute use decreases somewhat at Level 4, relative frequency of use continues to rise, albeit more modestly, in Level 4: from 18 percent to 20 percent of overall subordination, or the highest average use of 13 relative clauses per learner and almost double the individual average from the previous level (see Table 7). The analysis of relative clause length was only suggestive of largely variable but overall positive increases in relative clause length, whereas position of relative clauses (whether center-embedded or not) sheds little light on developmental progression.

The second and most striking finding, however, is that only weak support was found for an implicationally constrained development of relativization along the typological hierarchy so often used in previous SLA research. First, the present data added firm support to the observation by others (Hyltenstam, 1984; Ortega, 2000; Pavesi, 1986) that OPREP is at least produced, if not acquired, before IO by L2 learners. Jointly interpreting our findings with previous ones, we can conclude that this is true across at least four target languages (English, German, Spanish, and Swedish). Second, and even more importantly, the results for OPREP are particularly noteworthy in light of NPAH claims. Already in Level 1, two students may have reached a supposedly advanced OPREP stage in a non-experimental environment. Furthermore, the fact that all types of relative clauses, even the supposedly difficult ones, appear in the present data by Level 2, suggests that several students in the program have acquired the more "difficult" relative clauses by the end of the first year of intensive study of German or by the end of the second year in a non-intensive track.

Third, contrary to theoretical predictions of advancedness in relativization, the implicational scaling findings strongly suggest that relativization progresses through Levels 3 and 4 towards an intensification of SU relativization and a reduction of the range and complexity of more marked types (coupled with a steady increase in overall frequency of relativization). This was seen in implicational data both per curricular level (Figures 5 through 8) and in terms of individual longitudinal profiles (Figures 9 through 11). Therefore, the analyses of SU and DO types appear to be more productive and more reliable than the analyses of the more marked (and rare to extremely rare) OPREP, IO, and GEN types.

Discussion and conclusion

Several caveats are in order to help qualify these findings. A first consideration when interpreting our findings is that of possible task-effects, since at each level the PPTs involved quite different genres. Level 1 and Level 2 PPTs favor a personal and narrative textual organization and register, which results in a preference for congruent semiosis with its emphasis on the verbal paradigm and various circumstantial clausal structures, a tendency that is heightened at Level 2, where the task asks students to emulate a literary narrative voice. By contrast, the genres of the tasks in Level 3 and Level 4 demand compact thematic development and an increasingly distanced writer stance—all features that can be presumed to lead to greater use of nominalizations and therefore the likelihood of greater incidence of relative clause structures. This must have facilitated in part the increase in overall frequency of relativization that was observed from each level to the next. In the end, and in keeping with the Hallidayan framework that we chose for the development of our curriculum and our educational predictions for instructed development of advanced capacities, we suspect that relative clause use would be most usefully observed not in isolation but in the context of an array of syntactic and lexicogrammatical resources whose likelihood of occurrence is genre-based, developmentally influenced, and a matter of individual choice. These are the kinds of analyses currently being undertaken for the longitudinal data.

A more general concern pertains to the representativeness of the sample. It should be remembered that the data analyzed come from extended written production rather than experimental elicitation, and that the available evidence amounts to one piece of writing (one PPT) per learner at each level. For these two reasons, an absence of a certain type of relative clause in an essay cannot be taken as a direct representation of the underlying linguistic system. In other words, more exhaustive sampling would be needed before we can confidently conclude "a lack of emergence" of more marked (and therefore typically low-frequency) relative clauses. This general point was made by Norris and Ortega (2003) when they advised: "where interpretations are to be made about the emergence of linguistic phenomena which exhibit both variational and developmental characteristics . . ., measurement will need to elicit behaviors across numerous linguistic and communicative contexts in order to show that interpretations are not based on a lack of evidence, as opposed to evidence for the lack of emergence" (p. 733). It should be noted, however, that the same caution needs to be applied to previous relative clause studies, which oftentimes have been based on even smaller sampling slices of learner data. By comparison, the longitudinal analyses we offer come with a high warrant of trustworthiness. The data came from writing that took place under nearly ideal circumstances with a motivated progression of writing tasks, and the corpus yielded a not insignificant number of relative clauses ($n = 454$), with a relatively reasonable average relative clause production per learner at Levels 2 and higher (5, 7, or 13 per learner). Most importantly, the analyses trace a cohort of 23 students across a minimum of three, at times four, curricular levels, a "length of time" which, in many programs, would equate to the lion's share of an undergraduate program as far as attained L2 ability is concerned.[7] Nevertheless, we acknowledge that gaps in the implicational scales may in part reflect a paucity of evidence, rather than counter-evidence against the NPAH.

On the other hand, the presence of more marked types already from Level 1, and most robustly in Level 2, unequivocally supports our interpretation that several students in the program have acquired the more "difficult" relative clauses by the end of the first year of intensive study of German or by the end of the second year in a non-intensive track. As it turns out, the data of this study show the greatest variety of use of relativizations (though, quite naturally, not frequency) at Levels 1 and 2, the beginning and intermediate levels, and a remarkable and progressive reliance on su use, toward 79 percent of relativizations at Level 4 from a 39 percent use in Level 1. Although the NPAH makes no direct claims about the length of time necessary for learners to develop the ability to form relativizations at the lower end of the hierarchy, its implied theoretical meaning and its actual research practice typically consider these forms to be "advanced," one reason why most studies are located with intermediate to advanced learners. Our findings challenge this assumption by conclusively showing that relativization in an optimal instructed context need not be a late-acquired feature of advancedness. They also extend Pavesi's (1986) claim about the superiority of instruction over naturalistic acquisition for ultimate attainment of L2 relative clauses by uncovering a striking advantage in rate of relative clause acquisition for these 23 instructed German learners.

Another challenge to commonly accepted practice in the study of L2 relativization that our findings have uncovered is that most marked relative clauses can be usefully considered a sign of advancedness. In essence, the paucity of the more marked relative clause types at the more advanced levels, such as oi and GEN (but even OPREP), at the very least makes them less useful as indicators of advancedness—unless other valid criteria for that designation can be adduced. Issues of optionality and acquisition are likely to intersect, and further interpretation and generalization will require more fine-grained analysis beyond the overall quantitative findings presented thus far. More radically, the longitudinal data warrant two initial conclusions: not only is relativization in and of itself not a useful predictor of advancedness, it also does not support developmental claims about the nature of an evolving advancedness. At least it does not do so in the way it has been theorized and entered SLA consciousness, namely in terms of an underlying processing difficulty that is based on formal grammatical features.

What the data do point to, however, is a complex set of relationships that include as particularly prominent features dynamic and shifting relationships between syntactic and lexicogrammatical features, genre-related probabilities of language use at the simplex and complex clausal level, and, within that set of options, learner choices that show significant variation for different learners, even though certain "syndromes," as Systemic Functional Linguistics refers to register- and genre-related bundles of features, are discernible (see Matthiessen, 2006). Precisely because there is every indication that these relationships cannot be captured by single-source approaches that seek to establish causalities but that they come about within the nexus of socioculturally embedded textual probabilities and individual users' choices, their longitudinal study would seem no longer to be an add-on to research practice but a necessity if we wish to gain a more differentiated understanding of the nature of second/foreign language development and language use, particularly at the advanced level.

Notes

1. Unless otherwise noted, examples are taken from student writing in the longitudinal corpus.

2. The same curricular context was the site for the instructional longitudinal studies reported by Sprang and Liamkina (Chapters 8 and 9, this volume).
3. As befits a curricular project and one that was explicitly conceived as a whole-departmental collaborative effort, much of the conceptualization and programmatic and pedagogical implementation reported on in this chapter, along with its supporting documents, are communal property. Particularly outstanding contributions were made by individuals and groups whom we would here like to acknowledge. Syntactic analysis of the PPTs was undertaken by a group of graduate students whose dedicated and diligent coding work is at the heart of the project: Matt Adams, Teodora Atanasova, Shana Semler, Marianna Ryshina-Pankova, and Ellen Titzkowski. Co-author Castle Sinicrope handled much of the data management during the study and focused analysis on the longitudinal data. Tim De Marco, then an undergraduate student, assisted in various roles. Hiram Maxim, a faculty member in the German department, has been a valuable co-participant in this study since its inception. John Norris of the University of Hawai'i not only lent his expansive vision about the role of assessment and his expertise in making it happen within the department's curriculum; he also continues to be a co-researcher on the project. We particularly acknowledge with thanks his insights and analyses regarding the cross-sectional data (see also note 5). Finally, the specific analysis of the longitudinal development of relativization that this chapter reports on was undertaken by co-author Castle Sinicrope in conjunction with her undergraduate senior honors thesis in the spring of 2006.
4. A second major effort of data collection refers to the so called base line writing task, or BWT. While the PPTs explicitly and intentionally tapped into curriculum-dependent writing performance that both magnifies the well known task effect on writing and reduces comparability of learner performances across curricular levels, additional, curriculum-independent data on writing ability were obtained from students across all curricular levels (1–5). In that study, all students regardless of level wrote in response to an identical prompt, a book review. Writing occurred spontaneously in a timed lab setting that lasted a total of 50 minutes (as contrasted with the untimed at-home setting for production of the PPTs). A total of 124 students participated in that study, of whom 86 also provided PPTs; the total word count is 34,716 words for the BWTs and 84,850 words for the data provided by students belonging to both groups. Byrnes *et al.* (2005) presented on aspects of the inter-relation between findings from the PPTs, the BWTs, and the longitudinal data. Ryshina-Pankova (2006a, 2006b) reports on issues of coherence and cohesion as they can be discerned from the data, with particular focus on the BWTs at Levels 3–5.
5. Additional analyses of the longitudinal data, using the categories of Systemic Functional Linguistics, are underway for examining the interrelated shifts in syntactic behavior at the clausal and sentence level, particularly between Levels 2 and 4.
6. When Guttman scaling was applied to the data following the original theoretical hierarchy of su > do > io > oprep > gen, the obtained coefficients of reproducibility ranged from 0.87 to 0.95; the coefficients of scalability were markedly unsatisfactory, ranging from 0.40 to 0.71.
7. While writing ability is, of course, distinct from speaking ability, the results for SOPI tests obtained in the same curricular context reported by Norris and Pfeiffer (2003) provide additional information on learners in the curriculum. Median ratings attained at the end of curricular levels were: Level 1: IM; 2: IM; 3: IH; 4: AH.

References

Byrnes, H. (2001). Reconsidering graduate students' education as teachers: It takes a department! *Modern Language Journal, 85*, 512–530.

Byrnes, H. (2002). The role of task and task-based assessment in a content-oriented collegiate FL curriculum. *Language Testing, 19*, 419–437.

Byrnes, H., Crane, C., Maxim, H. H., and Sprang, K. A. (2006). Taking text to task: Issues and choices in curriculum construction. *ITL—International Journal of Applied Linguistics, 152*, 85–110.

Byrnes, H., Maxim, H. H., Norris, J. M., and Ryshina-Pankova, M. (2005). Revisiting writing development: A curriculum-based study of syntactic complexity. Symposium presented at the 14th World Congress of Applied Linguistics (AILA). Madison, WI.

Byrnes, H., and Sprang, K. A. (2004). Fostering advanced literacy. A genre-based cognitive approach. In H. Byrnes and H. H. Maxim (Eds.), *Advanced foreign language learning: A challenge to college programs* (pp. 47–85). Boston, MA: Heinle Thomson.

Crane, C. (2006). Modelling a genre-based foreign language curriculum: Staging advanced L2 learning. In H. Byrnes (Ed.), *Advanced language learning: The contribution of Halliday and Vygotsky* (pp. 223–241). London: Continuum.

Developing Multiple Literacies: A curriculum renewal project of the German Department at Georgetown University, 1997–2000. (n.d.). www1.georgetown.edu/departments/german/programs/undergraduate/curriculum.

Doughty, C. (1991). Second language instruction does make a difference. Evidence from an empirical study of SL relativization. *Studies in Second Language Acquisition, 13,* 431–469.

Eckman, F. R., Bell, L., and Nelson, D. (1988). On the generalization of relative clause instruction in the acquisition of English as a second language. *Applied Linguistics, 9,* 1–20.

Ellis, R. (2005). Planning and task performance: Theory and research. In R. Ellis (Ed.), *Planning and task performance in a second language* (pp. 3–34). Philadelphia, PA: John Benjamins.

Gass, S. (1979). Language transfer and universal grammatical relations. *Language Learning, 29,* 327–345.

Gass, S. (1980). An investigation of syntactic transfer in adult second language learners. In R. C. Scarcella and S. D. Krashen (Eds.), *Research in second language acquisition* (pp. 132–141). Rowley, MA: Newbury House.

Gass, S. (1982). From theory to practice. In M. Hines and W. Rutherford (Eds.), *ON TESOL '81* (pp. 129–139). Washington, DC: TESOL.

Halliday, M. A. K. (1993). Towards a language-based theory of learning. *Linguistics and Education, 5,* 93–116.

Halliday, M. A. K. (1996). On grammar and grammatics. In R. Hasan, C. Cloran, and D. G. Butt (Eds.), *Functional descriptions: Theory in practice* (pp. 1–38). Philadelphia, PA: John Benjamins.

Halliday, M. A. K. (2002). Spoken and written modes of meaning. In J. J. Webster (Ed.), *On grammar* (pp. 323–351). London: Continuum.

Hawkins, R. (1989). Do second language learners acquire restrictive relative clauses on the basis or relational or configurational information? The acquisition of French subject, direct object and genitive restrictive clauses by second language learners. *Second Language Research, 5,* 155–188.

Hyltenstam, K. (1984). The use of typological markedness conditions as predictors in second language acquisition: The case of pronominal copies in relative clauses. In R. Anderson (Ed.), *Second languages: A crosslinguistic perspective.* Rowley, MA: Newbury House.

Hyltenstam, K. (1987). Markedness, language universals, language typology, and second language acquisition. In C. Pfaff (Ed.), *First and second language acquisition processes* (pp. 55–78). Rowley, MA: Newbury House.

Keenan, E. L., and Comrie, B. (1977). Noun phrase accessibility and Universal Grammar. *Linguistic Inquiry, 8,* 63–99.

Kuno, S. (1974). The position of relative clauses and conjunctions. *Linguistic Inquiry, 5,* 117–136.

Martin, J. R. (2000). Design and practice: Enacting functional linguistics. *Annual Review of Applied Linguistics, 20,* 116–126.

Matthiessen, C. M. I. M. (2006). Educating for advanced foreign language capacities: Exploring the meaning-making resources of languages systemic-functionally. In H. Byrnes (Ed.), *Advanced language learning: The contribution of Halliday and Vygotsky* (pp. 31–57). London: Continuum.

Maxim, H. H. (2005). Integrating syntactic complexity in curriculum-based writing development. Paper presented in the symposium, Revisiting L2 writing development: A curriculum-based study of syntactic complexity. 14th World Congress of Applied Linguistics (AILA). Madison, WI.

Norris, J. M. (2005). Investigating syntactic complexity from cross-sectional, longitudinal, and multitask perspectives. Paper presented in the symposium, Revisiting L2 writing development: A curriculum-based study of syntactic complexity. 14th World Congress of Applied Linguistics (AILA). Madison, WI.

Norris, J. M., and Ortega, L. (2003). Defining and measuring SLA. In C. Doughty and M. H. Long (Eds.), *Handbook of second language acquisition* (pp. 717–761). Malden, MA: Blackwell.

Norris, J. M., and Pfeiffer, P. C. (2003). Exploring the use and usefulness of ACTFL oral proficiency ratings and standards in college foreign language departments. *Foreign Language Annals, 36*, 572–581.

Ortega, L. (2000). Understanding syntactic complexity: The measurement of change in the syntax of instructed L2 Spanish learners. Unpublished doctoral dissertation. University of Hawai'i, Honolulu, HI.

Ortega, L., and Iberri-Shea, G. (2005). Longitudinal research in SLA: Recent trends and future directions. *Annual Review of Applied Linguistics, 25*, 26–45.

Pavesi, M. (1986). Markedness, discoursal modes, and relative clause formation in a formal and informal context. *Studies in Second Language Acquisition, 8*, 38–55.

Pienemann, M. (1998). *Language processing and second language development: Processability theory.* Philadelphia, PA: John Benjamins.

Ryshina-Pankova, M. (2006a). Constructing coherent and cohesive textual worlds in advanced foreign language learner writing. Unpublished doctoral dissertation, Georgetown University, Washington, DC.

Ryshina-Pankova, M. (2006b). Creating textual worlds in advanced learner writing: The role of complex theme. In H. Byrnes (Ed.), *Advanced language learning: The contribution of Halliday and Vygotsky* (pp. 164–183). London: Continuum.

Schachter, I. J. (1974). An error in error analysis. *Language Learning, 24*, 205–214.

Schleppegrell, M. J. (2004). *The language of schooling: A functional linguistics perspective.* Mahwah, NJ: Lawrence Erlbaum.

Sheldon, A. (1974). The role of parallel function in the acquisition of relative clauses in English. *Journal of Verbal Learning and Verbal Behavior, 13*, 272–281.

Stenhouse, L. (1975). *An introduction to curriculum research and development.* London: Heinemann.

Tarallo, F., and Myhill, J. (1983). Interference and natural language processing in second language acquisition. *Language Learning, 33*, 55–73.

Terrell, T., Tschirner, E., and Nikolai, B. (2004). *Kontakte. A communicative approach.* Boston, MA: McGraw Hill (5th ed.).

Wertsch, J. V. (2006). Generalized collective dialogue and advanced foreign language capacities. In H. Byrnes (Ed.), *Advanced language learning: The contribution of Halliday and Vygotsky* (pp. 58–71). London: Continuum.

Yule, G. (1998). *Explaining English grammar.* Oxford: Oxford University Press.

Appendix: Prototypical performance writing tasks (PPTs), Levels 1–4

Thematic focus	Textual focus	Audience	Lexicogrammatical and discourse features
Level 1 Issues of personal well-being and planning ["Krank in Deutschland" Letter to a friend "Sick in Germany"]	Narrating about personal circumstances, expressing wishes and plans	Personal and familiar	Chronological narrative structures Hypothetical structures Coordination and subordination
Level 2 Imaginative treatment of personal relationships ["Alternatives Ende zu Patrick Süskinds Roman "Die Geschichte von Herrn Sommer" Alternative ending to Patrick Süskind's novel *The story of Herr Sommer*]	Placing narration about personal lives into the context of a literary work, literary conventions	Personal and public	Narrative structures Description Dialogue Coordination, subordination. embedded clauses
Level 3 Multicultural lives in contemporary German ["Zu Hause in Deutschland? Porträt einer vietnamesischen Familie" Journalistic treatment "At home in Germany? Portrait of a Vietnamese Family"]	Placing personal experiences into a broader social context	Public	Lexicogrammatical realizations of comparison and contrast Coordination, subordination, embedded clauses
Level 4 Germany's role in the EU; issues pertaining to creation of the EU constitution ["Die Verfassung der Europäischen Union und der Vereinigten Staaten: Mögliche Vergleiche und Lehren" Speech before a German Rotary Club audience "The constitution of the EU and the US: Possible comparisons and lessons"]	Making an argument about social, political, economic developments in societies	Public	Lexicogrammatical realizations of comparison and contrast, logico-semantic relationships, classification and laws, argumentation Coordination, subordination, embedded clauses, nominal structures: nominalizations, extended attributes

8 Advanced learners' development of systematic vocabulary knowledge

Learning German vocabulary with inseparable prefixes

Katherine A. Sprang

Abstract

The literature on advanced learners' word knowledge (e.g., Nation, 1990) assumes that learners can build upon their base vocabularies by adding derivational morphemes to known root words. Recent evidence shows, however, that learners neither do this systematically (Schmitt and Meara, 1997) nor with ease (Schmitt, 1998), even at relatively advanced stages of lexical development. The study reported in this chapter employs a case study methodology to examine the developing lexicogrammatical knowledge of word families experienced over the course of a semester by two advanced learners who received different forms of instruction on the meaning of the two German prefixes *be-* and *er-*. These prefixes prototypically convey the linguistic concepts of durativity, goal-/outcome-orientation, intentionality, telicity, and/or abstraction; thus, they are informationally dense and are often used to take a perspective on a given activity. Two learners participated in a 14-week-sustained input flood, including three concordancer activities. One learner also received explicit instruction on the linguistic concepts that form the meaning distinctions between root and prefixed verbs. Over the semester she used this knowledge to deduce prefixed words' meaningfulness as she encountered them in texts read for class. The other learner did not receive any instruction. Thus, her task was inductive as she sought to understand prefixed words in context. I examine the knowledge sources that the two learners used to develop a systematic understanding of these word classes over the semester, concluding with a discussion of the benefits and limits of instruction in this area.

Introduction

One of the hallmarks of advanced second language (L2) users is that they display literate capacities in multiple languages. This ability entails both recognizing and using a language other than one's L1 with conscious choices about the way one is expressing oneself to an audience that may have different notions of appropriate expression in a given context than those of one's L1 (Byrnes, 2006). This means that advanced L2 users, ideally, can display an "insightfulness regarding human knowing through language" (Byrnes, 2006, p. 5) that may transcend the capacities of a monolingual person.

If they are to achieve this capacity, advanced L2 users must be able to recognize and express nuances in meaningfulness in the L2, such as ascribing intentionality, purposefulness, or achievement of a goal or expected outcome to an activity. These notions are abstract, linguistic concepts used to express a perspective (Carroll, 2000; Slobin, 1996; Talmy, 1986, 1991; von Stutterheim and Carroll, 2006); and they are a critically important element of literate language use. They are construed through language (Langacker, 1991, 2006), and they may not reveal themselves as an explicit part of the definition of the words in which they reside. In L1 usage, this linguistic knowledge is implicit: most users of a language do not attend to the linguistic concepts that are part of their ways of thinking for speaking (Slobin, 1996). This makes recognizing them even more difficult for the advanced L2 user, because the L1 user cannot explain their meaningfulness even if the L2 user is astute enough to ask the right questions. Indeed, Slobin (1996, p. 89) has hypothesized that this type of restructuring would be very difficult for adult L2 users, because the meaningfulness is nonsalient and, for some features, covert. Studies by Carroll and von Stutterheim (e.g., von Stutterheim and Carroll, 2006) have confirmed that even highly advanced L2 users tend not to use the same linguistic means with the same frequency to express a perspective that native speakers do.

The converse of the question of whether these grammaticized distinctions can be learned through exposure is the question whether they can be *taught*. Indeed, as early as 1940, Whorf hypothesized that consciousness-raising techniques could be used to overcome the nonsalience of such features, if they could be "explained in such a way that they become semiconscious, with the result that they lose their binding power over [the language user] which custom has given them" (Whorf, 1940/1956, pp. 224–225, cited in Odlin, 2005). Recently, Ellis has argued that it is precisely this type of feature that requires focal attention to be learnable: "The learners are encountering novelty, wherein . . . a more conscious involvement is needed for successful learning and problem solving, yet they do not realize it because these aspects of language are neither salient nor are they of significant communicative value" (Ellis, 2005, p. 322).

The study reported in this chapter is drawn from a larger study, reported in Sprang (2003), which sought to address precisely these issues by asking: Is it possible to provide explicit instruction that will promote noticing of linguistic concepts for advanced learners? The features in question were two inseparable prefixes in German, *be-* and *er-*. Learners in the study were exposed regularly to *be-* and *er*-prefixed verbs as they worked through texts and performed tasks in an advanced-level four-credit course taught in the German department at Georgetown University by myself, the teacher-researcher. They all had competencies equivalent to three years of college-level German study. In this report I will focus on a case study of two learners. Via the chosen case study methodology (see Harklau, Chapter 2, this volume), I explore the most beneficial level of "consciousness-raising" intervention for meaningfulness to be recognized, understood, and useful for systematic word learning, with a longitudinal focus in recognition of the time required for learners to begin to develop systematic lexicogrammatical knowledge along these lines. More specifically, I track the two learners' developing understanding of the prefixes' meaningfulness, operationalized as vocabulary knowledge, over the course of a 14-week semester that included explicit, intensive exposure to prefixed words via, among other activities, three sessions of concordancing activities (Johns, 2000) and, for some learners only, concept-based explicit instruction on the meaningfulness of the two prefixes. I interviewed the learners at three points during the semester to see whether their knowledge of the prefixed words increased, and whether an understanding of the prefixes' role in word meaning was recognizable to them and used by them to comprehend unknown words as they were encountered during classroom reading and listening tasks.

Vocabulary development of advanced L2 users: exposure vs. instruction

Vocabulary size is critical to success at advanced levels of performance, both for receptive and productive tasks; however, most SLA researchers argue that teaching vocabulary at advanced levels is impractical (e.g., Nation, 1999, p. 10). Instead, it is assumed that advanced learners encounter large numbers of unknown vocabulary words through extensive exposure to oral and written texts (Laufer, 1997), and they need to use comprehension strategies such as inferring the meanings of words in context in order to succeed (Nagy, Herman, and Anderson, 1985; Paribakht and Wesche, 2006). Over time, with repeated exposure to vocabulary items, learners develop some level of word knowledge.

However, even when advanced learners grasp the meanings of vocabulary to accomplish the task of comprehending the texts at hand, it can be argued that comprehension during reading and listening does not necessarily lead to deep levels of vocabulary knowledge. As Faerch and Kasper (1986) note, learners engaged in comprehension tasks often process the vocabulary to which they are exposed as intake for comprehension rather than intake for learning. Thus, advanced learners must be proactive about their continued language development, if they want to move beyond low levels of word knowledge for comprehension in context to fully productive, appropriate usage.

Given that most advanced L2 learners are expected to attend on their own to their continued vocabulary development, the amount of focal attention that they need to provide to this endeavor becomes crucial. Learners tend to believe that they know a word even if they have only low levels of receptive knowledge of the word in context (Paribakht and Wesche, 2006). Herein lies a quandary for continued vocabulary development, because developing semantic links in a strong L2 mental lexicon requires explicit learning (Ellis, 1997). Learners do not have to look up every unknown word in a dictionary—indeed, that would prove deadly to contextualized comprehension; but they do have to *attend* to word meaning if they wish to deepen their understanding of L2 vocabulary. Sternberg (1987, p. 91) has presented three attentional processes as sufficient for development of vocabulary knowledge through exposure to L2 texts. *Selective encoding* is the process by which learners decide what contextual information is relevant to understanding a word within a text; *selective combination* is the process of formulating a context-specific definition; and *selective comparison* is the process by which the learner compares the new knowledge about this word to other, related words in the mental lexicon. According to Sternberg, the latter two of these involve deliberate, conscious processing of vocabulary for the word learner, while reading or listening with the broader goal of comprehending the meaningfulness of an L2 text. Jiang (2004) goes further and posits that even L2 users who have lived in immersion environments for a number of years may continue to mediate their L2 comprehension of words through their L1 concepts unless they are made aware that the L2 words and their L1 translations are not isomorphic. He argues that instruction may be required for the semantic restructuring process to occur, whereby L2 users become aware of meaning differences between L2 words and the L1 translations. "A combination of explicit explanation and contextualized input and interaction specifically designed to target a particular word or set of words can be . . . effective" (Jiang, 2004, p. 427).

While the number of vocabulary items known (*breadth* of word knowledge) is critical to advanced capacities, an even more important element of advanced L2 ability is related to precision of understanding, both for comprehension and production. This requires a focus on developing *depth* of word knowledge (Henriksen, 1999). Henriksen has categorized vocabulary knowledge along three dimensions, shown in Figure 1.

One might expect that developing an understanding along these various scales would require both focused exposure and conscious effort. Likewise, building a word web in the L2 that is both broad and deep requires a number of years. Thus, it is important to recognize that any systematic development of vocabulary knowledge along the three dimensions elucidated by Henriksen (1999) will occur gradually. Indeed, Melka (1997) has shown that in first language development children initially integrate new vocabulary through imitation or mimesis. This fixed usage gradually gives way to comprehended production that is strongly linked to the original context in which the vocabulary was initially learned, and finally develops into fully productive vocabulary use in novel contexts. Combining Henriksen's and Melka's models provides a framework for understanding word knowledge along a continuum, with a variety of different types of knowledge needed to complete a learner's understanding of a given vocabulary item. This suggests that vocabulary knowledge needs to be conceived developmentally, and learning opportunities should recur over a much longer period than has been traditionally expected, so that functionally differentiated and contextualized vocabulary knowledge is accrued over time, strengthening L2

1. Partial to precise knowledge (recognition for reading/pronouncing; meaning; function; grammatical status; semantic associations, including figurative uses)

2. Depth of word knowledge

    ❑   **intensional ⇔ extensional links**: intensional, e.g., members of word family: *stable, stabilize, stabilization, restabilization*, synonyms, antonyms vs. extensional, e.g., relationship between *meander, stroll, walk, march, jog, run*

3. Receptive ⇔ productive use knowledge

    ❑   comprehend, define, translate are all measures of receptive knowledge

    ❑   recall for production that is appropriate semantically, pragmatically, and syntactically

Figure 1 Dimensions of vocabulary development (following Henriksen, 1999)

lexical networks along a variety of dimensions, while word learning can be both item learning and system changing, as proposed by Henriksen.

Yet, longitudinal research into vocabulary development in adult L2 tends to focus on describing how individuals learn words through exposure alone, and primarily in immersion or second language settings (Altman, 1997; Grabe and Stoller, 1997; Parry, 1997; Schmitt, 1998). While the literature on advanced learners' word knowledge (e.g., Nation, 1990) assumes that learners can build upon their base vocabularies by adding derivational morphemes to known root words, evidence shows that learners neither do this systematically (Schmitt and Meara, 1997) nor with ease (Schmitt, 1998). Certainly learners report that they comprehend unknown members of a word family containing affixes if they already know the root word or a related word; but this research has shown that learners do not attend to developing an understanding of the meaning or function of the affixes with any degree of sophistication, nor do they develop levels leading to productive ability with the related words. Clearly, these abilities are needed for continued development, and it is important for educators to provide appropriate pedagogical support for learners to recognize that this focus is of value to them. Despite Jiang's call for explicit, differentiated vocabulary instruction, advanced learners are generally not taught vocabulary. And yet there are opportunities for highly productive, exponential vocabulary growth precisely for learners who already have a strong base vocabulary, for instance, through the teaching of derivational morphology. Thus, research is needed that tracks gradual accrual of vocabulary knowledge with the aid of an optimal combination of exposure and instruction and along a longitudinal trajectory.

The present study, then, was designed to explore the effectiveness of different types of exposure to the meaningfulness of prefixes, in an effort to determine how these features might be best taught in the foreign language classroom environment.

Context of study: classroom environment and design

The study described in this chapter took place within a semester-long intensive German course in a university environment in the United States. (The full four-year collegiate curriculum in which the present course was situated is described in *Developing multiple literacies*, n.d.) The advanced course, entitled "Text in context," requires threshold advanced learners (who have typically completed 18 credits of instruction) to read or listen to, both extensively and intensively, a large number of texts arranged around three thematic units of instruction. Learners are expected to mine texts to create semantic fields, and to use literate forms of expression congruent with secondary discourses when performing a series of scaffolded spoken and written tasks for the class. They are provided with lists of lexical sentence stems that are generically appropriate to the tasks they must perform. Learners expend significant cognitive effort reformulating ideas mined from the texts through structured outlines and thematic semantic webs, which are scaffolded activities that thereupon enable the learners to express these complex ideas orally and in writing, using the lexical sentence stems provided, all the while monitoring and maintaining cohesion and both morphological and syntactic accuracy across performances.

Through the texts, creation of semantic fields, and usage of the lists of lexical sentence stems, the learners in this study were exposed again and again to vocabulary with the *be-* and *er-* prefixes. They encountered them in readings, and they were required to use them in discussions and retellings or analyses of textual content. Above and beyond these multiple exposures that were part of the general instructional sequence, the learners participated as intact groups in a study that examined their levels of prefixed word knowledge. A graphical display of the time frame for the study is provided in Figure 2.

During the second week of the semester, I conducted interviews with all the learners in the class. As part of the interview, I administered a test with 30 of the words that they had encountered in a recent reading. Following the first interview, the learners participated in three computerized concordancer sessions. After the week-long intervention, the learners were interviewed a second time, during which they were again tested on 30 prefixed words, which they had encountered through the intervention or through readings in the same week as the test. And, finally, they participated in a third interview two weeks before the end of the semester, during which they were once again tested on 30 words to which they had been exposed in the previous week of class readings, some of which had also appeared on the first or second test. Thus, the design of this study purposefully respected classroom practices and goals in order to maintain ecological validity (see Harklau, Chapter 2, this volume; Spada, 2005). Maintaining the contextualized nature of the study within an intact classroom setting allowed a triangulated approach combining qualitative and quantitative measures. These multiple measures, in turn, strengthened the ability to detect qualitatively, through learner reports, and to measure quantitatively, through learner performances, whether systematic vocabulary growth occurred over the semester.

Inseparable prefixes *be-* and *er-*: systematic, prototypical meaningfulness

German prefixes *be-* and *er-* prototypically convey the linguistic concepts of durativity, goal-/outcome-orientation, intentionality, telicity (accomplishment of goal or anticipated outcome), and/or abstraction. Thus, they are informationally dense and are often used to take a perspective on a given activity (Carroll and von Stutterheim, 2003; Slobin, 1998). Learners tend to believe that they know the prefixed words when they encounter them because they are familiar with the root verbs (Sprang, 2003), so they tend to overlook the deeper meaningfulness that the prefix conveys.

The inseparable prefixes *be-* and *er-* combine with root verbs in German to form literally hundreds of words. Some of these polymorphemic words have a strong meaning relationship to the root word; others are less transparently related. Because the meaning shift of the prefixes is prototypically instantiated, it is not easy for a learner to perceive a pattern among the various meaning potentials that the prefixes

Week	1	2	3	4	5	6	7	8	9	10	11	12	13	14
		First interview		Three-day concordancer intervention	Second interview							Third interview		

Figure 2 Time frame of study

convey. On the other hand, if learners could decipher the meaningfulness of the prefixes and use it systematically, this would give them a powerful advantage when tackling the task of learning the meanings and uses of the hundreds upon hundreds of words in this word class.

Therefore, the analytical tools of Cognitive Grammar (Fauconnier, 1997; Johnson, 1987; Lakoff, 1993; Langacker, 1991, 2006) were utilized to develop a pedagogical explanation for the prefixes' meaningfulness. As Taylor (1993, p. 220) points out, "the challenge of applying cognitive linguistic insights to a pedagogical grammar lies precisely in searching for descriptively adequate, intuitively acceptable, and easily accessible formulations of these meanings." Since my goal was to develop a pedagogically sufficient explanation of their prototypical meaningfulness, I started with the diachronically more transparent meaning of the prefixes as grammaticized concepts. I developed an image schema that depicted one of two possible meaning shifts that the *be-* and *er-* prefixes conveyed; the image schema derives from the *event structure metaphor* (Lakoff, 1993) and is shown in Figure 3. It displays graphically the relationship of the linguistic concepts to the prefixes sufficiently that L2 learners can begin to grasp the prefixes' various contributions to the prefixed words.

The other meaning potential that the prefixes can convey to root verbs is a shift from the concrete, perceptual meaning to a metaphorical, abstract, conceived meaning. For instance, consider the difference between the following two uses of the verb "to see": "I see you" vs. "I see what you mean." Indeed, many of the prefixed words are doubly metaphorical, in that they convey the purposeful, goal-oriented core meaningfulness, as well as a shift from concrete to abstract. An example is the meaning shift from *gehen* to *begehen* and *ergehen: gehen* is among the most basic verbs of movement in German, translating most commonly as "to go" and "to walk"; it is also used abstractly in the semi-fixed expression *Wie geht es Ihnen?*, which translates literally to "How goes it with you?" ("How are you?"). The word with the *be-* prefix can be used in a concrete or an abstract sense: *den Weg begehen* means "to move along a path (concrete) over a period of time, headed towards some implied endpoint." *Den Tag begehen* means to "move through the day," translated most commonly as "to spend the day," generally used in the sense of marking time through some momentous event. And finally, *ergehen* is used only in an abstract sense, to connote the achievement of a

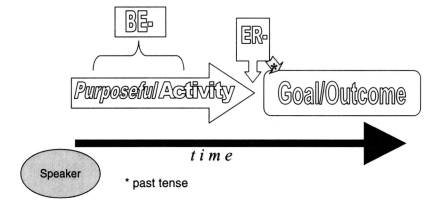

Figure 3 Image schema diagram for *be-* and *er-* prefixes (Sprang, 2003)

personal or public accomplishment: *es ist mir gut ergangen* means "things fared well for me," in the sense of "my goals or wishes were accomplished."

Instructional intervention

The two learners in this case study were chosen from two larger groups of learners studied over the course of one semester (see Sprang, 2003 for details). They were selected based on their similar performances during the first interview, conducted at the beginning of the semester, during which they achieved the same or very similar scores on various measures of vocabulary knowledge. Neither of them exhibited any recognition of the linguistic concepts as part of the prefixed words' core meaningfulness at the start of the semester.

   The treatment for each learner shared a core of exposure (the regular classroom activities plus three concordancer sessions), but differed in the instructions each received prior to the concordancing tasks and in the availability of explicit explanations about the meaningfulness of *be-* and *er-* prefixes. Both Learner A and Learner B participated in an input flood using a computerized concordancer which explicitly focused the learners' attention on words that they had recently encountered in texts read for class. The concordancer activity was based on findings from Hulstijn (1992), in that the learners were asked first to hypothesize a meaning for the word seen in context before they clicked on the word to see a definition of the prefixed word and a definition of the root verb. Over a period of one week, both Learners A and B were exposed to three interventions of 30 minutes each, during each of which they used the concordancer to consider 10 words with the *be-* prefix and 10 words with the *er-* prefix. Thus, over one week and three concordancing activities, the learners focused their attention on 60 prefixed words, 30 in each subclass, which they had encountered in texts read for class. An example of the computerized concordancer screens is provided in Figure 4.

   Prior to the three concordancer activities, only Learner A was provided with a 30-minute explanation of the core meaningfulness of the prefixes, similar to the explanation provided in the previous section. This concept-based instruction focused on prototypical conceptual distinctions, which the learner was required to transfer into semantic distinctions as they are manifested in each prefixed word (Odlin, 2005). During the computerized concordancer intervention, Learner A, who had received the concept-based instruction, was asked the question: "For each word, do you see how the explanation you were given for the meaning of the prefix works in this word?" Thus, Learner A's task was to use the pedagogical explanation to deduce prefixed words' meaningfulness as she encountered them in the input flood as well as in texts read for class over the course of the semester. Learner B, by contrast, received exposure to the computerized input flood without any metalinguistic explanations. She was therefore asked the question: "Does the prefix contribute to the meaning of the prefixed word?" She sought from this to determine the meanings that the prefixes lend to the root verbs. Thus, both interventions were explicit: the former was (concept-based) explicit-deductive, while the latter was (uninstructed) explicit-inductive. This distinction is important because, while we know that explicit mediation is necessary for semantic knowledge to accrue, I am not aware of any effects of instruction study that has examined longitudinally

Partial rendition of screen 1 for Intervention 1:

... , begann er, aber er beendete den Satz nicht. "Unten hat jemand "Jude"...
... Auch der Rabbiner begrüßte Friedrich viel feierlicher als die übrigen...
... niemand hat je seine Wege erforscht." Schloime und Gittel verschleuderten ...
... gestellt. Wir müssen sie erfüllen. Immer sind wir verfolgt worden ...
... mit Friedrich zum Arzt", ergänzte sie und ... fragte: "Ist es Ihnen recht?" ...

Screen 2, after the learner clicked on *ergänzte*:

Context
... "Ich wollte zu Ihnen", sagte Frau Schneider und reichte Frau Penk die Hand. "Ich wollte Sie bitten am Freitag nicht so früh zu kommen; ich muss nämlich mit Friedrich zum Arzt", ergänzte sie und zuletzt fragte sie: "Ist es Ihnen recht, Frau Penk?" ...
"Die Reinemachefrau" (1935), *Damals war es Friedrich*

Screen 3, after the learner had hypothesized a meaning for *ergänzte*:

Bedeutung
... "Ich wollte zu Ihnen", sagte Frau Schneider und reichte Frau Penk die Hand. "Ich wollte Sie bitten am Freitag nicht so früh zu kommen; ich muss nämlich mit Friedrich zum Arzt", ergänzte sie und zuletzt fragte sie: "Ist es Ihnen recht, Frau Penk?" ...
GANZ= ungeteilt, vollkommen ERGÄNZEN= vervollständigen (etwas vollständig/fertig machen)
Zurück zur Liste

Figure 4 Computerized concordancer

the development of systematic vocabulary knowledge via intensive and explicit exposure with instruction versus without instruction. Therefore, the question of which approach to take—enhanced exposure or focused concept-based instruction—is crucial to the ability to create effective pedagogies in support of learners' systematic development of vocabulary with derivational morphology.

Quantitative and qualitative measures

Modified Vocabulary Knowledge Scale test (VKS)

As part of each interview, learners participated in a vocabulary knowledge test to determine their evolving knowledge of prefixed words, and whether an awareness of the prefixes' meaningfulness was aiding them in developing systematic knowledge of vocabulary in those word classes. Students were told that this was not a "test" in the traditional sense of the word, but was an opportunity for them to explore their levels of word knowledge for a group of 30 complex words.

A modified version of the Vocabulary Knowledge Scale (VKS) test (Paribakht and Wesche, 1997) was used to test both productive and receptive word knowledge. I provided the learners with 30 one-page forms, with one word at the top left of each form. An example is provided in Figure 5.

As they progressed through each page, learners read the word aloud to activate

---

WORD
Please read each word aloud before responding to the following prompts. Consider each prompt before moving to the next one.

    A.   I understand* this word. (Please write a sentence to demonstrate your understanding.)

    B.   I associate this word with ideas or other words or parts of words. (Indicate those words or ideas in the space below. Please try to use German; only if your German is unavailable should you switch to English.)

    C.   I can't write any sentences with this word right now, but I understand this word when I see or hear it in context.

    D.   I can't tell you anything about this word.

*Understand = know how the word is used in a context and what it means in that context

---

Figure 5 Modified Vocabulary Knowledge Scale (from Paribakht and Wesche, 1997)

their memory; and they were asked to provide as much information as they could for each word by responding to the prompt(s) A and B, or B and C, or D, for each word. The learners were encouraged to produce a sentence-level context for each word if possible. They were told that there were no points subtracted if the sentence wasn't "native-like." Thus, learners used response prompt A of the self-assessment instrument to demonstrate the ability to produce a sentence with no context available to support their word knowledge. In response prompts B or C, they demonstrated partial knowledge; and they demonstrated their word associations in response prompt B. In an earlier pilot study I had found that requesting both a sentence and a definition for these words at the same time created cognitive dissonance in some learners (see Sprang, 2003, for details), so in response prompt B of the VKS form the learners were only asked for any connections they had with these words. Learners could supply definitions, but they were not required to do so.

Stimulated recall

After the learners completed the modified VKS test, we re-examined each page of the test. The learners could comment on any aspect of their performance, and I asked questions, for example, about what they had meant by certain word associations, or how they had thought of the sentences they produced. I took note of the order in which the elements were filled in by the learners, and I asked them about any interesting test-taking behaviors. Since the interviews were audiotaped, all retrospective comments by the learners were captured and later transcribed. Learners could also take this opportunity to offer any comments on their own performances.

Definition task

Following the modified VKS test and the stimulated recall session, learners were shown paragraph-level contexts for each word; the contexts were taken from texts they had read for class. The task at this point was to define the word, in German if possible, and to comment on the accuracy of the information they had written on the VKS form at the same time. I prompted learners to tell me what cues they used to define the word in its context.

Supplying a context with which the learner was somewhat familiar facilitated the learner's suppliance of existing partial knowledge of the word when seen in context. This allowed learners who had marked response prompt C on the modified VKS test to demonstrate their partial word knowledge upon seeing the prefixed word in context, which simulated the conditions under which the learner would encounter the word while reading. The definition task also allowed me to ascertain whether learners were able to distinguish linguistic concepts as part of word meaning when they were asked to provide a definition for a word in a paragraph-level context.

Transfer task

During the second interview, the modified VKS test included 10 word pairs that shared the same root word and both of the prefixes. This list was presented again to the learners following the word definition task. The transfer task required each learner to consider a root word that uses both the *be-* and the *er-* prefixes, and to explain what the difference is in the meaning of the two prefixed words. To do this in the absence of any context, learners needed to use their understanding of how the prefix impacts word meaning.

During the third interview, after the word definition task, I showed the learners a list of eight common verbs and ensured that they knew the meanings of each of those verbs. I then explained that I had placed the *be-* and *er-* prefixes with each of these root verbs, and that some of these words existed while others did not. The learners' task was not to tell me whether the word really existed or not; rather it was to tell me what the prefixed verb *would* mean *if* it existed. Thus, the transfer task on the third interview required learners to state the meaning of a hypothetical extensional word family where both the *be-* and the *er-* prefixes had been added to the root word, but the learner did not know whether the word was a real word or a pseudo-word. This task required learners to use their knowledge of the meaningfulness of the prefixes to determine a hypothetical meaning for the word. In instances where the learners identified that they knew a word was truly a word and could supply its definition, only portions of the explanation that referred specifically to the meaning of the prefix were considered during scoring of the data.

Scoring learner performances

In order to score the modified VKS test, I adapted the coding protocol developed by Nagy, Herman, and Anderson (1985). The resulting scoring system is provided in Table 1.

Using this protocol, learner performances were coded for the sentence production task and the word definition task for each of the three interview sessions conducted during the semester. These data were analyzed along an ordinal scale, because the individual differences in learners' word knowledge cannot be said to be equivalent from one level on the scale to another.

Table 1 Coding protocol for production task (VKS) and definition task

Scale	Ability to use	Ability to define
0	No sentence written OR completely inappropriate	No ability to define
1	Sentence written displays minimal partial knowledge (at least some real, correct knowledge)	Definition shows minimal partial knowledge (at least some real, correct knowledge)
2	Incomplete appropriateness—displays substantial correct knowledge but missing important component of meaning	Incomplete definition—displays substantial correct knowledge but missing important component of meaning
3	Word used with semantic appropriateness but some form-related problem	Definition conveys a complete understanding of at least one meaning of the word
4	Word used with semantic appropriateness and grammatical accuracy	

Table 2 Coding protocol for transfer task

Scale	Evidence for use of linguistic concept as part of explanation
0	Informant unwilling or unable to hypothesize a meaning for the word OR meaning provided exhibits no evidence that the informant used any portion of the linguistic concept in his or her explanation, e.g., only root word's meaning was considered.
1	Incomplete knowledge: evidence that informant used either temporal, intentional, telic, goal-/outcome-orientation, or abstraction senses of the linguistic concepts; however, more than one of these was needed for a complete explanation of the meaning of the prefixed word.
2	Complete knowledge: evidence that informant used all of the meanings of the linguistic concepts present in that word to explain the meaning of the prefixed word.

The learners' performances for each word tested on the transfer tasks were also coded using the three-point ordinal scale shown in Table 2.

Since the number of items tested on the transfer test varied from the second interview to the third interview, the numbers were converted to percentages for comparability from one test to the next. The transcriptions of the interviews were also coded for any appearance of a linguistic concept during the definition task, and the number of times a linguistic concept was used to help define the word was tallied for each concept.

Findings

Recognizing linguistic concepts

The first question is whether the learners could recognize in the prefixed words the linguistic concepts of durativity, goal-/outcome-orientation, intentionality, telicity,

Table 3 Demonstrations of ability to perceive linguistic concepts as part of prefixed word meaning

Linguistic concepts	Learner A			Learner B		
Week	2	5	12	2	5	12
Durativity	0	5	9	0	0	0
Goal-/outcome-orientation	0	3	8	0	0	0
Intentionality	0	2	7	0	0	0
Telicity	0	4	6	0	0	0
Abstraction	0	0	1	0	0	2

and the shift from concrete to abstract that the prefixes convey. The number of times a linguistic concept was used by each learner during the definition task to help define the word is shown in Table 3.

Over the course of the semester, Learner A demonstrated an increasing awareness of the presence of the linguistic concepts as part of the meaning of prefixed words. Whereas at the start of the semester she showed no awareness at all, on the second interview she provided multiple examples of the concepts as part of the prefixed words' meanings. And during the third interview, she reported that she was able to use the linguistic concepts to help her comprehend words in context. An example is provided in Excerpt 1.

Learner A's reporting of the meaningfulness of *er-* was incomplete, and she appeared not to remember the potential for shift from concrete to abstract meaningfulness; but she clearly recalled and used the "purposeful orientation to a goal or outcome over time" meaningfulness during the second interview; and she demonstrated continued ability and willingness to use the prefixes' meaningfulness to help her develop a richer understanding of the prefixed words than the context alone could provide

Excerpt 1 Learner A's increasing awareness of the presence of linguistic concepts in the prefixed words' meanings

Second interview, during definition task	*[besehen] Vielleicht sehen ist sehr kurz, ich sehe das aber ich denke nicht davon, aber mit besehen ist, oh ich sehe und etwas damit ist wichtig oder ich denke an das.*	[besehen, be- see- to observe] Perhaps *sehen* [to see] is for a very short time, I see it but I don't think about it, but with *besehen* it is, oh I see and something about it is important or I think about it.
Third interview, stimulated recall after definition task	I	You just looked at contexts with these pairs: *befolgen/erfolgen, bedenken/erdenken*, etc. When you see these in context, when you were just reading the cards, how do you understand these words?
	A	From the root word. And then knowing just that the *er-* prefix makes something deeper or more intensive or yeah. And *be-* is a goal and one is working towards the goal. And just the root word and knowing that meaning comes mostly from the root word but that it's changed a little bit.

Continued

Excerpt 1 Continued

I   So you use your word knowledge?
A   Mm hmm . . . I use the context too . . . I use the context, but I use the context more to understand the whole thing, I use the context, but also then in conjunction with my root word knowledge . . . If I was always using the context, I wouldn't even make a connection.
I   And does the prefix play a role?
A   Yeah, because I make that connection.

A = Learner A, I = Interviewer

Excerpt 2 Learner B's lack of awareness of the presence of linguistic concepts in the prefixed words' meanings

Speaker	Transcription	Translation of transcript
B	Beschlossen ist nicht offen. Ja. Und das kann nicht nur wirklich meinen, aber hier [pointing to her sentence, produced as part of VKS test] ist das uhm ja, es ist nicht Ideen oder, ja.	*Beschlossen* is "not open." Yeah. And that can mean not only concrete, but here it is [pointing to her sentence, produced as part of VKS test] uhm, yeah, it is not ideas or, yeah.
I	Ja, also hier in Ihrem Satz ist es konkret?	So here in your sentence it is concrete?
B	Ja.	Yes.
I	Und hier ist es abstrakt [pointing to the context pasted on the 5 × 7 card]?	And here it is abstract [pointing to the context pasted on the 5 × 7 card]?
B	Ja.	Yes.
I	Aber beschlossen hat die gleiche Bedeutung, nicht offen?	But *beschlossen* has the same meaning, "not open"?
B	Ja!	Yes!

B = Learner B, I = Interviewer

her, with increasing confidence in the usefulness and reliability of this prototypical meaningfulness over time. This growth in awareness can also be seen through Learner A's noticeably higher scores on the transfer tasks between the second and third interviews, as will be discussed in the next section (cf. Table 4).

In contrast to Learner A, by the end of the study Learner B had yet to develop a sensitivity to the presence of linguistic concepts as part of the prefixed words' meanings. This was despite her having experienced intensive exposure to many prefixed words over the semester. During the third interview, she provided evidence that she recognized a shift from a concrete meaningfulness to an abstract sense for two words. An example is provided in Excerpt 2.

However, Learner B did not provide any evidence that she used this reported meaningfulness to help her decipher the meanings of the words. During the third interview, when I asked her whether the prefixes helped her understand the words in context, she provided the following interlanguage hypothesis for the difference between words with be- and er-: "Er- is used more with objects and the be- prefix is more with people, but I don't know." She reported that she had a general sense of the meanings of the words, which aided comprehension, but this sense did not support productive abilities.

Prefix and prefixed word knowledge

The second question of interest in the present study is the extent to which learners' systematic knowledge of the prefixed words grew over the semester. The scores obtained on the three administrations of the modified VKS are shown in Table 4.

Measurements of partial vocabulary knowledge did not yield large differences in scores between Learners A and B, because both learners could quite often display partial word knowledge even if they relied solely on the meaning of the root verb to explain the meaning of the prefixed verb. For example, let us consider the verb *beschliessen*: there is a large difference between *schliessen*, "to close," and *beschliessen*, "to decide or conclude after deliberation." However, Learner B's explanation of the definition of *beschlossen* (past tense of *beschliessen*), provided in Excerpt 2, displayed partial word knowledge. The translations of the two words are not in any way similar; yet in English we use the metaphorical collocation "to keep an open mind"; and presumably, once one decides, one closes one's mind to alternatives. So Learner B's explanation that *beschlossen* is an abstract sense of "not open" was scored as a 1 (see Table 1). A complete understanding of the meaning of the word is not conveyed, but real partial knowledge is identifiable.

I would like to conclude the presentation of findings with a more qualitative analysis of the two learners' evolving knowledge of the meaningfulness of the *be-* and *er-* prefixes, as manifested through the stimulated recall data.

Learner B: Inductive exposure to prefixed words

Learner B reported during the third interview that, due to working with me over the course of the semester, she gave more sustained attention to the prefixed words when she encountered them in texts read for class. However, during the 14 weeks of this study, Learner B maintained the same strategies for recalling vocabulary, as evidenced in her test-taking behaviors and through stimulated recall and introspective

Table 4 Performance on tests of vocabulary knowledge and prefix knowledge

Measures of word knowledge	Learner A			Learner B		
Week	2	5	12	2	5	12
VKS test: *be-* words	7	13	15	7	7	10
VKS test: *er-* words	13	11	15	13	4	11
Definition task: *be-* words	15	14	19	13	10	18
Definition task: *er-* words	22	19	32	17	14	21
Transfer test: *be-* words		20	81.25		0	6.25
Transfer test: *er-* words		15	68.75		0	6.25

Note
Transfer test scores are percentages.

comments during the interviews. She reported that she relied on context to comprehend the vast majority of prefixed words encountered while reading, and that she knew only a few of the prefixed words well enough to use them for production with any degree of comfort.

On the VKS tests, she routinely activated her vocabulary knowledge by using the "connections" area as a brainstorming space: "I did B first so when I got to A I knew what I was talking about." She regularly wrote definitions in this area of the form, although I reminded her that she wasn't required to do so. Several times she recalled looking up a word in a dictionary while she was reading it for class or for subsequent in-class tasks, and she sought to recall those definitions, reporting that the definitions were helpful to her in her attempts to produce sentences with the words. She remembered several sentences as chunks or formulas, and could state exactly what experience she was recalling to activate her memory of the word in question, e.g., "The teacher said that," "I remember this from the computer activity," and "I used that phrase in my presentation."

On the definition task, she continued to rely heavily on context to help her determine the meaning of the prefixed words. Her knowledge of root verbs' meanings or functions continued to support her comprehension of the prefixed words throughout the semester, and she continued to rely on the root verb's meaning to provide definitions for the prefixed words, even if indirectly. For example, she provided the following general definition for *Bestimmung* ("legal provision, ruling," among others):

> *es ist man wählt und sie sagen, sie wollen das oder, ja*. I don't know how to explain it . . .

> . . . it means they vote and they say they want that or, yeah. I don't know how to explain it.

This example is of interest because of the inductive abilities Learner B displayed through this definition. Through class activities, she was well aware of the semi-fixed expression *ich stimme damit überein* to express agreement with someone's opinion. She almost certainly utilized the root verb of the separable prefixed verb *übereinstimmen* to induce a meaning for *Bestimmung* when she stated "they say they want that."

As for developing an understanding of the prefixes' meaningfulness, Learner B reported making no headway at all. At the beginning of the second test, which occurred one week after the computerized intervention, she reported that the concordancer activity was not very useful:

> The only problem was, I think I can figure out the connection [between the root word and the prefix] and then I get to a different word and I have no idea what the difference with the prefix is, so.

At the end of the second interview, during the transfer task, when I showed her the 10 word pairs and asked how she was able to differentiate them, she reported the following:

> In a couple of instances, the *be-* like *beachten* or *bedenken* is like a different way of saying *denken an etwas* or *achten auf*, but it [the prefix] doesn't really help . . . I really have no idea

of that [the *er-* prefix] ... really, it doesn't really help me to figure out what the word means to have a prefix there.

During the third interview, on the transfer test, she rejected a number of words as possibly having prefixes, stating that some of the root verbs can't have objects so they don't take the prefixes. Because the prefixed words convey purposeful activity toward a goal, the verbs often require that the trajectory, the path, or the goal be named. Pedagogical grammars tend to explain this requirement as a syntactic requirement, that the prefixed words require a direct object. Since Learner B specifically mentioned this "rule" as part of her decision-making process about words during the transfer task in the third interview, she may well have sought an explanation outside of the context of the study. I did not query her explanation, so it is uncertain whether this is the case; but if so, the explanation did not aid her in her attempt to explain the contribution of the prefixes to the meanings of the prefixed words.

During the second transfer task, Learner B mentioned a notion of activity involving an idea twice, which earned her some points on the transfer test, since this may have indicated some implicit knowledge of the metaphorical shift from perception to conception that both prefixes can convey. But Learner B did not develop a sense of the prefixes' contribution to prefixed word meaningfulness that she could use in comprehension or production. She did not develop a systematic sense of a shift in meaningfulness, and she continued to over-rely on the root verb's meaning to achieve partial comprehension of the prefixed words in context.

Learner A: Deductive exposure to prefixed words

In the week following the computerized intervention, Learner A had reported in her second interview with me that she had found the concordancer activity helpful but also frustrating. Excerpt 3 illustrates this.

Excerpt 3 Learner A's perceptions of the concordancer activity

A	The general idea is helpful, but I'm not at that point yet of getting exactly, some examples are good, but because I still don't get it enough
I	What do you not get?
A	Exactly how it works
I	How what works?
A	How it changes the meaning
I	The prefixes?
A	Yeah. I mean, I understand the idea, but it doesn't do the same thing in every single word
I	Right
A	So that's more frustrating because it's not enabling me to use it yet, because I don't know what the differences are or what the differences in how it changes each time.
I	What do you think the general idea is?
A	For which prefix? *Continued*

Excerpt 3 Continued

I	Both
A	Well, it's the process idea, and focus on the goal. But I understand that, and when I'm looking at it, I can say, oh I see the difference, but I could definitely not use it in my own vocabulary. And even when I understand it, yeah, I'm getting the general idea, but I'm often thinking a completely different concept than the definition [translation].

A = Learner A, I = Interviewer

During the third interview, however, Learner A reported that she had continued to use the explanation for the prototypical meaningfulness of the prefixes when she read for class, and that she had developed a level of comfort for the prototypical meaningfulness of the prefixes for each word encountered:

> When I see a word I specifically try to think about how I'm getting the same meaning out of it. I guess I see *erwarten* [er- = focus on an anticipated outcome or accomplishment + *warten*, to wait = to expect], I think about why it means to wait. Why, knowing what I do about the prefix, it means to wait. No, it means to expect, so wait for something specifically.

By the third interview, then, Learner A was able to adopt portions of the prototypical meaningfulness of the prefixes that she was taught in the 30-minute instructional session prior to her work with the concordancer activity. Indeed, on the modified VKS tests that she took as part of the second and third interviews, she provided many examples of recognizing the interdependence of the prefix and the root verb for the prefixed words' meaningfulness. A few of them are provided in Excerpt 4.

Learner A's explanations in Excerpt 4 were provided during all phases of the second and third interviews. Although she did not have a complete understanding of the meaningfulness of the prefixes—she did not remember to ascribe a shift from concrete to abstract as part of the verb's meaningfulness—she developed a strong interlanguage hypothesis that she was able to use with or without a context to help her understand and use the prefixed verbs. She recognized the durative, goal-/outcome-oriented, purposeful activity elements of the prefixed verbs again and again during the second and third interviews. She accepted the richness of the prefixed verbs' meaningfulness, as the complexity of her explanations in Excerpt 4 shows. And she rejected the idea that the root verb and the prefixed verb could be synonyms, which had been her basic assumption during the first interview at the start of the semester.

All in all, Learner A had come a long way in one semester towards recognizing and understanding the increased meaning density that a text containing prefixed verbs conveys. This is a major step towards developing advanced capacities in the foreign language, and it was attained through relatively brief instruction combined with sustained exposure over the course of the semester to the prefixed words during course-related activities, such as thematically organized extensive reading followed by text-mining activities and structured text reconstruction tasks.

Excerpt 4 Learner A's recognition of the role of the prefix on the modified VKS tests

Interview	Transcription: Learner A	Translation of transcript
Second interview, during stimulated recall after VKS test	*[bedenken] Ich weiß jetzt, was be- bedeutet, und ich kann mit denken ein bißchen zusammensetzen, und dann verstehe ich, es ist tiefer als denken. Man muß etwas tiefer denken. Nicht nur erinnern oder sehr kurz denken an etwas.*	[*bedenken, be-* think – to ponder] I know now what *be-* means, and I can put it together with *denken* [to think], and then I understand that it is deeper than "to think". One must think somewhat more deeply. Not just remember or think for a very short time about something.
Third interview, during stimulated recall after VKS test	I think *ergreifen*, you grab something and then you hold it.	I think *ergreifen* [*er-* grasp – to seize and hold onto], you grab something and then you hold it.
Third interview, during definition task	*Erweitern* is to further, but to achieve something. To further it to make it better . . .	*Erweitern* [*er- weiter* + verb (n) – to expand, enhance, broaden] is to further, but to achieve something. To further it to make it better. . . .
	Erfolgen ist das Ende von was folgt, nicht die Konsequenzen, aber der Resultat.	*Erfolgen* [*er-* follow after in a sequence – to take place, to happen (in the sense of "and so it happened that . . .")] is the end of what follows, not the consequences but the result.
	Erstrebt . . . wie für etwas kämpfen, sehr schwer aber nicht nur kämpfen, sehr schwer und lang und man muß immer für das arbeiten.	*Erstrebt* [*er-* strive – to accomplish through great effort] . . . is like to fight for something, really hard but not just to fight, to fight very hard and long and one must always work towards that.

Discussion

Acquisition of the inseparable German prefixes has long been held to be a difficult hurdle, both for teachers and for learners. Finding a systematically adequate explanation that accounted for the many variations at the word level has been an elusive task. This study has shown, based on Learner A's performance, that a pedagogical explanation utilizing the framework of Cognitive Grammar (Langacker, 1991, 2006) enables learners to recognize the prefixes' meanings and functions, which are motivated by earlier, more concrete meanings that have shifted through metaphorical and metonymic processes of diachronic semantic change. Through appropriate instruction, these meanings are comprehensible and, although perhaps differing from L1 conceptualization patterns, are applicable to the challenging endeavor of acquiring prefixed words.

Zareva, Schwanenflugel, and Nikolova (2005) argue that one should expect the quality of L2 lexical networks to differ from those of native speakers. They argue that this is based on different experiences and, though different, is equally valid to the word association patterns displayed by native speakers of a language. Following this logic, the fact that L2 conceptualization patterns may take a different form than those of L1 users may in fact contribute to the proficient L2 users' sophisticated "insightfulness regarding human knowing through language" that Byrnes (2006) describes. Interestingly, the performances of the learners in this study followed the same trajectory outlined by Melka (1997) for L1 vocabulary acquisition—initially learners were only comfortable using the word if they could recall the context in which the word had been learned, i.e., imitated or mimetic use; only gradually did the learners delink the word from the original context, with eventual use in new contexts.

Both Whorf and Ellis proposed that consciousness-raising activities are needed to raise learners' awareness of nonsalient forms in the foreign language. The most efficacious form that this consciousness-raising should take varies, depending on the feature under consideration. In this study, both learners participated in consciousness-raising activities through the repeated concordancer activity; but that activity does not appear to have been sufficient to develop an understanding of the contribution of the prefixes. Indeed, both learners reported finding it unsettling to discover through the concordancer activity that the meaningfulness of the prefixes shifted from one word to the next. Thus, in this instance, the concordancer activity increased the salience of the prefixes, but it did not reveal the "significant communicative value" (Ellis, 2005, p. 322) that the prefixes convey.

Perhaps because of the shifting meaningfulness of the prefix from word to word, Learner B was unable to develop a systematic understanding of the contribution of the prefixes to the root words' meanings. Exposure alone, albeit enhanced exposure, did not bring about a change in Learner B's understanding of the contribution of the prefixes to the prefixed words over the course of a semester. By contrast, brief, concept-based instruction preceding the concordancer activity allowed Learner A to recognize and adopt a systematic explanation for the meaning shift that occurred across the prefixed words. The instruction did not provide an immediate recognition and validation of the prefixes' contribution, however, because Learner A was required to transfer the prototypical conceptual meaning shift into a semantic distinction for each word as she encountered it in context. In the second interview she expressed some distress over this additional cognitive effort; but seven weeks later she had become comfortable with the task of considering each word, in its context, and figuring out how the conceptual pattern fitted the individual word. She was required to use Sternberg's (1987) processes for each word encountered, if she wanted to understand its meaning more fully: she had to use *selective encoding* and *selective combination* to recognize which elements of the prototypical meaningfulness of the prefixes were involved for the word's meaning, and she certainly used *selective comparison* to recognize the contribution of *be-* and *er-* during the transfer tasks, although it is uncertain whether she made this additional effort during reading for class, based on her own reports.

For Learner A, the additional cognitive effort was rewarded with enhanced, emergent systematic vocabulary knowledge for words with *be-* and *er-* prefixes. By contrast, Learner B did not recognize a pattern to the additional meaningfulness conveyed by the prefixes, and therefore had no basis on which to compare the contribution of the prefixes from one word to the next. Thus, as Whorf hypothesized, an adequate explanation for a grammaticized meaning shift was needed for the learners to escape the "binding power" of their L1's way of thinking for speaking; and only Learner A was able to do this with any degree of success. This contributed to a more developed sense of the individual words' meaningfulness, but also to a shift in the systematic understanding of how the prefixes contribute a sense of intentional, goal-oriented activity or accomplishment of a goal or expected outcome; or a metaphorical shift from concrete to abstract activity; or, in many cases, both. Had there been the opportunity to continue this research project, it would have been valuable to discover whether this emergent knowledge allowed Learner A to begin to use the prefixed words in activities outside of the interview setting, and possibly with an enhanced understanding of their nuanced meaningfulness. It is only through such documentation that we can hope to understand with any degree of sophistication the complexities of advanced L2 capacities.

Let us recall Jiang's (2004) claim that even advanced learners mediate their L2 comprehension of words through their L1 concepts. Although translation into L1 was not required by either learner to achieve general comprehension of the prefixed words in context, both learners resorted to translation to define the words; and in the case of the meaning density of the prefixed words, this strategy could not aid them to recognize the patterned conceptual meaningfulness that the prefix conveys. English translations of the prefixed words are often very different than the translations of the root words, e.g., *warten/erwarten* = "wait/expect" and *schliessen/beschliessen* = "close/decide." Thus, patterned meaning shifts between the root words and the prefixed words are virtually impossible to recognize through translation. As Jiang proposed, combining explicit instruction with contextualized exemplars is far more effective for grasping the systematicity that the prefixes' meaningfulness conveys to the vast numbers of prefixed words. Learning these words through translation can never lead to a systematic understanding of the contribution of the prefixes. But the proper form of instruction must be applied—in this case, concept-based instruction was necessary for a systematic understanding to emerge, because at the semantic level the meaningfulness of the prefixes changes from one word to the next.

Limitations and conclusion

A study of longer duration with more differentiated forms of data would be required to discover whether this emergent knowledge progressed to systematic productive knowledge of prefixed words. The duration of this study was sufficient only to show some movement towards understanding the meaningfulness of the prefixed verbs, and only for one of the two learners studied. It also indicated that instruction may be needed for this feature to be learnable, based on Learner B's performance across the span of the semester. Though she expended considerable effort and expressed a sincere desire to understand the contribution of the prefixes, Learner B was unable to recognize their systematic meaningfulness without a pedagogically appropriate explanation.

The design of the study precludes its generalizability to other populations of learners; however, this finding provides a first step in a larger research agenda that seeks to determine whether appropriate instruction can facilitate advanced learners' development of levels of L2 ultimate attainment superior to those which have been found for learners through naturalistic exposure. In this paradigm, the study of vocabulary development breaks the boundaries of individual word accrual. Indeed, understanding how the advanced learner develops a deep, broad L2 mental lexicon over time, including the contribution of derivational morphology to the L2 lexical network, is a critical facet in our understanding of the longitudinal development of advanced L2 capacities.

Note

The views expressed in this chapter are those of the author and do not necessarily represent the views of the Department of State.

References

Altman, R. (1997). Oral production of vocabulary: A case study. In J. Coady and T. Huckin (Eds.), *Second language vocabulary acquisition* (pp. 69–97). New York: Cambridge University Press.

Byrnes, H. (2006). Locating the advanced learner in theory, research, and educational practice: An introduction. In H. Byrnes, H. Weger-Guntharp, and K. A. Sprang (Eds.), *Educating for advanced foreign language capacities: Constructs, curriculum, instruction, assessment* (pp. 1–14). Washington, DC: Georgetown University Press.

Carroll, M. (2000). Representing path in language production in English and German: Alternate perspectives on figure and ground. In C. Habel and C. von Stutterheim (Eds.), *Räumliche Konzepte und sprachliche Strukturen [Spatial concepts and linguistic structures]* (pp. 97–118). Tübingen: Niemeyer.

Carroll, M., and von Stutterheim, C. (2003). Typology and information organisation: Perspective taking and language-specific effects in the construal of events. In A. Ramat (Ed.), *The structure of learner language* (pp. 365–402). Berlin: Walter de Gruyter.

Developing multiple literacies: A curriculum renewal project of the German department at Georgetown University, 1997–2000 (n.d.). http://www1.georgetown.edu/departments/german/programs/undergraduate/curriculum/curriculumoverview/

Ellis, N. (1997). Vocabulary acquisition: Word structure, collocation, word class, and meaning. In N. Schmitt and M. McCarthy (Eds.), *Vocabulary: Description, acquisition and pedagogy* (pp. 122–139). New York: Cambridge University Press.

Ellis, N. (2005). At the interface: Dynamic interactions of explicit and implicit language knowledge. *Studies in Second Language Acquisition, 27*, 305–352.

Faerch, C., and Kasper, G. (1986). The role of comprehension in second language learning. *Applied Linguistics, 7*, 257–274.

Fauconnier, G. (1997). *Mappings in thought and language.* New York: Cambridge University Press.

Grabe, W., and Stoller, F. L. (1997). Reading and vocabulary development in a second language: A case study. In J. Coady and T. Huckin (Eds.), *Second language vocabulary acquisition* (pp. 98–122). New York: Cambridge University Press.

Henriksen, B. (1999). Three dimensions of vocabulary development. *Studies in Second Language Acquisition, 21*, 303–317.

Hulstijn, J. (1992). Retention of inferred and given word meanings: Experiments in incidental vocabulary learning. In P. J. Arnaud and H. Bejoint (Eds.), *Vocabulary and applied linguistics* (pp. 113–125). London: Macmillan.

Jiang, N. (2004). Semantic transfer and its implications for vocabulary teaching in a second language. *Modern Language Journal, 88*, 416–432.

Johns, T. (2000). Data-driven learning: The perceptual challenge. In B. Kettemann and G. Marko (Eds.), *Teaching and learning by doing corpus analysis: Proceedings of the Fourth International Conference on Teaching and Language Corpora* (pp. 107–118). New York: Rodopi.

Johnson, M. (1987). *The body in the mind: The bodily basis of meaning, imagination and reason.* Chicago, IL: University of Chicago Press.

Lakoff, G. (1993). The contemporary theory of metaphor. In A. Ortony (Ed.), *Metaphor and thought* (pp. 202–251). New York: Cambridge University Press.

Langacker, R. W. (1991). *Concept, image and symbol: The cognitive basis of grammar*. Berlin: Mouton de Gruyter.

Langacker, R. W. (2006). The conceptual basis of grammatical structure. In H. Byrnes, H. Weger-Guntharp, and K. A. Sprang (Eds.), *Educating for advanced foreign language capacities: Constructs, curriculum, instruction, assessment* (pp. 17–39). Washington, DC: Georgetown University Press.

Laufer, B. (1997). The lexical plight in reading: Words you don't know, words you think you know, and words you can't guess. In J. Coady and T. Huckin (Eds.), *Second language vocabulary acquisition* (pp. 20–34). New York: Cambridge University Press.

Melka, F. (1997). Receptive vs. productive aspects of vocabulary. In N. Schmitt and M. McCarthy (Eds.), *Vocabulary: Description, acquisition, pedagogy* (pp. 84–102). New York: Cambridge University Press.

Nagy, W. E., Herman, P. A., and Anderson, R. C. (1985). Learning words from context. *Reading Research Quarterly, 20*, 233–253.

Nation, I. S. P. (1990). *Teaching and learning vocabulary*. New York: Newbury House.

Nation, I. S. P. (1999). *Learning vocabulary in another language*. Victoria University of Wellington: English Language Institute Occasional Publication no. 19.

Odlin, T. (2005). Crosslinguistic influence and conceptual transfer: What are the concepts? *Annual Review of Applied Linguistics, 25*, 3–25.

Paribakht, T. S., and Wesche, M. (1997). Vocabulary enhancement activities and reading for meaning in second language vocabulary acquisition. In J. Coady and T. Huckin (Eds.), *Second language vocabulary acquisition* (pp. 174–200). New York: Cambridge University Press.

Paribakht, T. S., and Wesche, M. (2006). Lexical inferencing in L1 and L2: Implications for vocabulary instruction and learning at advanced levels. In H. Byrnes, H. Weger-Guntharp, and K. A. Sprang (Eds.), *Educating for advanced foreign language capacities: Constructs, curriculum, instruction, assessment* (pp. 118–135). Washington, DC: Georgetown University Press.

Parry, K. (1997). Vocabulary and comprehension: Two portraits. In J. Coady and T. Huckin (Eds.), *Second language vocabulary acquisition* (pp. 55–68). New York: Cambridge University Press.

Schmitt, N. (1998). Tracking the incremental acquisition of second language vocabulary: A longitudinal study. *Language Learning, 48*, 281–317.

Schmitt, N., and Meara, P. (1997). Researching vocabulary through a word knowledge framework: Word associations and verbal suffixes. *Studies in Second Language Acquisition, 19*, 17–36.

Slobin, D. I. (1996). From "thought and language" to "thinking for speaking". In J. Gumperz and S. Levinson (Eds.), *Rethinking linguistic relativity* (pp. 70–96). New York: Cambridge University Press.

Slobin, D. I. (1998). Verbalized events: A dynamic approach to linguistic relativity and determinism. Unpublished manuscript.

Spada, N. (2005). Conditions and challenges in developing school-based SLA research programs. *Modern Language Journal, 89*, 328–338.

Sprang, K. A. (2003). Vocabulary acquisition and advanced learners: The role of grammaticization and conceptual organization in the acquisition of German verbs with inseparable prefixes. Unpublished doctoral dissertation, Georgetown University.

Sternberg, R. (1987). Most vocabulary is learned from context. In M. McKeown and M. Curtis (Eds.), *The nature of vocabulary acquisition* (pp. 89–105). Hillsdale, NJ: Lawrence Erlbaum.

Talmy, L. (1986). *The relation of grammar to cognition*. Berkeley, CA: University of California Press.

Talmy, L. (1991). Path to realization: A typology of event conflation. *Proceedings of the*

17th Annual Meeting of the Berkeley Linguistics Society (pp. 480–519). Berkeley: University of California at Berkeley.

Taylor, J. R. (1993). Some pedagogical implications of cognitive linguistics. In R. Geiger and B. Rudzka-Ostyn (Eds.), *Conceptualizations and mental processing in language* (pp. 201–223). Berlin: Mouton de Gruyter.

von Stutterheim, C., and Carroll, M. (2006). The impact of grammatical temporal categories on ultimate attainment in L2 learning. In H. Byrnes, H. Weger-Guntharp, and K. A. Sprang (Eds.), *Educating for advanced foreign language capacities: Constructs, curriculum, instruction, assessment* (pp. 40–53). Washington, DC: Georgetown University Press.

Whorf, B. L. (1940/1956). *Language, thought, and reality*, Ed. J. Carroll. Cambridge, MA: MIT Press.

Zareva, A., Schwanenflugel, P., and Nikolova, Y. (2005). Lexical competence and language proficiency. *Studies in Second Language Acquisition, 27*, 567–595.

9 Teaching grammatical meaning to advanced learners

A cognitive-semantic perspective

Olga Liamkina

Abstract

Recent second language acquisition research has found that explicit instruction utilizing adult cognitive capacities is conducive to acquisition (Norris and Ortega, 2000). However, existing explicit L2 instructional models target primarily beginning and intermediate levels, often teach discrete-point morphosyntactic rules, and do not consider long-term effects of instruction. This chapter begins to address these issues by reporting on a semester-long pedagogical treatment designed to help advanced college-level learners acquire the conceptual system of the German Dative case. Case usage is a highly problematic area for learners due to its semantical polysemy, contextually determined distribution patterns, perceptual non-saliency of case markings, and possibility of using alternative—albeit often inappropriate— means consistent with L1 grammatical patterns. Cognitive Linguistics theory (Langacker, 1999) served as the framework for metalinguistic, semantic explanations provided to students, which highlighted four major meanings of the clausal Dative. This core information was presented to students over the course of two weeks and was intended to function as advanced organizers that would facilitate subsequent noticing of the Dative in instructional materials and its appropriate usage in learner production. Additional text-based learning tasks were implemented throughout the semester to further refine learner understanding of case semantics and strengthen the form–meaning connections established initially. Thus, the study documents the acquisition of Dative's meanings over the course of a semester through the analysis of students' written work and traces the development of their declarative knowledge about Dative's semantics and functions through interviews and stimulated recall procedures.

Introduction

As a grammatical category that is absent in English, the German Dative case would seem to pose obvious acquisitional challenges for English-speaking learners of German. Indeed, even quite advanced learners do not employ the full range of Dative case uses as they strive to achieve precision of expression and nuanced meanings. This is true although they normally encounter the Dative in the first year of formal instruction and although they are quite able to recite the formal markers of the case. In other words, the Dative is clearly an acquisitional phenomenon whose developmental trajectory evolves over long periods of time and, therefore, can be captured most adequately longitudinally. However, not only are longitudinal studies in second language (L2) learning a rarity (see Ortega and Iberri-Shea, 2005), but advanced instructed L2 learners are almost completely absent in such research.

That fact motivates the goal of this chapter: to lay the groundwork for describing how advanced learners who received semantically oriented instruction over the course of a semester evolved in their ability to expand the range of uses for the Dative and how those uses, by and large, became more native-like in functionality and accuracy. Extending over the typical one-semester period of college courses, the study might be categorized as an instructional intervention study. However, my intention is not so much to relate "successful acquisition" of formal features in a certain domain, here the Dative, on the basis of a carefully controlled intervention that has little connection to ongoing instruction; instead, I want to provide an extended look at the complexity of acquiring capacities for use of such a fundamental and simultaneously semantically rich category as the German Dative case. I claim that this complexity can only be captured by longitudinal study, which also entails the following: first, both researchers and teachers require functionally oriented descriptions of language use in order to be able to trace long-term development; second, those descriptions must be translated into meaning-based pedagogies in order to give learners an optimal environment for growth of their meaning-making capacities (in a Systemic Functional sense; see Achugar and Colombi, Chapter 3, this volume); and, third, both research and teaching/learning activities should take place within explicitly stated, extended curricular contexts in order to gain the benefits of a coherent instructional proposal. The profession can then begin to describe adult instructed learning in a fashion that can result in substantive theoretical and practice-oriented statements about how to enhance it.

Exploring the developmental challenges of the German dative case: A cognitive-semantic view

As already indicated, the acquisitional problem that advanced learners of German face with the Dative is not form-based. If that is so, then a first challenge for the longitudinal study of the Dative is to explore its semantic properties in order to be able to trace learners' development. Four interrelated sets of issues highlight the phenomenon: cross-linguistic, processing, semantic, and discourse-oriented.

First, cross-linguistic investigation shows the difference between English and German to be less in what grammatical means are available for expressing similar meanings and more in the patterns that are preferred. While English expresses semantic relationships between clause participants through lexical means, such as prepositions or possessive pronouns, in German the same relationships are preferentially grammaticalized into the Dative case markings of definite and indefinite articles, possessive and demonstrative pronouns, or adjective endings (if unpreceded by an article). This is shown in (1):

(1)   *Quickly, I described the suspect **to the police officer**.*
      *Schnell habe ich **dem Polizisten** den Verdächtigen beschrieben.*
      Quickly have I **the police officer** [DAT] the suspect described.

By contrast, learners tend to rely on prepositional constructions, in a kind of transfer from the native into the target language, as in (2):

(2) *Schnell habe ich den Verdächtigen **zu dem Polizisten** beschrieben.*
     Quickly have I the suspect **to the police officer** described.

Because such formulations are partially acceptable and, in any case, semantically transparent to the interlocutors, learners rarely receive negative feedback regarding appropriateness of their linguistic choices and, therefore, have no need or possibility to reformulate their hypotheses of case usage (cf. Carroll *et al.*, 2000; Long and Robinson, 1998).

Second, because case in the clausal realm is unmarked and perceptually less salient, it is most likely hard for learners to notice in the input and control in production (VanPatten, 1990). In and of itself, the overwhelming frequency with which Dative clausal constructions appear in both written and oral input seems to have very little corrective influence. In the case of developing the ability to express temporality, functionally oriented studies (Bardovi-Harlig, 1992; Dietrich, Klein, and Noyau, 1995; Klein and Perdue, 1992) have posited three interlanguage stages: pragmatic, lexical, and morphological (cf. Givón, 1979). This sequence implies that lexical resources are more easily acquired than morphology. Applying this insight to case, one might say that, on account of their predominant use of prepositional constructions, advanced learners are at the lexical stage, with little ability to move forward to the morphological stage on their own.

Third, as a polyfunctional case, the Dative codes a host of seemingly disparate participant roles, from denoting someone receiving something to someone from whom something is taken away. As a result of traditional instruction, learners acquire only Dative's most prototypical concrete meanings of Recipient or Beneficiary and can apply them to a limited range of contexts. However, they seem unable to see conceptual connections between the variety of the Dative's meanings, which are situated on a continuum from concrete to abstract and have various scopes of application, and to link them to a single grammatical form.

Finally, beyond clause-level functionalities for the Dative case, learners encounter another set of challenges at the discourse level: in line with Halliday's (1982) observation, case is also a supra-sentential phenomenon that contributes to expressing given–new movement and creates textual organization and textual coherence. Thus, while Germans prefer to use clausal Dative constructions, as shown in (3) below, they choose prepositional phrases to mark the Dative participant as particularly prominent, as new in the information flow, or to indicate even finer gradience for the information status of clause participants, as shown in (4):

(3) *Zum Geburtstag habe ich **meiner Mutter** Blumen gekauft.*
     for birthday have I **my mother** [DAT] flowers bought
     I bought flowers for my mother's birthday.
(4) *Zum Geburtstag habe ich **fü meine Mutter** Blumen gekauft.*
     for birthday have I **for my mother** flowers bought

Thus, in (3) the new information is *Blumen*, and *Mutter* must be recoverable from the previous discourse, but it shares listener's attention with *Blumen*. By contrast, in (4) *Blumen* is still new information, but it is implicitly contrasted with something else that could have been bought; the prepositional phrase *für meine Mutter* indicates the non-intimateness of the purchasing of the flowers, so that listener's attention is not taken away from *Blumen*.

Cognitive factors may also lead to a choice of either a clausal or a prepositional construction. Smith (1987) argues that "despite similarity in meaning, the two constructions differ with respect to the conceived degree of independent potential for action or thought on the part of the [Dative participant]" (p. 407). In other words, speakers actively choose a construal that best reflects the situation, as shown in (5):

(5)   a. *Das Wasser ist **dem Baby** [DAT] zu warm.*
      b. *Das Wasser ist **fü das Baby** zu warm.*
      The water is too warm for the baby.

In (5a), the baby has to be in the water and it is projected to experience the water as too warm; in (5b), the baby may or may not be in the water, but its experience is not foregrounded; the judgment with regard to the water's appropriate temperature for the baby is made by the speaker.

The complexity of discourse factors described above helps explain why the challenges that the Dative presents to the learners become apparent only at the advanced level when students are faced with the task of learning how to make discursively motivated choices in increasingly monologic environments that are characteristic of public and academic contexts, where precision of expression and subtlety of meaning becomes of paramount importance. At the same time, the highly abstract nature of these factors makes it unlikely that the learners will discover the patterns of Dative's use and its significant role in the flow of discourse on their own (cf. von Stutterheim and Klein, 1987). Ironically, precisely at the advanced instructional level, explicit attention to "language" issues ceases to become a priority in typical collegiate foreign language programs—a result of bifurcation of language departments into separate "language" and "content" components, where the task of fostering learners' linguistic abilities is relegated to the first two years of the program (Byrnes, 2002; Byrnes, Crane, and Sprang, 2002).

The late emergence of the Dative as an acquisitional phenomenon whose complexity is rooted in its meaning points not only to the need for longitudinal study but also to the necessity of adequate pedagogical support for its development. I argue that careful attention must be paid to the nature of pedagogies within a classroom's ecology and that longitudinal studies involving "instructional interventions" are likely to be more meaningful when they are in harmony with the pedagogies that otherwise characterize an entire course and program. Only then can research practices respond to the kind of ethical challenges Ortega (2005) has identified for SLA; and only then are they likely to yield important insights about actual and potential instructed learner development in complex semantic domains of language use.

At this early stage of longitudinal study of advanced learners, we are urgently in need of posing and answering questions such as the following that address the acquisition of the German Dative case:

- Which aspects of the Dative's semantic structure and discourse use can students reasonably be expected to learn on their own, and which should, or even must, be taught?
- What pedagogical treatments (e.g., explicit vs. implicit) should be employed for targeting various aspects of the Dative's meanings and uses?
- How might different pedagogical treatments affect the length and shape of acquisitional paths?

The study reported in this chapter grappled with the above issues within the advanced-level course, "Text in context," taught in the German department at Georgetown University (for a description of the four-year curriculum, see *Developing multiple literacies*, n.d.). A four-credit-hour course taken after 18 credit hours of instruction, it occupies a critical place in the department's curriculum inasmuch as it focuses on oral and written genres typical of public and academic contexts in order to foster the development of advanced language capacities and a more sophisticated understanding of meaning–form links at all levels of the language system. Among other features, its pedagogy devotes explicit attention to the development of grammatical metaphor and to a shift from the verbal to the nominal paradigm (Halliday and Martin, 1993; see also Achugar and Colombi, Chapter 3, this volume) to realize coherent text-building. Increased use of nominal structures, which is characteristic of German academic language, not only leads to increased complexity and information density of sentences; it also provides an environment for extensive use of the clausal Dative case to express various relationships between nominal clause participants.

In the remainder of the chapter I relate how four delimited instructional vignettes were implemented to raise learner awareness for the semantics of the Dative and I describe learners' engagement with it longitudinally over a semester period.

Teaching the Dative to advanced learners: instructional choices

The question arises how one might effectively stage the complex learning tasks surrounding the Dative, particularly in its clausal form, within a course that holds an overall text and content orientation. In my own teaching of the course, I determined that students must first become familiar with the array of semantic roles that are coded by this case at the clause level before moving on to the more nuanced discursive functions of the Dative.

Developing semantically oriented instructional materials

When we move from a formal to a functional conceptualization of case, case markings are no longer understood as empty formal features; instead they denote a particular semantic relation that holds between a noun phrase and a verb or between two noun phrases. In that case, the central pedagogical task is to teach the preferred means for coding these relationships in the target language along with the contextual factors that are instantiated by divergent forms. In short, it is oriented toward enabling students to go beyond observing rules of accuracy and to make meaning-full choices with appropriate grammar resources.

A linguistic framework that views case in this manner is Cognitive Linguistics (CL), an umbrella term for a variety of research approaches and agendas within a larger functional movement in modern linguistics. What links CL to other usage-based theories is its recognition of the embeddedness of language in a social-interactional context (Sinha, 1999). What distinguishes CL from them is its firm grounding in human neurobiology. CL views language as an integral part of cognition that is shaped by the functions it serves as well as by a variety of historical, biological, psychological, and sociocultural factors that are "prerequisite and foundational" to the characterization of a linguistic structure (Langacker, 1999, p. 14).

Relying on CL as a theoretical framework, I established a limited number of semantic categories that would account for the majority of the Dative uses. My aim was to aid learners in the acquisition of the entire heterogeneous Dative concept in the short period of time I could allocate to explicit instruction of the Dative, while being specific enough to set the Dative case apart from the Accusative, a major source of error. At the same time, explanations needed to be both descriptively adequate and intuitively plausible for the learners so as to be easily accepted and accessed. Those considerations led to the decision to concentrate on four Dative meanings (or participant roles) that were most often found in course texts and that also cover the majority of Dative uses in German. I presented them with the help of visual aids in the form of graphics for each role. Figures 1–4 represent the schemas for the roles of Recipient, [–]Possessor, and Experiencer used in instruction; because the schema for the fourth role, Beneficiary, is very similar to that of Recipient, it was not included in instructional materials (captions in the figures below are in English; in instruction, German captions were used).

Role 1: Recipient

I identified recipient of a concrete object as the central Dative role (cf. Janda, 1993; Rudzka-Ostyn, 1996), from which all other roles can be derived by profiling various aspects of the prototypical image schema depicting transfer. Originating from a

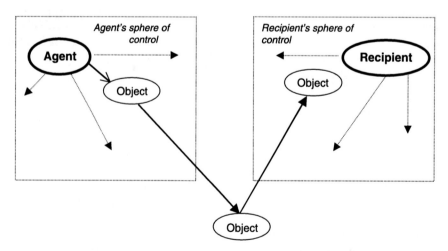

Figure 1 Recipient role schema

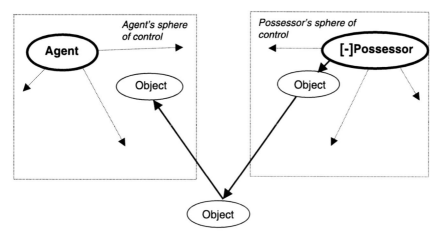

Figure 2 [–]Possessor role schema

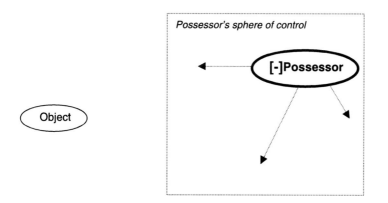

Figure 3 [–]Possessor role schema in non-prototypical cases

ubiquitous spatial scene depicting transfer of a concrete object between two human participants, this role has developed metaphorical extensions not only in the realm of transfer of abstract objects, but most prominently in the realm of human communication. Examples of verbs that prompt for a Recipient role include *geben* "to give," *schicken* "to send," *schenken* "to give as a present," *sagen* "to tell," *versprechen* "to promise," *empfehlen* "to recommend," etc.

Role 2: Beneficiary / Maleficiary

This role is closely related to the Recipient role since a beneficiary of someone's actions often comes to possess a concrete object that was intended for him or her. For example, in the sentence *My mother has knit me a scarf*, the beneficiary of the action of knitting gets the scarf as a result. However, the object could already be in the possession of Beneficiary, as in example (6); it could be a part of Beneficiary's body, as in (7); or it may not have anything to do with possession at all, as in (8).

(6) *Hans repariert **mir** das Fahrrad.*
     Hans repairs **my** [DAT] bicycle.
(7) *Die Mutter wusch **mir** die Hände.*
     Mother washed **my** [DAT] hands.
(8) *Ich öffnete **ihm** die Tür.*
     I opened the door **for him** [DAT].

Furthermore, the actions of the Agent do not have to be beneficial for the Dative participant; they can achieve the opposite, that is, harm the participant, damage his or her possessions, or generally incur an unfavorable situation for what I called a "Maleficiary":

(9) *Der Polizist schlug **ihm** ins Gesicht.*
     The policeman hit **him** [DAT] in the face.

Since there is an infinite number of actions involving two participants, this is the broadest category with the greatest potential for learning how to use the Dative in a wide variety of novel contexts.

Role 3: [–]Possessor

Possession means having an object within one's control, often as a result of a transfer. This category is represented by one verb only, namely *gehören* "to belong." A number of verbs represent the reverse process of either losing control over the previous possession (e.g., *wegnehmen* "to take away") or not possessing something that is highly valued or desirable (e.g., *fehlen* or *mangeln* "to lack"). A rather large group of verbs derived with the help of prefix *ent-*, usually described as "prefix of separation," depict the object as falling out of the sphere of control or interest of the Dative entity: e.g., *entziehen* "to take away," *entfallen* "to slip, fall from," *entkommen* or *entfliehen* "to escape." I called this role "Minus Possessor" ([–]Possessor), as illustrated in (10):

(10) *Um bei BMW zu arbeiten, fehlt **mir** [[–]Possessor] die nötige Erfahrung [Object].*
      I [[–]Possessor] am lacking necessary experience [Object] to work at BMW.

Diagrams for the Recipient and [–]Possessor roles differ mainly in the directionality of the transfer: to or away from the Dative participant (cf. Figures 1 and 2). In prototypical situations, involving the verbs *geben* and *wegnehmen*, all three participants (Agent, Object, and Recipient or [–]Possessor) are profiled; in less prototypical situations involving such verbs as *fehlen* and *mangeln* "to lack," only the Object (which is the syntactic subject) and [–]Possessor are necessarily profiled (Figure 3).

Role 4: Experiencer

The notion of sphere of control or "personal sphere" is an inherent aspect associated with all Dative roles; it ties Experiencer to the other roles. A Dative participant is "an individual who is perceived as affected by an action, process, or state taking place within or impinging upon his [*sic*] personal sphere" (Dabrowska, 1997, p. 16). It is

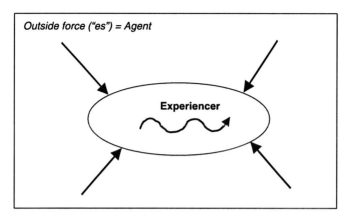

Figure 4 Experiencer role schema

those processes—physical, mental, or emotional—taking place within the Dative participant and being conceived of as externally induced and not intentional that lie at the heart of the Experiencer category (see Figure 4):

(11)   *Das Wasser ist **dem Baby** zu heiß.*
       The water is too hot **for the baby** [DAT]. (physical)
(12)   *Das ist **mir** wohl bewusst.*
       That is very well-known **to me** [DAT]. (mental)
(13)   ***Mir** ist Angst und Bange.*
       I [DAT] am scared. (emotional)

This is the category with the highest number of adjectival predicates, since what is often profiled is not the process itself but a resulting state. Because reflecting on internal processes requires awareness, Experiencers are always animate and predominantly human.

I conclude this section with a brief comment. I am aware that the above descriptions may appear to be overly technical and therefore of little relevance for classroom practice. However, I would argue that, if learners are to benefit from semantically oriented awareness to deal with complex areas of learning, then the profession must provide descriptions of this type and also enable practitioners to translate them into suitable pedagogies.

Implementing pedagogical treatments

I divided pedagogical treatment of the Dative into four sessions, one for each role, spread over two weeks at the beginning of the semester. Because each session lasted between 20 and 30 minutes and students' homework assignments probably required another 25–30 minutes, total focused time working with the Dative was slightly over two hours. In all four treatments I started explanations with prototypical examples, in which all roles were played by concrete entities. Questioning based on the examples led students on the path of gradual discovery of the case meanings; diagrams presented these meanings in a more abstract and schematic way; and, finally, students applied the newly gained insights to less prototypical examples of the Dative, often with abstract participants. Handouts provided diagrams and examples that, in general, were taken from course texts. For the rest of the semester I gave students feedback on their use of the Dative and drew their attention to those Dative constructions in texts that carried more abstract and metaphorical meanings but that could nevertheless be traced to the four major roles.

Assessing instructional benefits

To assess whether and how learner understanding of the case's semantics changed as a result of instruction, three tests were administered throughout the semester: before and immediately after the instructional treatments and at the end of the semester. The first two tests, which I will refer to as pre- and post-test, took place two weeks apart. The end-of-semester test, which I will refer to as the delayed post-test, took place two months after the Dative-focused instruction had concluded.

The testing procedures were as follows. Students received a list of verbal and adjectival predicates and were asked to produce in writing as many sentences as possible for each predicate, varying the quantity of objects and their case and considering whether they can be used without prepositions. In this fashion, students demonstrated their awareness (or lack thereof) of semantic roles that the Dative exhibits in given contexts. The tests had a staggered design: the pre-test had 5 items each under the Recipient and Beneficiary categories and 3 items under the [–]Possessor and Experiencer categories (for a total of 16 test items); 4 verbs that are not combinable with Dative complements served as distractors. Each subsequent test added one item for each role as well as one distractor. The number of verbs tested under each category was in part dictated by relative frequency of occurrence of each role in the texts, where Recipients and Beneficiaries represented a much larger category than [–]Possessors and Experiencers. Because roles do not have clear-cut boundaries role assignment is somewhat subjective. Therefore, learners received credit as long as they were aware of either of the roles that contribute to the semantic input of a verb. A list of all verbs tested, classified by Dative roles, can be found in Figure 5.

Immediately following the test, I used learner responses for a stimulated recall session in order to tap into learners' procedural (during production) and explicit (during stimulated recall) knowledge about the meaning of the Dative as well as individual lexical items. Evidence from the out-of-class tests of the study exists side by side with analysis of student writing as it regularly occurs for "Text in context" throughout the semester. Three writing assignments were analyzed: condolence letter, letter to the editor, and public speech as parts of pre-, post-, and delayed post-tests respectively.

Results: uncovering acquisitional trajectories

Analysis of test results, learner production on the semester's writing tasks, and learner self-report data on the stimulated recall interviews revealed several trends in the development of learners' knowledge about, and ability to use, the Dative.

On all three tests (n = 20)	Added on post-test (n = 5)	Added on delayed post-test (n = 5)
Recipient *schicken* – to send *bringen* – to bring *beschreiben* – to describe *versprechen* – to promise *gratulieren* – to congratulate	Recipient and Beneficiary *erlauben* – to allow	Recipient *vermitteln* – to convey, transmit, provide
Beneficiary/Maleficiary *waschen* – to wash *brechen* – to break *vergeben* – to forgive *öffnen* – to open *helfen* – to help	Beneficiary/Maleficiary and Experiencer *vorstellen* – to introduce; to imagine	Beneficiary/Maleficiary *bieten* – to offer
[–]Possessor *stehlen* – to steal *entziehen* – to take away *wegnehmen* – to take away	[–]Possessor and Maleficiary *schneiden* – to cut	[–]Possessor *entgehen* – to escape
Experiencer *scheinen* – to seem *kalt sein* – to be cold *wichtig sein* – to be important	Experiencer *unbekannt sein* – to be unknown	Experiencer *schwer fallen* – to be difficult
Distractors *besprechen* – to discuss *vermissen* – to miss *konzentrieren* – to concentrate *umziehen* – to move; to change clothes	Distractors *entscheiden* – to decide	Distractors *bitten* – to ask, to plead

Figure 5 Verbs used in test items

Table 1 Descriptive statistics for the base items on prompted production task

Test	n	Mean	SD	Minimum	Maximum
Pre-test	12	59.9	20.5	33.3	92.3
Post-test	12	83.8	19.0	30.8	100
Delayed post-test	12	84.0	23.1	21.4	100

Note: Results are given in percentage scores. Total number of items for all three tests was 20 (16 base plus 4 distractors).

Accuracy in use of clausal Dative constructions

As can be gleaned from Table 1, the group's rate of appropriately used clausal Datives significantly improved from the pre- to the post-test ($p < .05$) and this improvement was sustained throughout the semester.[1] When the results were inspected by individual learner, these group trends were reflected in the individual performance of all learners but one, Bonny, who scored at about 40 percent accuracy on the pre-test and consistently decreased in her performance over the two post-tests, scoring slightly over 20 percent on the delayed post-test.

Another way to interpret test results is through group data on clusters of verbs representing the same role relationships. Table 2 summarizes mean group scores on the base items broken down into role categories; Figure 6 graphically presents these results.

Table 2 shows that the improvement was experienced on all four semantic roles introduced in instruction, and particularly on [–]Possessor and Beneficiary. The results also indicate that the group initially performed most strongly with verbs calling for a Recipient, followed by Beneficiary, Experiencer, and [–]Possessor roles. That slope reflects past instructional emphases on the prototypical Recipient role of the Dative and the presence of verbs on the pre-test that are highly frequent and seman-tically prototypical for this category (*bringen* "to bring" and *schicken* "to send"). In reverse, difficulties with the [–]Possessor role reflect its limited inclusion in instruction,

Table 2 Mean learner performance by targeted Dative role

	k	*Pre-test*	*Post-test*	*Delayed post-test*
Recipient	5	75.9	88.3	85.0
Beneficiary	5	59.3	81.8	89.1
[–]Possessor	3	36.0	79.2	76.9
Experiencer	3	52.9	82.4	79.4

Note: Results are given in percentage scores. *k* = number of base items.

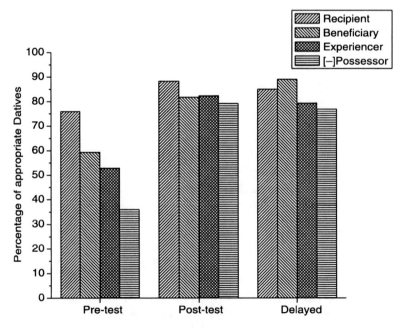

Figure 6 Group performance on the four targeted Dative roles

textbooks, and pedagogical grammars. Within the short time span of one semester, however, the group increased the usage of Dative complements with [–]Possessor verbs and sustained it on the delayed post-test: from 36 percent to 79.2 percent—in fact, the largest improvement across all categories—to 76.9 percent. The group improved equally well from the pre-test to the post-test on the two remaining categories: Beneficiary (by 22.5 points, and by an additional 7.3 points on the delayed post-test) and Experiencer (by 29.5 points, but then dropped 3 points on the delayed post-test). Together with accuracy rates (i.e., using Dative instead of Accusative), there was also an increase in the scope of application of Dative clausal constructions: tests and particularly the three writing tasks showed learners taking more risks by attempting to use the Dative with semantically complex and opaque predicates that lie further away from the Dative prototype.

Changes in learner awareness of the semantics of Dative

These positive developments reflect a shift in learners' declarative knowledge about the Dative that can safely be attributed to the semantically based instructional treatment. During the stimulated recall session on the pre-test, learners reported being often unsure about using the Dative and relying on a limited range of "rules of thumb" when deciding case assignment. "How it sounds" or using prepositions as a sort of "litmus test" were high-frequency strategies. In other words, if inserting a preposition (usually *zu* "to" and, for some, *von* "from") before a complement or using an English equivalent of a predicate in question with the preposition "to" seemed possible, then the use of clausal Dative appeared to them to be warranted. As a testament to the hurdles posed by well-established meaning–form assignments, students reported being more comfortable using a prepositional phrase although they realized that they were transferring English structures to German and although they suspected that a non-prepositional complement might be possible. Concurrently, learners most commonly described their reasoning about the use of the Dative by appealing to the notion of an indirect object, defined as someone "to whom an action is done." Emphasis on the preposition *to* not only suggests that the concept most often associated with the Dative is that of Recipient, but that [–]Possessor meaning is effectively excluded and the scope of Beneficiary is restricted to those instances when the participant is directly involved in the action (rather than simply benefiting from it, which in English would be expressed with the preposition *for*).

   While learners typically associated Dative with the Recipient meaning, they received no or, at best, imprecise semantic cues that signaled to them a need to use the Dative. Most importantly, in learners' opinion early in the semester, there was no discernible pattern behind the usage of the Dative. While they recognized similarities in use between several verbs (e.g., between *bringen* "to bring," *schenken* "to give as a present," and *schicken* "to send"), no learner at the beginning of the semester was aware of semantic ties between predicates used with the Dative, nor did anyone report having learned or formed a semantically based category of predicates that would necessitate the use of the Dative. Thus, for example, while most of the students used the Dative with the predicate *kalt sein* ("to be cold") and were able to name at least one more adjectival predicate that could be used like *kalt sein*, these items did not form a coherent semantic group for any learner. Instead, most reported learning separate verbs either as a set phrase, used with a particular Dative complement, or as a rule stating the need for a Dative object. Such memorization, however, turned out to be a flawed strategy: several students reported having to learn the standard lists of so-called "Dative verbs" but remembering only few—*helfen* "to help," *gratulieren* "to congratulate," *schenken* "to give as a present," *passieren* "to happen," and *glauben* "to believe." This is hardly surprising given the fact that no explanations as to why the verbs on the lists required Dative were given and learners could not discern any reasons for the Dative use on their own.

A different picture emerges from the two post-test interviews. After instructional treatment, students demonstrated an increased and much more sophisticated awareness of the range of the Dative's meanings and reported becoming more certain about using the Dative and gaining a better understanding of its use. By appealing to the notions introduced during the instructional treatments, all learners but one reported using semantic cues to justify their use of the Dative, at least in some instances. Some appropriated the labels for the roles that I provided and referred to them when commenting on their use of the Dative on the tests; others reported recognizing some items on the test as the ones discussed in class in conjunction with certain roles or remembering certain aspects of the Dative semantics and use discussed in class. Students also became much more adept at grouping the predicates calling for a Dative complement according to their semantics. Their ability to generalize information received during instruction can be illustrated with the predicate *wichtig sein* ("to be important"). While only four students used *wichtig sein* with the Dative on the pre-test, 11 used it on the post-test and 10 on the delayed test. This particular predicate was not mentioned in instructional materials, but learners seem to have been able to generalize the Experiencer concept to it. Only within a longitudinal orientation was it possible to capture these kinds of developments.

Decreased reliance on alternative means of expression

Students' newly gained knowledge and increased learner confidence also promoted less reliance on prepositional phrases and possessive pronouns (two main manifestations of apparent L1 influence on learner production): from 18 percent on the pre-test to 3.6 percent on the post-test to 4.5 percent on the delayed post-test. But even though students started to rely more on clausal Dative constructions, as these were appropriate in sentential context, the test does not allow gauging, with the necessary confidence and precision, learners' ability to choose between the use of clausal Dative or alternative means in relation to textual context. Even so, post-tests and delayed post-tests provide early evidence that learners were starting to realize the possibility of using clausal Dative in discursive contexts where alternative means had been the only option earlier on.

Test directions gave students the option of using the test items without any objects as long as the sentences made sense. By eliminating the need to choose an appropriate case for one or two complements altogether, this becomes the easiest option. The second easiest option is the use of transitive predicates with a single object in the Accusative. 13.2 percent of the sentences on the pre-test either did not contain any objects (in prepositional or in clausal constructions) or contained only a direct object in the Accusative. This number grew smaller on the post-test (9.1 percent) and diminished even further on the delayed test (7.3 percent). This suggests an increase in learners' comfort with using clausal Dative objects, either as a single complement of the predicate or in combination with an Accusative complement, a conclusion that is supported by learner comments during the stimulated recall interviews.

Overgeneralization

Two naturally occurring behaviors in a new learning context are oversuppliance and overgeneralization. Therefore, it is to be expected that, as learners incorporate new semantic concepts into their understanding of the Dative, they will initially produce clausal Dative constructions where Accusative is a correct option before more exposure to the input and instruction will allow them "to sort things out." To test for overgeneralization of the four semantic roles to inappropriate contexts, distractor items were included on the tests.

Initially, only two students used the wrong Dative with distractors. Mary could not decide whether *vermissen* ("to miss") is one of the "Dative verbs" she had learned before or a transitive verb (a decision that did not involve considering verb semantics or participant roles). Elise decided to use the Dative to code a conversational partner with *besprechen* ("to discuss") on the basis of how it sounds. On the post-test, however, the number of overgeneralized Datives increased to seven on the base items, the majority of them with *umziehen* (in its meaning "to change clothes"). Although no learner comments are available to explain use of the Dative with *umziehen*, in three sentences the Dative was used to code the presumable Beneficiary of the action – not an improbable generalization, given the verb semantics (e.g., *Er hat **sich** den Anzug umgezogen*, "He changed himself [DAT] the suit").

An interesting example of overgeneralization was provided by Michael, who referred to the Experiencer role to justify his decision to use the Dative with *entscheiden* ("to decide"), considerably misinterpreting the semantics involved in it:

> From my high school class . . . I slightly remember that you had to use not reflexive, but like a pronoun there. So I tried to place it within one of the four [categories], but I wasn't sure which, I was leaning towards Experiencer, I was thinking that I need to make a decision, I am experiencing decision-making process, it seemed to work.

Indeed, for him the notion of Experiencer was a kind of "catch-all" category that could be extended to cover the use of the Dative with other verbs, like *bitten* "to ask," *gratulieren* "to congratulate" ("I am an experiencer of congratulatory feelings," he explained), and *brechen* "to break."

On the delayed post-test, incorrect uses of the Dative increased even further: 8 instances with the base items (the majority again with *vermissen* and *umziehen* "to change clothes") and 8 more on two added items (2 with *entscheiden* and 6 with *bitten*). Such overwhelming use of Dative complements with *bitten* might reflect gener-alization of a use of the Dative with "verbs of communication" that was discussed during instruction. One learner, though, offered another explanation for her use of the Dative with *bitten* by appealing to the [–]Possessor role that was allegedly evoked by *bitten*, at least in her sentence, *Ich bitte **meiner Mutti** Taschengeld* ("I ask my mother [*DAT] for money"—"mother" becoming a [–]Possessor as a result of this action).

Beyond being inherent to language development, overgeneralization also provides evidence for learners' cognitive and affective engagement in meaning-focused ways of thinking about language and their active interpreting of the information presented in instruction, surely the processes at the heart of any learning (cf. Belz and Kinginger, 2002; Lantolf and Ahmed, 1989). As Larsen-Freeman (2002) puts it, "we attempt to make sense of [language that we encounter] using processes such as deduction, induction, and abduction. We seek patterns. We categorize frequently occurring items by abstracting from them underlying schema, prototypes, generalizations, and so forth . . . We do not only organize the data, we look for meaning in the patterns. If we cannot find it, we make it" (p. 280).

Implications of the study

At the most general level, the study indicates that participation in meaning-based instruction resulted in learners' increased ability to recognize and understand linguistic concepts inherent in the Dative's semantic structure and, subsequently, to apply this understanding to written production. Moreover, students' sustained score gains from the post-test to the delayed post-test two months after completion of the focused instructional treatment attest to the durability of the effects of this kind of instruction, which, it will be remembered, encompassed four sessions spread over two weeks and totaling slightly over two hours. This accords with Norris and Ortega's (2000) conclusion that explicit instructional treatments lasting more than two hours are in fact durable.

Looking at the results more closely from both an acquisitional and a methodological perspective permits the following additional observations. As Slobin (1993) indicates, L1 semantic concepts are exceptionally resistant to restructuring in L2 learning. In this study, no learner was able to use the Dative with complete appropriateness both in targeted tests and in unconstrained writing. In other words, the acquisition of the conceptual structure of the Dative case is a long-term process that stretches well beyond the span of one college semester. At the same time, this longitudinal investigation uncovered that significant changes in learner behavior can and did occur with a metalinguistically and metacognitively based semantic instructional approach. A similar conclusion was reached by Sprang (Chapter 8, this volume), who also observed beneficial effects of meaning-driven explicit instruction on the development of adult advanced learners' conceptual knowledge of German inseparable verbal prefixes *be-* and *er-*, where, once more, concepts are grammaticalized differently in English and German.

If that is so, it is worth looking more closely at pedagogies in relation to their effect on meaning-oriented language learning. Here, three observations deserve to be highlighted. First, an unexpected semantic "twist" in the explanations of a phenomenon that students believed to have learned a long time ago made the case forms salient enough to be noticed in subsequent input and interpreted in a new light. Second, instruction grounded in principles of Cognitive Linguistics provided a framework that guided both me as the instructor and the learners in analysis and categorization of clausal Dative instances encountered in texts throughout the semester; such

instructional support enhanced and guided implicit learning process based on frequency effects (cf. Larsen-Freeman, 2002). Finally, conscious metalinguistic reflection
on the Dative concept, promoted by instructional treatments, facilitated learning by
encouraging students to verbalize and exteriorize their knowledge in the process of
"languaging" (Swain, 2006) and to actively link meaning with form.

As already hinted at, length itself becomes an issue. On the research-methodological
level, Ortega and Iberri-Shea (2005) note that, while little is known about the optimal
length of observation for a longitudinal study, one can expect it to be related to the
complexity of language phenomena under consideration. However, as this study has
indicated, that factor is itself in need of empirical evidence through longitudinal
studies. In a reprise of the Focus on Form dictum that "instruction does make a difference," complexity itself can no longer be seen as a fixed and given phenomenon,
but as shaped differentially by learners in light of curricular and pedagogical contexts and approaches. While the present study has illuminated only a part of a long
acquisitional trajectory, it provided ample evidence for the fact that this trajectory is
different for different learners and can be expected to continue to be different
depending on their future experiences with the German language in and outside
of instructional settings. At the same time, an overall positive effect occurred even
within the short window of the study design, which involved a limited but semantically
oriented pedagogical approach.

Moreover, the nature of "complexity" is a function not only of pedagogical intervention but of the larger instructional context—that is, a curricular framework.
Precisely because these concepts require extended exploration, both a coherent curricular and a coherent pedagogical approach can be expected to add substantially to
longitudinal studies. In other words, beyond factors of time, principled program and
pedagogical proposals must accompany valued longitudinal studies of instructed
learning (Byrnes, 2001; Byrnes and Sprang, 2003; Byrnes *et al.*, 2006; also see
Georgetown German department's website www1.georgetown.edu/departments/
german/programs/undergraduate/curriculum/). It is no secret that the vast majority of collegiate L2 programs work with a textbook-based "curriculum" for their two
to four semesters of language requirement. The absence of true curricular contexts
that extend over multiple years may therefore be one of the greatest obstacles to the
longitudinal study of advanced L2 capacities.

Only within extended curricular proposals might we be able to find answers to
fundamental questions such as the following. First: Is it possible, desirable—perhaps
even necessary—to employ explicit concept-based instruction at earlier stages of
language study? With some restrictions, I would argue positively on all counts. While
early instruction surely cannot fully address the textual character of the Dative and
fine differences in construal that motivate the selection of clausal Dative, important
groundwork should be laid that enables learners to discern the relatively transparent
Dative roles of Recipient, Beneficiary, [–]Possessor, and Experiencer (and possibly a
few other minor ones). If L2 learners are taught and come to recognize semantic
motivation behind grammatical categories and principled differences between
information organizations in their L1s and L2s from the very early stages of L2 study,
they will be able to make meaning in the L2 in terms of specific choices within the
overall system of the language, one of the crucial abilities in L2 language use. A
second question is: Can such semantically driven information about a complex

grammatical phenomenon at the sentence level facilitate students' independent discovery of the discursive factors and cognitive differences in construal that determine the choice between a clausal Dative construction and alternative means, such as prepositional phrases and possessive pronouns? The answer can only be provided through empirical study that would target these differences in a textual environment. Finally, it is important to elucidate whether this kind of semantically orientated instructional approach can influence learners' ability to make flexible and situated choices at all levels of the language system that is so critical for advanced L2 competence with its fundamental characteristic of creating textual worlds through language. Only longitudinal studies will be able to tell.

Note

1. Due to space limitations, I present only the statistics on the base items used in all three tests. Analysis of learner performance on all task items (base and added) revealed a similar pattern.

References

Bardovi-Harlig, K. (1992). The use of adverbials and natural order in the development of temporal expression. *International Review of Applied Linguistics, 30*, 299–320.

Belz, J., and Kinginger, C. (2002). The cross-linguistic development of address form use in telecollaborative language learning: Two case studies. *Canadian Modern Language Review, 59*, 189–214.

Byrnes, H. (2001). Articulating foreign language programs: The need for new, curricular bases. In C. Gascoigne (Ed.), *Foreign language program articulation: Current practice and future prospects* (pp. 157–180). Westport, CT: Bergin and Garvey Press.

Byrnes, H. (2002). Towards academic-level foreign language abilities: Reconsidering foundational assumptions, expanding pedagogical options. In B. L. Leaver and B. Shekhtman (Eds.), *Developing professional-level language proficiency* (pp. 34–58). New York: Cambridge University Press.

Byrnes, H., Crane, C., Maxim, H., and Sprang, K. A. (2006). Taking text to task: Issues and choices in curriculum construction. *ITL—International Journal of Applied Linguistics, 152*, 85–110.

Byrnes, H., Crane, C., and Sprang, K. A. (2002). Nonnative teachers teaching at the advanced level: Challenges and opportunities. *ADFL Bulletin, 33*(3), 25–34.

Byrnes, H., and Sprang, K. A. (2003). Fostering advanced L2 literacy: A genre-based cognitive approach. In H. Byrnes and H. Maxim (Eds.), *Advanced foreign language learning: A challenge to college programs* (pp. 47–85). Boston: Thomson/Heinle.

Carroll, M., Murcia-Serra, J., Watorek, M., and Bendiscioli, A. (2000). The relevance of information organization to second language acquisition studies. *Studies in Second Language Acquisition, 22*, 441–466.

Dabrowska, E. (1997). *Cognitive semantics and the Polish Dative.* Berlin: Mouton de Gruyter.

Developing multiple literacies: A curriculum renewal project of the German department at Georgetown University, 1997–2000 (n.d.). www1.georgetown.edu/departments/german/programs/undergraduate/curriculum/

Dietrich, R., Klein, W., and Noyau, C. (1995). *The acquisition of temporality in a second language.* Philadelphia, PA: John Benjamins.

Givón, T. (1979). From discourse to syntax: Grammar as a processing strategy. In T. Givón

(Ed.), *Syntax and Semantics*. Vol. 12, *Discourse and syntax* (pp. 81–112). New York: Academic Press.

Halliday, M. A. K. (1982). How is a text like a clause? In S. Allen (Ed.), *Text processing: Text; analysis and generation; text typology and attribution* (pp. 209–247). Stockholm, Sweden: Almqvist and Wiksell International.

Halliday, M. A. K., and Martin, J. R. (1993). *Writing science: Literacy and discursive power*. London: Palmer Press.

Janda, L. A. (1993). *A geography of case semantics: The Czech Dative and Russian Instrumental*. Berlin: Mouton de Gruyter.

Klein, W., and Perdue, C. (1992). *Utterance structure: Developing grammars again*. Philadelphia, PA: John Benjamins.

Langacker, R. W. (1999). Assessing the cognitive linguistic enterprise. In T. Janssen and G. Redeker (Eds.), *Cognitive linguistics: Foundations, scope, and methodology* (pp. 13–59). Berlin: Mouton de Gruyter.

Lantolf, J., and Ahmed, M. (1989). Psycholinguistic perspectives on interlanguage variation: A Vygotskyan analysis. In S. Gass, C. G. Madden, D. Preston, and L. Selinker (Eds.), *Variation in second language acquisition*. Vol. 2, *Psycholinguistic issues* (pp. 93–108). Clevedon, UK: Multilingual Matters.

Larsen-Freeman, D. (2002). Making sense of frequency. *Studies in Second Language Acquisition*, *24*, 275–285.

Long, M. H., and Robinson, P. (1998). Focus on form: Theory, research and practice. In C. Doughty and J. Williams (Eds.), *Focus on form in classroom second language acquisition* (pp. 15–41). New York: Cambridge University Press.

Norris, J. M., and Ortega, L. (2000). Effectiveness of L2 instruction: A research synthesis and quantitative meta-analysis. *Language Learning*, *50*, 417–528.

Ortega, L. (2005). For what and for whom is our research? The ethical as transformative lens in instructed SLA. *Modern Language Journal*, *89*, 427–443.

Ortega, L., and Iberri-Shea, G. (2005). Longitudinal research in SLA: Recent trends and future directions. *Annual Review of Applied Linguistics*, *25*, 26–45.

Rudzka-Ostyn, B. (1996). The Polish Dative. In W. van Belle and W. van Langendonck (Eds.), *The Dative*. Vol. 1, *Description studies* (pp. 341–394). Amsterdam: John Benjamins.

Sinha, C. (1999). Grounding, mapping and acts of meaning. In T. Janssen and G. Redeker (Eds.), *Cognitive linguistics: Foundations, scope, and methodology* (pp. 223–255). Berlin: Mouton de Gruyter.

Slobin, D. I. (1993). Adult language acquisition: A view from child language study. In C. Perdue (Ed.), *Adult language acquisition: Cross-linguistic perspectives*. Vol. 2, *The results* (pp. 239–252). New York: Cambridge University Press.

Smith, M. B. (1987). The semantics of dative and accusative in German. Unpublished doctoral dissertation, University of California, San Diego.

Swain, M. (2006). Languaging, agency, and collaboration in advanced second language proficiency. In H. Byrnes (Ed.), *Advanced language learning: The contribution of Halliday and Vygotsky* (pp. 95–108). London: Continuum.

VanPatten, B. (1990). Attending to form and content in the input. *Studies in Second Language Acquisition*, *12*, 287–301.

von Stutterheim, C., and Klein, W. (1987). A concept-oriented approach to second language studies. In C. W. Pfaff (Ed.), *First and second language acquisition processes* (pp. 191–205). Cambridge, MA: Newbury House.

10 L1–L2 translation versus no translation

A longitudinal study of focus-on-formS within a meaning-focused curriculum

Marie Källkvist

Abstract

Translation as a pedagogical tool represents a focus-on-formS activity since target structures have been selected in advance for deliberate attention in the L2 classroom (Ellis, 2005). Although focus-on-formS approaches have fallen out of favor, translation can be a suitable awareness-raising and learning activity particularly for advanced learners who may be aiming for a career where a translation competency is relevant (such as teaching, or professional translation and interpreting). This chapter reports on the results of a longitudinal, experimental study carried out with advanced L2 learners of English within an authentic educational program. The effects on L2 morphosyntactic accuracy of engaging in two different focus-on-formS classroom learning activities were investigated: (i) L1-to-L2 translation activities versus (ii) fill-in-the-blank and transformation exercises. Both instructional regimes targeted the same set of relatively sophisticated English structures of the kind that challenge advanced native Swedish-speaking learners. The instructional treatment lasted for 13 weeks and was provided within one of the English courses the students took during the semester, namely a course in English grammar. Thus, the overall curriculum was communicative and the focus-on-formS activities were used only judiciously and in the context of the grammar course. The learners were Swedish (L1) university-level learners of English (L2), who had had nine or ten years of classroom exposure to English prior to taking part in the study. They were randomly assigned to two different groups, and a comparison meaning-only group was also added to the design. The effects of the two types of focus-on-formS exercises were measured by pre-tests (in week 1) and post-tests (in week 13). Results indicate that (i) the "translation group" students showed greater gain from pre-test to post-test when translating from L1 to L2; the difference in gain between "translation group" and "no-translation group" was not significant, but approached significance ($p = 0.07$); (ii) the "no-translation group" students showed somewhat greater gain from pre-test to post-test when doing a written retelling task directly in L2; and (iii) both focus-on-formS groups outperformed the meaning-only comparison group, at least on these relatively controlled measures of L2 grammatical knowledge.

Introduction

Translation has been used for hundreds of years in language teaching and as a way to learn foreign languages (FL) through self-study. It was once the main avenue for teaching and learning classical FLs. The 20th century saw a rapid decline, however, in the use of translation in L2 classrooms to enhance language learning, notably in the United States. At the same time, translation remains part of language instruction in many other parts of the world, particularly in FL or EFL settings (see Fotos, 2005; Gorsuch, 1998; Klapper, 2006; Newson, 1998; Schjoldager, 2004; Sewell, 1996; Shih, 1999). For students completing a degree in a FL, competency in translation is relevant for careers in teaching or translation and interpreting, leading to an interest in the kind of detailed comparative analyses of their L1 and the L2 that translation typically engenders.

This chapter addresses the general question of whether translation is a valuable component in university-level FL classes. It reports on a longitudinal study covering a treatment period of 13 weeks, in which two groups of randomly assigned advanced-level learners of English were given two different types of forms-focused exercises, only one of which involved translation.

I begin by describing how translation tends to be used in the first semester of English instruction at universities in Sweden, which is where the study was carried out. This will be followed by a review of attitudes among experienced language educators and translation studies experts toward translation as a way of enhancing L2 learning. I then discuss how the use of L1–L2 translation relates to recent approaches to form-focused instruction. Following this, I present theoretical considerations in cognitive psychology and empirical work in classroom language learning that support the use of translation for enhancing L2 learning. On this background I present details of the study and its major findings. The chapter closes with discussion of possible pedagogical implications.

Focus-on-form and focus-on-formS in EFL curricula in Sweden

Form-focused instruction (FFI) typically refers to teaching the grammatical form of the target language in two major approaches. According to Ellis (2005), "focus-on-formS" "requires a planned approach to FFI (i.e., the prior selection of a specific form for treatment). Learners are required to treat forms as discrete entities that can be accumulated systematically one at a time" (p. 716). By contrast, "focus-on-form" involves attention to form only when this is needed in "tasks" that are otherwise meaning-centered (see Long, 1991).

Curricula of English departments at Swedish universities have a communicative meaning focus rather than a formS focus. That is, only when problems arise does instruction devote attention to language features. These meaning-focused curricula aim to help students develop enhanced proficiency (fluency and accuracy) in spoken and written English; to introduce them to English linguistics, literature, and literary analysis; and to enhance their knowledge of culture and society in the English-speaking world. Only a few designated courses—grammar and translation courses in particular—incorporate focus-on-formS exercises. In an approach reminiscent of Contrastive Analysis these designated courses often emphasize grammar points in which Swedish and English differ and structures that, in teachers' experience, present particular challenges to students. Thus, while focus-on-formS instruction does occur, it plays but a minor role with regard to course credits in the overall language program.

Within the context of this discussion, the use of translation constitutes a limited but well-established practice of focus-on-formS: target structures have been selected in advance for deliberate attention in the classroom. For example, at Halmstad University, where data for the present study were collected, translation exercises form part of the course "Written proficiency: English grammar," which contributes 15 percent of the credits earned by English majoring students during their first semester.

Given the limited use of focus-on-formS instruction, the relative benefits of translation as compared to other kinds of focus-on-formS exercises in the context of a communicative, meaning-oriented curriculum become an issue in need for well-documented answers. Since the 1970s, a great deal of research on grammar instruction has been carried out, followed more recently by meta-analyses of published work (Ellis, 2002; Norris and Ortega, 2001). Ellis (2005) examines this research and concludes that grammar instruction results in greater accuracy in test-like performance but is much less likely to lead to improved accuracy in spontaneous oral language use. He argues as well that, when grammar instruction does have an effect, this effect is durable. Ellis further states that more research in the area of grammar instruction is needed since

> [t]he crucial question is . . . not whether instruction works but rather what kind of instruction works best . . . The research to date does not provide definite answers. It is not possible to declare that one type of focus-on-formS instruction results in better learning than another. (p. 726)

The present study takes up that challenge by investigating the potential benefits of two different types of focus-on-formS instruction: translation exercises versus fill-in-the-blank and transformation exercises.

Using translation for L2 learning: expert opinions

Given the generally negative attitude towards translation as a pedagogical tool in the mainstream of FL education, translation would seem to be a curious pedagogical choice for instruction. However, an entirely different view comes to the fore in publications written by translation studies scholars and L2 educators, who express an overwhelmingly positive view of the merits of translation-related activities for language learning. I surveyed 40 publications (all published in the last 25 years) and a mere three of these express a negative view, with concerns being raised about its use as an overall test of L2 proficiency in German BA programs (Klein-Braley and Franklin, 1998; Newson, 1998) and reservations being expressed about the way it has traditionally been incorporated in FL courses (Nott, 2002).[1]

As summarized in Table 1, experts publishing in this area unanimously advocate the *judicious* use of translation and there is no intention of reverting to the much-maligned Grammar-Translation Method nor to a structural syllabus.

Elaborateness of processing and translation in L2 learning

Beyond such practitioner support, the literature also provides theoretical arguments from cognitive psychology in support of translation, particularly through the

Table 1 Benefits to be gained from the judicious use of translation for L2 learning

Judicious *use of translation*	*Publication*
Presents real-life tasks that (1) foster interaction in the L2 classroom, and (2) introduce students to the complex processes of real-life translation.	Allford (1999); Cunico (2004); Duff (1989); Fraser (1996); Gonzàlez Davies (2004); Klapper (2006); Malmkjær (1998); Nott (2002); Rivera-Mills and Gantt (1999); Satorres and Closa (2003); Schjoldager (2003)
Involves a natural cognitive process that many L2 users already engage in; particularly beneficial with learners who share an L1.	Gonzàlez Davies (2001); Malmkjær (1998); Owen (2003)
Links L1 and L2 in ways that may enhance retention in memory.	Hummel (1995)
Suits L2 users with an analytical bent.	Malmkjær (1998)
Clarifies certain complex grammatical points.	Gonzàlez Davies (2001)
Directs attention to accuracy and demands the use of complex structures.	Gonzàlez Davies (2001)
Raises awareness of similarities and differences between languages and cultures.	Gonzàlez Davies (2001)
Caters to advanced L2 users who tend to be introverted.	Sewell (2004)

notion of elaborateness of processing (Anderson, 1990; Lockhart and Craik, 1990). As Hummel (1995) explains, "[e]laboration refers to extensiveness of processing and number of encoded features. It is suggested that a more extensive and more elaborated analysis of a stimulus is associated with greater retention" (p. 450). Indeed, Hummel explicitly connects elaborateness of processing and translation:

> an elaborated trace is characterized by additional information which allows the formation of an increased number of interconnections. When translating, a dual set of structures are activated: (a) the first language structures from which the meaning or message is derived, and (b) the second language structures which are constructed to match the message. Thus the translation process should entail just such an increased set of interconnections, resulting in a more elaborate set of memory traces associated with the L2 structures. And, according to the "elaborateness of processing" view discussed earlier, the L2 structures should therefore be more resistant to forgetting. (p. 452)

To support her argument that translation can enhance learning, Hummel refers to empirical work focusing on retention of L2 vocabulary. For example, watching subtitled films, learners retain the highest proportion of L2 vocabulary when subtitling is reversed (i.e., L1 sound—L2 script). This condition was more conducive to learning vocabulary than a condition where both sound and text were in L2 (Danan, 1992). Similarly, Holobow, Lambert, and Sayegh (1984) found benefits for reversed subtitling for "enhancing comprehension of verbal information" (Holobow, Lambert, and Sayegh, 1984, p. 59), and Lambert (1986) for learning French vocabulary.

Empirical evidence in support of using the L1 and/or translation for L2 learning

Hummel extends her hypothesis from vocabulary to the retention of L2 morphosyntax. Unfortunately, empirical work on the effect of translation exercises on L2 learners' morphosyntax is scant. To my knowledge, only one previous study has been published, reporting on preliminary findings of the present project (Källkvist, 2004), together with two immediately relevant, unpublished studies, both carried out on learners receiving classroom instruction in a FL (Berggren, 1972; Slavikova, 1990). Berggren (1972) found no noticeable differences between a translation treatment and a close reading treatment, but she did not submit her results to any inferential analyses. Slavikova (1990) found statistically non-significant differences that she nevertheless interpreted as trends for the most part favoring a translation group over a no-translation group. Thus, neither study provides robust evidence and they both leave the issue of the effect of translation for the enhancement of L2 learning very much unresolved.

There is, however, another body of published empirical work that lends indirect support to the use of translation for enhancing L2 learning, summarized in Table 2. This research involves contrastive input targeting L2 structures where there are specific differences between the L1 and L2 and was carried out with both adolescent and adult L2 learners, covering a range of language pairs. The results across these studies converge to suggest that contrastive input may facilitate learning. More specifically, the findings uniformly suggest that explicit contrastive information coupled with error correction enhance the learning of certain grammatical structures in which key differences between the L1 and L2 are implied. Kaneko's (1992) and Kupferberg and Olshtain's (1996) findings constitute empirical support showing the value of integrating L2 and L1 input to facilitate L2 acquisition. Two other studies, Rolin-Ianziti and Brownlie (2002) and Spada and Lightbown (1999), did not directly address the role of the L1, but their results led the authors to hypothesize that explicit instruction which includes contrastive information may be necessary for certain structures to be learned.

This background sets an overwhelmingly positive scene for the usefulness of translation for developing advanced L2 capacities.

Method

Research questions

Two main research questions are addressed in the present study:

1. Do students who have been exposed to translation exercises for a substantial period of time perform equally well on morphosyntactic accuracy in English as students who have done exercises in the L2 only (but targeting the same structures) when (a) *translating writing* from Swedish into English, and b) *writing directly* in English?
2. Are some learners able to do equally well in both types of task, regardless of exercise type?

Thus, the relative effectiveness of two types of focus-on-formS instruction was

Table 2 Studies of contrastive input targeting L2 structures

Study	Participants / Methodology	Main results
Kaneko (1992)	*Participants*: Japanese (L1) high-school level learners of English (*n* = approx. 552). *Methodology*: non-experimental; protocols of classroom interaction based on audio recordings, and uptake questionnaires completed by the participants.	For student uptake of grammar, teachers' L1-and-L2 mixed utterances were more influential than non-mixed utterances.
Kupferberg and Olshtain (1996)	*Participants*: Hebrew-speaking (L1) 16-year-old learners of English (*n* = 137). *Methodology*: Experimental treatment involving two types of structure that are difficult for Hebrew-speaking learners due to contrastive differences. Experimental groups received metalinguistic statements in Hebrew summarizing the differences between Hebrew and English. Control groups did communicative tasks targeting the same structures.	There were no significant differences between experimental and control groups on pre-tests. On post-tests and delayed post-tests, the experimental groups scored significantly higher for both recognition and production tasks. This suggests that contrastive explicit input facilitates the learning of structures that are difficult due to contrastive differences.
Rolin-Ianziti and Brownlie (2002)	*Participants*: Teachers teaching beginner-level university courses in French (*n* = 4). *Methodology*: Audio recordings of the teachers' speech.	Teachers used the L1 for giving translation equivalents, for commenting on forms and for managing the class. On the basis of these findings, Rolin-Ianziti and Brownlie hypothesized "that a few strategic uses of NL [native language] may introduce input modifications that affect FL learning positively. In particular, the two categories of *Translation* and *Contrast* within an FL matrix may expose learners to quality input."
Spada and Lightbown (1999)	*Participants*: French (L1) 11- to 12-year-old learners of English (*n* = 144). *Methodology*: Experimental treatment study of learners' command of English questions.	Learners continued to accept and produce ungrammatical question forms when using English. These forms were traced to properties of learners' L1. Spada and Lightbown hypothesize that there may be a need for explicit instruction and error correction in areas of L2 grammar where learners tend to form incorrect interlanguage rules.

investigated, both targeting the same set of L2 structures presented the same number of times in the same grammar book and in class. One type of instruction involved translation exclusively (the "T" treatment, for "Translation treatment") and the second type involved fill-in-the-blank and transformation exercises in the L2 (the "NoT" treatment, for "No Translation").

On the basis of previous research and on logic, my hypothesis was that two groups of participants exposed to the same explicit grammar instruction, and where only the ensuing exercises differed, would perform similarly on tests of morphosyntactic accuracy. Therefore I decided to expand the study by including a third group of learners of similar proficiency level who were studying English but without a grammar component:[2] The treatment received by this group will be referred to as "NoG" (for "No Grammar") treatment. Students in this group took an elective English course that entailed reading fiction in English and writing papers based on their reading. At no point during the treatment period of 13 weeks was their attention drawn to grammar. This added element in the study allowed for a comparison of the two types of focus-on-formS exercise treatments with a true focus-on-meaning treatment. Including this additional group led to a third research question:

3.   Do students who have had input through extensive reading and writing in English as an L2, but no explicit instruction in the use of morphosyntactic structures, perform equally well as students who have had "translation exercises" or "target-language-only exercises" on morphosyntactic accuracy when (a) *translating writing* from Swedish into English, and (b) *writing directly* in English?

Methodology

Experimental methodology was adhered to for research questions 1 and 2, and data were collected at Halmstad University, Sweden. Students (approximately 55) admitted to studying English (first-semester level) were divided into two groups on the basis of matched-pair random assignment. This was done on the basis of students' results on a forms-focused multiple-choice test of English grammar, which they sat on their first day of the semester. Matched-pair random assignment ensured that both experimental groups included students with good, intermediate and poor levels of grammatical accuracy at the onset of the study.

The instructional treatment was given to them in the course unit entitled "Written proficiency: English grammar" (which, as readers will remember, constitutes only 15 percent of the total credit load the students enrol in during their first semester of study in the program). One group (the "T" group, for "Translation") was consistently engaged in translation exercises targeting structures presented in their grammar book and by their teacher. For the same period of one semester, the second group (the "NoT" group, for "No Translation") performed fill-in-the-blank and transformation exercises in L2 targeting the same structures the same number of times. Both groups were taught by myself. Most of the lessons were audio-recorded, as one of the aims of the project was to examine the classroom discourse that developed from the two different kinds of exercise. The course content of other course units the university participants took this semester was identical for both groups.

It should be noted that the inclusion of the third (NoG) group, although a strength in some ways, gave rise to some weaknesses in other ways, because it meant departing from the experimental design. Thus, several variables besides translation differed between the NoG group, on the one hand, and the T and NoT groups, on the other. For one, the NoG students were in their final year of senior high school, and were taught by a different teacher. Moreover, they were an intact group (since no random assignment was possible with them), and they were taking other courses apart from their English classes. For these reasons, any differences in results between the NoG and the two experimental groups give rise to further hypotheses rather than conclusions.

Participants

All participants that were eventually retained were native speakers of Swedish and had had all their prior education in Sweden in order to control for as many extraneous variables as possible. Students in the experimental groups (T and NoT) ranged in age from 19 to 37 (although few were older than 25). Students in the NoG were 18–19 years of age. All participants had had nine to ten years of classroom instruction in English prior to data collection. They all had good communicative competence in English. The distribution of participants is indicated in Figure 1.

In the two experimental groups, only students who had 100 percent attendance over all 13 weeks were included as participants of this study. This was important, since all exercises which constituted the treatment were done in class in order to ascertain that the time students were engaged in the exercises would be similar in both the T and NoT groups. No such exercises were given as homework. The fact that both T and NoT comprise 15 students is coincidental.

For the NoG group, on the other hand, attendance was not taken into consideration, since they were doing an essential part of their English coursework outside of class time, reading fiction and writing papers as homework. The NoG learners completed identical tests under identical conditions and with the same time interval of 13 weeks intervening between them.

All participants agreed beforehand to be part of this research project. They were aware that they were taking part in a research project whose aim was to develop

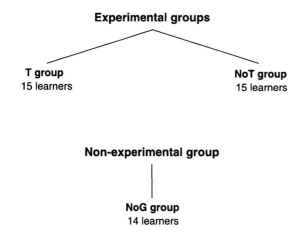

Figure 1 Distribution of participants across the three groups

teaching and learning methods and materials, but they were unaware of any further details. At the end of the instructional treatment, they all filled in a questionnaire describing relevant parts of their background (such as mother tongue, years of English instruction prior to university, etc.).

Instructional treatment

The instruction and exercise materials were designed specifically for the purposes of this study, taking into consideration what the course unit "English grammar" would normally contain. The aim was to introduce students to the grammatical analysis of the English language, and to improve their accuracy in English through explicitly teaching them certain structures and then having them do production exercises.

The instructional treatment covered 13 weeks and included 15 lessons, each 90 minutes long. In these 15 treatment lessons, students in the T group were consistently provided with exercises involving translation of full sentences or, in some cases, part of a sentence. All exercises were done in class with students working in pairs or small groups before the teacher conducted a full class discussion.

Students in the NoT group were provided with exercises targeting exactly the same structures the same number of times, but these exercises never involved translation; instead NoT students engaged in fill-in-the-blank and transformation exercises. When target structures were presented and discussed in class with the NoT group, no mention was made of differences between English and Swedish.

A noteworthy difference between the two treatments pertains to time on task. The language the NoT students were required to encode involved shorter sequences than T students when they were translating full sentences. Therefore, the NoT exercises were usually completed more quickly than the translation exercises in the T group. When the NoT students had finished their exercises, we had to shift our attention to something else in order not to provide the NoT participants with more exercise tokens for the target structures than the T participants.

As stated earlier, the NoG group read fiction in English, discussed works read in class, and wrote essays, which were handed in to their teacher for comments.

Testing instruments

All participants completed an identical pre-test and post-test battery consisting of three tests: (i) a multiple-choice test, (ii) a translation test, and (iii) a written retelling task (see Figure 2). The multiple-choice test and written retelling task did not require them to translate, whereas the translation test (Swedish into English) obviously did. The multiple-choice test was administered first, followed by the translation test and written retelling task. Participants spent approximately one hour completing the tests. In addition to the pre- and post-test battery, students were asked to complete two considerably shorter tests in week 3, with the purpose of measuring learning over one week, covering one target structure only (zero article). These results are not reported in this chapter for space considerations, but are presented in Källkvist (2004).

The target structures covered in the 13-week treatment period are of the kind that

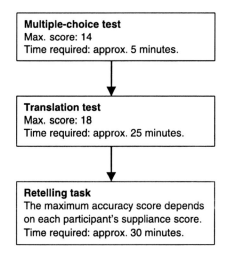

Figure 2 The tests included in the pre-test and post-test battery

we know from previous studies present Swedish university-level learners particular difficulty (Gyllstad, 1998; Karlsson, 2002; Rahm, 1998; Ruin, 1996). They were included in all tests, except for the multiple-choice test, since this test format is unsuitable for testing binary structures. The design of the multiple-choice and trans-lation tests was relatively straightforward, but gathering relatively free production data that would for certain elicit target structures of the kind studied here was a great deal more difficult. A written retelling task was developed for this purpose, and in what follows I explain in more detail the purpose and design of this task.

The written retelling task

It was considered necessary to give students verbal stimuli that would trigger the use of the target structures. A written retelling task proved to elicit tokens of the target structures in small pilot tests that were carried out prior to this study.

The retelling data were collected in the following way. When all students had completed the multiple-choice test and translation test, they were given a text entitled *Gold*, which covered three-quarters of an A4 page. It is a crime story with an unexpected ending.[3] Once students had read the text, it was collected and they were given a blank sheet of paper and were asked to write down exactly what they had read in as much detail as possible and in good English. *Gold* contained a total of 21 target structure tokens, distributed across seven different target structures. Thus, the total number of possible test item tokens a student could recall and supply was 21, although naturally no one achieved a full perfect score on either administration.

One drawback inherent in retelling tasks that are used as pre-tests and post-tests is that, if the original text to be retold in writing is identical in the pre-test and the post-test, there will inevitably be a memory effect. However, with the 13 weeks intervening this was not assumed to be a major problem. In addition, all groups completed the tasks under identical conditions, so the memory effect would affect all groups equally.

Testing procedure

The research schedule is presented schematically in Figure 3. It should be noted that teaching continued for a further three weeks after students had completed the post-tests. The reason was that the curriculum stipulated that there be a written exam at the end of the course, and it was considered important that data collection was complete before students started working in their spare time towards the exam. English was the medium of instruction for both groups.

As the majority of the participants in this study scattered immediately following the end of the course, it was not possible to include a delayed post-test. Several of the students left Halmstad University to study elsewhere or to go abroad. Some students took the course as preparation for study at university in English-speaking countries. A further shortcoming of this study is that it includes no free spontaneous production data. However, it would have been very difficult, if at all possible, to ascertain that students were using the target structures in free production, since several of these are relatively infrequent and can easily be avoided.

Results

Gains on the multiple-choice and translation tests

Tables 3 and 4 present pre-test and post-test results for each group. Table 3 provides results for the multiple-choice test. On the pre-test, the three means were similar, and a Mann-Whitney U Test revealed that there were no statistically significant differences among the three groups.

As expected, when pre-to-post gains over the 13 weeks of the study were inspected, the T and NoT groups had considerably greater gain on the multiple-choice test than the NoG group. These gains were significant in both the T ($p = 0.001$) and NoT groups ($p = 0.007$), whereas there was no statistically significant gain for the NoG group ($p = 0.321$). The only statistically significant difference in gain scores between the groups was between the T group and the NoG group ($p = 0.003$). Although the T group had greater gain than the NoT group, this was not significant ($p = 0.228$). The lack of significance can be attributed to the small number of test items

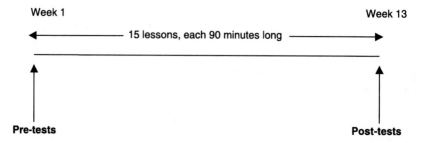

Figure 3 Research schedule

Table 3 Group means and gain scores for the multiple-choice test

	Pre-test			Post-test			Gain	Gain in % (out of possible gain)
	mean	median	SD	mean	median	SD		
T	8.87	9	1.85	10.73	11	1.79	1.86	21%
NoT	9.0	9	2.17	10.27	10	1.79	1.27	14%
NoG	8.43	8.5	1.55	8.86	9	1.35	0.43	5%

Note: Maximum possible score was 14. On both administrations, *n*-sizes were 15 for T and NoT and 14 for NoG.

Table 4 Group means and gain scores for the translation test

	Pre-test			Post-test			Gain	Gain in % (out of possible gain)
	mean	median	SD	mean	median	SD		
T	11.1	11	2.71	14.1	14	2.59	3.0	27%
NoT	10.4	11	2.10	12.8	13	2.31	2.4	23%
NoG	9.6	9.5	2.50	10.1	10	2.21	0.5	5%

Note: Maximum possible score was 18. On both administrations, *n*-sizes were 15 for T and NoT and 14 for NoG.

(the maximum score being 14) and the relatively limited number of participants (15 in either group).

Table 4 illustrates the results for the translation test, whose maximum score was 18. There were no significant differences between the pre-test scores of the three groups. On the post-test, a similar pattern to that of the multiple-choice test was revealed. The T and NoT groups had significantly higher gain scores than the NoG group (T vs. NoG: $p < 0.001$, and NoT vs. NoG: $p = 0.014$). The T group again had a higher gain score than the NoT group (27 percent vs. 23 percent), but this difference was non-significant ($p = 0.07$), although it approaches significance. This finding is all the more noteworthy because, as can be seen from the pre-test mean scores, the T group scored a mean of 11.1 compared to 10.4 for the NoT group and, thus, it had less scope for gain than the NoT group.

The results support the hypothesis that the T and NoT groups would perform better than the NoG group. The hypothesis that the T and NoT groups would have similar gains was also supported. The fact that the difference in gain between the T and NoT groups approaches significance ($p = 0.07$) in the translation test, but not in the multiple-choice test ($p = 0.228$) must be due to the smaller number of test items in the multiple-choice test (where the maximum score was 14 as compared to 18 in the translation test). It would obviously have been desirable to have longer tests, but students were already spending approximately an hour completing the pre-test battery, and another hour on the post-test.

Gains on the written retelling test

Because a written retelling task like ours is relatively rarely used or reported on in the literature, making it desirable to evaluate it as an elicitation task, a group of four native speakers of English was asked to do the task and was used as a reference group. Their results will be presented along with the learner groups in the tables below. The reference group participants were North American exchange students at Lund University and had no knowledge of Swedish when they completed the retelling pre-test. They completed the retelling task under identical conditions (i.e., 13 weeks' intervention time between pre-test and post-test).

Calculating the results for the retelling task is less straightforward than for the multiple-choice and translation tests, as each student has his or her own maximum accuracy score (based on his or her suppliance score); it was therefore not possible to compute group means and perform inferential statistics. Instead, two alternative in-depth descriptive analyses of the written retelling data were undertaken: (i) an accuracy score for each group simply on the basis of all suppliances of the target structures (Table 5), and (ii) an accuracy score for each group on the basis of the mean accuracy scores for each of the seven target structures (Table 6).

Since the accuracy score is dependent on participants' suppliance score, Table 5 provides also the mean suppliance score for each group. The number of tokens of the target structures in the text to be retold was 21. Table 5 shows that, of these, informants supplied on average between 4.29 (NoG) and 10.5 (NSs). The mean suppliance score is higher for all groups on the post-test. This is a memory effect, since the text was the same in the pre-test and post-test. NSs supplied more tokens of the target structures than any of the other groups, as a consequence of the NSs writing longer texts. This suggests that the task was easier for them than for the three groups of L2 users of English. The NSs also performed with 100 percent accuracy on all target structure tokens in both test administrations.

The gains in relative accuracy scores (percentages) suggest that there was greater gain from pre-test to post-test in the NoT group (from an accuracy score of 74 percent to 86 percent: up by 12 percentage points) than for the T group (82 percent to 86 percent: up by 4 percentage points), and for NoG (72 percent to 75 percent: up by 3 percentage points).

Table 6 presents the mean accuracy scores for each group based on the mean

Table 5 Mean number of test item tokens and standard deviation produced by each group

Group	n	Mean suppliance score	SD	Mean accuracy score	SD
T pre-test	15	5.93	3.26	4.86 (82%)	3.59
T post-test	15	9.07	3.75	7.80 (86%)	3.00
NoT pre-test	15	6.33	3.48	4.67 (74%)	2.61
NoT post-test	15	8.67	3.56	7.47 (86%)	3.11
NoG pre-test	14	4.29	2.46	3.07 (72%)	2.23
NoG post-test	14	5.71	3.02	4.29 (75%)	2.55
NSs pre-test	4	8.75	1.26	8.75 (100%)	1.26
NSs post-test	4	10.50	2.52	10.50 (100%)	2.52

Table 6 Mean accuracy scores for each group based on the means
for each of the seven target structures

Group	Mean accuracy score across seven target structures
T pre-test	72.7%
T post-test	84.0%
NoT pre-test	66.9%
NoT post-test	85.8%
NoG pre-test	67.5%
NoG post-test	65.3%

accuracy score for each of the seven target structures.[1] These results corroborate
those above: the NoT group has a greater pre-to-post test gain (18.9 percentage
points) than the T group (11.3 percentage points), and the NoG group has a drop in
accuracy rather than a slight gain (–2.2 percentage points). This decrease in accuracy
for the NoG group is due to them supplying more tokens on the post-test of certain
target structures (zero article, subject–verb agreement and pronominal reference
with U nouns, and partial inversion) that proved to be particularly challenging for
them on the pre-test. As they supplied more such tokens, there were more tokens to
commit error on.

As stated above, it is not possible to perform inferential analyses on the results
presented in Tables 5 and 6, but the descriptive patterns uniformly suggest[5] that the
NoT students had somewhat greater gain than the T students, which in all likelihood
is an exercise effect; the NoT students had done exercises in this mode (i.e., no
translation required).

I have presented so far the results that speak to research questions 1 and 3.
Research question 2 asked whether some learners are able to do equally well in both
test conditions (i.e., translation vs. retelling) regardless of exercise type (T/NoT). The
complete record of results for each student in the T and NoT groups was examined
in order to find out whether some learners are able to do well in both the translation
test and the retelling task, despite having been exposed to only one of the exercise
conditions.[6] I decided to go by the following criteria for a student to be considered to
be "doing well": (i) to have pre-to-post test gain in the translation test that equaled the
group mean gain or was above the group mean gain, and (ii) to have supplied at least
8 out of the 21 target structure tokens in the retelling post-test correctly, or to have an
accuracy score on the retelling post-test of 100 percent.[7]

The results are shown in Table 7 for the NoT group and in Table 8 for the T group.
The analysis revealed that 5 (33 percent) in the NoT group experienced gain from
the translation pre-test to the translation post-test that was equal to the group mean
(2.40) or above. These 5 students also exhibited good gain from the retelling pre-test
to the post-test. In the T group, 6 (40 percent) performed very well in both the retelling and translation tasks, following the criteria for "doing well" above. As many as
11 (73 percent) of the T group students performed very well in the retelling post-test.

The gain exhibited by the five NoT students (in bold typeface in Table 7) is
impressive and interesting. They were able to use target structures in a test condition

Table 7 Individual performances for the NoT group

Student	Translation test			Retelling	
	Pre-test	*Post-test*	*Gain*	*Pre-test*	*Post-test*
NoT1	**8**	**12**	**4**	**2/2 (100%)**	**6/6 (100%)**
NoT2	7	8	1	0/2 (0%)	4/5 (80%)
NoT3	**13**	**16**	**3**	**4/10 (40%)**	**14/17 (82%)**
NoT4	10	10	0	4/4 (100%)	5/5 (100%)
NoT5	13	14	1	6/8 (75%)	4/7 (57%)
NoT6	11	13	2	11/13 (85%)	12/12 (100%)
NoT7	10	12	2	4/5 (80%)	9/11 (82%)
NoT8	12	14	2	5/5 (100%)	6/6 (100%)
NoT9	**6**	**12**	**6**	**6/11 (55%)**	**9/10 (90%)**
NoT10	13	15	2	7/9 (78%)	5/10 (50%)
NoT11	11	12	1	7/9 (78%)	9/12 (75%)
NoT12	**10**	**15**	**5**	**5/6 (83%)**	**7/7 (100%)**
NoT13	**10**	**16**	**6**	**2/2 (100%)**	**11/11 (100%)**
NoT14	11	10	−1	3/4 (75%)	7/7 (100%)
NoT15	11	10	−1	4/5 (80%)	4/4 (100%)

Note: Translation test maximum score was 18; there was no maximum score for the written retelling task. Bolded scores signal the individuals who met "good performance" criteria.

Table 8 Individual performances for the T group

Student	Translation test			Retelling	
	Pre-test	*Post-test*	*Gain*	*Pre-test*	*Post-test*
T1	9	12	3	1/1 (100%)	5/7 (71%)
T2	11	13	2	3/7 (43%)	7/8 (87.5%)
T3	11	14	3	5/5 (100%)	6/7 (86%)
T4	**13**	**18**	**5**	**7/8 (87.5)**	**11/11 (100%)**
T5	**10**	**13**	**3**	**3/5 (60%)**	**6/6 (100%)**
T6	8	9	1	9/11 (82%)	8/12 (67%)
T7	14	16	2	6/6 (100%)	9/9 (100%)
T8	**6**	**12**	**6**	**7/8 (87.5%)**	**12/14 (86%)**
T9	14	16	2	4/4 (100%)	10/13 (77%)
T10	**13**	**17**	**4**	**3/3 (100%)**	**5/5 (100%)**
T11	11	12	1	3/3 (100%)	2/2 (100%)
T12	9	12	3	5/6 (83%)	6/7 (86%)
T13	15	17	2	7/10 (70%)	13/13 (100%)
T14	**14**	**17**	**3**	**9/11 (82%)**	**10/15 (67%)**
T15	**8**	**14**	**6**	**1/1 (100%)**	**7/7 (100%)**

Note: Translation test maximum score was 18; there was no maximum score for the written retelling task. Bolded scores signal the individuals who met "good performance" criteria.

(translation) which is known to be particularly demanding, and even though they had never used the target structures as a result of L1 prompts over the 13-week treatment period. Nevertheless, the results from this analysis also suggest that the T group had an overall superior pre-to-post test gain, in that more of them (73 percent) experienced good gain in the task for which they had had no exercises during treatment lessons.

These patterns in individual gain are in all likelihood due to the retelling task being easier than the translation test, and to the retelling task having an exercise effect for both groups. When reading the text to be retold, all informants were exposed to input of correct tokens of the target structures. Since all informants had had forms-focused exercises on the target structures, it is likely that their awareness was enhanced and noticing of these structures occurred while reading the text to be retold. The translation task, in contrast, does not provide input of correct usage of the target L2 structures. Thus the T group informants had experienced forms-focused input of both types: (i) L1-to-L2 translation, and (ii) a text (read twice) in L2 which was rich in target structure tokens.[8] It seems obvious that such a combination of input should result in enhanced learning.

Discussion

In this study, the gains in grammatical accuracy on forms-focused tests by three groups have been compared: two experimental groups (the T and the NoT groups) and a reference group (the NoG group). The study aimed to measure gains in accuracy as an effect of two different focus-on-formS treatments: translation exercises for the T group, and fill-in-the-blank and transformation exercises for the NoT group. The NoG group had no grammar instruction at all.

It was hypothesized that the two experimental groups, who had been engaged in forms-focused exercises, would have greater gains in the tests, which all measured grammatical accuracy in a number of target structures. This hypothesis was confirmed, as the T and NoT groups showed greater gains than the NoG group in all three tests. This result needs to be tempered by two qualifications, however. First, only test-like elicitation instruments were used. On tasks requiring participants to communicate spontaneously in speech or writing, we do not know whether the T and NoT groups would sustain their superiority in grammatical accuracy over the NoG focus-on-meaning group. Second, having a delayed post-test would have been desirable, but proved to be impossible, as the participants in the two experimental groups scattered on completion of the post-test battery. Nevertheless, this result agrees with previous research on the effect of focus-on-formS exercises on grammatical accuracy (reviewed in Ellis, 2005). We thus have strong support for focus-on-formS exercises being effective in terms of grammatical accuracy when measured through test-like elicitation tasks.

It should be noted that the NoG group did make progress in terms of accuracy on the target structures, but the gains were consistently modest in relation to the T and NoT groups. In the retelling task, moreover, the overall loss in accuracy scores observed for the NoG group must be attributed to their reproducing more tokens on the post-test for target structures that are particularly challenging to the Swedish learner, and therefore committing a relatively large number of errors on these. Thus, the results for the NoG group suggest that participants who are exposed to the target language without forms-focused exercises can still progress in grammatical accuracy, albeit more slowly, and that for the more challenging target structures input without attention to form is not sufficient.

The focus of the study were the results for the T and NoT groups, as these data were collected under experimental conditions. As this study was launched, it was hypothesized that the two groups would have similar gains in grammatical accuracy on all tests, since both groups were receiving explicit explanation of the same target structures the same number of times. What differed was exercise type only. The results support the hypothesis in that there were no statistically significant differences between the groups in pre-to-post test gains in the multiple-choice and translation tests (for which inferential analyses were possible). The results also suggest, however, that there is an exercise effect in two of the three tests, namely the retelling task and the translation test, where the greater gain for the T group approached the level of significance ($p = 0.07$). If the number of informants had been larger and/or the test had contained more test items, it is likely that the difference between T and NoT in the translation test would have been significant.

The exercise type effect is rather small, however, in comparison with the effect of explicit instruction on the target structure. In other words, the differences between the T and NoT groups, on the one hand, and the NoG group, on the other, were always greater than the difference between the T and NoT groups. This supports the hypothesis that explicit instruction with ensuing forms-focused exercises does make a difference when grammatical accuracy is measured by test-like elicitation instruments, but the *type* of focus-on-formS exercise makes a minor difference. The majority of the participants of the present study experienced greater gain when the test condition was the same as the exercise condition. However, 33 percent of the NoT informants had gains on the translation test that were equal to or above the mean gain for the T informants, and 73 percent of the T group informants performed very well in the retelling task. This shows that a portion of the learners are capable of performing well in forms-focused tests regardless of exercise type. Naturally, the categorical division in exercise type (one group had translation only, whereas the other had no translation at all) was made in an effort to address strictly the main research questions of this study. If one were to teach a focus-on-formS unit within a FL program without being constrained by the design of a research project, it would be more pedagogically sound to have learners engage in a combination of different types of exercises as well as receiving enhanced input. The findings gleaned in the present study further support the claim that combining both types of exercises would be sensible, good practice.

Since results suggest superior performance by the T group only in translation tasks, this study provides little support for the elaborateness of processing view advanced in Hummel (1995). According to this view, L1-to-L2 translation should lead to enhanced interconnections, which in turn should enhance elaborate memory traces that are more resistant to forgetting. Hummel may be right that L1-to-L2 translation leads to enhanced memory, but this effect may hold primarily when participants translate from L1 to L2, that is, the mode in which they operate is identical to exercise mode. On completion of translation exercises, perhaps exposure to a number of examples of the target structure in L2 is needed for learners to be able to encode the structure in conditions which do not involve translation. The T students had this, at least to a limited extent, since they read the text to be recalled, but their gain in the retelling task was still not superior to the NoT group. Ultimately, brain-scanning techniques involving some participants being engaged in translation and some not should be used if the elaborateness of processing hypothesis is to be properly put to the test.

This longitudinal study covering a period of 13 weeks was conducted within the limits of an existing syllabus and involved relatively little intervention in the way the course was normally run. Naturally, these circumstances led to a number of weaknesses: (i) it was the admission policies of Halmstad University rather than the needs of the research project that determined the number of possible participants; (ii) the fact that the treatments covered a relatively long period of time led to attrition in the number of informants, since 100 percent attendance was required for an informant to be exposed to the treatment; (iii) it was important to control for L1 interference, and for this reason only students whose L1 was Swedish were included; (iv) delayed post-testing was not done, due to a number of the students leaving immediately on the completion of the course. Naturally, the findings of this study need to be corroborated by replication, preferably including a larger number of informants, and by the study of different language pairs.

Implications for pedagogy

This study does not provide support for forms-focused courses for advanced learners that involve translation only. My results suggest that advanced learners who have been engaged in forms-focused exercises in L2 that involve no translation have somewhat superior performance in a writing task which requires them to operate directly in L2, even when they use target structures that are known to be particularly difficult due to contrastive differences between their L1 and L2. Since my results suggest that translation exercises can lead to superior performance in translation tasks, L1-to-L2 translation of the kind used in the present study has a place, albeit limited, in advanced-level courses when students share the same L1. If we expect and aim for our learners to be able to use the L2 well when communicating in situations in which they are required to translate and in situations in which they need to express themselves directly in L2, it seems fully reasonable that we provide them with exercises and rich, varied, and enhanced input of either kind. This is in line with recommendations made by educators and by translation studies experts reviewed above, who advocate the judicious use of translation. Also, by combining both types of exercise, learners will be exposed to a larger number of tokens of the target structure than would be the case if they were restricted to translating, which is more time-consuming. Moreover, their minds are stimulated in two ways, one of which involves comparison with the L1.

Finally, a great deal more empirical research on the effect of translation exercises/tasks is needed for us to more fully understand when to opt for translation in the L2 classroom.

Notes

I gratefully acknowledge funding for this study from the Swedish Council for Research (no. F0576/97). I also wish to thank Mats Johansson and Ursula Wallin, who gave me permission to conduct this study at Halmstad University, and Ulla Ahlqvist at Per Brahe Upper Secondary School in Jönköping, Sweden, who allowed me to collect data in one of her groups.

1. A complete list of the 40 publications is available from the author.
2. It was not possible to form a proper control group (i.e., a randomly assigned group of students who would have no formS-focused treatment at all) among the students at Halmstad University due to their curriculum stipulating that a course in English grammar be included in the first semester.
3. *Gold* was written by Gillian Brown, Kirsten Malmkjær, and John Williams (see Brown, 1994), but was modified for the purposes of the present study.
4. The seven target structures were: capital letter; zero article with uncountable nouns with generic reference; subject–verb agreement and pronominal reference with uncountable nouns in English whose equivalents in Swedish are countable; nominalized adjective disallowed in English but possible in Swedish; the use of *would* in a main clause containing a conditional sub-clause; partial inversion; and the use of the preposition *in* preceding year (e.g., *in 1998*).
5. A by-structure analysis covering all seven structures (a total of 21 tokens) was also carried out. This analysis provided further support that the NoT participants experienced greater gain: they had greater gain than the T group on five of the seven structures; for the remaining two, it was not possible to measure gain, since the NoT group performed at 100 percent accuracy in the pre-test.
6. The multiple-choice test is excluded from this analysis, since, due its test format, it did not contain tokens of all target structures among its test items.
7. Stating criteria for "doing well" in the retelling task is less straightforward than the other tasks, as it is not possible to compute a group mean for this task.
8. All participants in this study were exposed to English through novels and other books that they read as part of their course, and in all likelihood via the media (for example, undubbed TV programs and the internet), music, etc. over the 13-week treatment period. As a result, the T students may actually have encountered a number of tokens of the target structures in English during the 13 weeks.

References

Allford, D. (1999). Translation in the communicative classroom. In N. Pachler (Ed.), *Teaching modern languages at advanced level*. London: Routledge.

Anderson, J. (1990). *Cognitive psychology and its implications* New York: W. H. Freeman and Co.

Berggren, I. (1972). Does the use of translation exercises have negative effects on the learning of a second language? In *Rapport 14*, Department of English, Gothenburg University, Sweden.

Brown, G. (1994). The role of nominal and verbal expressions in retelling narratives: Implications for discourse representations. *Working Papers in English and Applied Linguistics, 1*, 81–90.

Cunico, S. (2004). Translation as a purposeful activity in the language classroom. *Tuttitalia, 29*, 4–12.

Danan, M. (1992). Reversed subtitling and dual coding theory: New directions for foreign language instruction. *Language Learning, 42*, 497–527.

Duff, A. (1989). *Translation*. Oxford: Oxford University Press.

Ellis, R. (2002). Does form-focused instruction affect the acquisition of implicit knowledge? A review of the research. *Studies in Second Language Acquisition, 24*, 223–236.

Ellis, R. (2005). Instructed language learning and task-based teaching. In E. Hinkel (Ed.), *Handbook of research in second language teaching and learning*. Mahwah, NJ: Lawrence Erlbaum.

Fotos, S. (2005). Traditional and grammar translation methods for second language teaching. In E. Hinkel (Ed.), *Handbook of research in second language teaching and learning*. Mahwah, NJ: Lawrence Erlbaum.

Fraser, J. (1996). "I understand the French, but I don't know how to put it into English": Developing undergraduates' awareness of and confidence in the translation process. In P. Sewell and I. Higgins (Eds.), *Teaching translation in universities: Present and future perspectives*. London: CILT.

González Davies, M. (2001). Translation in foreign language learning: Bridging the gap. Paper presented at the APAC-ELT Convention, Barcelona.

González Davies, M. (2004). *Multiple voices in the translation classroom*. Philadelphia, PA: John Benjamins.

Gorsuch, G. J. (1998). *Yakudoku* EFL Instruction in two Japanese high school classrooms: An exploratory study. *JALT Journal, 20*, 6–32.

Gyllstad, H. (1998). A study of grammatical errors in free compositions by advanced Swedish learners and the significance of negative transfer. Unpublished Master's thesis, Department of English, Lund University, Sweden.

Holobow, N. E., Lambert, W. E., and Sayegh, L. (1984). Pairing script and dialogue: combinations that show promise for second or foreign language learning. *Language Learning, 34*, 59–76.

Hummel, K. (1995). Translation and second language learning. *Canadian Modern Language Review, 51*, 444–455.

Källkvist, M. (2004). The effect of translation exercises versus gap-exercises on the learning of difficult L2 structures: Preliminary results of an empirical study. In K. Malmkjær (Ed.), *Translation in undergraduate degree programmes*. Philadelphia, PA: John Benjamins.

Kaneko, T. (1991). The role of the first language in foreign language classrooms. Unpublished doctoral dissertation, Temple University, Japan.

Karlsson, M. (2002). *Progression and regression: Aspects of advanced Swedish students' competence in English grammar*. Lund: Lund University Press.

Klapper, J. (2006). *Understanding and developing good practice teaching languages in higher education*. London: CILT.

Klein-Braley, C., and Franklin, P. (1998). "The foreigner in the refrigerator." Remarks about teaching translation to university students of foreign languages. In K. Malmkjær (Ed.). *Translation and language teaching: Language teaching and translation* (pp. 53–63) Manchester: St. Jerome.

Kupferberg, I., and Olshtain, E. (1996). Explicit contrastive instruction facilitates the acquisition of difficult L2 forms. *Language Awareness, 5*, 149–165.

Lambert, W. E. (1986). Pairing first- and second-language speech and writing in ways that aid language acquisition. In J. Vaid (Ed.), *Language processing in bilinguals: Psycholinguistic and neuropsychological perspectives*. Mahwah, NJ: Lawrence Erlbaum.

Lockhart, R. S., and Craik, R. I. M. (1990). Levels of processing: A retrospective commentary on a framework for memory research. *Canadian Journal of Psychology, 44*, 87–112.

Long, M. (1991). Focus on form: A design feature in language teaching methodology. In K. de Bot, R. Ginsberg, and C. Kramsch (Eds.), *Foreign language research in cross-cultural perspective*. Philadelphia, PA: John Benjamins.

Malmkjær, K. (1998). Introduction: Translation and language teaching. In K. Malmkjær (Ed.), *Translation and language teaching: Language teaching and translation* (pp. 1–15). Manchester: St. Jerome.

Newson, D. (1998). Translation and foreign language learning. In K. Malmkjær (Ed.), *Translation and language teaching: Language teaching and translation* (pp. 63–69). Manchester: St. Jerome.

Norris, J., and Ortega, L. (2001). Effectiveness of L2 instruction: A research synthesis and quantitative meta-analysis. *Language Learning, 50,* 417–528.

Nott, D. (2002) "Translation from and into the foreign language." In LTSN Subject Centre for Languages, Linguistics and Area Studies (Ed.), *The guide to good practice for learning and teaching in languages, linguistics and area studies.* Accessed online on August 15, 2005 at www.lang.ltsn.ac.uk/resources/goodpractice.aspx?resourceid=427

Owen, D. (2003). Where's the treason in translation? Humanising Language Teaching Magazine, *49,* 1. Accessed online on August 15, 2005. www.htlmag.co.uk/jan03/mart1.htm

Rahm, J. (1998). ". . . to who it concerns . . ." A study of grammatical errors in students' translations from Swedish into English. Unpublished Master's thesis, Department of English, Lund University, Sweden.

Rivera-Mills, S. V., and Gantt, B. N. (1999). From linguistic analysis to cultural awareness: A translation framework for the Spanish language classroom. *JOLIB, 10,* 1–13.

Rolin-Ianziti, J., and Brownlie, S. (2002). Teacher use of learners' native language in the foreign language classroom. *Canadian Modern Language Review, 58,* 402–426.

Ruin, I. (1996). *Grammar and the advanced learner: On learning and teaching a second language.* Uppsala: Studia Anglistica Upsaliensia.

Satorres, B., and Closa, A. (2003). Translation in the classroom. Why not? *Associació de Professors d'Anglès de Catalunya, 49,* 22–30.

Schjoldager, A. (2003). Translation for language purposes: Preliminary results of an experimental study of translation and picture verbalization. *Hermes, 30,* 199–213.

Schjoldager, A. (2004). Are L2 learners prone to err when they translate? In K. Malmkjær (Ed.), *Translation in undergraduate degree programmes* (pp. 127–149). Philadelphia, PA: John Benjamins.

Sewell, P. (1996). Translation in the curriculum. In P. Sewell and I. Higgins (Eds.), *Teaching translation in universities: Present and future perspectives.* London: CILT.

Sewell, P. (2004). Students buzz around the translation class like bees round the honey pot—why? In K. Malmkjær (Ed.), *Translation in undergraduate degree programmes* (pp. 151–162). Philadelphia, PA: John Benjamins.

Shih, M. (1999). More than practicing language: Communicative reading and writing for Asian settings. *TESOL Journal, 8,* 20–25.

Slavikova, H. (1990). Translating and the acquisition of Italian as a second language. Unpublished doctoral dissertation, University of Toronto, Canada.

Spada, N., and Lightbown, P. M. (1999). Instruction, first language influence, and developmental readiness in second language acquisition. *Modern Language Journal, 83,* 1–22.

11 Longitudinal gain of higher-order inferential abilities in L2 English

Accuracy, speed, and conventionality

Naoko Taguchi

Abstract

Pragmatic comprehension entails understanding both the literal meaning of an utterance and the force behind the words imbued by speaker's intention (Thomas, 1995). Given these high-order inferential processing demands, pragmatic comprehension is an area for the development of advanced L2 capacities, requiring efficient listening abilities that draw on well-developed and subtle representations of implicit and explicit knowledge. Rapid, effortless, and accurate skill execution in pragmatic processing is a fundamental characteristic of advanced second language use (Segalowitz, 2003). Hence, accuracy and speed of pragmatic processing can be investigated as two distinct, yet complementary aspects of advancedness in language proficiency. The present study employed this framework to examine the longitudinal development of pragmatic comprehension ability among Japanese college students studying English. Twenty native speakers of English and 92 Japanese learners of L2 English completed a computerized listening test that measured their ability to comprehend implied meaning. The L2 learners completed the test twice, before and after a seven-week course that did not involve pragmatic instruction. Results showed that over a seven-week period these L2 learners made a significant improvement in accuracy (i.e., the number of items answered correctly) and speed (i.e., time taken to answer each item correctly). However, the magnitude of effect was smaller for the speed gain than that for the accuracy gain. In addition, the gain over the seven-week period for comprehension of more conventionalized and less conventionalized items was similar in size. The findings have important implications for theoretical discussions of whether accuracy and speed of pragmatic processing develop in a parallel manner and jointly characterize the course of second language acquisition. They also offer insights on how the gradual development of advanced pragmatic comprehension abilities can be fostered in foreign language contexts which offer limited opportunities for pragmatic awareness and associative practices.

Introduction

Pragmatic comprehension, an aspect of pragmatic competence, entails understanding both the literal meaning of an utterance and the force behind the words imbued by a speaker's intention (Thomas, 1995). Given the demands of higher-order inferential processing, pragmatic comprehension is considered as an aspect of more advanced second language (L2) capacities, because it requires efficient listening abilities that draw on well-developed and subtle representations of implicit and explicit knowledge. Because rapid, effortless, and accurate skill execution is a fundamental characteristic of advanced L2 use (Segalowitz, 2003), accuracy and speed of pragmatic processing can be investigated as two distinct, yet complementary aspects of "advancedness" in language proficiency. A further question is the extent to which accuracy and speed in pragmatic comprehension develops in foreign language contexts that offer limited opportunities for pragmatic awareness and associative practices. The present study employed this framework to examine the longitudinal gains in pragmatic comprehension ability experienced among 92 Japanese college students studying English as a foreign language context. It investigated whether there are gains in pragmatic comprehension over a period of a seven-week intensive course in terms of accuracy and speed of higher-order inferential processing, and whether the magnitude of gains differs over varying degrees of conventionality encoded implied meaning items.

Pragmatic competence and advanced L2 capacities

Interest in pragmatics in L2 teaching and assessment has increased a great deal over the last few decades, corresponding to the emphasis on the development of functional and sociocultural aspects of communicative ability (ACTFL, 1999; Council of Europe, 2001). It is now widely believed that being a proficient user of an L2 involves mastery of functional usage of the language in communicative contexts. Hence, pragmatic competence—the ability to use language to perform functions appropriately—has been recognized as an indispensable component of L2 communicative competence (Bachman and Palmer, 1996; Canale and Swain, 1980) and has attracted much interest in the study of advanced communicative ability.

Some aspects of pragmatic competence are considered difficult to acquire and potentially late-emerging in learners' systems for several reasons. First, pragmatic competence entails the ability to control the complex interplay of language, language users, and language use contexts (Levinson, 1983; Mey, 1993; Thomas, 1983, 1995). The complex nature of pragmatics is reflected in the distinction between pragmalinguistics and sociopragmatics (Leech, 1983; and see Kasper, 1992; Thomas, 1983). Pragmalinguistics refers to the linguistic resources available in context, while sociopragmatics refers to the user's assessment of the context in which the linguistic resources are put to use. In order to become pragmatically competent, one needs a range of usable linguistic resources, and at the same time one needs to be able to evaluate layers of contextual information, select the most appropriate linguistic resource in context, and use it effectively. It is the combination of linguistic ability and contextual sensitivity that makes fully mature pragmatic competence difficult to acquire.

Another difficulty related to the acquisition of pragmatic competence is the sociocultural nature of the construct. Sociolinguistic functions are often difficult to perform because the mappings of forms, functions, and contexts are culture-specific and vary across languages. Although some pragmatic functions are claimed to be universal (Kasper and Rose, 2002), linguistic means to encode and decode those functions exhibit considerable variation across cultures (e.g., Blum-Kulka, House, and Kasper, 1989). As Saville-Troike (1996) noted, interactional skills, a component of communicative competence, subsume the knowledge of social conventions that mobilize the use of linguistic knowledge in context. Thus, knowledge of social conventions, namely how linguistic behaviors are structured in a society, is an important aspect of L2 learning. However, because social conventions of speaking are not salient, it is often difficult to notice how people convey appropriate levels of politeness, or what linguistic means they use to communicate meaning indirectly (Wolfson, 1989). Furthermore, since learners already have their L1 norms, they may transfer them to the L2 and end up with what Thomas (1983) calls "pragmatic failure" when the two languages operate under different conventions.

These observations collectively suggest that full pragmatic competence is an aspect of more advanced L2 capacities that may be attained at a later stage of L2 development. Pragmatic competence involves multiple sub-competencies. It involves the mastery of linguistic and non-linguistic knowledge and efficient control of both types of knowledge when encoding and decoding language functions in sociocultural context.

Two attributes of pragmatic comprehension ability: accuracy and speed

Within the construct of pragmatic competence, pragmatic comprehension ability is an important aspect to examine. Pragmatic comprehension involves an inferential process of understanding what a speaker intends to accomplish in making utterances. Meaning is conveyed at two levels: utterance meaning, or literal sense of words uttered; and force, or speaker's intention behind the words (Thomas, 1995). Since pragmatic comprehension entails understanding meaning at both levels, it requires decoding linguistic and contextual cues and using them to make inferences of speakers' intentions behind the cues. Given these demands, pragmatic comprehension requires efficient inferential abilities that draw on well-developed and subtle representations of implicit and explicit knowledge. Pragmatic comprehension is an effortful task in the L2 because learners have to recognize the mismatch between the literal utterance and the intended meaning, and reprocess the literal information to infer the implied message. The greater the mismatch is, the greater the processing effort becomes. Thus, competence in pragmatic comprehension subsumes accurate understanding of the implied speaker message, as well as efficient and speedy processing of the message, regardless of the distance between the literal meaning and intended meaning.

Traditionally, the end state of L2 acquisition was considered as the acquisition of language knowledge or competence (e.g., the knowledge of grammar and vocabulary) (Chomsky, 1965). Recently, researchers have paid more attention to the processing dimension of L2 acquisition, by examining how learners access linguistic information in real time (Anderson, 1990; McLaughlin, 1987). Because rapid and accurate skill execution is the fundamental goal of L2 acquisition (Segalowitz, 2001, 2003), linguistic knowledge and processing capacity should form two distinct, yet complementary aspects of "advancedness" in L2 proficiency. Hence, analyses of accuracy and speed combined should inform us whether or not the two aspects develop in a parallel manner and jointly characterize the course of L2 attainment.

In L2 pragmatic literature, Taguchi (2005) is one of the few studies that measured both speed and accuracy in pragmatic comprehension. Forty-six native speakers of English and 164 Japanese EFL learners completed a listening task measuring ability to comprehend different types of implied meaning: indirect requests, indirect refusals, and indirect opinion expressions. Results showed that, for these L2 learners, comprehension of indirect requests and refusals was significantly easier and less time-consuming than that of indirect opinions. There was a significant L2 proficiency impact on accuracy, but not on speed. There was no significant relationship between accuracy and speed of comprehension.

Because Taguchi's study used a cross-sectional design, findings were limited to the descriptions of pragmatic abilities and did not provide developmental accounts of accuracy and speed in pragmatic comprehension. Therefore, questions remain whether or not the two dimensions, the acquisition of pragmatic knowledge (i.e., operationalized as accuracy of response during comprehension) and the achievement of automatic control in processing that knowledge (i.e., operationalized as speed of response during comprehension), develop in a parallel manner and jointly characterize the course of pragmatic development. These questions should be better addressed in a longitudinal study that aims to capture developmental patterns of accuracy and speed as two distinct, yet complementary aspects of more advanced capacities in pragmatic comprehension ability.

Conventionality and inferential difficulty

In pragmatic comprehension, one factor that affects the inferential process and its processing effort is the level of conventionality encoded in utterances. Morgan (1978) defined conventionality as common knowledge of how things are done, encompassing both knowledge of language and language use. Commonality of knowledge is understood at different levels. Knowledge can be common across languages and cultures, or knowledge can be common among in-group members of a specific culture. When meaning is based on shared knowledge and conventions, it may be easier to comprehend for L2 learners, not only because it poses fewer processing demands, but also because it allows for the possibility of successful transfer of pragmatic knowledge from the L1. However, when the knowledge of convention is culture-specific, or not shared between L1 and L2, it might be more difficult for L2 learners to recognize, because they have to learn the social conventions of the target community and the linguistic and non-linguistic means to encode the conventions in the target language. The knowledge of convention has also been discussed as "frames" or schemata (Kasper; 1984, van Dijk, 1977). Frames constitute the hierarchical organizing principle that relates purposes of utterances to contexts and events (van Dijk, 1977). Some utterances become relevant when interlocutors are aware of the sociocultural rules and conventions associated with certain frames.

Some indirect speech acts are rather conventional in use across different cultures, and thus their intentions are more easily recognized than other non-conventional speech acts, because certain language use patterns and a closed set of expressions may be shared among language groups for those speech acts (Gibbs, 1981, 1983; Morgan, 1978). For instance, both in Japanese and English, when refusing someone's invitation, it is customary that one provides a reason for not accepting the invitation (Beebe, Takahashi, and Uliss-Weltz, 1990; Nelson *et al.*, 2002). Then, for Japanese speakers leaning L2 English, comprehension of indirect refusals can be relatively easy because it does not require extensive L2 inferencing. Learners can understand the intended meaning based on the shared conventions of language use, and do not have to process a great number of contextual cues. Nevertheless, when a frame is conventionalized but also embedded in a culture-specific practice, L2 learners may find it difficult to process.

Different from conventionalized speech acts, there are less conventional speech acts that could impose greater processing demands. Expressing indirect opinions, as shown in B's response below, is an example of a less conventional speech act:

A: Did you like the gift?
B: The wrapping paper was OK.

These speech acts are less conventionalized because meaning is not simply attached to a single expression and, instead, the speech acts are open-ended in realization. In the example above, because utterances used to express opinions of the gift are wide open, comprehension requires more effort. Namely, a greater number of linguistic and contextual cues needs to be processed in order to arrive at the intended meaning. Contextual cues needed to comprehend these indirect opinions are not limited to situational characteristics which generally make up a frame. Comprehension also relies on a broad cognitive context, including the set of all the assumptions and facts that a language user has about the world (Sperber and Wilson, 1995). Due to the broader contextual cues to be processed, along with the open set of expressions, comprehension of non-conventional indirect expressions imposes greater processing demands.

In summary, conventional and non-conventional speech acts, when indirectly conveyed, present different types of comprehension demands for L2 learners. Knowledge of conventions of language use and sociocultural rules behind the conventions is indispensable for successful comprehension of conventional indirect speech acts. When learners are aware of the norms of interaction and language use, or when the norms are shared between their L1 and L2 (e.g., indirect refusals in Japanese and English), meaning becomes transparent for learners, as long as they have sufficient linguistic skills to comprehend the utterances. By contrast, because non-conventional indirect speech acts, such as indirect opinions, do not operate within predictable patterns of discourse or lexical items, comprehension involves intensive bottom–up and top–down processing in which learners analyze syntax and lexicon-level information as well as contextual cues to infer meaning. Due to a greater number of linguistic and contextual cues to process, there is more extensive searching for meaning in non-conventional implicatures. "Advancedness" in pragmatic comprehension, then, could be in part characterized as the ability to comprehend a wide range of implied meaning types, both conventional and non-conventional.

In L2 pragmatics research, a relatively small number of studies to date has examined conventionality within the inferential process of implied meaning (notably Bouton, 1992, 1994, 1999; Carrell, 1981, 1984; Cook and Liddicoat, 2002; Kasper, 1984; Koike, 1996; Roever, 2001; Takahashi and Roitblat, 1994; Taguchi, 2002, 2005). Cook and Liddicoat (2002) examined L2 comprehension of request expressions. Fifty native speakers and 100 ESL learners of two proficiency levels responded to a written questionnaire that had 15 brief scenarios followed by a request-making expression. The expressions had three directness levels: direct (e.g., *Pass me the salt*), conventional indirect (e.g., *Can you pass me the salt?*), and non-conventional indirect (e.g., *Are you putting salt on my meat?*). The high proficiency learners had difficulty in understanding non-conventional indirect forms, while the low proficiency group had difficulty in both forms.

Taguchi (2002) also documented different difficulty levels across implied meaning types of different levels of conventionality. Eight Japanese ESL learners listened to 15 dialogues that included three types of indirect information based on Holtgraves (1999): indirect refusals, indirect disclosure of information, and indirect expression of opinions and information. Analyses of the learners' verbal protocols revealed that comprehension of indirect refusals required less effort than indirect expression of opinion and information. The higher proficiency learners used fewer strategies to interpret indirect refusals than the other two types of implied meaning, suggesting differential comprehension load among indirect expressions.

These studies suggest a potential relationship between learners' proficiency levels and the range of implied meaning types that they can handle. Meanings that are more conventionalized, regular, and thus require fewer linguistic and cognitive resources are more easily processed, regardless of the proficiency levels, as long as learners can take advantage of the conventionality. In contrast, meanings that are more context-dependent and less common or highly culture-specific are more difficult to comprehend, particularly for lower-level learners. These findings imply that the difficulty order among implied meaning types could indicate the developmental order in pragmatic comprehension. This assumption is worth pursuing further, because very few studies to date examined this issue in a longitudinal design.

Pragmatic development and context of learning

The research context selected for the present investigation was a Japanese university where students first study English as a foreign language and then use it as the medium of their regular instruction. This context was chosen for several reasons. First, it was selected because it is a foreign language context, as opposed to a second language context. Several studies have documented the superiority of a second language over a foreign language context in fostering the development of pragmatic ability (Bardovi-Harlig and Dörnyei, 1998; Barron, 2002; Matsumura, 2001; Schauer, 2006). Foreign language learners are considered to have limited access to authentic, contextualized input that helps them to analyze patterns of indirect communication. In addition, foreign language learners may be slow in the development of processing speed due to limited incidental exposure to L2 input. It is claimed that performance speed develops with consistent, repeated association practices between input and learners' responses to them (Ellis, 2001, 2003). Such practices do not occur frequently in a foreign language context, suggesting little speed increase over time among foreign language learners.

Another reason for the choice of this context is to empirically document pragmatic abilities of Japanese university students who received six years of English education in junior and senior high schools. Although recent educational policies and curricular reforms emphasize the development of students' functional ability (Ministry of Education, Culture, Sports, Science, and Technology, 1999, 2003), empirical examinations of their abilities are still rare. Thus, pragmatic ability at the college level is an important aspect to address to see whether or not the current educational system helps foster the attainment of more advanced communicative ability by the time students enter the upper stage of their educational career. In addition, although foreign language learners with many years of English education may have developed quite advanced levels of "knowledge" in general areas of L2, including pragmatic knowledge, they may be less adept in terms of automatic processing of that knowledge. Therefore, accurate and speedy comprehension of pragmatic meaning is worthy of investigation among Japanese university students who have received six years of formal English education focused on "knowledge."

The need for a longitudinal perspective on L2 pragmatic development

Because some aspects of pragmatic competence are potentially late-developed, longitudinal analyses of the pathways towards becoming a competent pragmatic user of the L2 are important in order to document learners' progression from the initial state to their ultimate attainment. Yet, pragmatic development has been an under-represented area of longitudinal investigation (Kasper and Rose, 2002). In L2 pragmatics in particular, much research has been confined to snapshot descriptions of learners' pragmatic behaviors at a given point in time, and very few studies to date have employed a longitudinal research design to examine a route of pragmatic development, as evidenced by difficulty orders or discrete stages of development (Bardovi-Harlig, 1999; Kasper and Rose, 2002). Thus, longitudinal analyses of pragmatic competence would be valuable in order to situate L2 pragmatic research within the scope of acquisition research. Such analyses would also contribute to elucidating the defining characteristics of advanced L2 proficiency that are considered to take a substantial amount of time to attain.

Only one study to date has examined the development of pragmatic comprehension over time using a pre- and post-test design. Bouton (1992) investigated ESL learners' comprehension of implicatures by using a written test that had 33 short dialogues. Results showed that learners' comprehension of idiosyncratic, less conventional implicatures improved over three years along with their length of residence in the target country. Comprehension of formulaic, more conventional implicatures, which required culture-specific knowledge to comprehend meaning, showed much less pronounced development. Building upon Bouton's work, more longitudinal research is needed to examine whether the ability to understand different implied meaning types develops over time, and whether the developmental patterns vary across meanings of different conventionality.

Research questions

The present study examined comprehension ability of implied meaning among college students in a Japanese university (hereafter "EFL students"). The purpose of the study was twofold: to document any gains in accuracy and speed of comprehension over a seven-week term, and to analyze the gains in relation to varying degree of conventionality encoded in implied meaning to seek out the nature of the difficulty involved in particular types of implied meaning. The two research questions below guided the study:

1. Does EFL learners' comprehension of implied meaning improve over time in terms of accuracy and speed of comprehension? If so, does the degree of improvement differ for implied meanings of two degrees of conventionality?
2. What are the characteristics of the implied meaning items that showed little improvement in EFL learners' comprehension over time?

Methodology

Participants

Participants in this study were 92 Japanese EFL students enrolled in the first session of an intensive English program (IEP) in a Japanese university. There were 21 males and 71 females with an average age of 18.26. The learners received between 16 and 20 hours of English instruction per week over a half-semester period (seven weeks). There was no specific focus on pragmatic instruction. English was the instructional medium in the program. Among the 92 EFL learners, only three students had lived abroad (and, in these three cases, for a period no longer than nine months).

Instrumentation: pragmatic listening task

Participants' ability to comprehend implied meaning was assessed by a computerized listening task comprising 60 items: 2 practice items, 10 filler items, and 48 experimental items. The items were drawn from Taguchi (2003, 2005), who had adapted items from previous studies with permission (Bouton, 1992, 1994; Holtgraves, 1999; Kotsonis, 1981; Roever, 2005). Internal consistency reliability of the task based on the Cronbach's alpha was 0.85 for the full test, 0.72 for refusal items, and 0.71 for opinion items.

Each item had a short dialogue spoken by a male and a female native English speaker. In the experimental dialogues, the reply that appeared at the end violated the maxim of relevance (Grice, 1975) and did not provide a straightforward answer to the speaker's question. A yes–no question followed each dialogue to check the participants' comprehension of speaker intention.

The task was computerized using the SuperLab Pro Program for Windows (Cedrus, 2003). The 48 experimental items had two item types: indirect refusals ($k = 24$) and indirect opinions ($k = 24$). Examples of the items by conventionality type are given in Table 1.

Utterances in indirect refusals took the form of providing a reason and were written so as to avoid explicit linguistic markers of refusals such as *No* or *I don't want to*. Indirect refusals were considered conventional because all the utterances used to convey refusals took a form of providing a reason, which is considered as a shared refusal routine between Japanese and English (Beebe, Takahashi, and Uliss-Weltz, 1990; Nelson *et al.*, 2002). Indirect opinion items were expressions used to convey opinions in a non-literal manner. Indirect opinions were considered less conventional because they did not reflect discourse routines or conven-

Table 1 Sample pragmatic listening task items

Indirect refusals (k = 24)	Indirect opinions (k = 24)
Susan: Hi Dave. How are you? Dave: Hi Susan. I'm OK. What have you been up to lately? Susan: Well, not much new or exciting, but I'm having a party this Saturday, and it should be fun. I hope you can come. Dave: I already have plans on Saturday. Q: Can the man come to the party?	Mary: Hi John, I'm back. John: Hey Mary, welcome back. You must be really tired after rushing around for your friend's wedding. Mary: Yeah, I'm so tired. I haven't slept much in the last three days. John: How did you like the wedding? Mary: The cake was OK. Q: Did the woman like the wedding?

tions of language use specific to Japanese or English patterns. The number of words that appeared in the yes–no questions was also kept approximately the same, either six or seven words, in order to reduce the effect of extraneous variables (e.g., reading time).

Data collection procedures

The pragmatic listening task was given to the participants using Windows computers on campus. After sitting in front of the computer, the participants put on headphones and read instructions on the computer screen in their L1. Before starting the test items, they practiced two items. Immediately following each aural dialogue, a yes–no question appeared on the screen. Participants responded by pressing two keys that were adjacent to each other on the keyboard: "1" for "yes" and "2" for "no." Once they chose the answer, the computer automatically took them to the next item. Response time was measured between the moment when the question appeared on the screen and the moment when the participants pressed the key. The computer recorded all responses and their latencies in seconds. The same procedure was repeated seven weeks later for all 92 participants.

Data analysis

The first research question examined the short-term development of accuracy and speed of pragmatic comprehension over a seven-week term, over two types of implied meaning items: indirect refusals and indirect opinions. The independent variable was time, and the dependent variables were accuracy scores and response times in the pragmatic listening task. Accuracy had an interval scale between 0 and 24 for each item type. Comprehension speed, also interval data, was calculated by averaging the number of seconds taken to answer each item correctly. Gains in pragmatic comprehension were analyzed using four matched-pair t-tests by comparing the differences in accuracy scores and response times between the pre- and post-test sessions for each item type. Prior to the statistical analyses, distributions of the variables were examined for underlying assumptions. The significance level for hypothesis testing was set at 0.05; however, because the research used four statistical comparisons, the alpha level was adjusted to 0.0125 using the Bonferroni correction in order to avoid a Type One error (Jaeger, 1993).

The second research question asked about the characteristics of the implied meaning items that showed little improvement in EFL learners' comprehension over time. The question was addressed qualitatively, by identifying the items that had a low accuracy rate in the pre- and post-test and examining them for shared features.

Results

Gains in accuracy and speed in pragmatic comprehension

The results for accuracy and speed of responses on the listening task are shown in Table 2. Let us examine the results for accuracy first. As can be seen in Table 2, there was a significant mean score difference in accuracy of responses between pre- and post-tests for refusal items ($t = 6.78$, $df = 91$, $p < .0125$) as well as for opinion items ($t = 5.03$, $df = 91$, $p < .0125$), indicating that the EFL learners achieved a significant gain in accurate comprehension of implied meaning. When effect sizes for accuracy were compared, the change for opinions was medium-sized (eta-square = 0.22) and the change for refusals was relatively larger (eta-square = 0.33). Moreover, the descriptive statistics show that indirect, less conventionalized opinions were more difficult than indirect, conventionalized refusals for these 92 learners. Namely, both on the pre-test and on the post-test, the average response behavior on the opinion items was less accurate and slower than the average response behavior on the refusal items. Thus, the gains in pragmatic comprehension experienced among these 92 students over seven weeks seem to have partially depended on the degree of conventionality encoded in the items. The ability to comprehend more conventionalized meaning accurately was more established at the onset of the study and showed

Table 2 Gains in accuracy score and response times

		Mean	SD	t	p	Effect size
Accuracy gains						
Refusals ($k = 24$)	Pre-test	19.38	2.58			
				6.78	.012	.33
	Post-test	21.09	2.17			
Opinions ($k = 24$)	Pre-test	15.84	2.67			
				5.03	.000	.22
	Post-test	17.07	2.56			
Speed gains						
Refusals ($k = 24$)	Pre-test	5.18	1.65			
				2.55	.012	.07
	Post-test	4.81	1.62			
Opinions ($k = 24$)	Pre-test	6.35	1.70			
				3.08	.000	.09
	Post-test	5.69	2.01			

Notes: $n = 92$, k = the number of items. The time refers to the average number of seconds taken to answer each item correctly. Effect size is based on eta-square.

greater improvement over a short period of time. This pattern of results supports the prediction that conventional implied meanings (operationalized as indirect refusals in this study) pose fewer developmental demands than non-conventional implied meanings (operationalized as indirect opinions here).

Regarding the results for speed of processing, the response time difference between the pre- and post-test was statistically significantly different for refusal items ($t = 2.55$, $df = 91$, $p < .0125$) as well as for opinion items ($t = 3.08$, $df = 91$, $p < .0125$). The findings, therefore, suggest that the 92 EFL learners became not only more accurate, but also faster in responding to both types of implied meaning items over a seven-week period. However, compared with the accuracy gain, the effect sizes for the response time differences between the pre- and post-tests were much smaller for both refusal and opinion items (eta-square = 0.07 for refusals and eta-square = 0.09 for opinions). Moreover, unlike the pattern uncovered for accuracy scores, the degree of change in comprehension speed was almost equal for the refusal and opinion items.

In sum, the 92 learners demonstrated significant changes for both accuracy and speed of implied meaning comprehension over a seven-week period. However, the degree of change seemed to differ between accuracy and response speed over a seven-week period, since the magnitude of such change was sizable for accuracy and much smaller for speed. In addition, conventionalized refusals appeared to be easier and faster-developing than non-conventionalized opinions in terms of accuracy but not in terms of processing speed. This can be inferred from the finding that the longitudinal gain in processing speed was similarly small-sized regardless of the level of conventionality encoded in the implied meaning, whereas the longitudinal gain in accuracy was larger for the easier, conventionalized implied meaning (indirect refusals) than for the more difficult, non-conventionalized implied meaning (indirect opinions).

Analyses of difficulty features of implied meaning items

In order to address the second research question and better understand the sources of difficulty involved in processing conventionalized and non-conventionalized implied meanings, item difficulty on the pre-test was inspected for the 48 experimental items, by calculating the percentage of the learners who answered each item correctly. Then, the items that were found difficult (i.e., less than 60 percent of the students answered correctly) were compiled. Item difficulty was analyzed again in the post-test data for the same items. The average time taken to answer each of the difficult items was also recorded. Table 3 shows the item statistics for the pre- and post-test. In the pre-test, nine out of the 12 difficult items were indirect opinion items, whereas many of the refusal items were relatively easy at the beginning of the seven-week session. Another notable trend is that the opinion items that were difficult at the pre-test still remained difficult at the post-test. The accuracy rate for most of the items improved only by 3 percent to 15 percent, and for Item 53 the accuracy rate decreased by about 10 percent.

Response time for the nine "difficult" opinion items was longer than the average response time at the pre-test (indirect opinion average = 6.35 seconds per item). At the post-test session, the response time became shorter for five out of the nine items by two to four seconds (Items 6, 8, 10, 19, and 44), and for Item 34 by about 0.72 seconds.

Table 3 Item difficulty analysis

Item # (key word)	Item type	Item difficulty		Implied meaning utterances (simplified)
		Pre-test % (ave RT)	Post-test % (ave RT)	
6 (colorful)	opinion	45.7 (9.42)	49.5 (6.54)	A: Did you like the food? B: It's certainly colorful.
8 (parents)	opinion	51.1 (10.10)	64.5 (5.89)	A: How did you like Mary's parents? B: I still love Mary.
10 (movie)	opinion	39.1 (6.73)	51.6 (5.07)	A: Did you like the movie? B: I was glad when it was over.
11 (house)	opinion	29.3 (16.01)	33.3 (22.7)	A: Do you like your new house? B: There's nothing I want to change.
19 (time)	opinion	59.8 (9.72)	75.3 (7.24)	A: What did you think about my paper? B: How much time did you spend on it?
36 (TV)	opinion	38.0 (6.85)	40.9 (10.15)	A: Did you like the show last night? B: I couldn't wait to see the end.
44 (table)	opinion	43.5 (7.57)	48.4 (4.68)	A: Do you like the dining table? B: I don't wanna change a thing about it.
53 (class)	opinion	58.7 (6.14)	47.3 (6.28)	A: Do you like meeting new people? B: I try to get to know them right away.
56 (talk)	opinion	52.2 (7.34)	64.5 (10.15)	A: What did you think about my talk? B: It's hard to give a good talk, isn't it?
28 (seminar)	refusal	47.8 (7.62)	64.5 (8.14)	A: Can we meet on Saturday? B: I'm often out of town on weekends.
34 (Italy)	refusal	44.6 (7.51)	64.5 (6.72)	A: Let's celebrate this weekend. B: Cindy is going to Italy this weekend.
35 (exam)	refusal	52.2 (7.65)	58.1 (8.54)	A: Do you wanna go over some questions? B: I don't have much time now.

Notes: $n = 92$, $k = 48$, ave RT = average number of seconds taken to answer the item.

Average improvement in the response time was 0.7 seconds. Since this improvement was statistically significant, the gains by two to four seconds are considered notable. Item 53 showed almost no improvement in the response time. The response time was slower for Items 11, 36, and 56 by three to six seconds. These analyses suggest that some opinion items were difficult to comprehend, and the time lapse of seven weeks did not make comprehension of those items easier. Response time gains for those difficult opinion items were not stable; speed improved for about half of the items, but for other items speed remained approximately the same, or became slower.

Since questions remained as to what features made some opinion items more difficult than others, in what follows I provide more detailed comparisons of features between easy and difficult opinion items.

The four items shown in Exhibit 1 are indirect opinion items that received a relatively low item difficulty rate; more than 80 percent of the learners answered them correctly at the pre-test, and the accuracy rate increased at the post-test, in some cases to over 95 percent.

A striking commonality across these four items is that the target implied meaning utterance (i.e., the last utterance in the dialogue) had some lexical items that could prime positive or negative meaning. Because indirect opinion utterances conveyed

Exhibit 1 Non-conventionalized indirect opinion items with low difficulty level

---

Item 2 (book report)
Jane: Dr. White, do you have time?
Dr. White: Sure. Come in.
Jane: Ah . . . did you have a chance to read my book report? It was my
                     first time to write a book report, so I'd like to know how I did on it.
Dr. White: Oh, it's *exactly* what I *wanted*.
Question: Does Dr. White like the book report?

Item 9 (New Mexico)
Jane: Hello Dr. White.
Dr. White: Oh, hi Jane. How was your spring vacation?
Jane: Ah . . . My friends and I rented a car and drove to New Mexico for a
                     week.
Dr. White: Oh really. Did you have a good time?
Jane: Well, our car *broke down* three times during the trip.
Question: Did Jane have a nice trip?

Item 29 (restaurants)
Tom: What do you do on weekends Sally?
Sally: I like the theater—you know, plays and concerts. How about you?
Tom: Oh lots of different things. I like books, dancing. I like to try
                     interesting restaurants too. Do you like eating in restaurants?
Sally: They are *too expensive* for me.
Question: Does Sally often eat at restaurants?

Item 31 (children)
Dave: Hi Susan. What are you up to?
Susan: I've got to go to work in half an hour or so. I'm baby sitting my
                     neighbor's kids every Monday and Wednesday night.
Dave: Oh really. Do you like children?
Susan: I would *enjoy* being a kindergarden teacher.
Question: Does Susan like children very much?

---

expressions of likes or dislikes in a non-literal manner, some words with positive or negative connotations could make it easier to infer the likes or dislikes. Item 2 had the words *exactly* and *wanted*, which had positive connotation. The phrase *broke down* in Item 9 indicated less preferred meaning. Item 29 included the phrase *too expensive*, which evoked negative impression. The word *enjoy* in Item 31 evoked a positive expression. Although indirect opinions did not reflect any conventionalized routines or discourse patterns, the lexical items that were associated with negative or positive meaning seemed to have assisted learners' comprehension.

These lexical features sharply contrast with some of the difficult opinion items displayed in Exhibit 2, which received between a 30 percent and 50 percent accuracy rate (cf. Table 3). The implied meaning utterances in these items did not include any connotative words that could evoke preferred or less preferred meaning. In Item 6, when asked about her impressions of a particular dish, the woman replied negatively by saying, *It's certainly colorful*. Individual words in the reply did not imply negative meaning, and in fact, the word *colorful* often has a positive connotation. In order to comprehend hidden speaker intention in this item, the listener needs to realize the speaker's strategic intention for commenting on the off-target aspect of the dish

Exhibit 2 Non-conventionalized indirect opinion items with high difficulty level

---

Item 6 (colorful)

Tom:	Wow, look, Sally. There are so many different kinds of food here. I don't know where to start. Which do you think is good?
Sally:	So far I've only had some of that one, the yellow dish.
Tom:	Oh, that looks good. Did you like it?
Sally:	It's certainly colorful.
Question:	Does Sally like the yellow dish?

Item 8 (parents)

Tom:	Hi Sally. How was your weekend?
Sally:	Good. Mike and I went camping. How was yours?
Tom:	I went to Mary's parents' place for dinner. It was my first time to meet her parents.
Sally:	Oh, how did you like her parents?
Tom:	I still love Mary.
Question:	Does the man like Mary's parents?

Item 10 (movie)

Ben:	Good morning, honey. I can't believe I fell asleep in the middle of the movie last night. Did you watch it till the end?
Barbara:	Yeah, I did.
Ben:	How was it? Did you like it?
Barbara:	Well, I was glad when it was over.
Question:	Did the woman like the movie?

Item 11 (house)

Tom:	Hi Sally. Did you have a nice break?
Sally:	Yeah, I had a great vacation.
Tom:	I heard you moved to a new place out in the country. How do you like your new house?
Sally:	Oh, I don't want to change a thing about it.
Question:	Does Sally like her new house?

Item 36 (TV)

Mary:	Hey, John. You're up already.
John:	Yeah, I got to finish this homework for the English class.
Mary:	Oh . . . I have to do that too . . . Hey, by the way, did you like the TV show last night?
John:	I couldn't wait to see what happened at the end.
Question:	Did the man like the TV show?

(color) to avoid commenting on the target aspect (taste). Similar inferential calculations apply to Item 8, in which the speaker changed the subject to avoid disclosing his negative feelings toward Mary's parents.

When items did not include any connotative words that could assist comprehension of one's likes or dislikes, the inferential process inevitably required a word-by-word syntactic analysis of the target utterance to decode what the speaker intended to convey by using a circumlocution. In Item 10, when asked for an opinion about a movie, the woman replied, *I was glad when it was over.* Although the word *glad* has positive meaning, the listener needs to relate the word to *when it was over* to understand that it is the ending of the film that brought about positive feeling. Then, the listener needs to use a deductive process to draw a logical conclusion that the movie itself was not interesting. The same syntactic analysis and deductive decoding are necessary to comprehend Items 11 and 36. In Item 11, when asked about an opinion of the house, the speaker replied that she had nothing to change about the house, implying that the house is in perfect condition, and she likes the house as it is. These extensive inferential processes, combined with bottom–up analyses of the utterances, seemed to be the factors that made certain opinion items more difficult to comprehend than others.

Discussion

The EFL learners in this study made a significant improvement in accurate, speedy comprehension of implied meaning over a seven-week period, suggesting that the exposure to L2 input and culture is not the only contributing factor for pragmatic development. The overall findings support the claim that pragmatic comprehension develops naturally in formal classroom settings, even in foreign language contexts that afford limited opportunity for pragmatic awareness. Nevertheless, the gain of speed was much smaller than that of accuracy for the seven-week period. The effect size of the pre- and post-test difference for refusals was .33 for accuracy scores, while it was .07 for response times. The effect size of the pre- and post-test difference for opinions was .22 for accuracy scores and .09 for response times. These findings suggest that the development of accurate demonstration of pragmatic knowledge precedes the development of processing capacity of using that knowledge. Processing of pragmatic meaning involves a coordinated action of a number of constituent processes, including linguistic, cognitive, and sociocultural processes, which must be automatized to achieve speedy performance. For the foreign language learners in this study, these underlying components seem to take a longer time to be automatized. Thus, speedy processing of pragmatic meaning could be considered an aspect of language ability that develops among foreign language learners gradually and slowly, and probably over longer periods of time and at a slower pace than pragmatic knowledge per se.

The small gain in comprehension speed may stem from the fact that the learners in this study did not have enough opportunities for associative practices to develop speed. Because they had limited incidental exposure to the L2, mapping practices between form and meaning did not occur frequently, resulting in relatively small degrees of speed development. The associative practice in pragmatic processing involves processing a greater number of great features, including linguistic information, the use of sociocultural and contextual information, and knowledge of conventions of language. Access to these features was probably even more limited for the EFL learners in this study.

In this study, the size of speed gain was similarly small for refusals and opinions. This is counter-intuitive. The lower-level processing (e.g., word recognition and sentence decoding), as shown in the previous literature, usually becomes faster as learners gain more experience and proficiency (e.g., Bialystok, 1990; Hirai, 1999; White and Genesee, 1996). Since the pragmatic portion of processing did not require as much effort in indirect refusals as it did in indirect opinions, one would assume that comprehension speed of refusals would become faster over time, because the learners could devote more time to lower-level processing (i.e., processing words in yes–no questions). Why did the conventionality of refusals fail to boost the development of speed over time? According to Segalowitz (2000), performance fluency involves efficient operation of underlying component mechanisms, such as perception of stimuli and semantic access. With extensive practice, these lower-level operations become automatic, leading to fluent performance. Due to the limited processing practice, the EFL learners in this study were probably not at the stage where these component processes were automatized. As a result, comprehension speed of indirect refusals did not show a large gain, despite their relative ease in the higher-order processing, when compared with indirect opinions. Thus, the present findings could in part be a function of the context of learning, in that these EFL learners did not have extended processing practice of lower-level input in the foreign language context.

Developmental order of more and less conventional implied meaning

Another developmental pattern gleaned from this study is the difficulty order of implied meaning items. Comprehension of indirect opinions was more difficult and took longer than comprehension of indirect refusals. Accurate comprehension of indirect opinions also demonstrated a smaller improvement over time compared with that of indirect refusals. These findings suggest that comprehension of indirect opinions presents greater processing demands; as a result, accurate comprehension of opinions may lag behind that of refusals in pragmatic development.

Differential comprehension demands between the two item types seemed to stem from different degrees of conventionality encoded in them. Linguistic and non-linguistic contexts in English refusals are more conventionalized for Japanese learners because the means to encode refusals are shared between Japanese and English. The indirect refusals included fixed patterns of discourse exchange and specific patterns used to realize the goal of refusals (giving a reason). These features of conventionality, once activated, reduce processing effort in communication (Sperber and Wilson, 1991). In contrast, less conventionalized indirect opinions require more extensive analytical processing of both linguistic and non-linguistic cues, because meaning is not simply attached to particular linguistic forms, nor is it embedded in predictable patterns of exchange. In the development of L2 pragmatic comprehension among Japanese learners, then, ability to comprehend indirect refusals seems to pre-date the ability to comprehend indirect opinions, both in terms of accuracy and speed of comprehension, due to the greater conventionality encoded in the refusals. The largest gains in accuracy were observed for conventionalized meaning, although the gains in processing speed were unaffected by conventionality. The findings suggest that pragmatic processing speed might be a slow-developing ability, given the small magnitude of the changes in this area over seven weeks.

Item difficulty analyses revealed that some indirect opinions were easier to comprehend than others, possibly because of the availability of lexical inferencing. Words often conjure up particular images, attitudes, or feelings. Thus, it seemed that certain words used in opinion expressions evoked positive or negative connotations (e.g., The words *broke down* conjuring up a negative meaning). As a result, the learners could understand positive or negative opinions more easily. Because some lexical items functioned as symbolic representations of one's opinions, learners' inferential process was straightforward, associating the word meanings to the thoughts that the speaker intended to express. These analyses correspond to Ross's (1997) observations that key-word inferencing is a common processing strategy for L2 learners; learners hear the key word and go directly to the association of the key word and its referent.

A group of more difficult opinion expressions, on the other hand, did not contain any key lexical items that could assist comprehension (e.g., indicating a negative opinion of a movie by saying *I was glad when it was over.*) Since there were no constant symbolic representations (i.e., key words), comprehension of these indirect opinions demanded more word-by-word bottom–up processing, such as analysis of syntactic and lexical information, as well as analysis of a number of contextual cues. Using these analyses, learners had to first understand literal meaning of the opinion expressions, and then work deductively toward the implied speaker intentions. Due to the multiple levels of processing, along with more drastic deviation from the Gricean maxims for certain opinion items, the degree of inferencing that the learners had to make became extensive, resulting in more absolute difficulty as well as slower-paced improvement in comprehension over time.

In summary, analyses of difficulty features among implied meaning items suggest potential developmental sequences in learners' pragmatic comprehension ability. Comprehension of more conventional implied meaning may precede that of less conventional ones, as long as learners are aware of conventions of language and language use in the target sociocultural context. Once learners understand what expressions are used to encode what functions, their ability to infer illocutionary force behind the expressions may develop naturally as their overall listening skills mature. However, the ability to comprehend less conventional implied meaning, especially expressions that lack lexical cues, does not seem to develop in a parallel manner, due to the extensive inferential bridge needed to arrive at correct interpretations.

As Sperber and Wilson (1995) claimed, processing effort is reflected in the number of signals to be processed and the amount of searching involved. Because humans process information as economically as possible, when people interpret meaning they select the most immediate assumption that has the greatest contextual effects for the smallest processing effort. When expressions include conventional features or lexical cues, people use them immediately to comprehend meaning. When those cues are lacking, they process a greater number and variety of signals, resulting in more extensive searching of meaning. These claims could explain the developmental patterns of L2 pragmatic comprehension. The number and intensity of signals available for interpretation determine the level of difficulty in pragmatic comprehension. Learners' comprehension progresses from the stage where meaning has strong signals, to the stage where the message does not involve any obvious signals and thus requires a series of inferential stages to arrive at intended meaning.

Conclusion

Two major findings were gleaned from this study in relation to longitudinal L2 development towards more advanced L2 proficiency. First, the degree of change in pragmatic comprehension ability was greater for accuracy than for processing speed. Second, the comprehension gains were greater for more conventionalized implied meaning (i.e., indirect refusals) than for less conventionalized implied meaning (i.e., indirect opinions). These findings imply that the pathways toward the full attainment of L2 pragmatic capacities are at least two-dimensional, including the development of pragmatic knowledge and the achievement of automatic control in processing it in real time. The attainment of speedy pragmatic processing seems to develop at a slower pace, compared with the attainment of accurate pragmatic knowledge, at least for learners in a foreign language context. More advanced pragmatic comprehension ability, then, can be characterized as the ability to comprehend a range of less conventional, idiosyncratic implied meaning accurately and in a speedy manner. Because this study limited its longitudinal analysis to a short period of time, there is a need for more longitudinal studies that document learners' fuller developmental path toward attainment of more advanced pragmatic capacities. Such efforts will enhance our understanding of the interdependence between knowledge and processing aspects of advanced L2 capacities, and of the course of development of both in pragmatic comprehension.

Note

A portion of the data in this study is reported in Taguchi (2007).

References

American Council for the Teaching of Foreign Languages [ACTFL]. (1999). *Standards for foreign language learning in the 21st century*. Lawrence, KS: Allen Press Inc.

Anderson, J. R. (1990). *Cognitive psychology and its implications* (3rd ed.). New York: W. H. Freeman and Company.

Bachman, L. F., and Palmer, A. S. (1996). *Language testing in practice: Designing and developing useful language tests*. New York: Oxford University Press.

Bardovi-Harlig, K. (1999). Exploring the interlanguage of interlanguage pragmatics: A research agenda for acquisitional pragmatics. *Language Learning, 49*, 677–713.

Bardovi-Harlig, K., and Dörnyei, Z. (1998). Do language learners recognize pragmatic violations? Pragmatic versus grammatical awareness in instructed L2 learning. *TESOL Quarterly, 32*, 233–262.

Barron, A. (2002). *Acquisition in interlanguage pragmatics: Learning how to do things with words in a study abroad context*. Philadelphia, PA: John Benjamins.

Beebe, L. M., Takahashi, T., and Uliss-Weltz, R. (1990). Pragmatic transfer in ESL refusals. In R. Scarcella, D. Andersen, and S. Krashen (Eds.), *Developing communicative competence in a second language* (pp. 55–74). New York: Newbury House.

Bialystok, E. (1990). The competence of processing: Classifying theories of second language acquisition. *TESOL Quarterly, 24*, 635–648.

Blum-Kulka, S., House, J., and Kasper, G. (1989). *Cross-cultural pragmatics: Requests and apologies*. Norwood, NJ: Ablex.

Bouton, L. (1992). The interpretation of implicature in English by NNS: Does it come automatically without being explicitly taught? *Pragmatics and Language Learning Monograph Series*. Vol. 3 (pp. 64–77). Urbana-Champaign, IL: University of Illinois, Division of English as an International Language.

Bouton, L. (1994). Can NNS skill in interpreting implicature in American English be improved through explicit instruction? A pilot study. *Pragmatics and Language Learning Monograph Series*. Vol. 5 (pp. 88–108). Urbana-Champaign, IL: University of Illinois, Division of English as an International Language.

Bouton, L. (1999). Developing nonnative speaker skills in interpreting conversational implicatures in English. In E. Hinkel (Ed.), *Culture in second language teaching and learning* (pp. 47–70). New York: Cambridge University Press.

Canale, M., and Swain, M. (1980). Theoretical aspects of communicative approaches to second language teaching and testing. *Applied Linguistics*, *1*, 1–47.

Carrell, P. (1981). Relative difficulty of request forms in L1/L2 comprehension. In M. Hines and W. Rutherford (Eds.), *On TESOL '81* (pp. 141–152). Washington, DC: TESOL.

Carrell, P. (1984). Inferencing in ESL: Presuppositions and implications of factive and implicative predicates. *Language Learning*, *34*, 1–19.

Cedrus (2003). *SuperLab 3.0*. San Pedro, CA: Author.

Chomsky, N. (1965). *Aspects of the theory of syntax*. Cambridge, MA: MIT Press.

Cook, M., and Liddicoat, A. (2002). The development of comprehension in interlanguage pragmatics: The case of request strategies in English. *Australian Review of Applied Linguistics*, *25*, 19–39.

Council of Europe (2001). *Common European framework of reference for languages: Learning, teaching, assessment*. New York: Cambridge University Press.

Ellis, N. (2001). Memory for language. In P. Robinson (Ed.), *Cognition and second language instruction* (pp. 33–68). New York: Cambridge University Press.

Ellis, N. (2003). Constructions, chunking, and connectionism: The emergence of second language structure. In C. Doughty and M. Long (Eds.), *Handbook of second language acquisition* (pp. 63–103). Malden, MA: Blackwell.

Gibbs, R. (1981). Your wish is my command: Convention and context in interpreting indirect requests. *Journal of Verbal Learning and Verbal Behavior*, *20*, 431–444.

Gibbs, R. (1983). Do people always process the literal meanings of indirect requests? *Journal of Experimental Psychology: Leaning, Memory, and Cognition*, *9*, 524–533.

Grice, P. (1975). Logic and conversation. In P. Cole and J. Morgan (Eds.), *Syntax and semantics*. Vol. 3 (pp. 41–58). New York: Academic Press.

Hirai, A. (1999). The relationship between listening and reading rates of Japanese EFL learners. *Modern Language Journal*, *83*, 367–384.

Holtgraves, T. (1999). Comprehending indirect replies: When and how are their conveyed meanings activated? *Journal of Memory and Language*, *38*, 519–540.

Jaeger, R. M. (1993). *Statistics: A spectator sport* (2nd ed.). Newbury Park, CA: Sage.

Kasper, G. (1984). Pragmatic comprehension in learner-native speaker discourse. *Language Learning*, *34*, 1–20.

Kasper, G. (1992). Pragmatic transfer. *Second Language Research*, *8*, 203–231.

Kasper, G., and Rose, K. (2002). *Pragmatic development in a second language*. Malden, MA: Blackwell.

Koike, D. (1996). Transfer of pragmatic competence and suggestions in Spanish foreign language learning. In S. Gass and J. Neu (Eds.), *Speech acts across cultures* (pp. 257–281). New York: Mouton de Gruyter.

Kotosonis, M. (1981). Children's interpretations of conversationally implied meanings. Unpublished doctoral dissertation. University of Virginia.

Leech, G. (1983). *Principles of pragmatics*. Harlow: Longman.

Levinson, S. C. (1983). *Pragmatics*. New York: Cambridge University Press.

McLaughlin, B. (1987). *Theories of second language learning*. London: Edward Arnold.

Matsumura, S. (2001). Learning the rules for offering advice: A quantitative approach to second language socialization. *Language Learning*, *51*, 635–679.

Mey, J. (1993). *Pragmatics: An introduction*. Oxford: Blackwell.

Ministry of Education, Culture, Sports, Science, and Technology (1999). *The Course of Study for Secondary School*. Tokyo: Author.

Ministry of Education, Culture, Sports, Science, and Technology (2003). *Regarding the establishment of an action plan to cultivate Japanese with English abilities.* Accessed online on June 20, 2004 at: www.mext.go.jp/english/topics/03072801.htm

Morgan, J. (1978). Two types of convention in indirect speech acts. In P. Cole (Ed.), *Syntax and semantics.* Vol. 9, *Pragmatics* (pp. 261–280). New York: Academic Press.

Nelson, G. L., Carson, J., Batal, M. A., and Bakary, W. E. (2002). Cross-cultural pragmatics: Strategy use in Egyptian Arabic and American English refusals. *Applied Linguistics, 23,* 163–189.

Roever, C. (2005). *Testing EFL pragmatics.* Frankfurt: Gunter Narr.

Ross, S. (1997). An introspective analysis of listener inferencing on a second language listening test. In G. Kasper and E. Kellerman (Eds.), *Communication strategies: Psycholinguistic and sociolinguistic perspectives* (pp. 216–237). New York: Longman.

Saville-Troike, M. (1996). The ethnography of communication. In S. McKay and N. Hornberger (Eds.), *Sociolinguistics and language teaching* (pp. 351–382). New York: Cambridge University Press.

Schauer, G. (2006). Pragmatic awareness in ESL and EFL contexts: Contrast and development. *Language Learning, 56,* 269–318.

Segalowitz, N. (2000). Automaticity and attentional skill in fluent performance. In H. Riggenbach (Ed.), *Perspectives on fluency* (pp. 200–219). Ann Arbor, MI: University of Michigan Press.

Segalowitz, N. (2001). On the evolving connections between psychology and linguistics. *Annual Review of Applied Linguistics, 21,* 3–22.

Segalowitz, N. (2003). Automaticity and second languages. In C. Doughty and M. Long (Eds.), *Handbook of second language acquisition* (pp. 382–408). Malden, MA: Blackwell.

Sperber, D., and Wilson, D. (1991). Loose talk. In S. Davis (Ed.), *Pragmatics: A reader* (pp. 540–550). New York: Oxford University Press.

Sperber, D., and Wilson, D. (1995). *Relevance: Communication and cognition* (2nd ed.). New York: Cambridge University Press.

Taguchi, N. (2002). An application of relevance theory to the analysis of L2 interpretation processes: The comprehension of indirect replies. *International Review of Applied Linguistics, 40,* 151–176.

Taguchi, N. (2003). Pragmatic performance in comprehension and production of English as a second language. Unpublished doctoral dissertation. Northern Arizona University.

Taguchi, N. (2005). Comprehending implied meaning in English as a second language. *Modern Language Journal, 89,* 543–562.

Taguchi, N. (2007). Development of speed and accuracy in pragmatic comprehension in English as a Foreign Language. *TESOL Quarterly, 42,* 313–338.

Takahashi, S., and Roitblat, H. L. (1994). Comprehension process of second language indirect requests. *Applied Psycholinguistics, 15,* 475–506.

Thomas, J. (1983). Cross-cultural pragmatic failure. *Applied Linguistics, 4,* 91–109.

Thomas, J. (1995). *Meaning in interaction: An introduction to pragmatics.* London: Longman.

van Dijk, T. (1977). Context and cognition: Knowledge frames and speech act comprehension. *Journal of Pragmatics, 1,* 211–232.

White, L., and Genesee, F. (1996). How native is near-native? The issue of ultimate attainment in adult second language acquisition. *Second Language Research, 12,* 233–265.

Wolfson, N. (1989). *Perspectives: Sociolinguistics and TESOL.* Boston: Heinle and Heinle.

12 Histories of engagement and sociolinguistic awareness in study abroad

Colloquial French

Celeste Kinginger and Géraldine Blattner

Abstract

A hallmark of advanced language competence is the ability to understand the social meaning of linguistic variation in a range of different sociopragmatic contexts. Study abroad (SA) is commonly believed to complement or even to complete classroom foreign language learning in this domain. It is assumed that study abroad participants are socialized into language use, developing metacognitive awareness of linguistic variability and linking linguistic and pragmatic features of the languages they are learning. Research on SA participants' performance in relation to variable sociopragmatic features suggests that, while these learners may develop awareness of these features they tend to avoid use of forms perceived as non-standard or informal. Performance data alone are therefore insufficient to assess learners' knowledge in this domain. In this chapter, we present case studies of three undergraduates who studied in France during the spring semester of 2003. A Language Awareness Interview was designed and administered prior to the participants' departure and at the end of their sojourn. Participants were asked to comment on their knowledge of variable uses of French within several domains, of which two are reviewed here: colloquial phrases and pronouns of address. Findings suggest that learners develop awareness of sociopragmatic variability over the course of 15 weeks abroad, but that corresponding performance is related both to issues of identity and to the learners' history of participation and socialization in French-speaking contexts as documented in narrative data.

Introduction

Research on language learning in study abroad strives to refine the profession's evaluation of this multifaceted environment. Much of the research serves to challenge virtues often uncritically ascribed to this context, in particular, the commonly held opinion that study abroad leads directly to advanced foreign language competence. An astute reader of the contemporary literature can no longer take the view that study abroad consistently offers a superior learning situation with limitless, unproblematic, and productive access to second language interaction, leading to dramatic gains in language proficiency for every student.

To take just one recent example, the research reported in Freed, Segalowitz, and Dewey (2004) compared the development of French language fluency in three groups of students who had previously studied French for two to four years: those remaining at home, those who were enrolled in a domestic immersion program, and

those who participated in a study abroad program. The findings revealed a significant advantage for the domestic immersion program over the study abroad program,
a result that the researchers trace in part to the immersion students' reports of
greater amounts of time spent using French. Thus, it would appear that the sojourn
abroad is not, in fact, a cure-all for fluency problems. Sheltered programs can be
engineered to generate fluency by providing the requisite amounts of input and
interaction right here at home.

There is, however, the perennial question of how language ability is conceptualized, whether it is seen in abstraction or as intimately and concretely tied to language
use in social settings of seemingly infinite and unpredictable variety (Lantolf and
Thorne, 2006). If the latter view is accepted, the value of study abroad remains
apparent. Even the most expertly designed domestic immersion program cannot
provide learners with experience of participation in diverse social encounters where
interactive outcomes are as consequential as they are when students live abroad. The
domestic immersion student will eat whether or not she successfully manages a
service encounter. Her inexpert manipulation of pragmalinguistic features, if it is
noticed, is unlikely to result in incomprehension, social isolation, deep embarrass-
ment, or rage. Her successes will be measured more in levels of academic achievement, in measures of proficiency, or in the approval of a small cohort of teachers and
students, and less in the satisfaction of proven ability to get things done, to reveal her
intentions or personality, to engage in discourse with confidence in the meanings she
expresses, interprets, and negotiates (Savignon, 1983).

Moreover, the language of the classroom is by definition a representation of language. Classroom language is officially sanctioned, that is, it has been selected and
approved for acquisition by learners. Classroom work includes only those activities
that can be performed within the semantic bounds of this acceptable standard language, and this for good (perhaps even excellent) pedagogic reasons. No teacher
wishes to be accused of representing the "wrong" type of language or of carrying
out activities that violate classroom decorum. Pedagogic norms are established and
textbooks are written in part to cast a net of social neutrality over the language that
students acquire, so that their gaffes will not be attributable to their instruction. The
fact remains, however, that knowledge of language includes awareness of the social
meaning of variety and register, including registers that are banned even from the
classroom designed for advanced learners (Lippi-Green, 1997). Study abroad offers
students the opportunity and the challenge of discovering an expanded range of
linguistic variety and of choosing to use those aspects of the language that best reflect
their own identity.

In this study, we explore a methodology for investigating the relationship between
students' histories of engagement in diverse social settings and the claim articulated
by Freed (1995) that study abroad participants tend to display "highly developed
meta-cognitive awareness of sociolinguistic differences and potentially conflicting
pragmatic demands" (p. 27). Our argument rests on two assumptions: (1) that residence abroad, as an environment for language learning, is unique in its potential to
offer varied and consequential social activity in the second language to students who
seek and attain access to it; and (2) that much of the learning that goes on in study
abroad extends outside of the decorous boundaries of classroom language use and its
outcomes as measured in standard academic terms. We propose that an understand-

ing of "histories of engagement" requires a longitudinal view complemented by a significant qualitative dimension in which the learners' own representations of the study abroad experience are included.[1] We further suggest, for reasons to be outlined below, that investigation of developing sociopragmatic competence must focus to some extent on awareness, as the citation from Freed would imply, rather than examining performance alone (Kinginger and Farrell, 2004).

The core of this chapter is an inquiry into participants' histories of engagement in language learning abroad as reflected in their ability to decipher a series of colloquial phrases in informal French. The study focuses on selected data from a larger investigation of language learning in study abroad involving 23 students and their sojourns in France during the spring semester of 2003.[2] In presenting our rationale for the study, we first justify our focus on informal varieties of French, then examine the problem of investigating knowledge of colloquial language in terms of the manner in which using these forms indexes both context of situation and the identities of language users. We then explain how we attempted to connect our analysis of assessment results with the findings emerging from longitudinal, narrative study of the students' experiences as recounted in interviews and journals. Basic findings are presented for the entire group of participants, and three students' cases are examined in detail for the insights they provide on variation in sources of knowledge—or lack thereof—about colloquial French.

Awareness of variety: The case of French

The presence of social, geographic, and situational variation in language use is, according to Lippi-Green (1997), among the "linguistic facts of life." Furthermore, "the inability to use or recognize the social markings of linguistic variants is one of the most significant problems of second language learners, and one that is rarely dealt with in the classroom, where the myth of standard language has a stronghold" (p. 30). If awareness of linguistic variety is clearly a key component in advanced language competence, the pedagogical treatment of this variation is extremely complex.

In the case of French, the myth of the standard language is one that has exerted heavy influence not only in the second language classroom but in pervasive linguistic ideology gradually formed over the past several centuries. As documented in any textbook on French sociolinguistics, the political and administrative imposition of standard French began as one aspect of the centralization of power in the 17th century, with the express intention of wiping out regional languages and equating linguistic and national identity. This effort eventually prevailed after the institution of compulsory primary education, beginning in the 1880s. In this context, the standard language was framed as the universal language of rationality, endowed with inherent clarity, logic, and precision (e.g., Ager, 1994; Ball, 1997). Grammarians have since viewed their task as one of preserving the language in its pure form, and the grammar of standard French has remained essentially static for over two centuries.

According to Ball (2000), however, the language in its idealized form has never had universal currency; as the French speaking world has expanded and contracted over the centuries, non-standard usage of French has also had a long, parallel history in the segments of society that are socially, economically, or geographically distant from Parisian power. The situation today is one in which the normative view of the language has become a key component in Francophone culture, engendering deep veneration for the standard language (associated with writing) alongside continued, widespread use of non-standard forms (particularly, though not exclusively, in speech). The ordinary speaker of French is, according to Ball, "in the unenviable position of making daily use of a range of forms that are officially proscribed or 'blacklisted' " (p. 8). This situation in turn leads to linguistic insecurity, in which the average users' confidence in their ability to speak the language "properly" is undermined (Ager, 1999).

The existence of dual languages within French is perhaps better illustrated by a writer than by a linguist: the English language essayist Luc Sante, a native speaker of French, has the following to say about the topic of this chapter, the colloquial language. French slang is

> an entire language, a parallel verbal world that mocks the formal protocols of the master language. Unlike the American variety, it contains words for every sort of thing, for "door," and "table," and "cup." Some of it is ancient, dating back to the time of François Villon and beyond; some of it actually derives from Romany, and it continues to loot other languages, in pointed contrast to official French, which proscribes loan words. It is a highly metaphorical language, as slang tends to be, with an insolent, blaring music and a staccato beat: *Quand le bruit se répand que la poule tape aux fafs dans un coin, vous voyez les tapis se vider de tous les tricards.* Literally, this would mean: "When the noise spreads that the hen is tapping for papers in a corner, you see the carpets emptying themselves of all the tricksters." What it signifies is: "When the word gets around that the cops are checking IDs in the neighborhood, all the parolees instantly vanish from the bars." . . . It is almost as if French and American had mated in the night and produced another tongue with all the advantages of both, and none of the pomposity. (Santé, 2004, pp. 82–83, italics in the original)

Thus, it would seem that the French language is effectively bifurcated into standard and non-standard use, but that the significance of linguistic variety in the teaching of French has been slow to emerge as a matter of urgency. For one thing, as in the example above, non-standard language is popularly associated with its most lurid or pathological elements. Valdman (2000), however, attributes the profession's attitude on the one hand to the historical absence of empirical studies irrefutably demonstrating the significance of variation in French, and on the other to the traditional academic emphases on interpretation of literary texts and knowledge of grammatical rules. Now that many corpus-based studies of spoken language have definitively proven the existence of separate systems of syntax and lexis governing formal versus everyday, colloquial French used in all segments of society (e.g., Blanche-Benveniste, 1997), and that the aims of language instruction have shifted toward communicative competence, French teachers are confronted with the fact that the idealized language of instruction may or may not have anything to do with the way "Native Speakers" of French, "educated" or not, actually speak.

Valdman's proposed solution is the elaboration of a pedagogical norm based on the standard along with knowledge, on the part of teachers, of social and situational factors governing variation. Ball (2000), in the volume referenced above, proposes a

Colloquial French grammar designed specifically with the advanced-level foreign language learner in mind. Kinginger (1999) recounts a pedagogical experiment in which intermediate-level classroom learners who engaged in an exchange via videoconference with peers in France were utterly confounded by the qualities of the French they heard, and needed consciousness-raising sessions on the structure of colloquial French in order to follow their interlocutors' utterances. The results of this experiment suggested that the need for awareness of language variety at all levels may become increasingly apparent with the growth of learners' access to non-pedagogic language use through computer-mediated communication. The debate as to the desirability of teaching colloquial French for productive use by learners will no doubt continue for a long time, but many educators agree that awareness of variation is a key component of advanced competence in the language, an awareness that must be achieved at some point in the learning trajectory if a speaker is to be deemed "advanced." Even if this awareness is not among the desired developmental outcomes of classroom instruction, it may well emerge as an unintended outcome of study abroad, a by-product of learners' engagement in a variety of social settings.

Investigating awareness of linguistic variation

Despite an increased emphasis on sociolinguistic awareness for learners, and despite Freed's (1995) intriguing comment on the significance of study abroad participants' metacognitive awareness of sociolinguistic differences and conflicting pragmatic demands, few researchers to date have attempted to document changes in language awareness in study abroad. Many studies have examined the emergence of sociopragmatic competence, however, by focusing on performance. Researchers have scrutinized learners' use of speech acts (e.g., Barron, 2003; Hoffman-Hicks, 2001; Matsumura, 2001), use of communication strategies (Lafford, 1995, 2004), manipulation of pragmatic and stylistic variants (Dewaele, 2004; Dewaele and Regan, 2002; Regan, 1995), and the appearance of colloquial lexis in French–English interlanguage (Dewaele and Regan, 2001). The findings of these studies suggest that the study abroad context is a favorable if not ideal environment for development of pragmatic competence; learners do develop the ability to understand sociopragmatic features of their second languages, and to manipulate the corresponding pragmalinguistic elements, but their progress often appears to be less dramatic than anticipated, and the studies tend to show a great deal of individual variation in achievement.

In a series of publications on the development of address form competence (i.e., ability to use *tu* versus *vous*, in French, or *du* versus *Sie*, in German), a key variable feature of European languages, Belz and Kinginger (2002, 2003), Dewaele (2004), and Kinginger and Farrell (2004) have advanced the argument that the use of performance measures alone may serve to mask certain key aspects of this phenomenon. This is due to the fact that the use of variable sociolinguistic features, such as colloquial lexis or the second person pronouns of address, is doubly indexical (Morford, 1997; Silverstein, 1992, 1996). That is, choice of a certain feature over another from a different variety or register may index, or point to, features of the immediately obvious social context, such as the setting, the age, gender, or relative social status of interlocutors. In Silverstein's terms, this is known as first order indexicality. (We may say *Gimme a break!* to our friend over a beer, but will say *Pardon me, but I beg to disagree* to our boss at a board meeting.) However, and crucially in our view, this choice also indexes second-order aspects of the speaker's identity; that is, how she wishes to be perceived in the context of a particular interaction. (Speakers might feel that use of certain colloquial terms makes them come across as young, hip, or urbane—or, alternatively, as ridiculous.)

Thus, the use of variable sociolinguistic features is inherently ambiguous; we cannot tell the extent to which a certain form has been employed or avoided due to first or second order indexicality, or a combination of both. The double indexicality of sociolinguistic variables means that learners need to assess not only how these forms relate to contexts of use, but also the extent to which they want these forms in their communicative repertoire in the first place (see also Frank, 2002, on the inter-action of learner identity and pragmatic performance in Russian). When we add to this the finding that second language learners tend toward hesitance to claim iden-tities as second language speakers empowered to use informal variants (Belz and Kinginger, 2002, 2003; Dewaele, 2004), it becomes clear that performance data alone cannot reveal what learners know about sociolinguistic variation. We therefore suggest that research in this domain may benefit from the elaboration of methodolo-gies that will allow investigation of sociolinguistic and sociopragmatic awareness, whether this investigation takes place *in situ* or *post hoc* (Kinginger and Belz, 2005).

Research design

Data for the current study were selected from a larger, hybrid and multi-method investigation of language learning in study abroad. This study combines: (1) docu-mentation of development in language proficiency and awareness over the course of a semester-long sojourn in France; (2) narrative analysis of the participants' own accounts of the experience in interviews, logbooks, and journals providing qualita-tive data from multiple points in time during the sojourn; (3) continuous contact with the participants, including frequent on-site observation and informal interactions throughout the semester. The research design was inspired, in part, by recent post-structuralist investigations of language learning emphasizing the significance of learner identity and negotiation of access to learning opportunities (Kinginger, 2004; Lantolf and Pavlenko, 2001; Norton, 2000). A key assumption of the research design was that variation in the students' engagement in learning opportunities would be present; that is, that some students would seek out and attain access to the language through various means, whereas others might seek but fail to attain this access, and still others might not, in fact, position themselves primarily as language learners. As noted above, our study was designed to privilege the reconstruction of students' stories about study abroad, and to trace the extent to which these students positioned themselves as language learners, sought out opportunities for participation in inter-active discourse or other learning situations, and in fact gained access to these resources.

Because we wished to explore the full range of variability in learners' experience of study abroad, we opened the study to all who would participate, regardless of background or experience of language study. We also assume that the measures we are using to assess learning cannot adequately reflect the variation in language ability that emerges from these diverse experiences. The best we can hope for is to use these measures as a source of triangulation (Dewaele, 2005), one aspect of the stories we reconstruct based on the participants' own accounts.

Complete data sets are available for 17 participants, all undergraduate French majors or minors participating in six different study abroad programs in France during the spring semester of 2003. In this chapter, in addition to the quantitative results for the 17 participants, we present more detailed case studies of three participants: Benjamin, Camille, and Ailis. Here we briefly introduce each learner.

Benjamin was a 20-year-old student from the Washington, DC, area, in his third year of university study. When Benjamin was a young child, his father had been in the military, and the family had lived for three years in Germany. Benjamin's mother was of Quebecois extraction, although she had long since ceased to use French in her daily life. Benjamin had enrolled in French courses from the 8th through the 12th grade in high school, participating in a state-sponsored domestic immersion program during one of the summers. At the college level he had taken four semesters of French and was enrolled in third-year literature courses before his departure for France. He reported having one French friend living near his hometown, with whom he interacted sporadically in French. He had also spent ten days on an excursion to Paris during the previous academic semester. His initial score of 730 on the *Test de Français International* (TFI; see details later), which corresponds to Basic Working Proficiency, was among the highest in the group.

Camille was a 20-year-old Business major from the region of New York City, who had studied French continuously since the 8th grade. Camille's mother had been a high school language teacher of French and Spanish, and had retained close contact with a family near Biarritz. Camille had traveled to France with her own family once before, when she was in the 7th grade and her parents "dragged us to all these castles" (Pre-departure Interview). At the college level, she took four courses, and was enrolled in third-year courses on French history and literature before her sojourn in France. Her initial score of 455 on the TFI placed her at the Intermediate level.

Ailis was a 20-year-old from a small town in rural Pennsylvania in her third year of university study. She had enrolled in French classes throughout junior high and high school—that is, from the 7th through the 12th grade. At the college level she had completed three semesters of study, ending with the second-year level course in grammar and composition. Her pre-departure TFI score of 490 placed her in the Intermediate category.

Table 1 displays basic demographic data about the three focal participants, as well as information about their respective routine activities while in France.

Data collection

The Language Awareness Interview

The Language Awareness Interview (LAI) represents an initial, exploratory effort to design an instrument appropriate for investigation of learners' awareness of sociolinguistic variation in French. As no comparable instrument is available, the LAI was designed for this study and was loosely based on the classic sociolinguistic interview (Labov, 1989). In the LAI procedure for this study, students were presented with a

Table 1 Profiles of focal participants

Participant	Age/gender	French prior to college (years)	French in college (semesters)	Living arrangement	Routine activities	
					Weekly	Weekend
Benjamin	20/M	5	4	Homestay (w/ children)	– metro/FR newspaper – FR classes – Lunch w/ US students – Dinner w/ host family – TV	– w/US students – w/host family and children
Camille	20/F	4	4	Homestay (w/o children)	– Metro – FR classes – Lunch w/ US students – Computer lab (ENG-email) – Dinner w/ host mother – TV (news)	– w/FR boyfriend
Ailis	20/F	4	3	Homestay (w/o children)	– Bus – FR classes – Lunch w/ US students – Computer lab (ENG-email) – Dinner w/ host mother (not much talking)	– Excursions with US students exclusively

series of short texts or problems involving diverse aspects of variation in French and were asked to comment on their knowledge of the language featured within each text or problem. The LAI consists of six sections:

- Colloquial words (Part I): In this section, participants commented on the meaning and appropriate context for use of colloquial words.
- Address form situations (Part II): This section required the participants to select an appropriate address form (*tu* or *vous*) in a series of imagined interpersonal situations involving different configurations of hierarchical status, solidarity, and deference. (For initial results, see Kinginger and Farrell, 2004.)
- Interrogative syntax (Part III): This section requested that participants explain the reasons underlying choice among a range of question forms in French.
- Speech acts for leave-taking (Part IV): Here, participants were to scrutinize a range of forms appropriate for leave-taking (e.g., *adieu, au revoir, tchao*) and match them to a range of social contexts.

- Colloquial phrases (Part V): Participants were asked to provide the colloquial meaning of phrases along with information about the persons who would use them and the contexts in which they could occur.
- Genre analysis (Part VI): Participants were presented with a series of transcribed spoken and written texts and were asked to hypothesize about the social situation in which they occurred.

Only the "colloquial phrases" section of the Language Awareness Interview (Part V) will be scrutinized here. In the colloquial phrases section, the students were presented with a written list of ten phrases that were selected after consulting an expert on French youth culture and language.[3] These phrases illustrate several features of colloquial French grammar, including absence of interrogative syntax in questions, reduction of the subject pronoun *il*, and left or right dislocation of the utterance's theme. They are also replete with examples of colloquial lexis (e.g., *moutards* "kids," *canard* "newspaper," *louper* "to fail"). In an effort to avoid including only "easy" phrases, alongside phrases in widespread contemporary use we deliberately included examples of colloquial French whose currency may be questionable or whose use may largely be confined to certain age groups older or younger than the participants. A list of these colloquial phrases appears in Appendix A.

The participants were asked to provide the colloquial meaning of each expression, as well as information about the persons who would use it and in which context it could occur. To recall, the LAI is primarily a qualitative exploration of participants' knowledge in this domain. Initially, we were less interested in establishing a rigorous scoring procedure for each section than in understanding the depth and breadth of this knowledge. Nevertheless, in the case of the colloquial phrases section, in reviewing the participants' responses it seemed reasonable to classify these responses in terms of the extent to which understanding of the referential meaning of the phrase was displayed, and in terms of the extent to which the participants could match the use of the phrase to an appropriate context. Thus, in order to arrive at a rough quantification of the participants' overall progress, scores of this task were computed as follows: three points were allocated for each of the ten colloquial phrases, adding up to a maximum score of 30 points. One point was awarded for the partial comprehension of the phrase (individual words) (W), another point for the referential understanding of the whole phrase (R), and the last point was given for identifying the appropriate social context in which such a phrase would be meaningful (C). To illustrate this procedure, we provide examples in Appendix B.

The *Test de Français International*

A global assessment of academic proficiency in standard French was achieved via pre- and post-administrations of the *Test de Français International*, a standardized, multiple-choice test of grammatical competence, reading and listening comprehension. This test was designed on the model of the Test of English for International Communication (TOEIC) as a measurement of ability to communicate in French within professional contexts of international exchange. After a pilot version of the test was developed in 1998 by the University of Ottawa, the test was adopted and validated under the aegis of the Educational Testing Service (ETS). ETS continues to administer this test.

The test was administered to all participants in November of 2002, prior to their departure, and again in September of 2003 upon their return to campus. The test includes three listening sections, the first of which (Part I) requires the candidate to choose the appropriate rejoinder or second-pair part in a short exchange. The second and third parts (Parts II and III) are more traditional comprehension exercises involving short dialogues and other texts. The reading comprehension section (Part VI) includes only one part that is devoted to standard reading comprehension questions. The texts involved in the comprehension sections are varied in genre and drawn from a range of academic and professional settings. The remaining sections require candidates to identify errors within sentences (Part IV) and to complete sentences drawing on knowledge of lexis and morphosyntax (Part V). After the administration of the test, the students' test booklets were sent to ETS for scoring. The TFI yields global proficiency scores ranging from 0 to 990 and is interpreted in terms of the levels indicated in Table 2.

Although the TFI is not a direct test of speaking or writing ability, in the materials accompanying the test scores and their classification into proficiency levels, ETS includes additional guidance for interpretation of these levels in terms of learners' productive capabilities. Thus, for example, the following characteristics are to be associated with the Intermediate level:

- can participate in normal face-to-face conversations
- knows basic grammatical structures, but lacks consistency
- can express requests to meet daily survival requirements
- functions in most travel and lodging situations
- weak understanding of social conventions or conversations
- pronunciation is understandable to native speakers used to communicating with foreigners. (*Test de Français International* score interpretation from TOEIC Services Canada)

Although the materials for the test make no specific mention of direct correlation with the ACTFL Oral Proficiency Interview and the guidelines that inform score interpretation for that test, it would appear that the TFI proficiency levels are defined in relation to those guidelines or to interpretation guidelines of similar instruments. The materials accompanying the test do mention that links between TFI scores and evaluation of oral expression have been established:

Table 2 Test de Français International score interpretation

Level descriptor	Scores
Beginner	10–260
Elementary	265–400
Intermediate	405–600
Basic Working Proficiency	605–780
Advanced Working Proficiency	785–900
Professional Proficiency	905–960
Advanced Professional Proficiency	965–990

Le test TFI fournit néanmoins une mesure indirect et fiable de l'expression orale et écrite. Des études, menées au niveau mondial sur un nombre important de non-francophones, ont démontré un lieu étroit entre les résultats obtenus au TFI et ceux obtenus lors d'une évaluation rigoureuse de l'expression orale. (*Manuel du candidat*, p. 7)

(Nevertheless the TFI furnishes an indirect and valid measurement of oral and written expression. Studies carried out worldwide and involving a significant number of non-francophones have shown a strong link between scores obtained on the TFI and those obtained in rigorous evaluation of oral expression. [*Candidate's Handbook*, p. 7; authors' translation])

For our purposes, we interpret the TFI scores as primarily indicative of the participants' command of the standard language in professional and academic contexts, of their reading and listening ability, and of their ability to function in the rigorously academic task of taking a multiple-choice test.

Interviews and journals

At the time that the participants were recruited in the fall of 2002, they were offered the possibility of two levels of participation: (1) participation in the assessments only, or (2) participation in the full study, including assessment, biweekly journal entries, interviews, and maintenance of a language use logbook at three week-long periods during the semester abroad. The philosophy underlying the collection of qualitative data in this project was one of participatory research, in which the participants were encouraged to nominate and pursue topics they deemed relevant to a shared project of understanding language learning in study abroad.

Nineteen of the twenty-three participants recruited agreed to full participation. All of these students were interviewed a minimum of two times, before their departure and at the end of their sojourn. Nine among them were also interviewed at the mid-term. The interviews were semi-structured to include certain pre-selected themes related to the history of the participants' engagement in language learning, but to allow for the emergence of topics nominated by the participants and for flexibility in including themes that piqued our own interest in the course of the study. In addition, all full participants maintained a paper-and-pencil or emailed journal in which they recorded, on a biweekly schedule, any events they judged relevant to our project.

Interview and journal data are further complemented, in our project, by informal contact with many of the participants on the part of the researchers: the project director (and first author of this chapter) and a graduate-level research assistant who collected data in France while functioning as a near-peer mentor whose support and assistance were available to the participants on an ongoing basis throughout the study.

Bearing in mind the caveat that test scores from the LAI and the TFI are of secondary importance in the interpretation of learners' experiences, we turn now to our results. We first examine the results of formal assessment via the Language Awareness Interview colloquial phrases section and the *Test de Français International*. We then turn to the question of how the test scores relate to the students' own accounts of their engagement with French language learning.

Results

In Tables 3 and 4 we present findings of two formal assessments for 17 participants in our study. Table 3 displays scores on the LAI colloquial phrases section for the entire group. Table 4 presents pre- and post-test scores, gain scores, and the interpretation of final scores in terms of level from the TFI.

Table 3 Colloquial word scores

Name	Comprehension of individual words		Understanding of idiomatic reading		Social context		Total score (out of a possible 30 points)		Gain score
	Pre-test	Post-test	Pre-test	Post-test	Pre-test	Post-test	Pre-test	Post-test	
Deirdre	1	6	0	2	0	1	1	9	8
Jada	3	7	2	5	2	5	7	17	10
Jerome	6	6	2	5	4	5	12	16	4
Benjamin	4	6	0	6	1	8	5	20	15
Camille	3	6	1	2	2	4	6	12	6
Ailis	4	3	0	1	1	2	5	6	1
Beatrice	3	7	3	5	3	6	9	18	9
Olivia	3	8	1	4	2	6	6	18	12
Delaney	2	6	2	5	2	5	6	16	10
Hannah	4	6	1	4	1	6	6	16	10
Bela	3	5	1	3	1	5	5	13	8
Brian	4	7	1	3	4	6	9	16	7
Hailey	3	3	2	2	3	3	8	8	0
Bill	2	6	1	5	1	5	4	16	12
Myrilla	1	3	0	3	0	2	1	8	7
Valerie	3	3	0	2	0	2	3	7	4
Elke	0	5	0	2	0	3	0	10	10

Table 4 *Test de Français International* scores

Name	TFI pre	TFI post	TFI gain	Post-score interpretation
Deirdre	545	585	40	Intermediate
Jada	575	630	55	Basic Working Proficiency
Jerome	695	805	110	Advanced Working Proficiency
Benjamin	730	800	70	Advanced Working Proficiency
Camille	455	565	110	Intermediate
Ailis	490	510	20	Intermediate
Beatrice	715	750	35	Basic Working Proficiency
Olivia	425	535	110	Intermediate
Delaney	545	585	40	Intermediate
Hannah	655	760	105	Basic Working Proficiency
Bela	485	505	20	Intermediate
Brian	650	695	45	Basic Working Proficiency
Hailey	545	735	190	Basic Working Proficiency
Bill	315	505	190	Intermediate
Myrilla	400	480	80	Intermediate
Valerie	370	460	90	Intermediate
Elke	635	705	70	Basic Working Proficiency

As anticipated, Table 3 reveals that most of the students made some gains in the domain of interpreting colloquial phrases, and that there is great variation in the overall achievement of the participants, ranging from the case of Ailis, with a gain score of 1, to the case of Benjamin, whose score rose by 15 points. Similarly, scores on the TFI show individual variation in proficiency in standard French as revealed in a test of reading, listening, and grammatical knowledge. For example, Benjamin began with a score of 730, which rose to 800. Camille and Ailis both scored at the Intermediate level when the study began (Camille: 455; Ailis: 490), and remained at that level after the study abroad period. However, Camille gained 110 points on the TFI, whereas Ailis gained only 20.

In this chapter, we take the quantitative findings as a point of departure for the core investigation of students' longitudinal accounts of language learning. In the sections below, we present case studies of three participants: the highest and lowest scorers on the colloquial phrases section of the LAI (Benjamin and Ailis, respectively) and one of the students whose score was in the mid-range (Camille). The three students whose case studies we present here might be considered either to have arrived at the advanced level in the case of Benjamin or to have demonstrated a desire to achieve advanced competence in French in the cases of Camille and Ailis. All three had invested considerable classroom seat time to the learning of French; they were enrolled in courses beyond the basic language program at college; they had elected to study abroad in France with a stated goal of enhancing their language competence. An examination of the scores alone, even were it complemented by a study of initial stated motivation, would reveal little more than a mystery surrounding individual variation in the results of the assessments. Only a detailed, longitudinal study of participants' histories of engagement in language learning activity can begin to address the reasons for this variation. That is, we cannot venture an explanation of this variation without examining over time both how the participants positioned themselves in relation to language learning, and what learning opportunities were extended to them during their sojourn abroad.

Benjamin

Benjamin spent his semester abroad in Paris, enrolled in a business-related program where he took courses exclusively with other Americans and where a homestay arrangement for residence was a requirement. Benjamin's story contrasts with the others in that the host family proved to be the main source of his reported progress in French. In routine classes and outings, he remained close to the American group until the latter part of the semester, and reported that, with the exception of one evening out in the company of Camille's boyfriend and his circle, he did not make prolonged contact with any French peers during his academic experience or free time outside the home. Coming from a relatively worldly family, with significant travel experience, Benjamin did not construct his study abroad semester as his one-and-only chance to experience other cultures through travel, but instead limited his trips away from Paris and his daily routine.

Benjamin was placed in the home of a baron and baroness living with their two daughters (17 and 20 years of age) in the wealthy suburb of Boulogne. He was invited to a formal dinner with the family every night, as his schedule permitted, and

was also invited to join the family for weekend excursions to their castle near Char-
tres. The home was well appointed and equipped with high-speed internet access
and cable television. Unlike many other study abroad students in homestay situations, Benjamin felt entirely comfortable with the material circumstances of his
adopted home; for example, there was no need for him to travel into central Paris in
order to use the computer resources of the study abroad program. He used his access
to television as a self-directed course in listening comprehension and as a source of
topics for conversation with the family. Although he was initially somewhat intimi-
dated by the level of family discussions around the dinner table, claiming that he
could not understand a single word, as the semester continued he became "more
interesting to talk to" (Post Interview) and it was in this context that the family
engaged him in "philosophical conversations":

> I think my host family especially is very well educated . . . so um like dinner conversations,
> tend to be things that I don't think I could keep up with in English, ya know, like
> philosophical conversations and all that kind of stuff. I'm like hold on slow down ya
> know? but I think that's part of it. so . . . very willing to engage me in debates discussions I
> think. (Post Interview)

In his journal Benjamin is an astute observer of the language-related behaviors of
his host family, how they diverge from the pedagogical norm, and how they influence
his own use of French:

> I've picked up on a few ties that seem to reoccur w/ my host family. My host brother
> seems to say "fin". Almost every other sentence at times. (As in "enfin" "essentially" after
> reflexion, etc. . . .) My host dad does something that I always thought was just a stereo-
> type, but apparently is not. I'm not sure I can exactly explain it, but it's like he says "oui"
> while inhaling sharply. And the whole family seems to be a huge fan of the word "truc".
> And par conséquent I find myself adopting these when I speak. though I suppose it's the
> little things that make the difference . . . (Journal, 2/12/2003)

By the mid-semester, Benjamin was growing frustrated with the boisterous public
behavior of his American classmates, as well as their lack of engagement in the
language learning process. At the same time, his relationship with the host family was
growing more complex and compelling. By the end of the semester he was spending
most of his time at home or on weekend trips to the family chateau, in conversation
with his hosts. By the end of the semester, he expressed gratitude for the opportunity
to develop his command of colloquial French alongside the standard:

> I think I've learned a lot of vocabulary, but I've also—I think the fact that's it's not all
> textbook helped. Cuz all ya learn in school is textbook ya know but when you're here to
> learn—ya learn phrases and . . . ya know everyday spoken language is ya know especially
> valuable. (Post Interview)

In the colloquial phrases task, Benjamin showed the largest improvement of all 17
students between pre- and post-test. His score quadrupled (from 5 to 20 out of 30) by
the end of his sojourn.

Camille

Camille enrolled in the same business-related program in Paris where Benjamin was studying, and, as for Benjamin, the homestay arrangement was mandated by the program. She was placed in the home of an older woman with one grown daughter. Although she initially rejected this situation on the grounds that she needed constant contact with French youth in order to learn how to speak (especially "slang"), and wanted to be with a family with children, she developed a friendly relationship with her host mother, one that convinced her to abandon plans to switch residences.

Camille's journal focuses on her daily activities and, to a considerable extent, on her efforts to learn the language. In both interviews and journal entries, her early comments reveal the presence of a "folklinguistic theory" (Miller and Ginsburg, 1995) in which fluency operates like a switch that is turned on by one's mere presence in the host community. In the initial interview, she suggested that she would "pick up" the language through contact with the host family and "whatever French friends I need" to help her learn French. Nevertheless, her determination to practice the language is revealed in the fact that she was one of the few participants who chose to write her journal primarily in French, and in this context she repeatedly emphasizes that she is in France to "become fluent." When asked in the Post-Experience Interview to describe what "fluent" means to her, she says it means: "that I can like come into a conversation and speak and not have to think uh and translate in my head." Camille realized early in the program that she would need to strike out on her own, away from the American group, if she wished to achieve this goal:

> I want to stop speaking so much English. I feel that the whole point in being abroad is to become immersed in another culture and to learn the language. So from now on I am going to try to spend less time with Americans and more time with French people. So starting tomorrow I am going to make an effort to meet French students and make friends. I've been intimidated so far but I think that I need to stop being shy and go meet some nice French students and make friends. Otherwise, I may never learn this language, and if I don't become fluent by the end of my stay I will be very annoyed with myself. (Journal, 1/22/2003)

Camille's clear and frequently articulated expectation was that she could "become fluent" by the end of her four-month stay in Paris, but as the semester continued she began to understand the complexity of this goal as well as the time and perseverance it would require. She began to note particularities of her own linguistic performance in specific circumstances:

> Il me semble que je parle plus quand il est juste moi et un ou deux autres personnes. Je pense parce que je me sens plus comfortable. Aussi, je comprends meilleure les adultes que les jeunes gens. Parce que les adultes ne parlent pas avec l'argot, comme les adoles-cents. Mais ça n'est pas un excuse. Je ne peux pas être timide en France especiallement parce que je suis seulement ici pour 4 mois et pas pour un an. (Journal, 3/9/2003)
>
> (It seems that I speak more when it is just me and one or two other people. I think because I feel more comfortable. Also, I understand adults better than young people. Because the adults do not speak with slang, like the adolescents. But that is no excuse. I cannot be timid in France especially because I am only here for four months and not for a year.)

By the time the semester had ended, she had a much enhanced awareness of the extent to which language learning represents an investment of time and effort. She planned to rearrange her schedule for graduation in order to permit a second sojourn in France.

The most salubrious influence on Camille's language learning during her semester in Paris was undoubtedly the presence of a "second family," her mother's friends. Though they did not live in Paris, she visited them and was immersed in French during her week-long spring vacation. Through their influence she met a young Frenchman in Paris who became her boyfriend and who introduced her to a wide circle of other friends and acquaintances. Camille had rejected the strategy of meeting others, particularly men, in bars or dance clubs, but she was keenly interested in the linguistic advantage of having a French boyfriend (for a similar case, see Kaplan, 1993), particularly if he were pre-approved by her mother's family friends:

> I've been hanging out with this guy Gabriel lately, and if I continue to hang out with him and his friends then I think I can become fluent. I hope so. Alright, anyways, I'm definitely falling in love more and more with Paris. So I know my study abroad semester will be awesome I just want to make it make awesome by becoming fluent. (Journal, 1/28/2003)

As the end of her sojourn approached, Camille attributed much of her progress to her relationship with Gabriel. She had begun to incorporate some colloquial words into her journal writing, and she doubled her score in the colloquial phrases task (from 6 to 12 out of 30). Spending time with her French boyfriend and other native speakers appears to have played an important role in this student's score improvement.

Ailis

Ailis took part in a five-month study abroad program located in Montpellier, a populous university town in the south of France, where she elected a homestay arrangement for her residence and was placed in the suburban home of an older, single woman with an "empty nest." As recounted in journals and interviews, Ailis's experience in France included an initial phase of intense loneliness that was eventually relieved via her acquaintance with other young American women participating in the program. One of these became her travel companion for weekly excursions away from Montpellier, to destinations both within and outside of France. Ailis describes homesickness and worry about her friends and family in Pennsylvania throughout her stay, with particular emphasis on her boyfriend, a great deal of speculation about the future of this relationship, and comments on her decision to avoid contact with other young men. She focuses in her journal on the relationships she is able to maintain with the people at home, and the satisfaction she derives from letters, phone calls, and emails from her friends and family.

Ailis was aware of two settings where she might have had opportunities to engage in social interaction with speakers of French: the classroom, and the home where she was living. Ailis took courses with the program for foreign students, where she met only other foreigners, but she was also enrolled in an "integrative" course at the university, where she was in a group with French students. However, according to her account, interaction among students and teacher was not a prominent feature of this classroom, where the instructor lectured and the students took notes. At the beginning of the semester, when Ailis was able only to pick out single words from the lecture and write them down in her notebook, she borrowed notes from one of the French students. This was the only interaction with a French peer that she recorded in her journal.

Ailis's experience of the homestay was akin to that described in Rivers (1998), a study debunking the myth of the homestay as a consistent source of opportunities for second language interaction. At home, Ailis did not enjoy extensive interaction with her host mother, who worked full-time, returning in the evening for dinner. Dinner normally took place in front of the television, with the host mother continuing to watch TV after the dinner was over. As a result, the daily routine at home involved Ailis in exchange of greetings and short, formulaic requests but did not otherwise engage her. Ailis summed up her access to informal French in the journal entry below, from February 7:

> Since I only hang out w/ the US students, we always end up talking english. I haven't met any french kids so I only talk french in class (which isn't too often since usually just the teacher talks) and to my host mom. But since she works all day long I rarely see her. And the past week we've eaten dinner in front of the TV so we hardly talk. (Journal, 2/7/2003)

In a subsequent journal entry from the latter part of the semester, Ailis describes the strategy she has adopted (apart from frequent travel) for maintaining her comfort in this home:

> So overall, I really don't talk to my host mom. And when I do it's always just about my classes or plans. She never tells me anything about herself or what's going on in her life. Not like I need to know intimate details, just polite conversation stuff. She probably thinks I'm weird cuz I stay in my room a lot but I feel more comfortable in my bedroom. And this way I don't get in her way or bother her. Not like I think I do, but still. Even though I've been here for 3 months, I don't feel any more comfortable around her and the house than I did in the beginning . . . (Journal, 4/16/2003)

Thus, most of Ailis's interaction took place with other American students studying abroad, either in Montpellier or elsewhere, with French reserved for classes and service encounters. She made few attempts to interact with French peers, and the homestay situation did not generate significant opportunities to use French. Although she writes of her desire to expand her horizons, her comments on French culture and communicative style are often based on the point of view of a judgmental outsider:

> You could totally tell it was a French beach w/ all the topless women and guys in Speedos! It's going to be a relief going back to the US and seeing not scrawny guys and they'll be in normal trunks! Oh another odd thing, we saw 2 little girls pee right on the beach! Their parents were perfectly aware of what they were doing too! I mean either hold it or at least pee in the ocean, that's better than peeing where you might walk in it! The French just

have some odd traditions and cultural aspects that I still can't get used to! (Probably never will!). (Journal, 5/1/2003)

One thing I noticed about the French, it seems like they are always interrupting each other. I'm watching some talk show now and they all seem to be talking at once. And my host mom does that w/ her friends and even business people like the painter and window salesman. I think it's a little rude, but maybe it's normal for them . . . (Journal, 5/19/2003)

In the end, Ailis decided to shorten her sojourn, changing her reservations in order to leave for home as soon as her academic obligations had been fulfilled.

As noted above, Ailis received a gain score of 1 on the colloquial phrases task (from 5 to 6 out of 30). Given the limited amount of time that she spent in informal interaction with speakers of French, this modest outcome is hardly remarkable.

Discussion and conclusion

Although we have no intention of suggesting that a causal relationship exists between these students' scores on an assessment of their awareness of colloquial French and the qualities of their experiences while in France, it is nonetheless clear that some thematic unity obtains here. An advantage appears to accrue for the students who are more engaged in interaction, with interlocutors of more varied age and background.

Benjamin came to the study abroad program with a history of success in academic language learning, as witnessed by his high TFI score, and with the benefit of previous experience of spoken French in the domestic immersion program and during a short trip to France. Moreover, he came from a relatively worldly and well-traveled family, with a realistic understanding of the complexities of language learning. He was placed in the home of an educated, well-to-do, sophisticated family who practiced routine and somewhat ritualized nightly gatherings for conversation around the dinner table. These proved to be a predictable locus of "legitimate peripheral participation" (Lave and Wenger, 1991) in which Benjamin could first observe, then imitate and interact, and finally join the family with the status of a welcomed friend.

Camille gained access to a circle of French friends through her romantic interest in Gabriel, and thereby became engaged in routine, informal talk to complement her academic work in the program. However, she began the program with limited experience of spoken French and a score on the test of academic standard French (the TFI) placing her at the Intermediate level. She also brought to her experience a folklinguistic theory of language learning that downplayed the seriousness of the effort involved. Thus, she had further to go in language learning, and in her general appreciation of the problems involved than did Benjamin.

For Ailis, the experience of study abroad was doubly difficult in the sense that there was little in her background, in terms of access to travel or to an understanding of spoken French or language learning, to prepare her for her sojourn. Her home-stay, and its multiple TV dinners, only contributed to her loneliness and alienation, leading her to find refuge in the company of other Americans and to construct her experience as an opportunity to escape, via travel, from the possibility of establishing ties to the locale where she was studying.

Comparison of the three cases suggests that there is much more to the study abroad experience than meets the eye. The ways in which the sojourn will function as an environment for development of advanced competence will depend on the qualities of the sojourn itself—for example, on the role that the host family elects to take in welcoming, assisting, and instructing newcomers. However, and crucially, it will also depend on the histories of the participants, and how they position themselves with respect to the people they meet and the activities that become available to them. In the examples here, Benjamin was in some ways ideally positioned for language learning both within a highly privileged homestay environment and in terms of his own relatively sophisticated general cosmopolitanism and understanding of how language learning works. For Camille, although the study abroad program did not result in immediate, dramatic gains, it may be said to have furthered her desire to learn while enriching her awareness of the degree to which achievement of second language "fluency" represents a serious, long-term effort. Ailis, on the other hand, encountered few occasions for social engagement in French and made little effort to seek them out, preferring instead to interpret her experience as a one-time opportunity for general broadening of the mind through travel.

There can be no doubt that all three of these students profited from their sojourn in France; however, language learning is not necessarily highlighted in each case. Undergraduate study abroad participants clearly vary not only in terms of motivation for language learning but also in terms of the learning opportunities extended to them, and the ways in which they construe both study abroad and the process of language development within it. Only a longitudinal approach, including the voices of the researched and the ways they represent their experience, can provide insights into the relationship between language learning and social context, and thereby begin to unravel the mystery of individual differences that has traditionally plagued the interpretation of study abroad research.

In this study, we have taken a particular interest in study abroad participants' appreciation of colloquial language; that is, the sort of language that is unlikely to appear anywhere on a classroom radar screen, but that is in plain evidence to students who live abroad, find themselves in informal situations, and opt to take note of it. Appreciation of the social meaning of colloquial language is a hallmark of advanced competence, but one that has been infrequently studied. Nevertheless, a common complaint among teachers of French, particularly at the graduate level, is that study abroad veterans show a command of "street French" that works to the detriment of their writing and performance in formal academic settings. Future research could profitably examine awareness of colloquial and standard language in their finer points and in the differences between them among students deemed "advanced" and teachers at the beginning of their careers.

In the context of a research study, and given the problems associated with examining doubly indexical sociolinguistic features, it would likely be difficult to capture situations where this language is in use by participants and to perform a valid analysis of this use. Our relatively modest but realistic goal was therefore to explore students' awareness of colloquial French through an interview. Our results suggest that study abroad students do in fact develop their awareness and understanding of colloquial language and how it relates to context of situation; that is, the study abroad setting is potentially quite different from classroom-based or sheltered immersion programs in its impact on sociolinguistic competence. However, this awareness is not a simple effect of context. Rather, it is shaped by the students' histories of engagement in concrete, language-related activities within diverse social settings.

Notes

1. Research on study abroad tends to involve protracted periods of time in the sense that the length of programs or of other residence abroad defines temporal boundaries of the period under consideration, typically from a semester to a year or more. In US study abroad research, this period tends to correspond to the most popular, semester-long sojourn abroad, as for example in the influential studies of Brecht, Davidson, and Ginsburg (1995) and their colleagues, and in the collection edited by Freed and Collentine (2004). Reports of study-abroad-related research in Europe normally consider periods abroad of a year or more (e.g., Barron, 2003; Dewaele and Regan, 2001). In this chapter we are advocating a longitudinal approach involving collection of data of diverse kinds at multiple points during the period under consideration, in the hope of capturing some aspects of the dynamism characterizing participants' motives (Lantolf and Genung, 2002) along with evidence of their language learning. We agree with the assertion of Ortega and Iberri-Shea (2005), who underscore the value of longitudinal findings that would allow the SLA community to "contribute meaningful characterizations of the gradual process of attaining advanced second language and literacy competencies across various contexts" (p. 28).
2. "The Social Context of Language Learning in Study Abroad," Celeste Kinginger, Project Director. This research is supported by CALPER (Center for Advanced Language Proficiency Education and Research), a National Foreign Language Resource Center (United States Department of Education, CFDA 84.229, P229A020010–03).
3. Our sincere thanks to Professor Meredith Doran, of Penn State University, who offered us guidance on the selection of the colloquial phrases.

References

Ager, D. (1994). *Sociolinguistics and contemporary French*. New York: Cambridge University Press.

Ager, D. (1999). *Identity, insecurity, and image: France and language*. Clevedon, UK: Multilingual Matters.

Ball, R. (1997). *The French-speaking world: A practical introduction to sociolinguistic issues*. London: Routledge.

Ball, R. (2000). *Colloquial French grammar*. Malden, MA: Blackwell.

Barron, A. (2003). *Acquisition in interlanguage pragmatics: How to do things with words in a study abroad context*. Philadelphia, PA: John Benjamins.

Belz, J. A., and Kinginger, C. (2002). The cross-linguistic development of address form use in telecollaborative language learning: Two case studies. *Canadian Modern Language Review, 59*, 189–214.

Belz, J. A., and Kinginger, C. (2003). Discourse options and the development of pragmatic competence by classroom learners of German: The case of address forms. *Language Learning, 53*, 591–647.

Blanche-Benveniste, C. (1997). La notion de variation linguistique dans le français parlé. *Langue Française, 115*, 19–29.

Brecht, R. D., Davidson, D. E., and Ginsburg, R.B. (1995). Predictors of foreign language gain during study abroad. In B. Freed (Ed.), *Second language acquisition in a study abroad context* (pp. 37–66). Philadelphia, PA: John Benjamins.

Dewaele, J.-M. (2004). *Vous* or *tu?* Native and non-native speakers of French on a socio-linguistic tightrope. *International Review of Applied Linguistics, 42*, 383–402.

Dewaele, J.-M. (2005). Investigating the psychological and emotional dimensions in instructed language learning: Obstacles and possibilities. *Modern Language Journal, 89*, 367–380.

Dewaele, J.-M. and Regan, V. (2001). The use of colloquial words in advanced French inter-language. *EUROSLA Yearbook, 1*, 51–67.

Dewaele, J.-M., and Regan, V. (2002). Maîtriser la norme sociolinguistique en interlangue française: le cas de l'omission variable de "ne." *Journal of French Language Studies, 12*, 123–148.

Frank, V. M. (2002). The interlanguage pragmatic competence of classroom-based learners of Russian: "Ponimaesh', k tebe takoe delo." Unpublished doctoral dissertation, Bryn Mawr University.

Freed, B. (1995). Language learning and study abroad. In B. Freed (Ed.), *Second language acquisition in a study abroad context* (pp. 3–33). Philadelphia, PA: John Benjamins.

Freed, B. and Collentine, J. (Eds.) (2004). *Learning context and its effects on second language acquisition.* Special issue of *Studies in Second Language Acquisition, 26*(2).

Freed, B. F., Segalowitz, N. and Dewey, D. P. (2004). Context of learning and second language fluency in French: Comparing regular classrooms, study abroad, and intensive domestic immersion programs. *Studies in Second Language Acquisition, 26*, 275–301.

Hoffman-Hicks, S. (2001). The longitudinal development of French foreign language prag-matic competence: Evidence from study abroad participants. Unpublished doctoral disser-tation, Indiana University.

Kaplan, A. (1993). *French lessons: A memoir.* Chicago: University of Chicago Press.

Kinginger, C. (1999). Videoconferencing as access to spoken French. *Canadian Modern Language Review, 55*(4), 468–489.

Kinginger, C. (2004). Alice doesn't live here anymore: Foreign language learning and identity reconstruction. In A. Pavlenko and A. Blackledge (Eds.), *Negotiation of identities in multilingual contexts* (pp. 219–242). Clevedon, UK: Multilingual Matters.

Kinginger, C. and Belz, J. A. (2005). Sociocultural perspectives on pragmatic development in foreign language learning: Microgenetic and ontogenetic case studies from telecollabora-tion and study abroad. *Intercultural Pragmatics, 2*, 369–421.

Kinginger, C., and Farrell, K. (2004). Assessing development of metapragmatic awareness in study abroad. *Frontiers: The Interdisciplinary Journal of Study Abroad, 10*, 19–42.

Labov, W. (1989). Field methods of the project on linguistic change and variation. In R. Bauman & J. Sherzer (Eds.), *Explorations in the Ethnography of Speaking*, Second Edition (pp. 28–66). New York: Cambridge University Press.

Lafford, B. A. (1995). Getting into, through, and out of a survival situation: A comparison of communicative strategies used by students studying Spanish-abroad and "at home." In B. Freed (Ed.), *Second language acquisition in a study abroad context* (pp. 97–121). Philadelphia: John Benjamins.

Lafford, B. A. (2004). The effect of the context of learning on the use of communication strategies by learners of Spanish as a second language. *Studies in Second Language Acquisition, 26*, 201–225.

Lantolf, J. P., and Genung, P. G. (2002). "I'd rather switch than fight". An activity-theoretic study of power, success, and failure in a foreign language classroom. In C. Kramsch (Ed.), *Language acquisition and language socialization: Ecological perspectives* (pp. 175–196). London: Continuum.

Lantolf, J. P., and Pavlenko, A. (2001). (S)econd (L)anguage (A)ctivity Theory: Understanding second language learners as people. In M. Breen (Ed.), *Learner contributions to language learning: New directions in research* (pp. 141–158). New York: Longman.

Lantolf, J. P., and Thorne, S. (2006) *Sociocultural theory and the genesis of second language development.* New York: Oxford University Press.

Lave, J., and Wenger, E. (1991). *Situated learning: Legitimate peripheral participation.* New York: Cambridge University Press.

Lippi-Green, R. (1997). *English with an accent: Language, ideology, and discrimination in the United States.* New York: Routledge.

Matsumura, S. (2001). Learning the rules for offering advice: A quantitative approach to second language socialization. *Language Learning, 51,* 635–679.

Miller, L., and Ginsburg, R. B. (1995). Folklinguistic theories of language learning. In B. Freed (Ed.), *Second language acquisition in a study abroad context* (pp. 293–315). Philadelphia, PA: John Benjamins.

Morford, J. (1997). Social indexicality in French pronominal address. *Journal of Linguistic Anthropology, 7,* 3–37.

Norton, B. (2000). *Identity in language learning: Gender, ethnicity, and educational change.* New York: Longman.

Ortega, L., and Iberri-Shea, G. (2005). Longitudinal research in second language acquisition: Recent trends and future directions. *Annual Review of Applied Linguistics, 25,* 26–45.

Regan, V. (1995). The acquisition of sociolinguistic native speech norms: Effects of a year abroad on second language learners of French. In B. Freed (Ed.), *Second language acquisition in a study abroad context* (pp. 245–267). Philadelphia, PA: John Benjamins.

Rivers, W. P. (1998). Is being there enough? The effects of homestay placements on language gain during study abroad. *Foreign Language Annals, 31,* 492–500.

Sante, L. (2004). French without tears. In W. Lesser (Ed.), *The genius of language* (pp. 67–84). New York: Pantheon Books.

Savignon, S. (1983). *Communicative competence: Theory and classroom practice.* Reading, MA: Addison-Wesley.

Silverstein, M. (1992). The uses and utility of ideology: Some reflections. *Pragmatics, 2,* 311–323.

Silverstein, M. (1996). Indexical order and the dialectics of sociolinguistic life. In R. Parker, R. Ide, and Y. Sunaoshi (Eds.), *Proceedings of the Third Annual Symposium about Language and Society—Austin [SALSA]* (pp. 266–295). Austin: University of Texas at Austin, Department of Linguistics.

Valdman, A. (2000). Comment gérer la variation dans l'enseignement du français langue étrangère aux Etats-Unis. *French Review,* 73, 648–666.

Appendix A: Colloquial phrases and approximate translations

1. J'en ai marre. (I am sick/fed up with this.)
2. Qu'est-ce qu'elle est casse pied cette nana. (That girl is a pain in the ass.)
3. Ton boulot, qu'est-ce que ça donne? (What's going on with your job?)
4. Elle a une floppée de moutards. (She has a ton of kids.)
5. Tu me fais pas la bise? (Why don't you give me a kiss?)
6. T'as vu dans l'canard? On fait toute une tartine pour un clebs écrasé. Quelle salade pour un cabot! (Did you see the paper? There is a whole to-do about a dog that got run over. What fuss over a dog.)
7. Sa copine est hyper chouette. (His/Her girlfriend is really cool.)
8. Y'en a qui ont pas fait gaffe et qu'on loupé l'exam. (Some of them screwed up and flunked the exam.)
9. M'enfin tu vas la fermer? (When are you going to shut up?)
10. Elle est bonne cette meuf. (That girl is hot.)

Appendix B: Colloquial phrases scoring procedure

Example (1)

In Deirdre's pre-test, she clearly does not understand the meaning of Phrase #4:

Elle a une floppée de moutards.	W	R	C	D: somebody talking about mustard? u::m I don't know what *floppée* is though.
	0	0	0	

Example (2)

In Olivia's post-test, one point was assigned to her understanding of the term *nana* (Phrase #2) ("girl"), but no further points were assigned because she clearly did not understand the referential meaning of the phrase or the context in which its use would be appropriate.

Elle est casse pied cette nana.	W	R	C	O: uh . . . I don't know what *casse pied* means, but *nana* is like a girl so I think that it would be someone trying to get hit on—sees a good looking girl. trying to talk to them, that kind of thing so I think the person would be in a good mood. or . . . hanging out mood like playful mood, not really serious. I: uh uh so it' be like one friend to another? O: uh uh
	1	0	0	

Example (3)

In Delaney's pre-test, she identifies the mood associated with the phrase (#1) without recalling its referential meaning:

J'en ai marre.	W	R	C	D: um I recognize it? um but I really don't remember—I kinda feel like it mighta been when they were mad but I I don't remember= I: =ok= D: =I know I've heard it before=
	0	0	1	

Example (4)

In Jerome's pre-test, one point was assigned for word comprehension and one for context, although he did not indicate an understanding of the entire phrase (#3).

Ton boulot, qu'est-ce que ça donne?	**W**	**R**	**C**	
	1	0	1	J: … uh … talking about something … chat about how they make. I: alright, so who would say this and to whom they would say it? J: uh, I guess it would be said to a person, like between friends, talking about a third person. I: ok. J: like in his job, how much does he make. I: ok, and why would it be amongst friends? J: uh, because it's kind of impolite to ask people how much they make.

Example (5)

In her post-test, Beatrice identifies a potential social setting and referential meaning of the phrase (#10) in question:

Elle est bonne cette meuf.	**W**	**R**	**C**	
	1	1	1	B: … she's ((giggle)) she's good this girl like she is … I I think that it means she is hot this girl, like you know? I, I would say that's a few guys talking, I've never heard a girl use *meuf*. I: ok, so guys talking about a girl? B: that's what I would say.

13 Acquiring oral language skills over the course of a high school year abroad

What's in it for absolute beginners?

Allison J. Spenader

Abstract

The study of language learning in study abroad contexts has been primarily focused on the college level sojourner with several semesters of formal language instruction behind her. This study examines the learning experiences of two high school exchange students with no previous language ability to inform questions pertaining to how and why language acquisition takes place on the individual level, paying particular attention to how cross-cultural adaptation influences language learning over a year-long study abroad experience. Using a descriptive case-study design framed by cross-cultural adaptation theory (Berry, 2005), oral fluency and global proficiency gains are examined at the five- and ten-month marks of the two students' sojourn. Observations, interviews, and external measures of linguistic and cross-cultural development over the course of a year provide for rich descriptions of the personal challenges and triumphs of these adolescent sojourners. The results of the study indicate that even absolute beginning language learners can make impressive language gains during the course of a year abroad, both in terms of global proficiency and oral fluency. Linguistic success was found to be largely a result of satisfying relationships with host nationals and specific personality traits. Implications for study abroad programs are presented, with particular attention paid to how language learning can be maximized in study abroad programs at all levels.

Introduction

Study abroad is often considered a capstone experience in the foreign language curriculum. While research on language learning in college level study abroad dominates the field, studies of high school exchange students provide an interesting perspective in terms of highly naturalistic language learning in the host family and the mainstream classroom. In study abroad high school programs, students often benefit from extended access to native speakers through a complete immersion environment—a setting where they are completely surrounded by the host language and culture. In order to understand what it is about the study abroad context that allows for language learning, we must take a critical look at the personal experiences of sojourners over time. By examining language acquisition in study abroad longitudinally, we can be better informed about the processes involved in language learning in this context.

The experience of studying abroad is complex both programmatically as well as in terms of the lived experiences of the individual. Of particular interest is how an individual's ability to adapt to the host culture impacts language learning. Within the field of psychology, cross-cultural adaptation is readily explored in populations moving between cultures, including immigrants, refugees, and sojourners. Cross-cultural adaptation refers to the processes that occur on both personal and societal levels when an individual comes into contact with a new culture. A useful way of examining this process is through the analysis of *acculturative strategies*. Berry (1997, 2005) identifies four basic strategies for adapting to culture. These are *integration, assimilation, separation,* and *marginalization.*

This study constitutes an attempt to establish a link between the SLA literature on study abroad and existing theories on cross-cultural adaptation. It looks to describe the interplay between acculturative strategies and language learning in two adolescent sojourners who spent a year in Sweden.

Absolute beginner adolescent sojourners and cross-cultural adaptation theory

Much has been written about language learning in study abroad contexts. Research tells us that students who study abroad typically make linguistic gains as a result of their time spent abroad (Freed, 1995a). In particular, study abroad seems to benefit oral proficiency development (Brecht *et al.*, 1995; Magnan, 1986; Ryan and Lafford, 1992), and fluency development (Freed, 1995b; Lapkin, Hart, and Swain, 1995). Specifically, certain features of fluency, such as rate of speech and length of utterance, appear to improve as a result of study abroad (Freed 1995a). These studies have largely informed our current understanding of the linguistic benefits of study abroad. However, none of these studies included absolute beginners. In fact, it has even been suggested that the immersion environment may be "wasted" on the novice speaker (Engle and Engle, 2003).

Very little has been done to investigate the adolescent, absolute beginner sojourner, and the predominating belief is that these learners are at a real disadvantage in terms of adapting to life in a new culture. Yet for sojourners to nations where less commonly taught languages are spoken, it is unlikely that students will arrive with any previous knowledge of the language. These sojourners can help us to better understand how language learning takes place as a result of submersion environments. Furthermore, by looking at their oral language development over time, we can attain a better understanding of the real linguistic benefit of the semester and year-long study abroad program.

For decades, researchers in the field of second language acquisition have hypothesized about the relationship between language and acculturation. Schumann's (1986) acculturation theory states that a learner will learn the target language only to the degree to which he or she cross-culturally adapts. Early work by Guiora (1972) presents the concept of *ego-permeability*, which posits that a learner's ability to take on a new cultural identity is related to his or her ability to learn language. More recently, individuals who are able to engage in meaningful relationships with their hosts have been found to acquire more "native"-sounding pronunciation (Lybeck, 2002) and to develop more fluent use of formulaic routines (Dörnyei, Dorow, and Zahran 2004).

If language is viewed as a behavioral trait, as it often is in the fields of social psychology and cross-cultural psychology, then a link can be expected between acculturative strategies and one's ability and/or willingness to learn the host language (e.g., Bochner, 1982; Ward, Bochner, and Furnham, 2001; Ward and Kennedy, 1994). In his seminal cross-cultural adaptation model, Berry (1997, 2005) identifies four basic strategies for acculturation, based on one's preference for maintaining one's own heritage culture, and a relative preference for participating in the host society. In *assimilation*, individuals prefers to abandon their heritage culture and become absorbed into the host culture. *Integration* refers to a strategy where the heritage culture is still maintained and yet there is a willingness to participate in the host culture. When an individual wants to hold on to the heritage culture exclusively, *separation* occurs. Finally, when neither the heritage nor the host culture is valued or maintained, an individual is said to experience *marginalization*. Other research on the effect of cross-cultural adaptation on language learning in study abroad has identified a number of additional key relationships (see Ward, Bochner, and Furnham, 2001). Ward and Kennedy (1993), for example, found a link between the amount of language learned by high school study abroad participants and the kinds of relationships they forged with their hosts. Students who reported the most satisfying relationships with host nationals also reported fewer feelings of homesickness, and reported higher levels of language ability.

In the study reported in this chapter, I explore how acculturative strategies might impact language learning in sojourners. By collecting data from multiple sources, I describe in detail how the cross-cultural adaptive process during the course of a year abroad in Sweden impacts language learning in two adolescent sojourners who had no prior knowledge of Swedish when they began their year abroad. The study distinguishes itself from existing studies of cross-cultural adaptation in that, rather than relying solely on large-scale correlational analysis, as cross-cultural psychologists often do, I focus instead on the individual experience over time.

Method

Context

This study examines the experiences of sojourners who participated in a year-long high school exchange program to Sweden. Exchange Program (a pseudonym), or EP for short, has a long history of facilitating adolescent student exchange. The program works to maximize contact with host nationals through homestays and mainstream high school experiences. Students going to Sweden need not have any previous knowledge of Swedish, but are encouraged to attend "Swedish for foreigners" classes provided by their schools. They are expected to partake in either mainstream or immigrant classes to the best of their ability, which includes attending classes and completing assignments, as they are able.

Participants

The present report draws from a larger study that involved four adolescent sojourners participating in a year-long high school exchange to Sweden with EP (Spenader, 2005). In the study sampling I wanted to ensure a variety of experiences, including male and female students, students from rural and urban centers, students hosted in urban and rural centers, ages ranging from 16–18, both students who had and had not yet graduated from high school, and students with outgoing and more reserved personalities. Aware of these requirements, the EP office in Stockholm recommended the four individuals as potential participants. In the present chapter I will look at just two of the original four participants, Faith and Max. Table 1 summarizes their profiles. Neither Faith nor Max had had any prior experience with the Swedish language, nor had they ever visited Sweden.

Faith had graduated from high school before her year in Sweden. She was tall and fair, and came from a small city in the Midwest. Faith was a hockey player, and was placed in a community where hockey was a favorite pastime. Her host mother was the coach of the local hockey team, while her host sister was the goalie. Both of her older brothers had been EP students, and she chose Sweden because her brothers had not been there, and because she knew she'd be able to play hockey. She was also very interested in learning Swedish.

Max had graduated a year early from high school, and was looking to fill up a year before starting college with his friends. He had wanted to study in Japan or Italy, but because he applied late his choices were limited. He felt that Sweden "seemed like a good country," although he didn't know much about it. He was hosted on a dairy farm in southern Sweden, about 8 kilometers (5 miles) from the small town where his high school was located.

Research questions

The study is organized into individual cases characterized by in-depth descriptions of the personal sojourner experience over time. The qualitative description of each individual experience serves as the primary means for addressing the following research questions:

1.   What are the linguistic outcomes of sojourners who go abroad without any previous language skills, as measured in terms of proficiency and fluency?
2.   How does cross-cultural adaptation influence oral language development in high school study abroad participants?

The first research question delves into the linguistic benefits of study abroad to absolute beginners. The second research question is that of the role of cross-cultural adaptation in the learning of the target language. In order to attain a complete picture of these processes and how they are interrelated, a variety of data sources were employed.

Table 1 Overview of participants

Participant	Age at arrival	High school graduate	Personality traits suggested by EP program officials	Host community
Faith	18	Yes	Friendly and athletic	Medium-sized town
Max	17	Yes, one year early	Quiet, reserved, and thoughtful	Rural

Data collection

I used interpretive methods to capture the individual experiences of sojourners at two points during the year. I visited the participants first in January, after five months in Sweden, and again in May, after ten months, in order to obtain a "snapshot" of their lives in Sweden. During each visit, I shadowed each participant for a day. The shadowing process meant that I met each participant at their school and observed them from early morning (before classes) through evening, following students home after school. During the shadowing, I took extensive observation notes. Observations took place primarily in the schools and the homes of the students, but also "around town"—on buses, in cafés and shopping centers. This allowed me to witness each sojourner in multiple social contexts.

I also conducted interviews with the participants, their host teachers, and their host parents concerning issues related to the cross-cultural adaptation and language learning of each sojourner. All constituents were interviewed both in January and again in May, and interviews ranged from just under 20 minutes, to nearly 90 minutes in length. I transcribed all interviews and subsequently coded and analyzed them. In addition, email questionnaires were collected in February, March, and April, as a means of continuing to monitor the student's experiences during the second half of their year (see Appendix A for the questionnaire). Together, these methods of data collection provided an extensive, descriptive data set, with multiple perspectives on each sojourner experience over the course of a year.

As a means of informing the rich, descriptive data collected on the sojourners, the research aimed to link the study to existing theories on cross-cultural adaptation. Three external measures of cross-cultural adjustment were used to inform the qualitative findings. Only one of these, the Acculturation Index (AI) developed by Ward and Rana-Deuba (1999b), seemed to differentiate between the participants in a way that enlightened their approaches and ultimate ability to use Swedish. Therefore, I limit my report here to the AI.[1] This instrument consists of 21 items that ask sojourners to rate how they see themselves in terms of behavior and experiences with relation to their home and host cultural norms. A think-aloud protocol was used in administering the AI, so that sojourner commentary could be captured in relation to all items. These data were then transcribed, coded, and analyzed.

Linguistic development was measured in terms of oral proficiency and fluency development. Because sojourners in the EP program do not always partake in Swedish as a foreign language class, it was conceivable that their fluency might develop more rapidly than their overall proficiency. To account for their true oral language ability, both global proficiency and fluency measures were taken. Oral Proficiency Interviews (OPIs) were administered and scored according to the Foreign Service Institute's (FSI) protocol for Swedish for each sojourner in January and again in May. The OPIs were administered on the same day as the observations and interviews. Typically, I would sit with the sojourner in the school library and conduct the interview. The interviews were recorded and later transcribed. A native-speaker rater was employed to confirm the proficiency judgment, as well as to provide fluency ratings based upon those same interviews.

Analysis

The observation, interview, and email data were transcribed and analyzed in two primary stages. First, I analyzed the data deductively, using codes that had been suggested as relevant in previous research studies on adaptation and language learning. During the second round of coding, I used an inductive analysis in order to highlight those factors that appeared to influence participants' experiences of success with regard to language learning and cross-cultural adaptation.

The AI was filled out by the sojourners, and the scores reported here refer to the number of items where participants identified more strongly with Swedes (assimilation) or with US Americans (separation), equally strongly with both (integration), or identification with neither (marginalization).

The FSI provided the OPI scoring rubric for Swedish, which included 58 language features, and the samples were analyzed in terms of whether or not the features were used correctly in the majority of instances present. The scores reported here are thus according to the FSI scales. Fluency judgments were made in terms of ranking the four participants relative to each other, and rating them on a scale of 1 through 7, with 1 being "not at all fluent" and 7 being "totally fluent." As mentioned, in addition to my ratings, a blind judgment was provided by a trained OPI tester/rater in Swedish for both the OPI rating and the overall fluency rating. Another fluency indicator was the mean length of utterance. The proficiency and fluency scores were then compared to the qualitative descriptions to comprise a case study analysis of each individual's language learning experience as it relates to cross-cultural adaptation.

Findings

Table 2 displays the main results of the three linguistic measures: global proficiency rating, fluency score, and mean length of utterance. It can be seen that each of the two participants represented a different sojourner experience in terms of oral language development. Their ultimate proficiency scores ranged from FSI level 1.81 for Max to 3.81 for Faith (equivalent to Intermediate-High and Superior, respectively, on the ACTFL scales; see Lowe and Stansfield, 1988), while fluency ratings spanned from somewhat fluent for Max to totally fluent for Faith.

Table 2 Language outcome measures for the two participants

	Time	OPI level FSI scale	Fluency score	Mean length of utterance
Faith	January	3.13	5	8.9
	May	3.81	7	18
Max	January	1.81	2	2.9
	May	1.87	3.5	4.14

Note
January was the fifth month and May was the tenth month of residence abroad. FSI/ACTFL equivalences are: Levels 1+ through 2+ = Intermediate-High, Advanced, and Advanced-Plus; Level 3 and higher = Superior. Fluency scores ranged from 1 = not at all fluent to 7 = totally fluent. Mean length of utterance is given in words.

Thus, these two participants illustrate well the kinds of variation in linguistic development that exist even within a fairly specific study abroad context. Despite the fact that both had begun the experience at the same point of no prior knowledge of the Swedish language and no prior contact with Sweden, by the five-month mark (in January) it was clear that their learning curves were distinctly different, and the difference only accentuated at the ten-month hallmark (in May). Moreover, when their May AI scores were inspected (cf. Tables 3 and 4 later), it turned out that they also represented two very distinct acculturative strategies, namely a largely assimilative yet slightly separative strategy in response to Swedish culture for Faith, and a largely separative, even slightly marginalized strategy, for Max.

Looking solely at the quantitative data presented across Tables 1 through 4, an interesting pattern emerges where advanced second language capacity is associated with an assimilative acculturative strategy. The relationship between language learning and acculturation is more thoroughly illustrated in the wealth of information contained in the individual stories of each sojourner. In particular, the difference in success in language learning seemed to be linked to the ways in which the two sojourners had adapted to life in Sweden, including the kinds of relationships they had with Swedes, which in turn had a direct impact on how, where, and why they used Swedish.

Faith's story

Faith's acquisition of Swedish is by all accounts impressive. After only five months in Sweden, she had scored a 3.13 (ACTFL Superior) on the FSI scale, and by the end of ten months, she was a 3.81, approaching the ACTFL level of Distinguished. FSI Level 3 is characterized as speech containing infrequent grammatical errors, and the ability to use complex structures and a broad vocabulary. In her first OPI, her mean utterance length was 8.9 words, and in May it was 18. In order to understand her success with Swedish, it is crucial to understand her personal experiences with Swedes and Sweden.

Because Faith was a hockey player, EP placed her in a mid-sized town where hockey was a community pastime. Faith lived with the women's hockey coach's family, and played on the team as well. In January, Faith explained that she wasn't really experiencing any real troubles living in Sweden:

> "Well, there haven't really been that many [cultural differences], I mean I live in (Midwestern city) and this is Sweden, so of course there's some cultural things I mean, but like ethnic, not really. It's mostly white Norwegians, Swedish, and Finnish [people], that's how it is in my state, often . . . you know if I had gone to maybe Thailand or India, somewhere there, there probably would have been a bigger gap. It's been pretty easy so far." (Faith, January)

By January she had gained enough confidence in her Swedish that she felt very optimistic about the remainder of her year. At this point her FSI rating was 3, equivalent to Superior on the ACTFL scale, and her fluency was rated as a 5 (1 = not at all fluent, 7 = totally fluent):

> "It's a lot easier, and it's very sort of freeing because now, at first I would try and go and order a hot dog at the kiosk sort of thing and I couldn't get anything to work. And now I can go to stores and I can make the bus, and ask for directions or do what I want." (Faith, January)

She credited her family with helping her reach such a high level of Swedish, and also spoke very positively of her Swedish hosts. She also reported that she had stopped attending her "Swedish for immigrants" classes at school, because she felt she was learning more Swedish with her mainstream classmates. Faith's ability to participate in the mainstream classroom was apparent in both the January and the May observations. During our January visit, I witnessed numerous occasions where Faith would initiate or partake in jokes and humor, as in the following excerpt from my fieldnotes:

> They all move over to look at something that some girl has. They are in a big clump. They pass the paper to the middle, Faith holds one corner and reads through with them, and laughs at one point and reads aloud for the group, then looks up at the girl who brought it. They all laugh and then hand the paper back to the girl it belongs to. (Faith observation, January)

In her February email, she offered the following comment pertaining to her own role in initiating meaningful contact with Swedes. Here she points out a change in her personality, namely that she has had to become more extroverted in order to be successful in creating relationships with Swedes:

> "A lot of Swedes seemed reserved about coming up and talking to me, so if I want to talk to people, I often have to make the first move. I'm generally a more introverted person, so that's been a challenge." (Faith email, February)

Faith became increasingly more motivated as her Swedish improved. By February she was already feeling much better about her Swedish. She wrote:

> "Now that my Swedish is going really well, I've committed to doing all my papers and assignments in Swedish. This can be really hard when I have to write about, for example, why everyone should ascribe to the political philosophies of a certain party!" (Faith email, February)

By February she had also really begun to link her Swedish identity with her ability to speak Swedish:

> "It's all about blending in. Being able to eat with the Swedes and talk with the Swedes and act like a Swede makes you a Swede by association. If you act like everyone else, you seem more Swedish. Being able to speak the language is the biggest development I've experienced here, as my language skills progress, I feel more and more Swedish. The Vasaloppet ski tournament was held in Mora recently, and there were a lot of tourists in the area, and my friends and I would see them and make jokes about the tourists etc. And more than once it's been assumed that I was Swedish." (Faith email, February)

In March, she noted just how comfortable she had become living in Sweden:

> "I don't notice any specific feelings directed towards Swedes in general . . . I guess as I've assimilated more, I don't notice any real differences. Many days I sort of forget I'm an exchange student. It just seems like I belong here, like it's totally normal that I live in Sweden and can speak the language and everything." (Faith email, March)

The stories of Faith's ability to "blend in" with her Swedish friends illustrate the breadth and depth of her relationships with her classmates and her host family. As has been noted, she felt that learning Swedish was the most important factor influencing her contact with Swedes. While she admits that getting to know Swedes required her to be more assertive than she normally is, she also managed to make close friends as her Swedish improved.

Faith seemed to have successfully adapted both her perspectives and behaviors to allow her to exist comfortably in her Swedish community. She was fortunate to be involved in her cohort in school, as well as in the hockey community. She recognized that her ability to sustain contact with her Swedish hosts was beneficial to her learning of Swedish. She even felt that the mainstream classroom was more facilitative of language learning than formal Swedish instruction in her SFI class, primarily because the mainstream class allowed her to feel that she was part of the class.

Faith's AI score in May, presented in Table 3, supports the assertion that she was successful in adapting to life in Sweden. In fact, Faith identified more with Swedes than with US Americans in most categories on the AI.

Using a scale of 1 to 7, where 1 indicates "not at all similar to," and 7 indicates "totally similar to," there were in fact only five areas in which Faith felt she was more "American." Interestingly, she rated the category of "self-identity" as a 5 in similarity to US Americans, and a 4 in similarity to Swedes. This score indicates that, in terms of her own identity, she was incorporating aspects of each culture. Indeed, her interviews and observations exhibit evidence for an enthusiastic willingness to adapt her attitudes and behaviors, and a strong desire to belong to the host culture.

Over the course of the year, the ongoing development of acculturation and language skills were observed and documented. Faith made very impressive gains in Swedish language ability, both in her January assessment and again in May. For Faith, the willingness to shift her identity and include "Swedishness" in her own self-concept was strongly related to her ability to learn language. She seemed very aware of the connection between her ability to use Swedish effectively and her ability to "blend in" to Swedish society.

Table 3 Faith's Acculturation Index scores in May

	More like a Swede (assimilation)	Equally like a Swede and an American (integration)	More like an American (separation)	Like neither an American nor a Swede (marginalization)
Faith	14	2	5	0

Max's story

Max's Swedish score on the January OPI was 1.81, the equivalent of Intermediate-High on the ACTFL scale. This score meant that Max could use Swedish in many contexts with a fair amount of grammatical accuracy, although his speech could be described as very simple in nature. He was able to ask and answer simple questions and participate in short exchanges of information. However, his utterances were very short in length, only 2.9 words per sentence on average, and he used many non-native-like fills. Considering he had been an absolute beginner prior to coming to Sweden, the score of 1.81 obtained after only five months of immersion can be seen as an indicator of good progress in language learning. What is interesting, however, is that his second OPI did not show much improvement over the first. The May OPI score for Max was 1.87, and his mean utterance length had only increased to 4.14 words. The reasons for Max's apparent linguistic plateau are illustrated by the personal accounts of his year in Sweden.

Max was a bit reserved and quite soft-spoken. He was placed in a small community, and hosted by a family who ran a dairy farm. Being out in the country meant that he had to rely on rides from his host family or friends to socialize outside of school hours. Max's identity prior to his year in Sweden can be described as very independent. He was financing his EP year himself, and was used to having the freedom to drive around and to enjoy nightlife on the weekends. He had no personal connections to Sweden, and only chose it because it was in Europe and he thought it might have some good nightlife. His primary motivation for studying in Sweden was "to fill up a year so I could go to college with my friends" (Max, January).

While he largely lacked any tangible goals for his year in Sweden, Max did express a goal to learn Swedish. However, he did not follow through with this goal, and rationalized giving up on it by citing the "uselessness" of Swedish:

> "I did have a plan that I was going to start speaking Swedish after Christmas, but obviously I didn't follow through with that. I am just thinking though, there's no real practical application for Swedish outside of Sweden. So I don't really have that much incentive. I mean it would be nice, but I don't have that much incentive." (Max, January)

Max's disinterest in learning Swedish was reiterated in later interviews and in the email questionnaires. In February Max wrote:

> ". . . there's no incentive to speak Swedish. Everyone at least understands English and I can understand Swedish, so there's no need to speak it." (Max email, February)

In fact, the bulk of Max's interactions in Sweden were in English. Max reported speaking English to everyone, his host mother and brother, his teachers and his friends at school, most of whom were immigrants. Max's teacher also commented on his lack of assertiveness:

Teacher: He's a little bit mistreated. And coupled with the fact that he's not exactly the type who takes initiative, no. He really doesn't [speak Swedish]. And I think that the teachers sometimes forget to support him, to give him some extra help. No . . . he is really the kind of person, not so outgoing, maybe. And he's sort of been like this the whole time.

Researcher: Do you think he is really trying to learn Swedish?

Teacher: I actually can't really say, since I don't know how it's going in his Swedish classes and I don't know if he tries to address his friends in Swedish, for example. But with me and such, he doesn't try to speak Swedish with me, he starts out in English directly. And so I haven't seen him make any extra effort to carry out a conversation in Swedish. (Max's teacher, January)

By February, Max began to comment on his own identity, and a sense of pride in being able to remain an outsider. In his questionnaires he plainly stated his complete lack of Swedish identity, and even linked this to his lack of ability in the Swedish language:

"I don't feel Swedish at all and I'd like to keep it that way. The main reason I don't feel Swedish is because I don't (not can't) speak the language. I feel very American. This is (for me) a good thing. It seems that I get special treatment just because I am American." (Max email, February)

Max's final email correspondence in April included many negative comments concerning Swedes in general as well as Swedes he knew personally. He also states yet again his lack of any sort of Swedish identity, attributing this to the choice to not speak Swedish. He further distances himself from Swedes, by aligning himself with the immigrants in his school, in the following comments taken from his May interview:

"Oh, if there was another fight like that [a fight he witnessed between immigrants and Swedes], and I was near by, I would fight on the side of the immigrants. I just feel more connected to the immigrants. I guess since most of my friends are immigrants." (Max, May)

When I met with Max for the last time, he told me that he stopped attending classes altogether, and that no one in his school had seemed to notice. This was largely because he had been placed in two different cohorts—a mainstream cohort and an immigrant cohort. It seemed that this division in his school schedule meant that he didn't really belong anywhere. Furthermore, he had no particular teacher assigned to him, so no one from the school was checking to see how he was doing.

Max's AI scores in May, shown in Table 4, illustrate that he did not identify closely with Swedes. Interestingly, his scores also exhibit evidence that in some cases he did not identify with US Americans, either.

Table 4 Max's Acculturation Index scores in May

	More like a Swede (assimilation)	Equally like a Swede and an American (integration)	More like an American (separation)	Like neither an American nor a Swede (marginalization)
Max	3	1	13	4

Max's acculturative strategy is primarily one of *separation*, where he identifies more strongly with his US cultural identity than with Swedes on most topics. Overall, Max seems to retain his US identity to a great extent. Additionally, he gives signs of a bit of a *marginalized* acculturative strategy. In conversations with Max, it seemed as if his identification with immigrants caused him to question his allegiance to either cultural group, and instead adopt an identity as an outsider of sorts. His language skills stabilized at the Intermediate level, and his fluency increased only slightly during the second half of the year. He did not use Swedish on a regular basis, although he likely could have. Max made a choice not to use language, seemingly as a means of distancing himself from Swedes.

Discussion

The first research question in this study addressed the linguistic outcomes of sojourners like Max and Faith, who go abroad without previous language skills. This study demonstrated that, although the amount of language learned in a complete immersion environment can vary greatly, the linguistic benefits of study abroad for the absolute beginner are nevertheless potentially as high as for learners at other levels. Some in the field of study abroad have questioned the value of sending individuals abroad without having first studied the target language at home (Engle and Engle, 2003; Freed, 1995a). The linguistic gains documented in this study for both learners refute these claims, and illustrate that, in cases such as that of the EP program, there is sufficient support to allow for significant gains in language learning.

Faith's dramatic linguistic gains, despite her complete lack of previous exposure to Swedish, is in some respects unexpected. Her ultimate proficiency levels reached 3+ on the FSI scale, equivalent to Superior on the ACTFL scale. When compared with previous studies on sojourner language learning, this rating is higher than the ratings achieved by college level sojourners, including sojourners who had previous language ability. Consider Lafford's (1995) study on Spanish learners in Spain and Mexico. In that study, at the end of a semester abroad, the most common OPI rating of those students was Intermediate-Mid. Freed's (1995b) study, also involving students with a background in the foreign language, yielded OPI scores that ranged from Intermediate-Low to Advanced at the end of a semester abroad. Max's ratings, on the other hand, are more similar to the participants in Lafford's and Freed's studies, indicating that his pattern of learning is not atypical. These linguistic outcome findings suggest that, contrary to what many believe about the necessity of previous ability in the target language, absolute beginners can make equal and, in Faith's case, even more significant gains in the target language, as compared to sojourners with a background in the language.

Faith's story is significant not only because of what it tells us about absolute beginners' capacity for reaching advanced levels in oral proficiency after only five or ten months of study abroad, but more importantly because it helps us to understand *why* she was so successful. This is indeed the focus of the second research question, which asked how cross-cultural adaptation influences oral language development in high school study abroad participants. The reasons for the variation in linguistic achievement observed in the present study appear to be due, at least in part, to the kinds of relationships Max and Faith had with native speakers, and the ways in which each acculturated.

Faith's success can be seen as tied to her ability and willingness to adapt to the host culture. Berry (2005) asserts that, "For behavioral shifts, the fewest changes result from the separation strategy, whereas the most result from the assimilation strategy" (p. 707). The data in this study suggest that *assimilation* is associated with Faith's higher levels of fluency and oral proficiency. The best language learner was the student who experienced the greatest identity shift, and identified more closely with Swedish norms than any other participant as measured by the AI. This is not surprising, as others have suggested that the success with which one can acculturate will determine one's language ability (Guiora, 1972; Schumann, 1986). Similarly, this study finds support for the claim that individuals who are able to engage in meaningful relationships with their hosts will acquire more "native"-sounding pronunciation (Lybeck, 2002) and "smoother" levels of idiomatic vocabulary use (Dörnyei, Dorow, and Zahran, 2004).

Faith's willingness and ability to adopt the communication style of the new culture mirrors the *assimilative* strategy. In contrast, Max's strategies of *separation* and *marginalization* were associated with less successful language learning. Berry (2005) continues "... marginalization is often associated with major heritage culture loss and the appearance of a number of dysfunctional and deviant behaviors (such as delinquency) ..." (p. 707). In fact, Max did exhibit quasi-delinquent behavior in that he stopped attending all of his classes in March, and even expressed a desire to participate in a fight. In Max's case, this disassociation with the host culture seemed to be related to a reluctance to use language, resulting in lower and stagnant levels of language ability.

Implications for study abroad programs

The findings of this study have a variety of implications for those who design, manage, and support study abroad programs. If the goal of a study abroad program is to maximize language learning, then the following two recommendations can be made.

First, it is obvious that student placements should optimize opportunities for language use. The experiences of Faith and Max illustrate the importance of personal relationships in language acquisition. While Faith's placement was highly successful, Max's was not. Exchange programs must be mindful of the kinds of supports that are needed to ensure that sojourners have access to their host peers. In addition, the host family served as both an emotional and linguistic source of support. For Faith, the fact that her host family shared her interest in hockey seemed to facilitate an immediate kinship to both her siblings and her parents. On the other hand, Max reported having very little in common with his host family, and admitted he made no effort to learn about either his host father or his work on the farm. However, both Faith and Max reported their host families as a support for learning Swedish, something that was particularly helpful in the beginning of the year.

In order to maximize contact with host nationals, students should ideally be placed in a home where the language is spoken. Their host schools should support language learning, both by offering formal instruction, but more importantly by providing access to naturalistic language use. In Faith's case, the mainstream classroom was a far more useful setting to learn Swedish than was her "Swedish for immigrants" class. For Max, not belonging to a particular cohort seemed to allow him to "slip between the cracks." Schools need to provide opportunities for language study, but not to the point that they distract from a mainstream school experience.

This study has shown how significant language learning can take place over the course of a year abroad. Thus, a second recommendation is that students without previous language ability should be encouraged to study abroad. While it is certainly preferable that sojourners have some ability to use the language prior to studying abroad, for many students it is simply not possible. The results of this study show that how an individual learns language in study abroad is dependent on a variety of factors, and that absolute beginners have the capacity to make impressive gains, provided they are supported socially and emotionally. In particular, the study highlights how important interpersonal relationships are for supporting language use and mastery.

Limitations and suggestions for further research

It would certainly be inappropriate to claim that the results of this study are conclusive, or that they can be generalized to the sojourner public at large. This study is limited by the scope of its participants. Only four students participated in the main study (Spenader, 2005) and the goal was not to make claims concerning sojourners in general. This is an obvious area for further research. Additionally, the study looks only at learners of Swedish, a typologically related language that is relatively easy for English speakers to learn. Further research is needed to explore the processes of learning more difficult languages in more culturally diverse settings. This study focused only on oral language development, and future research should also incorporate multiple measures of language ability. In particular, it would be interesting to analyze sojourner language learning using conversational analysis, as has been proposed by Wilkinson (1998), or focusing on the development of sociolinguistic awareness of registers, as Kinginger and Blattner do in Chapter 12 of this volume. While the study of Max and Faith has begun to illuminate the very personal experiences of beginning language learners over the course of a year abroad, it at the same time urges us to continue to discover and analyze the complexities of the adolescent sojourner experience from the perspective of cross-cultural psychology as well as that of language learning.

Note

1. In addition to the Acculturation Index shown in Appendix B, the main study reported in my dissertation (Spenader, 2005) also used the Sociocultural Adaptation Scale (SCA), (Ward and Kennedy, 1999) and the Intercultural Development Index (IDI) (Hammer and Bennett, 2001). The SCA was administered at five and ten months, while the IDI was administered only at the ten-month mark. All three measures provided valuable insight, and the extensive analysis and results of these measures can be found in the dissertation. This chapter highlights only the AI, due to limited space and the particular salience of the AI results.

References

Berry, J. W. (1997). Immigration, acculturation, and adaptation. *Applied Psychology: An International Review*, *46*, 5–68.

Berry, J. W. (2005). Acculturation: Living successfully in two cultures. *International Journal of Intercultural Relations*, *29*, 697–712.

Bochner, S. (1982). *Cultures in contact: Studies in cross-cultural interaction*. Oxford: Pergamon.

Brecht, R. D., Davidson, D. E., and Ginsberg, R. B. (1995). Predictors of foreign language gain during study abroad. In B. Freed (Ed.), *Second language acquisition in a study abroad context*. Philadelphia, PA: John Benjamins.

Dörnyei, Z., Dorow, V., and Zahran, K. (2004). Individual differences and their effects on formulaic sequence acquisition. In N. Schmitt (Ed.), *Formulaic sequences* (pp. 87–106). Philadelphia, PA: John Benjamins.

Engle, L., and Engle, J. (2003). Study abroad levels: Toward a classification of program types. *Frontiers: The Interdisciplinary Journal of Study Abroad*, *9*, 1–20.

Freed, B. (Ed.) (1995a). *Second language acquisition in a study abroad context*. Philadelphia, PA: John Benjamins.

Freed, B. (1995b). What makes us think that students who study abroad become fluent? In B. Freed (Ed.), *Second language acquisition in a study abroad context* (pp. 123–148). Philadelphia, PA: John Benjamins.

Guiora, A. Z. (1972). Construct validity and transpositional research: Toward an empirical study of psychoanalytic concepts. *Comprehensive Psychiatry*, *13*, 139–50.

Hammer, M. R., and Bennett, M. J. (2001). *The Intercultural Development Inventory (IDI) manual*. Portland, OR: Intercultural Communication Institute.

Lafford, B. (1995). Getting into, through, and out of a survival situation: A comparison of communicative strategies used by students studying Spanish abroad and "at home." In Freed, B. (Ed.), *Second language acquisition in a study abroad context* (pp. 97–121). Philadelphia, PA: John Benjamins.

Lapkin, S., Hart, D., and Swain, M. (1995). A Canadian interprovincial exchange: evaluating the linguistic impact of a three-month stay in Quebec. In B. Freed (Ed.), *Second language acquisition in a study abroad context* (pp. 67–94). Philadelphia, PA: John Benjamins.

Lowe, P. J., and Stansfield, C. W. (Eds.). (1988). *Second language proficiency assessment*. Englewood Cliffs, NJ: Prentice Hall Regents.

Lybeck, K. (2002). Cultural identification and second language pronunciation of Americans in Norway. *Modern Language Journal*, *86*, 174–191.

Magnan, S. (1986). Assessing speaking proficiency in the undergraduate curriculum: Data from French. *Foreign Language Annals*, *19*, 429–438.

Ryan, J. M., and Lafford, B. A. (1992). Acquisition of lexical meaning in a natural environment: "ser" and "estar" and the Granada experience. *Hispania*, *75*, 714–722.

Schumann, J. H. (1986). Research on the acculturation model for second language acquisition. *Journal of Multilingual and Multicultural Development*, *7*, 379–392.

Spenader, A. J. (2005). Cross-cultural adaptation and language acquisition in high school study abroad. Unpublished doctoral dissertation, University of Minnesota.

Ward, C., Bochner, S., and Furnham, A. (2001). *The psychology of culture shock*. Philadelphia, PA: Routledge.

Ward, C., and Kennedy, A. (1993). Psychological and socio-cultural adjustment during cross-cultural transitions: A comparison of secondary students overseas and at home. *International Journal of Psychology*, *28*, 129–147.

Ward, C., and Kennedy, A. (1994). Acculturation strategies, psychological adjustment, and sociocultural competence during cross-cultural transitions. *International Journal of Intercultural Relations*, *18*, 329–343.

Ward, C., and Kennedy, A. (1999) The measurement of sociocultural adaptation. *International Journal of Intercultural Relations, 23,* 659–677.

Ward, C., and Rana-Deuba, A. (1999a). Acculturation and adaptation revisited. *Journal of Cross-cultural Psychology, 3,* 422–442.

Ward, C., and Rana-Deuba, A. (1999b). Home and host culture influences on sojourner adjustment. *International Journal of Intercultural Relations, 24,* 291–306.

Wilkinson, S. (1998). Study abroad from the participants' perspective: A challenge to common beliefs. *Foreign Language Annals, 31,* 23–39.

Appendix A: Standard email correspondence questionnaire

1. In general, how do you feel your year in Sweden is going?
2. What are your biggest challenges living with your host family right now?
3. What is the biggest challenge you face with Swedish friends?
4. What are the biggest challenges you face at school right now?
5. At this point in the year, how many hours a day are you spending speaking Swedish?
6. Where are you learning the most Swedish? What is it about these contexts that helps you learn?
7. In what contexts are you still using English at this point?
8. What are your feelings towards Swedes in general right now?
9. Have you learned anything new about "Swedishness"?
10. How "Swedish" do you feel at this point? Why?
11. How "American" do you feel at this point, and why?

Appendix B: Acculturation Index

Adapted from: C. Ward and A. Rana-Deuba (1999a). Acculturation and adaptation revisited. *Journal of Cross-cultural Psychology, 3,* 422–442.

This section is concerned with how you see yourself in relation to other Americans and Swedes. You are asked to consider two questions about your current lifestyle. Are your experiences and behaviors similar to Americans? Are your experiences and behaviors similar to Swedes? Use the following scale to indicate how similar your various experiences of daily life are compared to Americans and Swedes.

1................2................3................4................5................6................7

not at all similar   *very similar*

Enter your response (1, 2, 3, 4, 5, 6, or 7) in the parentheses. Please respond to all items.

	Americans	Swedes
1. Clothing	( )	( )
2. Pace of life	( )	( )
3. General knowledge	( )	( )
4. Food	( )	( )
5. Religious beliefs	( )	( )
6. Standard of living	( )	( )
7. Recreational activities	( )	( )
8. Self-identity	( )	( )

	Americans	Swedes
9. Family life	( )	( )
10. Accommodation/residence	( )	( )
11. Values	( )	( )
12. Friendships	( )	( )
13. Communication styles	( )	( )
14. Cultural activities	( )	( )
15. Language	( )	( )
16. Perceptions of Americans	( )	( )
17. Perceptions of Swedes	( )	( )
18. Political ideology	( )	( )
19. Worldview	( )	( )
20. Social customs	( )	( )
21. School activities	( )	( )

14 An ethnographic longitudinal approach to the development of assessment for advanced competencies of medical interpreters

Claudia V. Angelelli

Abstract

Medical interpreters are highly proficient individuals who are capable of processing and conveying information in two languages, often under conditions of critical and extreme pressure. Yet, our understanding of the language competencies used by advanced language users is only incipient, as these superior L1/L2 users have seldom been studied (Valdés and Angelelli, 2003). This chapter reports on the application of three-year-long ethnographic data (Angelelli, 2001, 2004a) from a bilingual medical setting to develop tests that assess linguistic, sociolinguistic, and interpreting competencies of medical interpreters across three languages. During a total of 37 months (22 for Spanish and 15 for Cantonese and Hmong) medical interpreters were observed and recorded as they worked with English-speaking healthcare providers and Cantonese, Hmong, and Spanish-speaking patients. The data were subsequently used to develop the tests in these three languages for the healthcare setting (Angelelli, 2003a). The rich data collected provided a unique window into the language competencies used by advanced/superior language users. The tests are now used to screen individuals who want to get into medical interpreting programs as well as those who want to work in healthcare settings interacting with monolingual speakers of languages other than English. This unique longitudinally driven and contextualized approach to the development of assessment of language proficiency and interpreting skills advanced proficiency presents challenges and strengths that are also discussed in this chapter.

Introduction

Today, as in the past, speakers of societal and non-societal languages come into contact via interpreters. All over the world, the phenomenon of languages in contact has gained unprecedented importance due to migration, the processes of nationalism and federalism (Grosjean, 1982), and globalization (Block and Cameron, 2002). Given the concomitant multilingual needs all these processes bring for education, trade, commerce, and intermarriage, there is an unprecedented and ever-growing need for interpreters to continue to bridge communication gaps between monolingual interlocutors.

In the United States, in particular, the end of the 20th century and the beginning of the 21st witnessed important demographic changes that have profoundly challenged all aspects of US society, and most particularly the delivery of healthcare services to limited-English-speaking patients (Angelelli, 2004a). Nearly every hospital in our country receives patients with limited English proficiency. As a result, we see an increasing need for professional interpreters in the medical setting. However, fewer than 25 percent of US hospitals are either staffed with skilled interpreters (Flores *et al.*, 2003) or have the adequate screening mechanisms in place to determine who can perform the job. As a result of this dearth, healthcare organizations in the USA have been forced to resort to creative solutions in order to bridge the linguistic barrier between providers seeking to assist patients and patients seeking help (*Hablamos Juntos*, 2005). These solutions range from attempts to match patients' and providers' language (Molina Healthcare Inc., 2005), to hiring face-to-face or remote professional or ad hoc interpreters (Angelelli, 2003b, 2004b), to utilizing family or community members as temporary alternatives.

If communication is complex, communication across cultures in the medical context is even more complex. In any communicative event, language is at the heart of communication. When two languages are involved, a highly sophisticated language professional facilitates that event. This extremely proficient individual is capable of processing and conveying information in two languages, often under conditions of critical and extreme pressure. The language interpreter has at least an Advanced/Superior proficiency level (Byrnes, Thompson, and Buck, 1989) in both languages, although in many cases Superior or Distinguished (Angelelli and Degueldre, 2002), as well as an ability to use those languages under pressure to convey messages in a socioculturally appropriate way. Yet, our understanding of the language competencies used by these individuals is only incipient, as these superior L1/L2 users have seldom been studied (Valdés and Angelelli, 2003, p. 68), and little is known on the development of language competencies beyond the advanced level in general (Leaver and Shekhtman, 2002).

This chapter reports on the application of three-year-long ethnographic data from several bilingual medical settings to develop tests that assess linguistic, sociolinguistic, and interpreting competencies of medical interpreters across three languages. An ethnographic study was conducted first for a period of 22 months in a bilingual English/Spanish hospital in California (see Angelelli, 2001, 2004a), where the medical interpreters were observed and recorded as they worked with English-speaking healthcare providers and Spanish-speaking patients. Subsequently, Cantonese and Hmong medical encounters were observed and recorded during an additional period of 15 months in order to obtain comparable linguistic data. The data resulting from recorded interpretation-mediated encounters, interviews with patients and providers, artifacts (e.g., educational brochures, consent forms, and other documents made available to patients), and observations were then used as a baseline to determine the content of the tests at a final phase (Angelelli, 2003a). In what follows I offer a brief journey through the three-year-long investigation and explain how its findings were used eventually to develop the tests. My goal is to show that an ethnographic approach to study these language professionals offers a unique opportunity to unveil their advanced language competencies, and to apply the empirical data to new ways of measuring them.

The context: interpretation of bilingual medical encounters in public hospitals in California

Public hospitals in California care for diverse multi-ethnic and multilingual communities and thus constituted a feasible site to collect data on bilingual medical encounters reflecting such diversity. In each of the participating organizations, the staff cares for thousands of hospitalized patients and provides one-half million outpatient and emergency consults annually. In addition to a high level of basic services, these hospitals also provide sophisticated medical specialty services that require the use of technical language. Among them are a rehabilitation program, a regional burn center, a trauma center, and a neonatal intensive care unit. Hospitals also offer a medical advice and appointment hotline available 24 hours a day, seven days a week to patients, most of whom are African-American, Asian, and Hispanic. The community that utilizes these services ranges from middle class to working class, but the average patient is sub-working class. Overall, moreover, patients and providers vary in terms of socio-economic status, level of education, gender, and age, and this diversity is reflected in their discourse. This point is important because, as we will see, the difference in level of education of the two main interlocutors—patient and provider—triggers differences in register during the medical encounters. The ability to switch registers and understand a variety of registers turned out to be a crucial part of the advanced competencies demanded from these interpreters in their renditions of the original message.

The medical interpreters

The focal interpreters in the two ethnographic studies were also the intended users of the tests that were eventually developed. They facilitated communication between patients and providers in what I will refer to in this chapter as interpreted communicative events (ICEs), which could occur both face to face and over the speakerphone. In general, several bilingual candidates are tested on a monthly basis from within and outside hospitals, and if they pass the test hospital employees are included into a bilingual-employee directory and are called upon to interpret if needed. Medical interpreters working in the sites involved in this study were either staff members of the hospital or independent contractors who worked in local interpreting agencies. Their educational background varied from holding a high school diploma to being physicians in their home country.

In order to work as healthcare interpreters, they had to pass an in-house test of medical vocabulary, interpreting skills, and memory retention in both directions (English into target language, and target language into English). At the time the ethnographical study was conducted, there were no guidelines for administering the tests, nor were there data available on its validity or reliability. Once they passed the test, hospital employees were included into a bilingual-employee directory and were called upon to interpret if needed, and they received a minimal monthly bonus for their interpreting services. Non-hospital employees who passed the test could then be subcontracted on a part-time basis. In addition to passing the test, interpreters had to meet two other requirements; namely, they had to have two years of experience in the field (as medical interpreter, translator, or bilingual medical assistant) and they had to demonstrate bilingual ability.

Ethical considerations: gaining entrée, negotiating, and maintaining trust

Collecting authentic patient–provider interactions was challenging. In addition to the regular internal review board for the protection of human subjects of my university, this project required hearings in each of the participating hospitals. Once the administrative boards of each hospital approved the project, I proceeded to seek consent from providers and interpreters. In addition, patient consent was requested at the beginning of each interaction. For hospital administrators, complying with the Health Insurance Portability and Accountability Act (1996) and changes in laws and regulations protecting patients' privacy were the main concern. For patients, getting the help they needed without distractions was the main concern. For the participating interpreters, quality control and the conclusions drawn on the basis of these observations that may affect their employment were the main concern. They feared for their jobs. As I went about requesting consent, I reassured interpreters that the goal of the study was not that of quality control. This was a crucial element in building trust.

Although healthcare providers had been briefed on the nature of the research and its implementation, they took several months to adjust to the request for consent, each time they called for an interpreter. During the data collection, I made an effort to minimize the intrusion of the researcher in the interaction and among the participants. By the time I started recording, I had already shadowed and monitored interpreters for over nine months. At the time the recording started, my "intrusion" was evident by an additional cable on the interpreter's desk—the one that connected my tape recorder to his or her phone—or by recording interpreters I had already shadowed during their face-to-face assignments.

Ethnographic insights: the advanced language capacities of medical interpreters

Thorough studies in discourse analysis and interpreting offer a window to explore the performance of these individuals (e.g., Bolden, 2000; Davidson, 2000, 2001; Metzger, 1999; Prince, 1986; Roy, 1989, 2000; and Wadensjö, 1995, 1998). I expanded on this work by studying a larger number of interactions (including, but not limited to, ICEs) over time. Additionally, I used discourse analysis and Hymes' (1974) theory of speech events to investigate in more depth the communicative functions that constitute the basis of communication in a medical setting. I did so guided by research carried out to date in oral language proficiency and testing (Johnson, 2000, 2001), the testing of heritage speakers (Valdés, 1989),[1] the identification of interpreting skills (Valdés *et al.*, 2003; Valdés, Chavez, and Angelelli, 2000), and medical interpreting (Angelelli, 2001, 2004a).

I found that the language used in each of the ICEs varied widely, reflecting among other factors the participants' social background, the complexity and content of the interview, and its length. Medical interpreters who possess advanced competencies in both languages facilitate communication between providers and patients face to face or remotely. They must learn about the ways in which both patients and providers speak, they must be familiar with the ways of speaking of the different speech communities (Hymes, 1974), even if they may belong to neither of them. Each speaker not only differs in terms of their native language, but also in many other social factors that affect communication, such as their gender, age, level of education, and socio-economic status (Angelelli, 2004b), so that, more often than not, interpreters juggle language and social factors and produce the type of discourse familiar, acceptable, or understandable to each of the two interlocutors during the various turns of the same conversation. I discovered over my 22 and 15 months of close observation of medical interpreters engaged in ICEs that this competency is essential in bridging communicative gaps.

Excerpt 1 illustrates how Mariana, one of the Spanish interpreters, brokered register to make messages understandable for both interlocutors. It comes from an interaction between Dr. Kim (a general medicine resident) and an outpatient, Jesús, who suffers from frequent indigestion and stomach aches. Mariana is in the room helping Jesús communicate with Dr. Kim. The excerpt starts when the doctor asks Jesús about his medicine intake. Jesús explains how he used to take care of his problems using a home remedy that his wife prepared for him. Clearly Mariana understood both the provider and the patient's way of speaking. In turns 35–36, she not only interpreted from Spanish to English, but she also switched the register of the utterance. From the patient's rural Spanish she relayed the message to the doctor in a modified register, in a more formal language, that she thought was adequate for Dr. Kim. The ability to interpret between languages and to process information

Excerpt 1 Mariana (Tape 9 #3 000–103)

30	D	Please ask him if he is taking any medicine.
31	I ▶	¿Está tomando algún medicamento ahora? Vio que esas medicinas vienen en unas cajitas, o frascos, bueno, él quiere que usted traiga esas cajitas para ver lo que está tomando. */Are you taking any medicine now? You know those little boxes . . . you know how medicine sometimes comes in little boxes or jars. Well, the doctor wants you to bring in those little boxes next time, so that she can see what medicine you are taking/*
32	P	No . . .
33	D	Anything over the counter, herbs, anything for this?
34	I	¿Está tomando algo que compra en la farmacia sin receta, algún tecito?
35	P ▶	Ay ay ay, no . . . ojalá estuviera mi vieja acá . . . ella sí que era sabia en estas cuestiones . . . me daba su juguito de penca de nopal . . . eso me aliviaba . . . pero ya no está . . . que va uno a hacerle pos . . . se la llevó la flaca . . . */ (Oh . . . no . . . if only my old lady???were here . . . she knew her stuff . . . she used to give me nopal juice . . . that hit the spot . . . but she's gone . . . what can I do? . . . she kicked the bucket/*
36	I ▶	I wished my wife were here with me . . . she really was knowledgeable about this. She used to make nopal juice for me . . . that was a relief . . . but she is not with me anymore . . . what can I do? She passed away.

Note: D = doctor, I = interpreter, P = patient

under pressure is coupled with the ability to produce messages in a socioculturally acceptable way, and in a way in which the other interlocutor can access it. This is what Mariana is doing when she changes registers to make the message understandable to the patient.

A second important finding was that the different modes in which the conversation is held also impact the language produced during the interview, thus positing a different challenge to interpreters. A particular communicative challenge that interpreters face in this respect arises when they join the interview via speakerphone (as in a teleconference) or a TV monitor (as in videoconferencing). In both cases, the three parties are not in the same room. This is done either for reasons of privacy, such as for example an examination with the gynecologist, or for the sake of efficiency. An important efficiency consideration, for example, is that interpreters who stay at a desk and work through the telephone/speakerphone increase productivity, since they can take on more interviews than if they had to walk to each of them around a big hospital. Speakers of the societal language (such as providers) generally receive guidance or training in the use of remote (i.e., non-face-to-face) interpreters. However, this is not the case for most patients, who discover how to communicate in this way during their medical interview. Oftentimes, both providers and patient must compensate for the interpreter's physical absence by making over-explicit statements.

For example, if during a speech event such as answering a question, the patient points to some part of their body illustrating the response, the provider must relay that fact to the interpreter. Excerpt 2 illustrates this issue. In this example we come into the conversation when the patient, Juan, who has broken his wrist and forearm in three pieces and has undergone surgery, and whose bone has not healed, is discussing the possibility of an infection with his orthopedic surgeon. Carmen, the interpreter, is helping them communicate. However, she is not in the room and instead has joined them via the speakerphone. Juan is now complaining about pain. The physician needs to know where the pain is located. In this example, the interpreter listens to the patient's utterance in Spanish and to the provider's clarification in English and then reproduces the utterance in the provider's language and register.

Excerpt 2 Carmen (Tape 43 # 220–226)

28	D	So, you need to tell me exactly where it hurts and how intense the pain is.
29	I	OK señor Gomez, el doctor quiere que le diga exactamente dónde le duele y cómo es de intenso su dolor /*OK Mr. Gomez, the doctor wants you to tell him exactly where the pain is located and how intense it is*/
30	P	*Me duele acá* (pointing to the left forearm next to the elbow) *mucho pero no me van a mochar mi alita, veda?"* /It hurts here a lot, but they are not going to chop my wing, right?/
31	I	Doctor, he says that the area he was pointing at hurts a lot, but he is worried about his arm being amputated and he hopes that will not happen.

Note: D = doctor, I = interpreter, P = patient

Evidently, communication via speakerphone differs from face-to-face communication in several ways. Since the interpreter is not sharing the same context with the other two interlocutors, she/he has no access to body language. In the case of interlocutors who have received guidance on how to speak through remote interpreters by rephrasing comments (the utterance *it hurts here* becomes *the patient is pointing at his left forearm near his elbow*), the interpreter only accesses one of the interlocutors' explanation/interpretation of the kinesics, not to the original message. This adds another component of complexity to the equation that the interpreter has to solve.

Finally, it should be noted that observing interpreters during a prolonged period of time also allowed me to gain a deeper understanding of how these competencies (e.g., the ability to slide an utterance up and down the register scale) interact with varied contexts for language use and increased my confidence about the varying typicality of such contexts. For example, long-term observations revealed that interpreters have to read consent forms for patients in both Spanish and English (since only some organizations already provide translations), as well as patients' medical records from their home countries, and instructions on how to take medicine or to follow a diet. These tasks tap into language competencies that a medical interpreter exhibits on a daily basis, and this finding proved valuable in the development of the test I will describe in the second half of this chapter. Not only tasks, but communicative functions, were found to be at the core of healthcare provider and patient communication. Particularly representative communicative functions were description of a condition, complaint about a condition, challenge of a decision.

To summarize, and following Hymes (1974), we may say that medical interpreters are temporary guests in a speech community (Angelelli, 2000), since they do not necessarily belong to the community of either patients or providers. They must, however, be able to navigate both. In the course of their jobs, medical interpreters process information in two languages and under pressure. They comprehend and produce language of various degrees of complexity, alternating between target and source languages, rural and urban speakers whose level of education ranges from second grade to graduate school, and in whose speech communities they are only a temporary guest. Herein lies the crux of their advanced capacities. A robust conclusion derived from the ethnographic engagement over 22 and 15 months is that interpreters must be able: (a) to understand what both interlocutors say (using both formal and informal registers, and both in face-to-face and from remote locations); (b) to relay information in both registers and delivery modes; and (c) to understand material written in the two languages of the interaction. Finally, the interpreters must be able to meet these three demands across tasks and communicative functions, several of which are highly typical and predictable in their daily interpretation encounters.

The application of ethnographic insights into the development of medical interpreting tests

With funding and support from The California Endowment, a consortium of five organizations in California,[2] I was commissioned to develop a language proficiency test and an interpreter readiness test in three languages: Spanish, Hmong, and

Cantonese. The tests were developed in conjunction with a team of research assistants and consultants in specific areas of the project (see Angelelli, 2003a). The first versions of these tests, completed in 2003, responded to the mandate to evaluate medical interpreters in the United States in a meaningful, valid, and reliable way. Their specific purpose was to identify and assign candidates to medical interpreting classes. This project constitutes to this date the first application of ethnographic data to develop tests that assess linguistic, sociolinguistic, and interpreting competencies of medical interpreters. The final product of the process I will describe below was a language proficiency test and an interpreting skills test for Cantonese-, Hmong-, and Spanish-speaking candidates. Unique features of these tests are: (1) they are data driven, which means they represent what real interpreters do in the field; (2) both the content and tasks are authentic; (3) response times are empirically established; (4) content and scoring units were validated by experts (e.g., both provider and patient sorted relevant and irrelevant information on the script); and (5) tests were conceptualized taking heritage speakers into consideration, since they constitute the majority of the population of test candidates in hospitals in California.

Establishing the need for the test

A review of commercially existing tests preceded the test development effort. Tests reviewed included those used by various national and international government agencies; private institutions; nonprofit agencies; and corporations. Results indicated that, although several of these tests seem to be effective for the various settings for which they were developed, they do not suit the needs required to test language proficiency and interpreting skills for the medical setting. The literature review supported the assessment that the existing tests were not suitable. Specifically, each test reviewed presented at least one of the following problems: (a) lacked empirical evidence to support the assessment criteria used (Johnson, 2001; Lantolf and Frawley, 1985; Savignon, 1985; Valdés, 1989); (b) was not conceived to measure accurately the language proficiency of heritage speakers (Valdés, 1989);[3] (c) did not measure authentic sociocultural interactions within any particular setting (Johnson, 2001); (d) could not be administered and interpreted locally (Johnson, 2001); and (e) involved steep cost factors. Additionally, many of the commercially available tests devoted significant efforts (in time and length) to measure writing, a component that empirical research (Angelelli, 2003a, 2004a; Metzger, 1999) demonstrated is not found among the tasks performed by a medical interpreter.[1]

Once the need to develop a new test was established, the following step was to conduct a job analysis at each of the five participating sites. In addition to observations, I also conducted interviews with hospital administrators and interpreter managers to understand whether and how the job of these healthcare interpreters would be different from healthcare interpreters in other sites of California that had already been studied (Angelelli 2001, 2004a).

The test development process

The data resulting from ICEs, interviews with patients and providers, artifacts (educational brochures, consent forms, and other documents made available to patients), and observations were used as a baseline to determine the content of the tests.

First, a database of 392 Spanish–English ICEs formed the basis for test development. This database expanded to 492 ICEs to include 50 Cantonese/English, and 50 Hmong/English ICEs. The smaller size of the Hmong and Cantonese empirical data was due to budgetary and time restrictions. In addition, community members, interpreters, and healthcare providers of each of the three ethnic groups participated in the test development study.

The ICEs data were subsequently transcribed, translated, and analyzed to develop the scenarios to be used in the tests in these three languages in the health-care setting (Angelelli, 2003a). Moreover, the ICEs data were supplemented with focus groups. The purpose of the focus group data was to have native informants validate the scenarios and the adaptations of the scripts. The focus groups also discussed the main cultural issues among their ethnic group. The scripts for Hmong and Cantonese were produced and checked in collaboration with the same language experts and informants who participated in the development of the tests. These tests would assess the required skills for medical interpreting candidates to accommodate the growing need to assess professionally trained interpreters in the medical field on a regular basis. More specifically, they were developed to measure skills in language proficiency (LP) and interpreter readiness (IR) with respect to Spanish, Cantonese, and Hmong.

Interpreted communicative events were selected on the basis of typicality/frequency (LeCompte and Schensul, 1999) and analyzed for medical content and language in the following manner. From the large pool of 392 Spanish/English interpreted events (Angelelli, 2001), the team analyzed the most frequent interpreted communicative events and randomly selected ten events from eight different interpreters. Those ten events were transcribed and analyzed. The most frequent interactions, aside from introductions and closings of a conversation (present in every interaction), included: (a) patients making appointments, (b) patients canceling appointments, (c) parents visiting with their child who is a patient, (d) doctors making a first-time visit, (e) doctors conducting a pre-operation visit, (f) hospital personnel admitting the patient, and (g) doctors making a follow-up visit. This analysis was the basis for the creation of the tests script. Subsequently, results were triangulated with the focus groups and by consulting medical research on the three ethnic groups of interest.

Tests description

This section briefly describes the goal, content, and form of the language proficiency (LP) and the interpreter readiness (IR) tests.

The Language Proficiency Test is a contextualized measure of language ability for the bilingual medical setting. A basic assumption is that interpreting students must be able at a minimum:

a. to understand what both interlocutors say (using both formal and informal registers);
b. to relay information in both registers; and
c. to understand material written in the two languages of the interaction.

The content of the LP is empirically driven. Thus, artifacts collected (patient's medical records, explanations of procedures, prescription labels) constitute the content for the reading comprehension exercise, and excerpts from recordings on provider/ patient interactions as well as interviews with patients and providers are used as prompts for the listening and speaking exercises. In addition, the LP is strongly reflective of register variation. This was a fundamental feature because the previous ethnographic studies (Angelelli, 2001, 2003a, 2004a) and other research conducted on bilingual medical encounters (Davidson, 1998, 2000, 2001; Metzger, 1999; Wadensjö, 1995) show that speakers (specifically patients) come from a wide range of socio-economic backgrounds. The types of tasks included in the LP tests also reflect this reality. Consequently, the LP measures linguistic proficiency in three primary areas: reading comprehension, listening comprehension across registers, and speech production in a variety of registers. Exhibit 1 illustrates these features of the LP. It shows the instructions presented to the candidate for a speech production exercise in which a patient is describing his health problems to a nurse. Both interlocutors speak Spanish, but they vary significantly in their educational background. The patient attended school up to second grade, he uses low register and a rural variety of Spanish. The nurse is a Superior (ACTFL, 1989) speaker of Spanish, and she learned it as a second language. The test candidate has to listen to the patient, take notes, and reproduce it in a Spanish that the nurse can understand.

It should be underscored that the LP is a criterion-referenced test that allows assessors to make inferences about how much language ability a test taker has, and not merely how well he or she performs relative to other individuals. The LP tests are not a measure of academic achievement, nor can they provide information about the various social and psychological factors that must be considered along with language ability in making decisions to admit students to an interpreter training program. However, the results of the LP tests can be very helpful in assigning students to interpreting classes, placing students in language enhancement programs, exempting students from a language enhancement program, and evaluating students' proficiency in the target language as they complete a language enhancement program. The test administration requires approximately 50 minutes, input and output is audio-based, and it lends itself to individual or group administration.

The IR, on the other hand, measures a candidate's ability to interpret in three

Exhibit 1 Listening item from LP subtest

Part II: Task 4

Here, a male patient is describing health problems related to an accident. He is from a small rural town, has attended school up to 2nd grade, and has not talked very often with people outside his community. The nurse who is helping him is an instructor in the School of Nursing. She studied Spanish at school and knows it well, but is not sure she understands everything the patient has said. After listening to him, please tell the information to the nurse in a way that you think she will best understand.

Now, listen to the story and remember you can take notes if necessary.

---

primary areas: (a) understanding the source language (English for healthcare providers and Cantonese, Hmong, or Spanish for patients) in two (low and high) registers; (b) processing the information presented in the source language; and (c) restating that information in the appropriate register of the target language/culture. Like the LP tests, the IR tests have been conceived for individual or group testing administrations. Additionally, also like the LP tests, the IR tests are not a measure of academic achievement, nor can they provide information about the various social and psychological factors that must be considered along with ability to interpret in making decisions to admit students to an interpreter training program. However, the results of the tests can be very helpful in assigning candidates to interpreting classes, placing candidates in interpreting training programs according to levels of ability, and evaluating students' interpreting skills after they complete an interpreting training program.

The IR tests are criterion-referenced tests, and they have a total of four segments each. The longitudinal approach once again provided a unique opportunity to obtain an extensive corpus of authentic data involving 392 medical encounters (Angelelli, 2001). These ICEs served as the basis for the selection of communicative functions that were at the core of healthcare provider and patient communication (e.g., description of a condition, complaint about a condition, challenge of a decision).

As in the LP tests, and within the framework of ethnographic studies, the first criterion used was typicality, that is, the communicative functions and their content represent the interactions in a medical setting during a provider–patient encounter. Various segments of data containing frequently used communicative functions were incorporated into a story. The end result was two four-segment stories that require the test taker to interpret between the patient and the healthcare provider. The final script was validated by focus groups of experts (provider and patient) who were asked to identify relevant units of information. The response times for the candidate were empirically established by averaging the performances of three candidates who were representative of the population working at the hospitals. They were: (1) a bilingual who is a native speaker of English and who has an Advanced/Superior competency in Spanish; (2) a bilingual who is a heritage speaker of Spanish and who has near-native competency of English; and (3) a bilingual who is a native speaker of Spanish and who has Superior command of English.

Once the script was finalized and the response times were established, the team proceeded to record the interactions on video. The recording of the Cantonese and Hmong versions of the tests posited challenges for the researcher who does not master those languages. The use of experts/informants, translators, and interpreters was once again important. Before the video shooting, they were responsible for writing the cue cards to assist actors with memory. During the shooting, they observed body language and checked the utterances to make sure they matched the language written on the cue cards. After the shooting, they helped in the editing process and in identifying turns that either had to be reshot or rewritten to match the oral and the written language.

Applications of the tests

The tests resulting from these longitudinal studies are now used to screen individuals who want to get into medical interpreting programs as well as those who want to work in healthcare settings interacting with monolingual speakers of languages other than English. One of the five organizations within Connecting Worlds, Healthy House for a MATCH Coalition, used the tests in their site and tested 60 candidates for Spanish and Hmong. Additionally, and as a result of a collaborative agreement between The California Endowment and Robert Wood Johnson Foundation's National Program *Hablamos Juntos* (a program to provide equal access to health services to Hispanics), the Spanish LP and IR tests were digitized and the video and audio tests were electronically piloted in ten sites across the United States (rural and urban locations included). In these healthcare organizations, the computer-based administration yielded 640 cases that are currently being analyzed and will contribute to reliability studies. Finally, under another grant from The California Endowment, Second Language Testing Inc. is currently conducting further piloting on both the video/audio and computerized tests in California.

Conclusion

My goal in studying medical interpreting was exploratory for the duration of the ethnographic studies, and it was only when the opportunity to develop a test arose that a more concrete and even practical use for the rich data emerged. I discovered that studying interpreted medical discourse for an extended period of time is as revealing as it is complex. It allows the exploration of issues that can only be addressed through time. Among those is the language used by these individuals in a professional setting. Conducting an ethnographical study meant being present to observe, record, and write down what was seen and heard, and ask what on the surface seemed like over-simplistic questions, but questions which turned out to be important ones indeed. It also required cross-checking, comparing, and triangulating the information obtained before it became the solid foundation on which to build my knowledge base.

Throughout the course of doing their jobs, interpreters' competencies manifest themselves to the observer. However, the challenges are not small. Observing phenomena as they naturally occur implies an important commitment on the part of the researcher to respect the reality that unfolds before the self, to resist the temptation to manipulate it, and to abandon the desire to impose on it the framework that would satisfy our inquiry. It also means rethinking and understanding time commitments. Researchers' and informants' notions of time vary and, when in conflict, informants' should prevail. At the hospitals where I conducted observations and recording for Cantonese, Hmong, and Spanish, plans get changed by the second. Anticipating and planning data collection acquires a different dimension. Additionally, ethnographic data collected in a language that is not mastered by the researcher also adds other layers of complexity. Researcher and language experts need to work together before, during, and after data collection. Coordination and teamwork are essential elements to obtaining the maximum benefit from each observation session.

In our multilingual society communication between speakers who do not share a linguistic code is only possible with the help of interpreters. An ethnographic approach to the work of medical interpreters offers a unique opportunity to study their linguistic competencies and interpreting skills in depth and over time. These longitudinal observations make it feasible to observe and describe the features that characterize these language professionals, and to understand advanced competencies as they unfold in situated practices. Additionally, as was shown in this chapter, ethnographic studies yield valuable data that can be used for educational purposes, in both curricular materials design and testing. The tests developed on the basis of three-year-long ethnographic insights will prove an invaluable resource to interpreter educators and interpreting-service managers in their efforts to improve cross-linguistic communication in healthcare settings. By measuring the language proficiency and interpreter readiness of a candidate, organizations will be able to select candidates efficiently and gauge the linguistic abilities of those who want to participate in professional development programs. Authentic and valid testing is the first step toward empowering interpreters to be ready for the challenges they face as they assist non-English-speaking patients to navigate the healthcare system in the United States. An ethnographic approach was key in addressing the content and construct validity of these tests.

This study has several practical and theoretical implications for the assessment of situated practices such as medical interpreting. The longitudinal data, such as observations and recording of patient/provider encounters, offer a unique opportunity to analyze the language and behaviors used by both interlocutors and to incorporate them into tasks that replicate the reality of practicing professionals. In so doing, this study sets new directions in interpreting testing by providing a basic framework to discuss the assessment of interpreting skills in a responsible, systematic, and valid way. As was described in this chapter, authentic interactions and artifacts which were used (intact or adapted) in tasks to measure skills expected of medical interpreters, such as listening comprehension or speech production at different levels of register, replicate the realities of medical interpreters at work. Acknowledging the authenticity of tasks observed during prolonged periods of time for both measurement and teaching purposes will lead to more meaningful educational opportunities for future medical interpreters.

An ethnographic approach to the study of medical interpreters proved to be an invaluable methodology to identify language competencies used by these professionals. Furthermore, it afforded not only a unique opportunity to unveil their advanced language competencies but also to apply the empirical data to new ways of measuring them. I am now convinced that the study of the linguistic competencies of an interpreter should occur in a natural setting and for a prolonged period of time. In Vygotsky's (1978, p. 65) terms (quoted from Angelelli, 2004a), "to encompass in research the process of a given thing's development in all its phases and changes means to discover its nature, its essence, for 'it is only in movement that a body shows what it is.' "

Notes

1. Those who grew up in the United States and were exposed to Spanish at home (i.e., first, second, or third generation children of native Spanish-speaking immigrants).
2. The five organizations were: Asian Health Services, Healthy House for a MATCH coalition, Las Clínicas de Salud del Pueblo, PALS for Health, and Vista Community Clinic.
3. Most of the commercially available tests were designed for educated native speakers (Valdés, 1989) without the inclusion of heritage speakers, who, according to our research, reflect the linguistic background of most US medical interpreters.

4. It is important to note that this review of the commercially available tests (expanded from what was done for the initial tests) comprises only the information that was available from March to September 2004, and therefore should not be considered exhaustive.

References

Angelelli, C. V. (2000). Interpreting as a communicative event: A look through Hymes' lenses. *Meta (Journal des Traducteurs)*, *45*(4), 580–592.

Angelelli, C.V. (2001). Deconstructing the invisible interpreter: A critical study of the interpersonal role of the interpreter in a cross-cultural/linguistic communicative event. *Dissertation Abstracts International*, *62*(9), 2953 (UMI No. AAT 3026766).

Angelelli, C.V. (2003a). Connecting World Collaborative testing project. Unpublished technical report submitted to The California Endowment, San Diego, CA.

Angelelli, C.V. (2003b). The interpersonal role of the interpreter in cross-cultural communication: Survey of conference, court, community, and medical interpreters in the U.S., Canada, and Mexico. In L. Brunette, G. Bastin, I. Hemlin, and H. Clarke (Eds.), *Critical link 3: Interpreters in the community* (pp. 289–302). Philadelphia, PA: John Benjamins.

Angelelli, C.V. (2004a). *Medical interpreting and cross-cultural communication*. London: Cambridge University Press.

Angelelli, C.V. (2004b). *The visible interpreter: A study of community, conference, court interpreters in Canada, Mexico, and United States*. Philadelphia, PA: John Benjamins.

Angelelli, C. V., and Degueldre, C. (2002). Bridging the gap between language for general purposes and language for work: An intensive superior-level language/skill course for teachers, translators, and interpreters. In B. L. Leaver and B. Shekhtman (Eds.), *From advanced to distinguished: Developing professional-level language proficiency* (pp. 91–110). Cambridge: Cambridge University Press.

Block, D., and Cameron, D. (Eds.) (2002). *Globalization and language teaching*. London: Routledge.

Bolden, G. (2000). Toward understanding practices of medical interpreting: Interpreters' involvement in history taking. *Discourse Studies*, *2*(4), 387–419.

Byrnes, H., Thompson, I., and Buck, K. (1989). *The ACTFL Oral Proficiency Interview Tester Training Manual*. Yonkers, NY: American Council of Teachers of Foreign Languages.

Davidson, D. (1998) Interpreting medical discourse: A study of cross-linguistic communication in the hospital clinic. Ph.D. dissertation. Stanford University.

Davidson, B. (2000). The interpreter as institutional gatekeeper: The social-linguistic role of interpreters in Spanish–English medical discourse. *Journal of Sociolinguistics*, *4*, 379–405.

Davidson, B. (2001). Questions in cross-linguistic medical encounters: The role of the hospital interpreter. *Anthropological Quarterly*, *74*, 170–178.

Flores, G., Barton Laws, M., and Mayo, S. J. (2003). Errors in medical interpretation and their potential clinical consequences in pediatric encounters. *Pediatrics*, *111*, 6–14.

Grosjean, F. (1982). *Life with two languages: An introduction to bilingualism*. Cambridge, MA: Harvard University Press.

Hablamos Juntos National Program (2005). Accessed online September 2005 on www.hablamosjuntos.org/default.about.asp

Health Insurance Portability and Accountability Act [HIPPA] (1996). Accessed online September 2005 on www.hep-c-alert.org/links/hippa.html

Hymes, D. (1974). *Foundations in sociolinguistics: An ethnographic approach*. Philadelphia, PA: The University of Pennsylvania Press Inc.

Johnson, M. (2000). Interaction in the oral proficiency interview: Problems of validity. *Pragmatics*, *10*(2), 215–231.

Johnson, M. (2001). *The art of non-conversation*. New Haven, CT: Yale University Press.

Lantolf, J., and Frawley, W. (1985) Oral proficiency testing: A critical analysis, *Modern Language Journal, 69*, 337–345.

Leaver, B. and Shekhtman, B. (Eds.) (2002) *From advanced to distinguished: Developing professional-level language proficiency.* Cambridge: Cambridge University Press.

LeCompte. M and Schensul, J. (1999). *Analyzing and interpreting ethnographic data.* Vol. 5. Walnut Creek: Altamira.

Metzger, M. (1999). *Sign language interpreting: Deconstructing the myth of neutrality.* Washington, DC: Gallaudet University Press.

Molina Healthcare Inc. (2005). Accessed online September 2005 on www.molinahealthcare.com/california/member/spanish/hf-faq.html

Prince, C. (1986). Hablando con el doctor: Communication problems between doctors and their Spanish-speaking patients. Ph.D. dissertation, Stanford University.

Roy, C. (1989). A sociolinguistic analysis of the interpreter's role in the turn exchanges of an interpreted event. Ph.D. dissertation, Georgetown University, Washington.

Roy, C. (2000). *Interpreting as a discourse process.* New York: Oxford University Press.

Savignon S. (1985). Evaluation of communicative competence: The ACTFL guidelines. *Modern Language Journal, 69*, 129–134.

Valdés, G. (1989). Teaching Spanish to Hispanic bilinguals: A look at oral proficiency testing and the proficiency movement. *Hispania, 72*, 392–401.

Valdés, G., and Angelelli, C. (2003). Interpreters, interpreting, and the study of bilingualism. *Annual Review of Applied Linguistics, 23*, 58–78.

Valdés, G., Chavez, C., and Angelelli, C. (2000). Bilingualism from another perspective: The case of young interpreters from immigrant communities. In A. Roca (Ed.), *Research on Spanish in the United States: Linguistic issues and challenges* (pp. 42–81). Somerville, MA: Cascadilla Press.

Valdés, G., Valdes, G., Chavez, C., Angelelli, C., Enright, K., Garcia, D., and Gonzalez, M. (2003). The performance of the young interpreters on the scripted task. In G. Valdés, *Expanding definitions of giftedness: The case of young interpreters from immigrant communities* (pp. 119–164). Mahwah, NJ: Lawrence Erlbaum.

Vygotsky, L. S. (1978). *Mind in society: The development of higher psychological processes*, Ed. M. Cole, V. John-Steiner, S. Scribner, and E. Souberman. Cambridge, MA: Harvard University Press.

Wadensjö, C. (1995). Dialogue interpreting and the distribution of responsibility. *Hermes, Journal of Linguistics, 14*, 111–129.

Wadensjö, C. (1998). *Interpreting as interaction.* New York: Addison Wesley Longman Inc.

Coda

15 Theorizing advancedness, setting up the longitudinal research agenda

Lourdes Ortega and Heidi Byrnes

Abstract

In light of the varied theoretical and empirical insights of the contributions assembled in the volume, the concluding chapter points out directions that appear to be particularly fruitful for the longitudinal study of advanced language L2 capacities. While at this early stage of inquiry into longitudinal study and into advancedness it is important to keep open diverse conceptual and empirical options, we argue that a reconceptualization of our notions of time, as the key factor in development, and a broadened understanding of the social and contextual nature of language itself will be needed in order to nourish and strengthen future research programs on the longitudinal study of advanced L2 capacities.

Introduction

As we declared in the introduction to this collection, we hope to put forth a linked claim: that there is a need for the longitudinal study of L2 development and that this need is particularly acute in the study of advanced L2 capacities. In this closing chapter we revisit this nexus by placing the project itself into the context of existing SLA discussions and by exploring additional issues the proposed focus uncovers and obstacles it may encounter.

Readers of the chapters assembled in this volume will likely have observed that their authors position themselves quite variably toward the theoretical and methodological link we propose. On the one hand, they affirm the validity of connecting longitudinal study and advancedness. On the other, they also project a certain independence of the two issues from each other, from conceptual, research methodological, and practical standpoints. Such diverging treatment serves as a healthy reminder that shifts in research focus (i.e., advancedness), not to mention shifts in research practices of a discipline (e.g., adopting a longitudinal research methodology), can be instantiated only over long periods of time. To our knowledge this collection is, after all, the first devoted to featuring that connection.

And, indeed, the full rationale to support our linking longitudinalness with advancedness is elusive and subtle. In the process of developing the present volume, we kept asking ourselves: Do we have ways of conceptualizing advancedness empirically under an encompassing interpretation of the longitudinal course of L2 development? And is *advancedness* the given, and *longitudinalness* the means for specifying it more closely? Or is longitudinalness the given, where extending it far enough would in due time bring advancedness under its purview?

We grapple with these questions in this closing chapter. The position we espouse is that longitudinalness is not captured by "longer," nor is advancedness captured by "more and better." Instead, a main goal in the development of a research program for the longitudinal study of advanced L2 capacities should be to craft sufficiently expansive and articulated understandings of language learning, in general, and advanced capacities, in particular, over time, so as to offer a frame of reference within which SLA researchers can imagine, specify, and research advanced L2 capacities in ways that match up with the interests of contemporary multilingual and multicultural societies. The central question of interest in the proposed research program is: How does learning over time evolve toward sophisticated second language capacities, indeed to high-level multiple-language capacities?

Our comments take this progression. We open with a critique of current theorizing of the two constructs that underpin the conceptual link that defines this volume—that is, advancedness and longitudinalness. The bulk of our remaining reflections is devoted to exploring current and alternative notions of time and of language itself. We place these considerations within the larger context of recent theoretical developments in SLA research in order to uncover affinities of interest that might provide initial ways for characterizing this project in the future. Our reflections address at some level of depth the kind of reconfiguration that appears to be necessary if SLA research is to fashion a robust longitudinal methodology that can capture advanced capacities.

Advancedness problematized

In Chapter 1, we referred to some ways in which the field generally goes about characterizing advancedness, such as institutional status, test scores or scale descriptors, L2 features that are posited to be late-acquired, and sophisticated language use in context. Norris (2006) rightly notes that "such a variety of measurement operationalizations for 'advancedness' will lead to little more than findings that defy comparison and interpretation" (p. 173). Another obstacle we see is that the existing criteria show a tendency to consider advanced levels of performance as essentially no more than "better than intermediate-level" structural and lexical ability for use, with performance often placed into the trajectory of greater accuracy, fluency, and complexity. This narrow focus on accuracy, fluency, and complexity traits in isolatable domains such as lexis and grammar does not capture defining aspects of advanced levels of ability, particularly the textually oriented, socially embedded, and situationally motivated nature of language use that addresses a vast array of concerns in human life. Shohamy (2006) laments the under-theorization of such dimensions in the construct of advancedness, and emphasizes their importance, reminding us that language is a complex, flexible, and personal creator of meaning and content, and that there are multiple ways of being an advanced multilingual user. Kinginger and Blattner (Chapter 12, this volume) agree when they view language ability as "intimately and concretely tied to language use in social settings of seemingly infinite and unpredictable variety" (p. 224). Harklau (Chapter 2, this volume) and Achugar and Colombi (Chapter 3, this volume) also highlight that speaker's identity is constituted through language and enmeshed in the social context. Angelelli (Chapter 14) reminds us of the very real importance that fluency in socially diverse registers may have for advanced L1/L2 users in certain workplaces. Certainly, in the awakenings of SLA as a field, interest in language learning as a form of cognitive learning meant that the focus was on the nuts and bolts of language as a system—that is, mostly on the morphological and syntactic domains. However, other contemporary theories of language and language learning have by now become available that highlight language learners' engagement in terms of emergent, and therefore variable, ways of creating intended meanings in context with the resources made available by an entire language system. Our current notions of advancedness wait to be transformed by these more contemporary theorizations of language competence.

We find two other aspects of current understandings of advancedness problematic: the insistence on the gold standard of native-likeness or near-nativeness and the apparent bias in favor of formal and school-based registers of language, which oftentimes also means privileging written language and standard national varieties.

The accumulated critique against the reification of the native speaker as a model and norm for L2 learning has been too strong to ignore among researchers interested in studying and understanding advancedness (e.g., Cook, 2002; Firth and Wagner, 2007; Leung, Harris, and Rampton, 1997; Seidlhofer, 2001). It is truly puzzling to us that the myth of the native speaker remains untouched in much discourse about advancedness in SLA, particularly given that (paradoxically) researchers in this field have a long tradition of cautioning against elevating native norms to the gold comparison in understanding the L2. Thus, in what many consider the awakenings of SLA as an autonomous field, Corder (1975) called to consider language learners' errors as a source of insights about the processes of second language learning and as windows into the development of interlanguage as a system of its own. Almost a decade later, Bley-Vroman (1983) identified many pitfalls in what he called the comparative fallacy. About 15 years later, once again, Klein (1998) raised the issue. Observing that SLA as a field had not yet exerted the expected theoretical impact on our general understandings of the human capacity for language, he reflected that this had to do

> with a particular perspective on the acquisition process: SLA researches learners' utterances as deviations from a certain target, instead of genuine manifestations of underlying language capacity; it analyses them in terms of what they are not rather than what they are. For some purposes such a "target deviation perspective" makes sense, but it will not help SLA researchers to substantially and independently contribute to a deeper understanding of the structure and function of the human language faculty. Therefore, these findings will remain of limited interest to other scientists until SLA researchers consider learner varieties a normal, in fact typical, manifestation of this unique human capacity. (p. 527)

For many years now, Vivian Cook (1992, 2002) has argued that L2 users are developing bilingual competence. He has proposed the notion of "multicompetence" as a way of capturing the important point that L2 competence is fundamentally different, in psycholinguistic terms, from the linguistic competence of a monolingual. And indeed, psycholinguistically oriented scholars of bilingualism have produced irrefutable evidence that the various languages of a multilingual interact at all levels.

Under such premises, development defined against a monolingual target norm is thoroughly misguided. For example, Leather (2002), an L2 phonologist, remarks:

> In the "process" of multiple acquisition the languages apparently interact, so that the acquisition of each individual language is qualitatively different from that of a monolingual. . . . Moreover, the very notion of a determinate target system against which transitional forms can be evaluated, though central to most acquisition studies, may not withstand close scrutiny. (p. 50)

It is about time that we free ourselves from analytical and conceptual pitfalls that equate L2 development with monolingual development. Quite simply, if multicompetence is not a clone of L1 competence, then the advancedness of multilingual users cannot be expected to be isomorphic with the advancedness of monolingual users.

The bias in favor of formal written registers presents a more subtle challenge for researchers interested in the longitudinal study of advancedness. Traditionally, the field of SLA has tended to see oral language as a privileged site for L2 learning, a tendency that became even more pronounced in the era of communicative language teaching (Harklau, 2002; Kern and Schultz, 2005; Kramsch, 2006). Within the area of advancedness, however, the balance seems to be tipped on the side of academic and written language registers (e.g., Byrnes and Maxim, 2004; Leaver and Shekhtman, 2002). To some extent, that orientation may be an artifact of the history of the language field itself, in research and in teaching practice. However, that historical accident should not unduly influence what notions of advancedness we should now carry forward. We therefore argue that advanced language capacities, much more than beginning or intermediate capabilities, can only be imagined in relation to language users who have access to a range of language resources and deploy them less or more successfully as the result of certain choices in particular social situations and contexts. Obviously, both oral and written modalities will be involved. Less obvious is the answer to the question whether a kind of oral advancedness should be privileged that shows strong influence from literate practices. This influence may be particularly noticeable in various educational, public-institutional, and professional contexts within which learners wish to be competent social actors. In that case an emphasis on academic usages of language that favors written modalities and standard national varieties as forms of advancedness is understandable. After all, such registers are associated with societal power and participation (Schleppegrell, 2004; Valdés, 2005).

However, advanced language use encompasses a much more varied landscape of registers. Some of the "advanced" things we do with language include "telling jokes and stories, writing funny letters, chatting expertly with friends on the phone or in Internet chat rooms, doing crossword puzzles, and so on" (van Lier, 2002, p. 143). As Harklau (Chapter 2, this volume) reminds us, "an immigrant learning English in a US high school learns more and different things about English than a peer who drops out of school and works as an unskilled laborer. Nevertheless, they could both arguably be classified as advanced language learners" (p. 28). If this is so, longitudinal research on advancedness would benefit from sampling across a variety of social settings that afford opportunities for diverse language repertoires, as this will enrich the developmental insights we obtain (e.g., Tarone and Liu, 1995). Moreover, definitions of advancedness will have to encompass and explain less traditional forms of language use—for example, the oral repertoires investigated in this volume by King-inger and Blattner (Chapter 12) and Angelelli (Chapter 14)—as well as less norma-tive and more hybrid written repertoires. This is necessary if we want to strike a balance between more equitable access to the discourses of power, on the one hand, and recognition of diversity, on the other, and if we want to support hybrid identities enacted in advanced language uses that are not necessarily rewarded by the main-stream (Lam, 2006; Villa, 2002).

In sum, we believe current definitions of advancedness are of limited usefulness in informing a principled research agenda. The kinds of answers that SLA research has drawn on to define advancedness seem too much of an atheoretical list, and therefore difficult to research consistently across studies that add up to a concerted research program. The conceptualizations that predominate are also too narrow in their morphosyntactic and formal focus and too biased in their reification of native-likeness and their emphasis on prestige registers and modalities. This being so, we are prone to missing important aspects of advancedness. Moreover, the answers we have sought are also oftentimes removed from educational practice and from an explication of the values that motivate research on advancedness. From our perspective, therefore, one area in dire need of future exploration is con-ceptualizations and theorizations of advancedness. We will return to this point later, when we explore Systemic Functional Linguistics as a theoretical framework that allows a reconceptualization of the notion of language and advanced capa-cities. First, however, we would like to examine notions of time in current L2 longitudinal thinking.

Longitudinalness revisited

Longitudinal study is fundamentally about time. The working definition of longitu-dinalness that Ortega and Iberri-Shea (2005) propose focuses on the joint contribu-tion of four criteria: study length, the presence of multi-wave data collection, the conceptual focus on capturing change by design, and the focus on establishing antecedent–consequent relationships through prolonged tracking of the phenom-enon in its context rather than through experimental controls or comparisons. And yet, that seemingly straightforward working definition of what counts as longitudinal is immediately problematized because even the most obvious questions cannot be answered in terms of linear chronological time. Consider, for example, the issue of the desirable distribution and number of data takes that should be employed within a multi-wave data collection effort. In their book-length treatment of applied longi-tudinal data analysis, statisticians Singer and Willett (2003) emphasize "that there is no single answer to the seemingly simple question about the most sensible metric for time" and encourage researchers to "choose a metric for time that reflects the cadence you expect to be most useful for your outcome" (p. 11). They argue for considerable flexibility regarding the spacing of waves of data collection. In child first language acquisition, a field closer to SLA, Tomasello and Stahl (2004) discuss questions regarding the appropriate temporal density of sampling, the likely capture rate enabled by different sampling choices, and the resulting impact on the validity and reliability of inferences made about child language growth. They take into account the relative frequency of occurrence of a language phenomenon in real time in order to propose shorter but denser, versus more extended but thinner, longitudinal data collection schedules. Their discussion sheds a sobering light on the complexity of methodological issues associated with notions of longitudinal sampling. However, at this point, at least, it appears that it is more the substantive *content* of what is to be captured through measuring development toward advancedness, and not primarily statistics or methodology, that requires considerable attention on the part of second language researchers.

As Ortega and Iberri-Shea (2005) have urged, it would be helpful to study L2 learning in longtime perspectives that document change around (i.e., before, during, and after) turning points, such as the transition from primary to secondary school (Lightbown, Halter, White, and Horst, 2002), from high school to college (Harklau, 2000), and the key L2 experience of study abroad (see, in this volume, Rees and Klapper, Chapter 6; Kinginger and Blattner, Chapter 12; Spenader, Chapter 13), particularly when examined against the full course of the four-year university curriculum (Klapper and Rees, 2003). These are rather macroscopic turning points, but some traditions may afford more importance to microscopic turning points of different grain size (contiguous turns in interaction, a few hours, or a certain number of days). This is the case in the microgenetic method that documents shorter-term or in-the-fly changes in "mental functions and processes" of Vygotskian sociocultural theory (Lantolf and Thorne, 2006, p. 19) or in the talk-in-progress emic methodology of Conversation Analysis (Brouwer and Wagner, 2004). We believe macroscopic and microscopic turning points afford context-rich windows into tensions in the social environment that may give rise to needs and pressures for language use and meaning-making which, in turn, are the fuel of L2 development. Note, however, that turning points are important in understanding L2 learning not in and of themselves, as raw reality, as it were, but as acted upon by learners, who are human agents. Social experience—in those few SLA theories that afford it a central theoretical status—is important not as externally documented experience, but as *lived* experience that emerges out of the engagement of human agents with others and with the physical and social environment (Ortega, 2006, p. 244). It follows, therefore, that macroscopic and microscopic turning points are not chronologically determined but are projected conceptually, on the basis of aspects of the language system, of the nature of development itself, of situated and lived contexts, and of performance characteristics language users reveal in particular situations of language use.

In fact, we would argue that the research interests of L2 longitudinal study may actually run counter to the notions of time that researchers have heretofore privileged. Diverse disclaimers notwithstanding, the bulk of existing research has, at least implicitly, suggested the existence of simple linearities and simple causalities, expressing these in terms of single features seen as decontextualized "variables" that change along a single time line—one development leading to or "causing" another. As Ortega and Iberri-Shea (2005) note, such thinking continues to prevail when longitudinal change is recast through the lens of repeated cross-sectional comparisons or when it emphasizes the discovery of continuities that, by and large, privilege notions of developmental stability over time. In this picture, the importance of two key characteristics of language learning, the phenomenon to be investigated, has been underestimated: variability and non-linearity.

Ortega (2006, pp. 226–228) examines the roles that the two constructs of systematicity and variability play across a range of SLA theories. Some theories in SLA, typically those affiliated with linguistic formal approaches, are motivated by the quest to uncover universal patterns of acquisition, and therefore treat variability as noise to be controlled for or eliminated in the studies. Other SLA theories, whether rooted in functional approaches or information processing psychological models, make the universal the center of inquiry and therefore afford variability a peripheral if complementary role in explaining observed findings. To our knowledge, only a few theories so far have made variability into the very center of their research programs, and they have done so from rather diverse epistemological approaches: interlanguage variationist theories (Tarone, 2007), Vygotskian sociocultural theories (Lantolf and Thorne, 2006), and a family of emergentist and dynamic complex systems theories as well as ecological perspectives (Ellis and Larsen-Freeman, 2006; de Bot, Lowie, and Verspoor, 2007b; Kramsch, 2002; van Lier, 2002, 2004).

In the study of advancedness, variability is by necessity a central concern, given that social uses for language become greatly diversified and result in increasing choices and expanded repertoires. If variability is taken seriously in longitudinal research, observed stabilities or monotonic increases or decreases would have to be described not in and of themselves but in relation to the kinds of environments and conditions—that is, the social contexts—under which aspects of language development may manifest themselves in such a fashion when they otherwise show greater dynamic variation. In reverse, seemingly nonconforming data would be queried for the insights they can provide about language development under both a language-systemic and a developmental perspective. In this light, one can conclude that the task at hand should be approached not in terms of uncovering high similarities between learners, which suggests uniformity across study participants, but in terms of uncovering the nature of within-individual variation in development where that is set in relation to inter-individual differences.

The second issue, non-linearity, is also complex. On the one hand, SLA researchers have always appreciated the non-linearity of interlanguage development, and have identified many mechanisms and processes that attest to such nonlinearity, including U-shaped behavior and backsliding (Kellerman, 1985), flooding and trickling (Huebner, 1983), restructuring (McLaughlin, 1990), and stabilization/fossilization (Long, 2003). However, ultimately the assumption of linearity prevails in much of the literature, partly because of the teleological concept of interlanguage as transitional and ever changing *towards* the target, and partly because the non-linearity is always discussed in terms of accuracy (or, at best, presence/absence or frequency of certain forms), rather than time. That is, it has often been acknowledged that L2 accuracy develops non-linearly, but it has seldom been noted that L2 development as a whole is also unevenly paced, with different rates of change (in accuracy, fluency, and repertoire of choices or so-called complexity) for different aspects of the system of language and different time distributions of stability and (gradual or sudden) change for different phenomena, different learners, and different contexts of use.

In sum, for longitudinal study to yield value-added information for a richer understanding of second language development, the necessary incorporation of "time" cannot stop at highlighting "process" over "product," or, in somewhat of a detour, preferring qualitative, ecologically rich forms of inquiry over more quantitative decontextualized approaches. Rather, what seems to be necessary, first and foremost, is a different kind of approach to the analysis of time and of language itself. In longitudinal SLA studies, "time" must be variously transformed in order to capture dynamic trajectories of development that include ranges of developmental change that leave play for potentially considerable individual variation, *both* within the overall non-linear and unevenly paced trajectory *and* in learners' actual performance profiles at a particular time. Ideally, such a novel approach would posit theoretically grounded systems of different grain size within the overall semiotic system of language that would yield researchable foci of different granularity. At the same time, such proposals for subsystems should provide well-motivated principles for beginning to specify just how language learners might negotiate them differently at a time and over time in a fashion that might inform us about development-in-and-beyond-variation.

Ultimately, we have argued, we may need to overturn simple chronological notions of time. But if we do so, what are the alternatives? By way of a general description, we would like to propose that the longitudinal study of advanced L2 capacities can benefit from the reconceptualization of time that is fostered in dynamic systems, emergentist, and ecological views of language development (de Bot, Lowie, and Verspoor, 2007b; Ellis and Larsen-Freeman, 2006; Kramsch, 2002; van Lier, 2004). In the next section, we present the alternatives to current thinking about time that these approaches afford L2 researchers. After we examine alternative thinking about the notion of time, we will return to the notion of language itself.

Exploring a dynamic understanding of time

Recently, the kinds of sophisticated understandings of time and timing that do exist elsewhere are gradually being brought to the attention of SLA researchers. Particularly important is a set of related proposals that could be characterized as cognitive-associative emergentist and drawing on dynamic systems, ecological systems, and complexity theories, as proposed initially by Larsen-Freeman (1997), Herdina and Jessner (2002), Kramsch (2002), and van Lier (2002, 2004). Most recently, similar and related perspectives have been championed by de Bot, Lowie, and Verspoor (2007b), Ellis and Larsen-Freeman (2006), and Larsen-Freeman and Cameron (forthcoming). The approaches share in common: (a) their empirical cognitive orientation within which social context can nevertheless be accommodated; (b) the notion of emergence and co-construction based on co-occurrence and environment–individual interactions; (c) the assumption of complete and mutual interconnectedness among subsystems and variables; and (d) the probabilistic nature of hypotheses, explanations, and analyses. The approaches also fare well with the requirement that variability be investigated as a central part of development rather than discarded a priori as noise. We believe for these reasons this family of theories offers promising alternatives to address longitudinalness in future research on L2 advanced capacities. In this section our goal is to highlight select elements of these theories that advocate for longitudinal study as the primary approach to developmental data and point at novel notions of time.

An important notion is that of *dynamicity*—that is, the complete and perpetual interaction of variables, at different levels, and all mutually interdependent. Proponents argue that this dynamicity can best be understood in longitudinal perspective. For example, de Bot, Lowie, and Verspoor (2007b) state that "the major property of a DS [Dynamic System] is its change over time" (p. 8) and propose that L2 researchers investigate the full course of development, and that they "look at the messy little details, the first attempts, the degree of variation at a developmental stage, and the possible attrition" (p. 19). One way to capture the dynamism of the system is in terms of *forces* that operate within it and lead to accelerations or decelerations; that is, to "rates of change, and that means amounts of change in amounts of time" (van Gelder and Port, 1995, p. 9) and forms of stability and instability. It is no surprise, then, that longitudinal methodologies are prioritized in these approaches. A dynamic approach to longitudinalness would seem to recommend itself highly for the study of advancedness, inasmuch as advanced language learning appears in some cases to show slow movement, at times so slow as to justify claims of "fossilization" (e.g., see the radically different individual cases in Kinginger and Blattner, Chapter 12, and in Spenader, Chapter 13, both this volume).

Variability and non-linearity are particularly central in this family of theories. *Variability* is thought to be "an inherent property of a changing system" (de Bot, Lowie, and Verspoor, 2007b, p. 14) and, even more importantly, in itself a source of development (Ellis and Larsen-Freeman, 2006, p. 564). In this respect de Bot, Lowie, and Verspoor (2007a) note that much L2 research in the past has documented variability at the one-variable, static level and has attempted to explain variability by recourse to one or two isolatable variables. According to these authors, the approach to variability in the dynamicity and complexity research program is novel because the goal is to capture how interactions of multiple variables change over time. Here, *non-linearity* ensues from the fact that any environmental change can lead to self-reorganizations of the various subsystems in ways that are not proportional to the initial change. The explanation given for this is that the objects of study (in this case, language learning) are made up of nested systems, all interconnected at different levels, and all responsive to the environment and always adapting to it as well as changing it. Thus, the "variables interact in non-additive ways" (Ellis and Larsen-Freeman, 2006, p. 560). These non-additive, non-linear and multivariate interactions are a function of time.

It follows that *causality* is questioned and reconceptualized in dynamic theories as well, in light of the centrality afforded to time and context. As Ellis and Larsen-Freeman (2006) assert, "[t]o attribute causality to any one variable (or even a constellation of variables) without taking time and context into account is misguided" (p. 563). In other words, causality is located at the interstices between time and context. For one, causes may be distal or proximal on any given scales of time that might be considered relevant. Secondly, causes and effects are disproportional in their magnitude (something that is known as the butterfly effect in this literature). Thirdly, given the central properties of dynamicity, variability, and non-linearity, what explains a change at some point may cease to explain change at a later point in development. Thus, it is no surprise that in their recommendation for new methodologies that address these needs, Larsen-Freeman and Cameron (forthcoming) criticize traditional, cause–effect linear predictions, which they call forecasting, and favor instead what they call "retrocasting" (p. 5). Retrocasting would entail retrospective explanation of growth based on what has already changed, or the traces of change to be found in the system (p. 5). Similarly, De Bot, Lowie, and Verspoor (2007a, 2007b), in their proposal of Dynamic Systems Theory, prefer to talk about precursors, successors, and connected growers rather than antecedent–consequent relations: "By looking at dense corpora, we should also try to discover which sub-systems are precursors of other subsystems and which sub-systems are connected growers" (de Bot, Lowie, and Verspoor, 2007b, p. 19). For them, the onset (gradual or abrupt) of an increase in variability signals a transitional phase, and the documentation over time of alterations in the degrees of variability for various interconnected subsystems allows for the mapping of precursors (or antecedents), successors (or consequents) and connected growers—that is, subsystems that are precursors of subsequent sub-systems (p. 19). The underlying logic is that "it is not the possible causes but the degree of variability in itself . . . that is taken as providing insight in the develop-mental process" (2007a, p. 53). In sum, in lieu of traditional cause–effect chains of causality, the task is that of capturing (a) amounts of change in (b) degrees of vari-ability over (c) amounts of time.

Last but not least, an important contribution in the family of theories we are considering is the proposal of *heterochrony* or the fact that there are multiple time scales that need to be considered in longitudinal research. Ellis and Larsen-Freeman (2006) identify at least the following: "evolutionary, epigenetic, ontogenetic, interactional, neuro-synchronic, diachronic" (p. 576). Language development as occurring along multiple time scales is also the concern of Lemke (2002), who arrives at that position via a social ecology of learning that draws on Hallidayan Systemic Functional Lin-guistics. He, too, proposes a dynamic model, but one that privileges an understand-ing of language as a semiotic resource where

> each level [of organization] is regarded as a metastable, dynamically emergent pattern of organization, which exists by virtue of interactions between the system and its environ-ment, and in which order is accumulated and disorder exported to higher levels . . . The units of analysis at every level are, most basically, *processes* . . . structures are epiphenom-ena of material interaction processes taking place one level below, and they may in turn function as virtual participants in processes at the next level above. (pp. 69–70; emphasis in original)

Particularly attractive for our concerns, and a consequence of Lemke's focus on language development as occurring within an ecosocial system, is the fact that, though all levels of organization "are in a continuous process of development, enabl-ing (from below) and constraining (from above) development at an intermediate level," each level will develop "at a significantly different characteristic timescale (i.e. rate)" (p. 71). As he emphasizes, one should expect this shift to a multiple-time-scale system view of development to have "profound implications for our views of educa-tion, language learning, and indeed the social order of relations among humans at different ages" (p. 71).

Taking the insights of ecosocial and dynamic systems theories to the longitudinal study of advancedness, more specifically, we feel our envisioned longitudinal research program might benefit from a certain two-directional perspective: Where did the features that can now be observed come from? And where do they point for potential development in the future? That probing would then have to admit the possibility of just such dynamic interactions between learners' attending to certain aspects in real time under certain conditions of timing that result in continuities and discontinuities, dependencies and indepencies of development. If researchers want to understand long-term L2 development, they will find rich environments for observing its fundamental features, such as its projected non-linearity and its dynamically different rates of change for different aspects of the system language, at certain turning points in the life of a learner (at the macroscopic level) and at critical points in interactions with others in their social and material environments (at the microscopic level). However, we would have to desist from applying "linear notions of time to complex multiscale systems" and, instead, would have to address heterochrony, or the fact that "certain events widely separated in linear time may be more relevant to meaningful behavior now than other events which are closer in linear time" (Lemke, 2002, p. 80).

Not only time but also language must inevitably be reconsidered if we are to embark in a substantive way on the longitudinal study of advanced L2 capacities. Where might the longitudinal study of advanced capacities turn in order to be informed by a conception of language that is congruent with such a new conception of time?

Reimagining language for the longitudinal study of advanced capacities

With Achugar and Colombi (Chapter 3, this volume), we think Systemic Functional Linguistics (SFL) offers the required global frame of reference while at the same time making available more local conceptual tools that can be harnessed for the longitudinal study of advanced capacities. In fact, a number of L2 researchers in the US and elsewhere who focus on advancedness (e.g., those working with heritage learners and graduate level EFL/ESL learners, and those interested in diverse aspects of academic level L2 performance) have already begun to pursue that very possibility (Byrnes, 2006a; Schleppegrell and Colombi, 2002; also Byrnes and Sprang, 2004). We now extend that possibility to incorporate longitudinalness.

Matthiessen (2006) explicitly addresses how SFL might aid conceptualizing and researching evolving advanced L2 capacities. He states that learning a language is fundamentally about learning how to mean. More precisely, and following Halliday's schema (e.g., 1999a, 1999b), he reminds readers that learning a language (language as substance) is always and at the same time learning through language (language as instrument) and learning about language (language as object). That engagement in learning proceeds along a number of intersecting semiotic dimensions within the overall semantic space that the system of a particular language makes available. The intent is to capture the fact that language is located within a context, meaning that one of the biggest challenges facing theoretical accounts of language, and one most such accounts have largely sidelined, is to relate the semiotic system language to that social context. Ultimately, under the systemic-functional project a description of language must be such that it captures language as a probabilistic and dynamic resource that enables its users to linguistically signal their construal of social contexts in ways that largely accord with the construals the entire language group makes while also enabling him or her to engage in more nuanced, more individual forms of meaning-making.

At the global level SFL handles this demand by positing three foundational dimensions. The first dimension is the *hierarchy of stratification*. Language is stratified into: (a) two content strata, the system of "meaning" (semantics) and the system of "wording" (the lexicogrammar of a language); and (b) two expression strata, phonetics and graphetics. Crucial for successful long-term learning is that emerging multilingual users "learn language **trinocularly**, from all stratal angles . . .: not only 'from below' (the resources of sounding and writing . . . and then the resources of wording) and 'from above' (the resources of meaning in context), but also 'from within' (the internal organization of a given stratum as a linguistic subsystem)" (Matthiessen, 2006, p. 37; emphasis in original). Once grammar is construed as the dynamic engine behind the semiotic capacities of language (see Halliday, 1996), it follows that it will be crucial for advanced learners to come to see lexicogrammar as a flexible resource, rather than an inventory, much less a set of rules. This involves being able to see probabilities of clusters of language forms—across the continuum of lexicon and grammar all the way to texts—in relation to "situations," "functions," "notions," "registers," or "genres," an approach that will require a textually oriented pedagogy and will best be instantiated by it.

One way to arrive at a longitudinal trajectory toward advancedness would be in terms of such system-internal features. For example, how is the learner moving toward expressing a greater range of social situations through oral and written texts in ways that show how clusters of features at the stratal subsystems of semantics and lexicogrammar (i.e., simplex clause and complex clause, group, word, morpheme) interact to instantiate ideational, interpersonal, and textual meaning? One should expect "earlier" advanced learners to be significantly engaged in still acquiring those stratal subsystems in a trinocular way; "later" advanced learners, by comparison, would be those who have acquired considerable flexibility in that regard *in terms of the functions* language expresses with high probabilities in different contexts of situation and the textual genres that signal them.

The second global dimension, the *spectrum of metafunction*, recognizes the fact that any language use is multifunctional in that it always accomplishes two things at once: it construes our experience in the world and inside us (its ideational function), and it enacts our social roles and relations (its interpersonal function). Both the ideational and interpersonal functions are handled at once through our staging of texts (the textual function). Accordingly, various registers, indeed even various genres, emerge that will more or less privilege an ideational or a personal function (Byrnes and Sprang, 2004). In this way, the three metafunctions allow us to develop something like a text typology/topology for tracing development on the basis of which one can probe learners' awareness and appropriate use in context of the resources the language makes available (for a graphic representation, see Matthiessen, 2006, p. 46). While this type of SFL analysis has been most richly developed in English (e.g., Martin and Rose's [2003] analysis of coherence), it is by no means English-centric. As Caffarel, Martin, and Matthiessen (2004) are at pains to stress in their discussion of an SFL-based language typology, considerable work with a context-sensitive, meaning and text orientation for the analysis of language and its various subsystems has been accomplished in non-English, even non-Indo-European language environments (e.g., Caffarel, 2007 for French; Teruya, 2007 for Japanese; not to mention Halliday's own lifelong engagement with Chinese). In other words, the kind of language-based analysis that will most definitely be necessary if the longitudinal study of advancedness is to be appropriately grounded is beginning to be modeled in various linguistic environments.

The third global dimension, the *cline of instantiation*, addresses the fact that each text instantiates only certain aspects of the overall potential of the system. Halliday (1996) felicitously phrases this dynamic relationship by saying that "a semiotic system is a meaning potential together with its instantiation in acts of meaning" (p. 4), thereby reconnecting what Saussure's ([1916] 1983) analysis of language into *langue* and *parole*—quite fatefully—separated. All language users, whether so-called native or nonnative, and whether they use one or multiple languages, will always position themselves somewhere on the cline in the unfolding act of meaning-making and with regard to the meaning potential they have assembled in their own repertoire of resources. Thus, one can describe advanced language learning as the learner being engaged in the complex task of instantiating the system in a particular text and, in reverse, coming to understand that each text is but a particular realization of the system that provides certain glimpses into the system's potential. In addition, the cline of instantiation is perhaps the key way in which one might describe how far an advanced learner has advanced or, for that matter, can advance.

However, it is at the local level of a particular stratal subsystem, rather than at the global level of the cline of instantiation, that these global dimensions are realized. In this area, one of the most prominent longitudinal trajectories for observing L2 development is likely to be the movement from congruent semiosis of everyday life to the noncongruent or metaphorical/synoptic way of construing experience, in the use of what is known in SFL as grammatical metaphor (see Achugar and Colombi, Chapter 3, this volume). Several dimensions make it a convincing way of capturing an evolving advancedness. From the standpoint of learning, as Halliday (1993) shows, there is a direct connection between this shift in semiotic resource and how we become competent languaging beings (Swain, 2006), particularly through the influence of schooling. There appear to be strong indications that this same sequence applies as well to adult L2 learners, even after they have already acquired noncongruent semiotic forms in their L1. Given its presence in all metafunctions and its outstanding effect on thematization and information-structuring patterns, the availability of grammatical metaphor in and of itself would seem to be a treasure trove of information regarding development (Halliday, 1999b; Ryshina-Pankova, 2006; Teruya, 2006). If one could also trace in L2 development the kinds of early stages for metaphorization that Derewianka (2003) has found for evolving child L1 development, it could take on even stronger longitudinal contours. With such an orientation, a genuine focus on longitudinal study might not only affect how we come to trace development toward advanced capacities but also how we come to teach toward it (Byrnes, 2006b), how we report it, how we assess the outcomes of learning, and, by implication, how we think about what it means to know a language.

Concluding thoughts

We began these reflections by highlighting the complexity of the longitudinal study of advanced language capacities by noting that both longitudinalness and advancedness have thus far been undertheorized. For that reason alone it is not surprising that both notions, separately and in combination, have also been thoroughly under-researched. To recapitulate, we have argued that a theoretical reconfiguration appears to be necessary if SLA research is to fashion a robust longitudinal method-ology that can capture advanced capacities—our notions of time and our notions of language itself will need to be reconceptualized.

A preferred approach to language and language analysis would: (1) place language in a sociocultural context and make explicit links between contexts of situation and the nature of language forms that instantiate those contexts; (2) foreground language as a meaning-making semiotic system; (3) provide analytical constructs for investigat-ing language use at the textual level, in both oral and written modes; (4) offer a functional approach to grammar that expressly engages the fact that all language use occurs at the utterance/textual level in a particular context; and (5) recognize and provide insights regarding the effect of educational practices on language use and language development toward public literacies. At the heart of the performance of advanced learners is situated language use. Such a theoretical positioning acknow-ledges and validates the fact that accumulated cultural experience affects any lan-guage use, including that of learners, and particularly so-called advanced uses of language. We believe Systemic Functional Linguistics offers a framework with the theoretical depth and analytical grain size necessary to underpin the longitudinal study of L2 advanced capacities.

In terms of conceiving of time and timing, we have suggested that the research interests of genuinely longitudinal study may actually run counter to the notions of time that SLA research has heretofore privileged, and that we may need to overturn them in the future by conceptually privileging an ecology of language development that puts dynamicity, variability, and non-linearity at the heart of the analyses and considers heterochrony or multiple time scales. Indeed, the longitudinal study of advancedness requires a dynamic two-way perspective, where the tentatively pro-jected destination would have a certain conceptual priority, but where an encompass-ing perspective of the full trajectory would guide the research. For example, how can we specify, right from the start, whether and how posited features of advancedness can become traceable at earlier stages of ability? And what might differentiate advancedness from "what comes thereafter"? Is it the notoriously fuzzy notion of near-nativeness, an acquisitional goal that many have begun to prominently disavow? We believe that without such a two-way longitudinal perspective, it will be difficult to arrive at insights that would warrant the methodological and practical complexities and burdens that longitudinal research clearly constitutes (see particularly the contri-butions in this volume by Angelelli, Harklau, Myles, and Skiba, Dittmar, and Bressem). Indeed, without this novel dynamic perspective, the knowledge generated by costly longitudinal studies would not be substantially deeper than that already contributed by sophisticated cross-sectional research.

We would like to raise some cautionary observations. First, Systemic Functional Linguistics and the family of dynamic systems, ecosocial systems, emergentist, and complexity theories are not the only frameworks that we consider useful, although they are our preferred choices in the research program we are envisioning. We recognize they are equipped to address some issues in the longitudinal study of advancedness better than others. For one, the study of how advanced meaning-making develops will necessitate a broad view of semiotic human communication that encompasses new forms of multimodality and goes well beyond language, even as broadly defined as in the SFL framework. Lemke (2002) explains why this is so: "You cannot, neither materially nor physiologically nor culturally, make meaning *only* with the formal linguistic sign system; other modes of meaning-making are always functionally coupled with language use in real activity" (p. 72). Critical literacy theories and theories of multimodality and semiotics—many of which show affinities and intersections with SFL—would also need to be brought to the fore in longitudinal investigations of advancedness (e.g., Gee, 1998; Kress, 2003; Street, 2003). Likewise, many if not all of the theories related to complexity/chaos, emergentism/associative cognition, and dynamic systems make use of cognitivist metaphors that often borrow from computational sciences and biology and emphasize blind, as it were, Darwinian evolutionary-like variability as the source of change. In that sense they place themselves in an ambivalent position regarding human consciousness and intentionality (or, following Vygotskian terminology, higher-order mental functioning). Indeed, despite the repeated claim by various proponents that these theories offer a comfortable integration of the cognitive and the social (de Bot, Lowie, and Verspoor, 2007b; van Geert, 1998), and despite evident efforts at accommodating "socialized consciousness" (Ellis and Larsen-Freeman, 2006, p. 571–572), it is unclear how this family of theories, at least as formulated so far, can deal as readily with intentional thought and the societal and sociopolitical influences on L2 learning as other frameworks clearly can (particularly Vygotskian and neo-Vygotskian theories and theories from anthropological and sociological traditions where human consciousness, agency, and power have been at the center of inquiry for many years now; but see Lemke, 2002, and van Lier, 2004, for proposals that address these difficulties by blending dynamic and ecological systems with socioculturally inspired principles). In addition, the application of dynamic longitudinal methodologies is new in applied linguistics and thus will require modifications and complementations along the way (Larsen-Freeman and Cameron, forthcoming).

Second, there are several other theoretical options that allow for the exploration of advanced meaning-making capacities across situated contexts and over time. Particularly interesting are theories which place variability into the very center of the research program. For example, Tarone (2007) has proposed a renewed interlanguage variationist approach that would be worth exploring in the context of the future research program we envision. Vygotskian sociocultural theories appear to be well suited for the longitudinal study of advancedness, as Byrnes (2006b) has indicated in her discussion of the proximity of Hallidayan and Vygotskian approaches to investigating advanced L2 development. As Lantolf and Thorne (2006) note, they are compatible with other linguistic frameworks as well, such as a semantically (as contrasted with a psycholinguistically) oriented cognitive linguistics represented by researchers like Fauconnier and Turner (2002) and Langacker (e.g., 1998), the cross-linguistically oriented work of the psycholinguist Slobin (1996), the usage-based inquiry by L1 researchers like Tomasello (1998), the dialogism of Bakhtin (1986), and the emphasis on an emergent rather than an essentialist, pre-existent grammar highlighted in Hopper's work (e.g., 1988). We see great potential in these frameworks for the longitudinally oriented study of advancedness as well.

Third, longitudinal research that focuses on language only, however broadly defined, will fall short of the task of illuminating the development of advanced L2 capacities. This seems to be the message implied in the position that van Lier (2002) espouses, when he poignantly warns: "Signs are not objects out there, nor thoughts in here, but relationships between the person and the world, physical and social" (p. 151). The full, longitudinal perspective needs to include nonlinguistic dimensions that are to be found in the interplay between the language learner (a socioculturally situated agent) and the context. Nonlinguistic dimensions in the development of advancedness can be explored through a range of theories and options, including ethonographically (Harklau, Chapter 2), via SFL-specific tools for the indexing and construal of identity (Achugar and Colombi, Chapter 3), by resort to sociocultural theories (Kinginger and Blattner, Chapter 12), or even by calling on cross-cultural psychological constructs (Spenader, Chapter 13) (all this volume). The relation between learner and the larger social world has also been investigated and theorized usefully in identity research that, as Norton (2006) characterizes it, is associated more with anthropological and sociological perspectives and less with psychological schools. They thus offer alternative perspectives to the more psychologically oriented sociocultural frameworks that are more commonly found in SLA. In identity theory and L2 learning, "the very articulation of power, identity, and resistance is expressed in and through language. Language is thus more than a system of signs; it is social practice in which experiences are organized and identities negotiated" (p. 503). Agency and identity will have to be incorporated in the longitudinal study of advancedness because what moves change and language learning, our engagements as humans, is "with becoming all the selves we want to be" (Lemke, 2002, p. 77). In sum, and this concludes our caveats, whatever choices L2 researchers make, if they are clearly articulated in dialogue, they should result in epistemological diversity (Ortega, 2005) that brings strength to our efforts to account for the dynamic pathways to multicompetence of nonlinguistic dimensions of advancedness as well as linguistic ones.

Our attempt in this chapter to elucidate central issues awaiting the longitudinal study of advanced L2 capacities can only be a first step in laying out how time in relation to advanced development might be reconfigured in a mutually facilitative fashion, not least because the dual focus of this volume, to our knowledge, has no precedent in the literature. That such a step is likely to be incomplete, perhaps even flawed, comes with the project. We suspect that the following dilemma will confront future researchers interested in the research program we are attempting to describe, as it has presented itself to the different authors in this collection as well: Is *advancedness* the given (though perhaps an undertheorized given, as we have argued in this chapter) and *longitudinalness* the means for specifying it more closely? Or is longitudinalness the given (though an underpracticed given, as Ortega and Iberri-Shea, 2005 and Tucker, 1999, claim), where extending it far enough would in due time bring advancedness under its purview?

How we choose to define, operationalize, and theorize the longitudinal study of advanced capacities is no longer a light choice to be made on the basis of disciplinary preferences but becomes a deeply ethical issue (Ortega, 2005). We live in a globalized environment where extensive migrations (Lam, 2006) and information and communication technologies enabling virtual transnational communication (Ess, 2002; Parayil, 2005) are the almost inescapable norm. As a result, our societies are increasingly multilingual. Thus, the urgent need arises to find ways of integrating highly diverse groups into interconnected communities that demand complex forms of multiple literacies if their members are to thrive. The focus of our research can no longer simply be "advancedness" as decontextualized "successful" language learning that has no consequences for human lives (Byrnes, 2006b). Nor can we imagine longitudinal development to be captured simply by "longer" investigations. For longitudinal study to yield value-added information for a richer understanding of advanced second language capacities, a different kind of approach to the analysis of time and of language itself is needed. But if we can arrive at a reconceptualized theoretical frame of meaning, then we will still need to clarify the values that ought to guide such a research program. For us, what gives meaning, purpose, and energy to the enterprise must be our search for answers regarding whether and how the longitudinal study of multicompetence can enhance our professional abilities to nurture advanced L2 capacities among people who, by choice or circumstance, need to mean in more than one language. We hope to have made a convincing case that the project itself deserves the best efforts of the SLA field, on its own merits and for its potential to affect how we imagine language development to take place at any level. A focus on longitudinal study of language development that extends to advanced capacities might well be the most readily available and credible way to bring about that desired change.

References

Bakhtin, M. M. (1986). The problem of speech genres. In C. Emerson and M. Holquist (Eds.), *M. M. Bakhtin: Speech genres and other late essays* (pp. 60–102). Austin, TX: University of Texas Press.

Bley-Vroman, R. (1983). The comparative fallacy in interlanguage studies: The case of systematicity. *Language Learning, 33*, 1–17.

Brouwer, C. E., and Wagner, J. (2004). Developmental issues in second language conversation. *Journal of Applied Linguistics, 1*, 29–47.

Byrnes, H. (Ed.) (2006a). *Advanced language learning: The contribution of Halliday and Vygotsky*. New York: Continuum.

Byrnes, H. (2006b). What kind of resource is language and why does it matter for advanced language learning? An introduction. In H. Byrnes (Ed.), *Advanced language learning: The contribution of Halliday and Vygotsky* (pp. 1–28). New York: Continuum.

Byrnes, H., and Maxim, H. H. (Eds.). (2004). *Advanced foreign language learning: A challenge to college programs*. Boston: Heinle Thomson.

Byrnes, H., and Sprang, K. A. (2004). Fostering advanced L2 literacy: A genre-based, cognitive approach. In H. Byrnes and H. H. Maxim (Eds.), *Advanced foreign language learning: A challenge to college programs* (pp. 47–85). Boston: Heinle Thomson.

Caffarel, A. (2007). *Systemic functional grammar of French*. New York: Continuum.

Caffarel, A., Martin, J. R., and Matthiessen, M. I. M. (2004). Introduction: Systemic functional typology. In A. Caffarel, J. R. Martin, and M. I. M. Matthiessen (Eds.), *Language typology: A functional perspective* (pp. 1–76). Philadelphia, PA: John Benjamins.

Cook, V. (1992). Evidence for multicompetence. *Language Learning, 42*, 557–591.

Cook, V. (2002). Background of the L2 user. In V. Cook (Ed.), *Portraits of the L2 user* (pp. 1–28). Clevedon, UK: Multilingual Matters.

Corder, S. P. (1975). The language of second-language learners: The broader issues. *Modern Language Journal, 59*, 409–413.

de Bot, K., Lowie, W., and Verspoor, M. (2007a). Authors' response: A dynamic view as a complementary perspective. *Bilingualism: Language and Cognition, 10*, 51–55.

de Bot, K., Lowie, W., and Verspoor, M. (2007b). A Dynamic Systems Theory approach to second language acquisition. *Bilingualism: Language and Cognition, 10*, 7–21.

Derewianka, B. (2003). Grammatical metaphor in the transition to adolescence. In A.-M. Simon-Vandenbergen, M. Tavernier, and L. Ravelli (Eds.), *Grammatical metaphor: Views from systemic functional linguistics* (pp. 185–219). Philadelphia, PA: John Benjamins.

Ellis, N. C., and Larsen-Freeman, D. (2006). Language emergence: Implications for applied linguistics—introduction to the special issue. *Applied Linguistics, 27*, 558–589.

Ess, C. (2002). Computer-mediated colonization, the renaissance, and educational imperatives for an intercultural global village. *Ethics and Information Technology, 4*, 11–22.

Fauconnier, G., and Turner, M. (2002). *The way we think: Conceptual blending and the mind's hidden complexities.* New York: Basic Books.

Firth, A., and Wagner, J. (2007). Second/foreign language learning as a social accomplishment: Elaborations on a reconceptualized SLA. *Modern Language Journal, 91*, 800–819.

Gee, J. P. (1998). What is literacy? In V. Zamel, and R. Spack (Eds.), *Negotiating academic literacies: Teaching and learning across languages and cultures* (pp. 51–59). Mahwah, NJ: Lawrence Erlbaum.

Halliday, M. A. K. (1993). Towards a language-based theory of learning. *Linguistics and Education, 5*, 93–116.

Halliday, M. A. K. (1996). On grammar and grammatics. In R. Hasan, C. Cloran, and D. G. Butt (Eds.), *Functional descriptions: Theory in practice* (pp. 1–38). Philadelphia, PA: John Benjamins.

Halliday, M. A. K. (1999a). Grammar and the construction of educational knowledge. In R. Berry, B. Asker, K. Hyland, and M. Lam (Eds.), *Language analysis, description and pedagogy* (pp. 70–87). Hong Kong: Language Centre, The Hong Kong University of Science and Technology and Department of English, Lingnan University.

Halliday, M. A. K. (1999b). The notion of "context" in language education. In M. Ghadessy (Ed.), *Text and context in functional linguistics* (pp. 1–24). Philadelphia, PA: John Benjamins.

Harklau, L. (2000). From the "good kids" to the "worst": Representations of English language learners across educational settings. *TESOL Quarterly, 34*, 35–67.

Harklau, L. (2002). The role of writing in classroom second language acquisition. *Journal of Second Language Writing, 11*, 329–350.

Herdina, P., and Jessner, U. (2002). *A dynamic model of multilingualism: Perspectives of change in psycholinguistics.* Clevedon, UK: Multilingual Matters.

Hopper, P. (1988). Emergent grammar and the a priori grammar postulate. In D. Tannen (Ed.), *Linguistics in context: Connecting observation and understanding* (pp. 117–134). Norwood, NJ: Ablex.

Huebner, T. (1983). *A longitudinal analysis of the acquisition of English.* Ann Arbor, MI: Karoma.

Kellerman, E. (1985). If at first you do succeed. In S. M. Gass and C. Madden (Eds.), *Input in second language acquisition* (pp. 345–353). Rowley, MA: Newbury House.

Kern, R., and Schultz, J.-M. (2005). Beyond orality: Investigating literacy and the literary in second and foreign language instruction. *Modern Language Journal, 89*, 381–392.

Klapper, J., and Rees, J. (2003). Reviewing the case for explicit grammar instruction in the university foreign language learning context. *Language Teaching Research, 7*, 285–314.

Klein, W. (1998). The contribution of second language acquisition research. *Language Learning, 48*, 527–550.

Kramsch, C. (Ed.) (2002). *Language acquisition and socialization: Ecological perspectives.* New York: Continuum.

Kramsch, C. (2006). From communicative competence to symbolic competence. *Modern Language Journal, 90*, 249–252.

Kress, G. (2003). *Literacy in the new media age.* New York: Routledge.

Lam, W. S. E. (2006). Culture and learning in the context of globalization: Research directions. *Review of Research in Education, 30*, 213–237.

Langacker, R. (1998). Conceptualization, symbolization, and grammar. In M. Tomasello (Ed.), *The new psychology of language: Cognitive and functional approaches to language structure* (Vol. 1, pp. 1–39). Mahwah, NJ: Lawrence Erlbaum.

Lantolf, J. P., and Thorne, S. L. (2006). *Sociocultural theory and the genesis of second language development.* New York: Oxford University Press.

Larsen-Freeman, D. (1997). Chaos/complexity and second language acquisition. *Applied Linguistics, 18*, 141–165.

Larsen-Freeman, D., and Cameron, L. (forthcoming). Research methodology on language development from a complex systems perspective. In K. De Bot (Ed.), *Second language development as a dynamic process.* Special Issue of *The Modern Language Journal, 92*(2).

Leather, J. (2002). Modeling the acquisition of speech in a "multilingual" society: An ecological approach. In C. Kramsch (Ed.), *Language acquisition and socialization: Ecological perspectives* (pp. 47–67). New York: Continuum.

Leaver, B. L., and Shekhtman, B. (Eds.). (2002). *Developing professional-level language proficiency.* New York: Cambridge University Press.

Lemke, J. L. (2002). Language development and identity: Multiple timescales in the social ecology of learning. In C. Kramsch (Ed.), *Language acquisition and socialization. Ecological perspectives* (pp. 68–87). New York: Continuum.

Leung, C., Harris, R., and Rampton, B. (1997). The idealised native speaker, reified ethnicities, and classroom realities. *TESOL Quarterly, 31*, 543–560.

Lightbown, P., Halter, R., White, J., and Horst, M. (2002). Comprehension-based learning: The limits of "do it yourself." *Canadian Modern Language Review, 58*, 427–464.

Long, M. H. (2003). Stabilization and fossilization in interlanguage development. In C. J. Doughty and M. H. Long (Eds.), *Handbook of second language acquisition* (pp. 487–535). Malden, MA: Blackwell.

McLaughlin, B. (1990). Restructuring. *Applied Linguistics, 11*, 1–16.

Martin, J. R., and Rose, D. (2003). *Working with discourse: Meaning beyond the clause.* New York: Continuum.

Matthiessen, C. M. I. M. (2006). Educating for advanced foreign language capacities: Exploring the meaning-making resources of languages systemic-functionally. In H. Byrnes (Ed.), *Advanced language learning: The contribution of Halliday and Vygotsky* (pp. 31–57). New York: Continuum.

Norris, J. M. (2006). Assessing advanced foreign language learning and learners: From measurement constructs to educational uses. In H. Byrnes, H. D. Weger-Guntharp, and K. Sprang (Eds.), *Educating for advanced foreign language capacities: Constructs, curriculum, instruction, assessment* (pp. 167–187). Washington, DC: Georgetown University Press.

Norton, B. (2006). Identity and second language. In K. Brown (Ed.), *Encyclopedia of language and linguistics* (Vol. 5, 2nd ed., pp. 502–507). Oxford, UK: Elsevier.

Ortega, L. (2005). For what and for whom is our research? The ethical as transformative lens in instructed SLA. *Modern Language Journal, 89*, 427–443.

Ortega, L. (2006). Second language learning explained? SLA across nine contemporary theories. In B. VanPatten and J. Williams (Eds.), *Theories in second language acquisition: An introduction* (pp. 221–246). Mahwah, NJ: Lawrence Erlbaum.

Ortega, L., and Iberri-Shea, G. (2005). Longitudinal research in SLA: Recent trends and future directions. *Annual Review of Applied Linguistics, 25*, 26–45.

Parayil, G. (2005). The digital divide and increasing returns: Contradictions of informational capitalism. *The Information Society, 21*, 41–51.

Ryshina-Pankova, M. (2006). Creating textual worlds in advanced learner writing: The role of complex theme. In H. Byrnes (Ed.), *Advanced language learning: The contribution of Halliday and Vygotsky* (pp. 164–183). New York: Continuum.

Saussure, F. de. ([1916] 1983). *Course in general linguistics*, trans. Roy Harris. London: Duckworth.

Schleppegrell, M. J. (2004). *The language of schooling: A functional linguistics perspective*. Mahwah, NJ: Lawrence Erlbaum.

Schleppegrell, M. J., and Colombi, M. C. (Eds.). (2002). *Developing advanced literacy in first and second languages: Meaning with power*. Mahwah, NJ: Lawrence Erlbaum.

Seidlhofer, B. (2001). Closing a conceptual gap: The case for a description of English as a lingua franca. *International Journal of Applied Linguistics, 11*, 133–158.

Shohamy, E. (2006). Rethinking assessment for advanced language proficiency. In H. Byrnes, H. D. Weger-Guntharp, and K. Sprang (Eds.), *Educating for advanced foreign language capacities: Constructs, curriculum, instruction, assessment* (pp. 188–208). Washington, DC: Georgetown University Press.

Singer, J. D., and Willett, J. B. (2003). *Applied longitudinal data analysis: Modeling change and event occurrence*. New York: Oxford University Press.

Slobin, D. I. (1996). From "thought and language" to "thinking for speaking." In J. J. Gumperz and S. C. Levinson (Eds.), *Rethinking linguistic relativity* (pp. 70–96). Cambridge: Cambridge University Press.

Street, B. V. (2003). What's "new" in New Literacy Studies? Critical approaches to literacy in theory and practice. *Current Issues in Comparative Education, 5*(2), 77–91.

Swain, M. (2006). Languaging, agency and collaboration in advanced second language learning. In H. Byrnes (Ed.), *Advanced language learning: The contributions of Halliday and Vygotsky* (pp. 95–133). New York: Continuum.

Tarone, E. (2007). Sociolinguistic approaches to second language acquisition research—1997–2007. *Modern Language Journal, 91*, 837–848.

Tarone, E., and Liu, G. Q. (1995). Situational context, variation, and second language aquisition theory. In G. Cook and B. Seidhofer (Eds.), *Principles and practice in the study of language* (pp. 107–124). Oxford: Oxford University Press.

Teruya, K. (2006). Grammar as a resource for the construction of language logic for advanced language learning in Japanese. In H. Byrnes (Ed.), *Advanced language learning: The contribution of Halliday and Vygotsky* (pp. 109–133). New York: Continuum.

Teruya, K. (2007). *A systemic functional grammar of Japanese*, 2 vols. New York: Continuum.

Tomasello, M. (Ed.) (1998). *The new psychology of language: Cognitive and functional approaches to language structure*. Vol. 1. Mahwah, NJ: Lawrence Erlbaum.

Tomasello, M., and Stahl, D. (2004). Sampling children's spontaneous speech: How much is enough? *Journal of Child Language, 31*, 101–121.

Tucker, G. R. (1999). The applied linguist, school reform, and technology: Challenges and opportunities for the coming decade. *CALICO Journal, 17*, 197–221.

Valdés, G. (2005). Bilingualism, heritage language learners, and SLA research: Opportunities lost or seized? *Modern Language Journal, 89*, 410–426.

van Geert, P. (1998). A Dynamic Systems model of basic developmental mechanisms: Piaget, Vygotsky, and beyond. *Psychological Review, 105*, 634–677.

van Gelder, T., and Port, R. F. (1995). It's about time: An overview of the dynamical approach to cognition. In R. F. Port and T. van Gelder (Eds.), *Mind as motion: Explorations in the dynamics of cognition* (pp. 1–45). Cambridge, MA: Bradford Books.

van Lier, L. (2002). An ecological-semiotic perspective on language and linguistics. In C. Kramsch (Ed.), *Language acquisition and socialization: Ecological perspectives* (pp. 140–164). New York: Continuum.

van Lier, L. (2004). *The ecology and semiotics of language learning: A sociocultural perspective*. Dordrecht: Kluwer Academic Publishers.

Villa, D. (2002). The sanitizing of US Spanish in academia. *Foreign Language Annals, 35*, 222–230.

Author index

Subject index

informants: attitudes 31, 50, 252–9, 260;
dropout rates 10, 31; engagement with
target language 224–5, 235–41; heritage
speakers 44, 49–50; relationships with
researchers 27, 30–1; rights 84, 267;
selection of 78–80, 117–18, 146, 189–90,
199, 228–9, 249–50
input 186, 187t
instantiation 293
institutional time 113–14
instructional treatments 190
integration 249
intentionality 144, 150–3, 295
Interagency Language Roundtable scale 7
Intercultural Development Index 260n
interlanguages 283; developmental
sequences 24, 165; influence of native
language 60, 157–9, 175–6; non-linear
development 287; variability 287, 295
interpreted communicative events 266, 272
Interpreter Readiness Test 271, 273–4
interpreters 17, 265–76; measurement of
proficiency 7, 271–5, 276
interviews 7, 144, 147–9, 229–31, 233, 251
intonation 5
Inventory of longitudinal studies in the social sciences
25
Italian-English learners 4

Japan, educational policies 208–9
Japanese-English learners 205–6, 206–7,
210, 212–14, 217–18
JDB (informant) 4
journals 233
Julie (informant) 5

L1 acquisition: advanced stages 28; case
studies 41, 43t, 73, 285–6; and culture 37,
38; developmental sequences 5, 39–41,
293; effect of literacy 28; vocabulary
development 143
L2 acquisition: academic language 43–53;
case studies 42, 43t, 229, 235–40, 249–60;
and culture 37–8; definition 26;
developmental sequences 4–6, 39–41;
flooding effects 4; importance of
longitudinal studies 3–6, 26–9; individual
differences 26–7, 28–9, 127–32; influence
of native language 60, 157–9, 175–6; and
learner perceptions 99; theories 9, 110–11;
and turning points 286; *see also*
advancedness; child second language
acquisition; classroom contexts; context;
foreign language learning; study abroad
language acquisition *see* L1 acquisition; L2
acquisition

language attitudes *see* attitudes
Language Awareness Interview 16, 229–31
language change 39, 295
language choice *see* choice
language domains 43–4
Language Proficiency Test 271, 272–3
language variation *see* variation
late-acquired language features 7–8, 11,
124–34
learnability 139–40; relativization 110–11,
112–13; vocabulary 140–3, 159
learners: acculturation strategies 16, 248–9,
253, 257–8, 258–60; engagement with
target language 224–5, 235–41; and
identity 227–8; individual differences
26–7, 28–9, 127–32, 174, 177–8, 179,
195–7, 235; measurement of proficiency
7–8; perceptions of target language 99;
relationships with host families 235–40,
249, 253–5, 256, 258–60
learning theories 9, 36–41, 53–4, 114–15,
290, 291–3, 294–5
lexical density 45–9
lexicogrammar
lexicon: developmental sequences 141–3,
157–9; *see also* vocabulary
linguistic concepts 144–7, 150–3, 156
linguistic theories: Cognitive Grammar 145,
157; and longitudinal studies 291–3,
294–6; relativization 11, 110–11, 124–6,
132, 133–4; Systemic Functional
Linguistics 9, 36–41, 53–4, 114–15, 290,
291–3, 294–5; thinking-for-speaking
hypothesis 140
listening tasks 208, 210–11
literacy: academic language 38, 43–53; and
L2 competence 28, 116–17, 139–40, 284;
oral-literate continuum 40–1
logogenesis 39
longitudinal studies: definition 6, 25–6, 78–9,
113–14, 281–2, 285–8; and dynamic
systems theory 288–91; ethnographic
methods 267–70, 271–2; FLLOC Project
10, 63–70f; importance 3–6, 26–9, 60,
209, 242n; large-scale projects 73–4; P-
MoLL Project 10, 74–8; planning/
preplanning 81–2; and pragmatic
development 209, 212–17; study abroad
93–6, 228–42; theoretical frameworks
291–3, 294–6; time required 29–30, 31–2,
179; validity 80–1, 94; *see also* methodology
Lucía (informant) 46–9

maleficiary role 169–70
Marcelo (informant) 51–3
marginalization 249, 253, 258, 259

CPSIA information can be obtained
at www.ICGtesting.com
Printed in the USA
FFOW03n1924290816
27225FF

9 780415 882194